Country Pine

Furniture Projects

*32 Classic Pieces to
Build for Your Home*

Bill Hylton

Illustrations by Sally Onopa

Photographs by Mitch Mandel

**Fox
Chapel Publishing**

1970 Broad Street • East Petersburg, PA 17520
www.FoxChapelPublishing.com

Country Pine Furniture Projects: 32 Classic Pieces to Build for Your Home is a reissue of the work originally entitled *Country Pine Furniture You Can Make With the Table Saw & Router.* This revision incorporates a new cover design and is printed on a premium grade paper, thus enhancing the reproduction of the photographs.

©1995, 2008 by AW Media LLC.
Illustrations ©1995 by Sally Onopa

The author and editors who compiled this book have tried to make all of the contents as accurate and as correct as possible. Plans, illustrations, photographs, and text have all been carefully checked and cross-checked. However, due to the variability of local conditions, construction materials, personal skill, and so on, neither the author, AW Media LLC, nor Fox Chapel Publishing Inc. assumes any responsibility for any injuries suffered or for damages or other losses incurred that result from the material presented herein. All instructions and plans should be carefully studied and clearly understood before beginning construction.

Printed in the United States of America

Prop credits: Aunt Daisy's, Wescosville, Pa.; Ethan Allen, Wescosville, Pa.; Geri Johnson, Orefield, Pa.; The Gifted Touch, Allentown, Pa.; New Look Interiors, Hatfield, Pa.; and Patchesk, Emmaus and Kutztown, Pa.

Published under license by:
Fox Chapel Publishing Company, Inc.
1970 Broad Street
East Petersburg, PA 17520
www.FoxChapelPublishing.com

Library of Congress Cataloging in Publication Data

Hylton, Bill.
    Country Pine : furniture you can make with the table saw and router /
  Bill Hylton : illustrations by Sally Oneopa : photographs by Mitch Mandel.
      p. cm.
    ISBN 978-1-56523-376-8
    1. Furniture making-- United States Amateur's manuals. 2. Country
  furniture-- United States Amateurs' manuals. 3. Furniture, Pine-
  -United States Amateurs' manuals. I. Title.
TT195.H93   1999
684.1'04—dc21   99-14913

Country Pine Furniture Projects: 32 Classic Pieces to Build for Your Home is printed on Williamsburg brand paper produced by International Paper Co. at its Ticonderoga, N.Y., plant. IP has earned chain-of-custody certification from the Sustainable Forestry Initiative for all of its brands of paper, which means all trees used to manufacture its products are replaced through reforestation or natural regeneration. The certification also ensures harvesting practices that are used to protect the air, water, soil, and wildlife. SFI is the largest of two primary independent forest certification standards in North America and is the recipient of the United Nations Environmental Program/International Chamber of Commerce's 2002 World Summit Business Award for Sustainable Development Partnerships.

CONTENTS

Introduction iv

Five-Board Bench 1

Open Bucket Bench 7

SHOPSMARTS: *Making a Board* 13

Drop-Leaf Kitchen Table 19

Hanging Display Shelf............................ 29

Step-Back Cupboard 37

SHOPSMARTS: *Gluing Up Panels* 49

Candle Boxes 55

Half-Round Table 63

Quebec Bonnet Cupboard 71

SHOPSMARTS: *Cutting Mortise-and-Tenon Joints*.............. 83

Candle Shelf 89

Dry Sink 95

Case of Drawers 103

SHOPSMARTS: *Resawing on the Table Saw* 112

Tool Trays 115

Schoolmaster's Desk 123

Post-and-Panel Chest 131

SHOPSMARTS: *Raising Panels* 140

Side Table 143

Corner Cupboard 153

SHOPSMARTS: *Coving on the Table Saw*...................... 170

Stage Box... 175

Splay-Leg Table 183

SHOPSMARTS: *Tapering Legs on the Table Saw* 189

Blanket Chest 193

Narrow Amish Cabinet 201

Sideboard 213

SHOPSMARTS: *Routing Dovetails*...................... 232

Bookshelves... 237

Footstools 243

Maritimes Chest of Drawers 251

SHOPSMARTS: *Routing an Edge Joint*...................... 264

Bench Table 267

Dome-Top Chests 275

Amish Wardrobe 287

SHOPSMARTS: *Country Finishes* 305

INTRODUCTION

Simple is best. In woodworking and furniture making, as in all other aspects of life, simple is best.

So this book has about 30 projects that any woodworker, even the woodworker with fledgling skills and only a modest shop, can build using lumberyard pine. What could be more simple? Each project is presented in detail, with lots of drawings, a table listing all the parts with their dimensions, and step-by-step construction directions.

I'm biased, of course, but I think this is a great collection. Now that the book is finished, I can lean back and take the time to admire the furniture that's collected here. A large (but not ostentatious) corner cupboard, a dry sink, footstools and candle boxes, four different tables ranging from a three-legged half-round table to a drop-leaf kitchen table, small dome-topped chests, a post-and-panel chest, a blanket chest, even a chest of drawers. (If you build everything, you'll have 32 pieces altogether.) All are nicely proportioned, I think; and while fully representative of country furniture, a number of the pieces may be just a little different from what you might expect. The Quebec bonnet cupboard is a good example of this, as is the narrow Amish cabinet.

Setting the Focus: Country pine furniture is the focus of the collection for a couple of good reasons.

Country furniture, first of all, is extraordinarily popular. It isn't stylish or trendy. It transcends fashion with its low-key, timeless beauty. There's something warm and friendly and inviting about the best of it. We're comfortable with it. It's furniture we live with, that we enjoy having around.

Too, country furniture is relatively easy to build. Sure, the doors are assembled with mortise-and-tenon joints, but this time-honored joint is easy to craft. You do the mortises with a plunge router and the tenons on the table saw. Yes, some of the projects have dovetailed drawers or cases, but, again, dovetails are easy to cut with a router. You just need

to read how, then try it once or twice. And building a project or two will give you the hands-on experience you need to fully master the technique.

(Let me interject a comment here about the ten *ShopSmarts* features interspersed among the projects. [I call them *ShopSmarts* because that's what you'll get from them.] Each *ShopSmarts* zeros in on a common woodworking procedure, such as cutting those mortise-and-tenon joints or routing those dovetails, and it explains, step by step, just how to do it. The operation is shown in a sequence of photos. Often, plans for an important jig or fixture are included. As you build the country furniture projects, you'll refer to these features again and again. I'm biased, I know, but I really think the approaches shown simplify the procedures. And as I said, simple is best.)

Narrowing the collection's focus to furniture built of pine simplifies, too. It eliminates a significant variable—what wood to use. Left a variable, the choice of a wood can complicate design, lumber selection, acquisition, and preparation, and even project construction.

In the early years of our country, the woodworkers building the furniture used by people like you and me made it of pine. Pine was a utilitarian wood, just as it is today. Yes, they did make a lot of furniture entirely of pine. I didn't realize myself just how much until I started looking. There are truckloads of it out there—in homes and museums, in antique stores, and at flea markets. The furniture is old, yes. It is pine, yes. But it nevertheless is sturdy and attractive. It is still in use, one hundred years, one hundred fifty years, even two hundred years after its construction.

So restricting the collection to pine pieces did not degrade it in any way.

Equally important here is pine's availability today. All across the country, pine is readily available in standard dimensions. Your local building center has stacks of pine boards, so it's convenient to buy, and thus to use. A lot of us hobby woodworkers butchered pine first and are still most comfortable working it. Pine is friendly, approachable, comfortable. Just like country furniture.

Picking the Projects: Having set the focus, all I needed was projects. About 30 of them would do. Looking for a mix of small items and large pieces, I wanted to embrace all the traditional forms—a cupboard or two, several different tables, small boxes or chests, maybe a wardrobe, a dry sink, a hanging cabinet or shelf. I think *Country Pine* gets its arms around these forms.

While this is a personal collection, I had nothing to do with the designs. Rather than design pieces "in the country style," I chose to reproduce real country pieces. I located a few pieces in private collections, but none of them are museum pieces. Most were borrowed or rented or (as a last resort) purchased from antique dealers. The collection is representative of the old country furniture that is on the market.

If you like how they look, you need to thank a couple dozen anonymous woodworkers who lived and worked ninety to two hundred years ago. *They* designed and executed the "prototypes." And dozens of families have since conducted years of real-time tests of the utility of the designs and the durability of the constructions. Each piece is engineered for long life, believe me. Though there's nothing fancy about the joinery, none of it is in any way slipshod. These are solid, durable pieces, able to stand up under hard use.

Building the Book: After I settled on a piece for inclusion in my little collection, I spent hours photographing and measuring it, analyzing its design and construction. Then, with the help of my computer, I drafted all the illustrations except the exploded view. I drew up a cutting list, scouted out appropriate hardware, chose a finish. I drafted step-by-step construction directions. THEN we set to work building a reproduction following the drawings and draft instructions. Throughout the construction process, the text and drawings were under scrutiny, and corrections and alterations were made as the reproductions were completed and finished. The result is, I think, a tested, proven collection of plans.

Let me point out that I did not build all the reproductions. I did build some, but the majority, including all the big pieces, were built by Phil Gehret of the Rodale Press Design Shop.

Likewise, the drawings you see are not exactly mine. Illustrator Sally Onopa created the exploded views, and she put a professional finish on what I had done in RoboCAD on my computer (in some cases "professional finish" is a euphemism for "she did it over and got it right").

Others contributed greatly to the book. Pat Corpora, the publisher, wasn't simply supportive about doing this book, he was downright insistent that it be done. Jeff Day provided the initial concept for the book, and indeed the first couple of projects—the step-back cupboard and the Amish wardrobe. As I started collecting projects, doing drawings, and drafting the text, he served as a sounding board. Mitch Mandel took the photos. Mitch's specialty, beyond lighting and focus, is framing a shot to eliminate distractions, so your attention is concentrated on the technique being shown. Jerry O'Brien designed and laid out the book. He consulted on the photography and illustrations, always working to make the book attractive but also instructive and easy to follow. Barbara Webb copyedited every word and checked every drawing, which is a lot more demanding than it may sound.

I hope you won't see the result of our collaboration as simply a project book. I see it as a compendium of woodworking tips, tricks, and techniques that makes woodworking easy by methodically covering all the details, by anticipating questions and providing realistic answers.

I see the projects as confidence builders. Some may seem daunting, maybe because of their size or their seemingly complex joinery. Yet, as I keep saying, none of these are really difficult to build. The blanket chest, for example, might intimidate you. But once you get the major panels glued up and sanded, you're practically done! The joinery is basic: butt and rabbet joints secured with glue and nails. The results are nothing short of impressive. As you apply the final coat of finish, you'll find yourself brimming with enough confidence to tackle any other project in the collection.

So go ahead; you can do it! They're simple.

Bill Hylton

FIVE-BOARD BENCH

A five-board bench may not sound like a home furnishing. I know I see scenes from summer camp or flash back to smelly locker rooms if you say "Five-board bench."

But this particular bench has been around my home for years with no such mental impact that I remember. And for my wife, Judi, this bench brings back pleasant memories of her grandparents doing the wash. They'd set up the sturdy wringer-washer beside the cellar drain, then get out this bench and set a couple of washtubs on it. (To a three- or four-year-old, this didn't seem like work; Nana and Papa probably wouldn't remember it that way.) They'd hook up a hose to fill the washtubs and the washer. The washer would hum and churn, and water would cascade from the wringer, and the air would be damply scented with soap and bleach. The stuff of nostalgia.

By the time my wife was part of the scene, the bench had already migrated with her family through a dozen or more different homes around Pennsylvania's Lehigh Valley. The family would move as jobs and finances and family size and landlords would dictate, and household furnishings were bought and sold, built and given away, broken and left behind. But this bench was sufficiently useful (and durable) that it remained among the family's chattel.

Eventually, Judi's parents came to possess the bench, and she liberated it from their basement quite a few years ago. It's spent some time in our basement, it's true, but usually it serves as a plant stand—indoors during the winter, out on the deck in the summer.

Of course, this little bench isn't really a locker-room/summer-camp kind of five-board bench. The engineering and construction are the same, but the size and proportions are different. It's easy easy easy to build, a veritable saber saw, hammer, and chisel project. All it requires is one 12-foot 5/4 × 12 pine board and a handful of cut nails.

The original (*above*) was used as a laundry bench. The reproduction (*opposite*) is more likely to see use on a deck.

1

EXPLODED VIEW

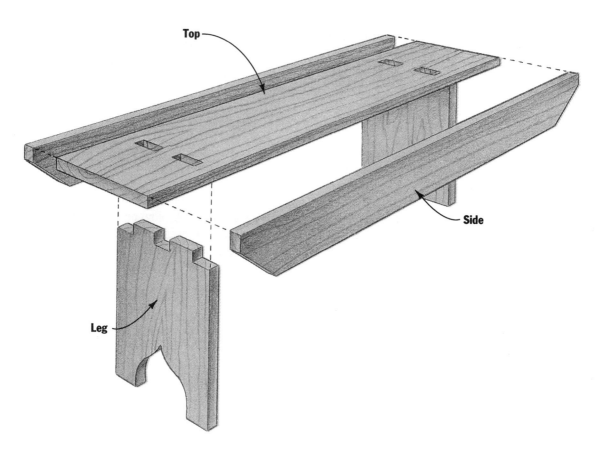

CUTTING LIST

Piece	Number	Thickness	Width	Length	Material
Top	1	$1^{1}/_{16}$"	$11^{1}/_{4}$"	$49^{1}/_{2}$"	5/4 pine
Legs	2	$1^{1}/_{16}$"	$11^{1}/_{4}$"	$15^{5}/_{16}$"	5/4 pine
Sides	2	$1^{1}/_{16}$"	$4^{1}/_{2}$"	$49^{1}/_{2}$"	5/4 pine

HARDWARE
8d cut finish nails

1. Cut the parts. The original bench was built with a couple of those reeeeally wide pine boards that, though once commonplace, are darn near impossible to find these days. I trimmed the width a bit to allow you to use a stock 5/4 × 12 board, which is $11^{1}/_{4}$ inches wide (usually).

Thus glue-up isn't necessary.

Cut one 12-foot board into the five that form the

bench. Make the parts the sizes specified by the Cutting List.

Lay out the angle cuts on the sides, as shown in the *Side View,* and make the cuts with a circular saw or saber saw. Then set these parts aside until assembly (Step 4).

2. Shape the legs. The tops of the legs are notched to form the two tenons that join them to the top. Lay out the tenons, as shown in the *Leg Layouts,* and cut the tenons on the table saw, as shown in the photos on page 5.

Each leg has a cutout that forms two feet. You can enlarge the pattern provided here, or you can freehand your own version of the cutout. In any case, lay out the cut lines on each leg and make the cut with a saber saw. Sand away any visible saw marks, and soften the edges of the legs with the sandpaper.

3. Cut the mortises. Laying out the mortises on the top is as critical a step as this project has. The size and spacing of the mortises MUST match the tenons; otherwise, the bench won't be assemble-able. So use the leg to lay out the mortises.

Measure and mark the location of the leg at

Use a Scrap Wood Layout Tool

Because the length of each leg tenon equals the thickness of the top, you can use a scrap of the working stock as a layout tool. Lay the scrap across the leg, flush with the top edge, and scribe the shoulder line along the scrap.

---

each end of the top. Stand the leg on the top at the line, and trace around the tenons. It is likely that the legs are slightly different, so don't use the same leg to lay out both pairs of mortises.

Drill out the bulk of the waste with a large-diameter bit, then square up the mortises with a chisel. Position the individual holes very carefully inside the layout lines. To minimize the paring that's necessary, try to overlap the holes as much as possible. Whereas most bits tend to wander into a previously bored hole if you try this, a Forstner bit won't. After you've bored out as much of the waste as you can, finish up the mortise with the chisel. As you work, trim to the layout lines, but do leave the lines. (If you cut away the lines, the mortises definitely will be too big.) Test fit the leg, and pare the mortises as necessary.

LEG LAYOUTS

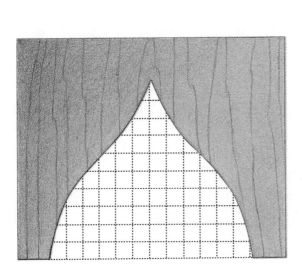

1 Square = ½"

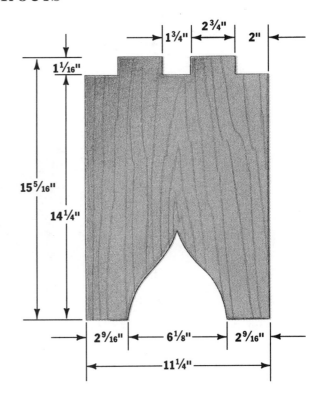

PLAN VIEWS

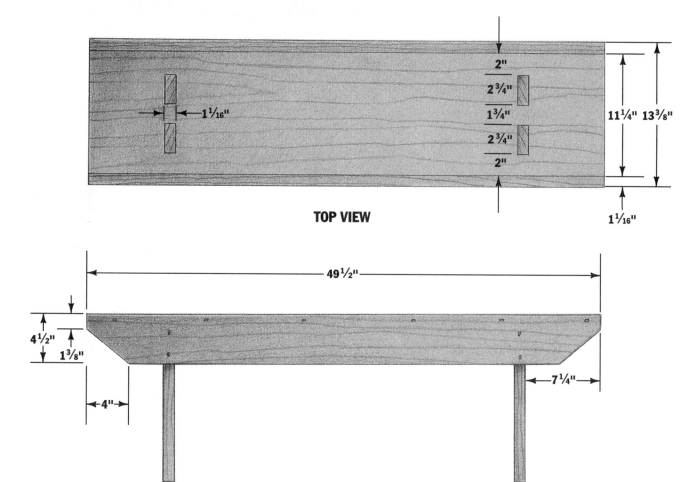

2"

2¾"

1¾"

2¾"

2"

1¹⁄₁₆"

11¼" 13⅜"

1¹⁄₁₆"

TOP VIEW

49½"

4½"

1⅜"

4"

7¼"

32⅞"

SIDE VIEW

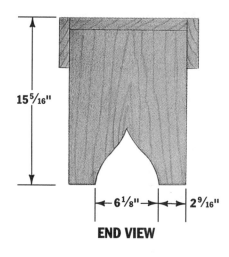

15⁵⁄₁₆"

6⅛"

2⁹⁄₁₆"

END VIEW

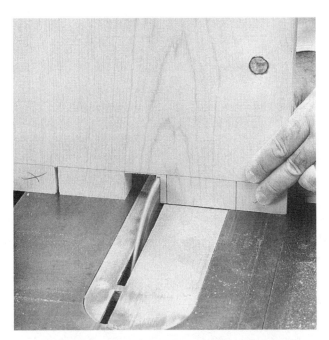

The table saw makes quick work of forming the tenons. Crank up the blade until its height matches the stock thickness. Stand the leg on end, and guide it with the miter gauge. Kerf to the waste side of each layout line. Then open the gap between the two tenons by making repeated kerfs.

Complete the tenons by turning the leg on edge, raising the saw blade to align with the kerf, and cutting away the waste in a single pass. Guide the workpiece with the miter gauge.

4. Assemble the bench. Glue the tenons into the mortises and nail the sides in place. I'd suggest laying the top and legs on edge, then setting the side in place. Drive two or three nails through the side into the top's edge, then square up the legs and drive nails through the sides into the legs. Drive a few more nails to finish up this first side, then roll the bench over and repeat the process to attach the second side.

5. Apply a finish. The bench doesn't beg for any particular finish. The original was painted several times, it would appear from the different colors of flecks found here and there. But it is virtually free of paint now. It's been outdoors enough to have weathered—mildly eroded surfaces, that UV gray color, rusty nailheads, some mature splits and deep cracks.

To duplicate this, we've simply parked the new bench out on the deck. We softened the exposed edges with a spokeshave (rounding them over with a router would have given them too uniform an appearance), but we didn't sand it or apply any finish whatsoever. After one summer and part of a fall, the bench is getting there.

You may have another appearance in mind. Tips on applying a selection of different finishes can be found in the *ShopSmarts* feature "Country Finishes" on page 305.

OPEN BUCKET BENCH

Will people 200 years from now—that's in the year 2195—be collecting and copying the utility shelves we're making today?

I find it hard to imagine. Yet that's what we're doing with this bucket bench. When it was constructed, back in the 1790s, it was strictly utilitarian. Though this particular bucket bench is a fairly sophisticated example of the genre, it represents only a midpoint along the evolutionary timeline.

In the country two hundred years ago, water for drinking, cooking, and the very occasional washing was taken in buckets from a spring or stream to the house (such as *it* was). To minimize bending once you got the buckets to the house, you'd set them on a bench. So the very earliest bucket benches were simply *benches,* not unlike the Five-Board Bench included in this collection (page 1). It was something that could be made with a minimum of wood, using primitive tools. Strictly for utility.

As the family got larger, more water was needed. Just a bucketful wasn't enough. Maybe there was now a bucket of milk from the family cow to have at hand. Too, a place was

needed for the ladle, or for the crude block of home-made soap. So the first, primitive bucket bench had to be replaced with a more commodious piece.

The "second generation" of bucket bench is what we have here. It has room for a couple of buckets. On the upper shelf, at a comfortable working height, there's room for a cooking pot, mixing bowl, or washbasin. The back kept the piece from swaying and wracking while the cook worked, but it also contained spills to a degree, at least keeping them off the wall. And the narrow top provided a convenient place to stash that soap and communal drinking cup. The slightly stepped configuration meant the cook could dip into the water buckets without moving them.

Later generations of bucket benches sported doors and other embellishments. They became less austere, more stylish. And in their new forms, they became known as water benches, dry sinks, and washstands.

The original of this project was built of pine boards and painted. The top and sides were joined by hand-cut dovetails. If you've never tackled dovetails, this

---

Bare, the original bucket bench (*above*) looks like an ill-proportioned bookcase. Stocked with crocks, bowls, and a bucket, its use is clear (*opposite*).

is an ideal project. The pins are large and widely spaced, so it is easy to cut them. Moreover, the project itself is a utilitarian country piece. It's a style that forgives the workmanship of inexperience. The original doesn't have the perfectly proportioned, tightly fitted dovetails that a fine furniture piece does. They're more than a trifle gappy, to be candid.

While the piece was built to be practical and functional, its proportions are pleasing. It reflects the builder's pride in his work. Time was taken to scratch a double bead along the front edges of the sides—just a little decoration. Two hundred years later, it's still sturdy, still useful, still attractive. It's worth keeping.

---

1. Cut the parts. The bucket bench is constructed from six boards. Their thicknesses and widths dictate that you will do some resawing and/or planing, followed by some gluing up. Check the *ShopSmarts* features "Making a Board" on page 13, "Resawing on the Table Saw" on page 112, and "Gluing Up Panels" on page 49 for sequences and useful tips on these procedures.

After the stock is thicknessed and glued up, rip the parts to the required widths. Then crosscut the parts to the lengths specified by the Cutting List.

2. Shape the sides. Study the *Side View,* then lay out the two sides. Include the following in your layout:

- Arched cutout that forms the feet
- Notch for the back
- Two tapers—the first from the top to the upper shelf, the second from the upper shelf to the lower shelf

Cut these elements. The arch can be cut with a saber saw or on the band saw. The notch can be done with a saber saw. The tapers are probably best done with a circular saw.

3. Cut the dovetail pins on the sides. Lay out the two sides, and mark one as the left and one as the right. Then lay out the dovetail pins, as shown in *Joinery Details.*

Begin by scribing baselines (one on each side of the workpiece), which might best be done by using an offcut of the 1-inch stock used for the top and sides. Align one face of the scrap flush with the top of the workpiece, and trace along the other face, thus capturing the actual thickness of the top. On each side of the workpiece, scribe in the verticals between the baseline and the top edge, then complete the layout by connecting them across the top end.

With a backsaw, cut the verticals, cutting only

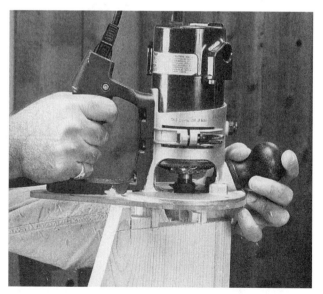

Laying out the pins doesn't require anything fancier than a square and a pencil. As you delineate the pins, x out the waste, so it's clear on which side of the lines you must cut.

Form the pins by cutting down to the baseline with a backsaw. Then remove the waste between pins quickly using a router and a straight bit. The stock is thick enough to support the router, and the saw cuts define the waste.

EXPLODED VIEW

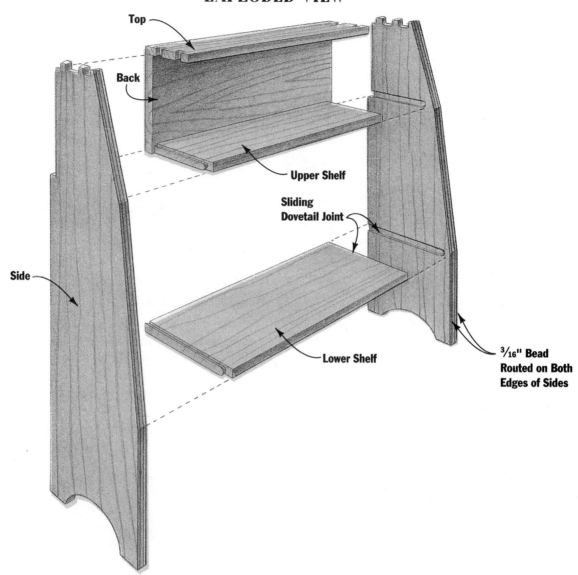

Top

Back

Upper Shelf

Sliding
Dovetail Joint

Side

Lower Shelf

3/16" Bead
Routed on Both
Edges of Sides

CUTTING LIST

Piece	Number	Thickness	Width	Length	Material
Sides	2	1"	12 1/8"	43 3/4"	5/4 pine
Top	1	1"	6"	31"	5/4 pine
Upper shelf	1	7/8"	8 3/4"	29 1/2"	5/4 pine
Lower shelf	1	7/8"	11 1/2"	29 1/2"	5/4 pine
Back	1	3/4"	9 7/8"	31"	1-by pine

HARDWARE

8d cut finish nails

Lay out the tails from the pins, as shown. Stand the side on the top, and get the edges lined up perfectly. Then use a knife to scribe the outline of the tails in the top along the edges of the pins. To make them more visible, run a pencil over the knife marks.

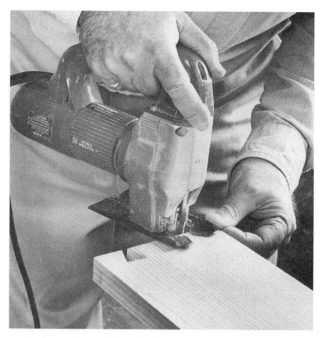

The slots between the tails are large enough that you can use a saber saw to rough them out. Trim them to the knife marks with a sharp chisel.

as deep as the baseline. Use a saber saw or coping saw to cut along the baseline. Clean out the areas you can't reach with the saw, using a chisel.

4. Cut the tails on the top. Lay out the tails from the pins. Rest the top on the workbench, then upend a side and set it in position against the top. Use a knife of some kind—a utility knife or even a penknife will do—to scribe around each pin.

With the tails thus laid out, cut them using a backsaw or coping saw. You can even use a saber saw to rough out tails this large. Be sure you cut shy of the layout marks. With a chisel, carefully pare the tails to fit.

5. Rout the sliding dovetail slots. As you can see from *Joinery Details*, the dovetail slots for the shelves are 7/8 inch wide but only 1/4 inch deep. And they are stopped.

Rest the sides on the bench top with their inner faces up. Lay out the slots for the upper and lower shelves. The drawings show where to position the slots and how long to make them. Rout the slots in one side at a time. Clamp a fence to the workpiece to guide the router, outfit the router with the proper bit, and adjust the bit height to 1/4 inch.

To make the cut, set the router against the fence at what will be the back edge of the side. Switch on the router and feed it along the fence, routing the slot. Return the router to the starting point before switching it off and lifting it from the work.

If you have a 7/8-inch dovetail bit, the slots are completed. If you are using a smaller-diameter bit, you have to shift the fence position slightly and make a second pass.

When the first slot is completed, move the fence and cut the second in the same manner. Then do the second side.

6. Rout the sliding dovetail tails. With the slots done, rout the tails on the ends of the shelves. Fit your router with an edge guide, and set its position so the bit just nicks the board. You want to form a tail that perfectly fits the slots, and do it in just two passes, using the same guide setting for both. Make test cuts on scraps of the working stock, fitting them in the slots. When the setup is right, cut tails on the ends of both shelves.

Pick the front edge of each shelf and mark it. Then trim back each tail so it ends 1/2 inch shy of the front edge. Two cuts made with a backsaw will do the job on each tail.

PLAN VIEWS

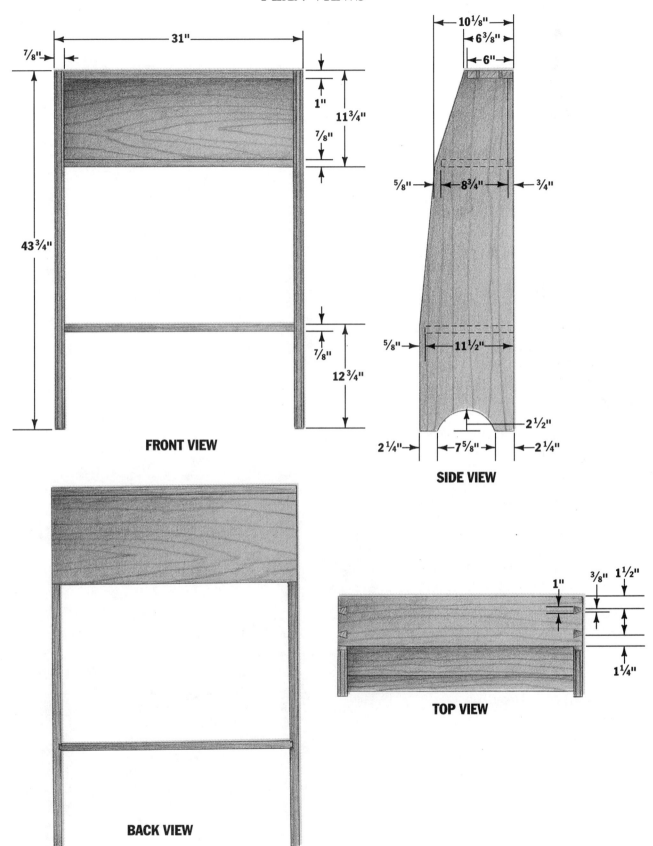

FRONT VIEW

SIDE VIEW

BACK VIEW

TOP VIEW

7. Rout the beads on the sides. The original bucket bench has a pair of tiny beads along the front edges of the sides. Though 1/4-inch-diameter edge-beading bits are widely available, a bit that cuts a 3/16-inch-diameter bead is tough to find. Try Cascade Tools (800-235-0272); their bit number C1125 does the job.

8. Assemble the bucket bench. Drive the shelves into their slots in the sides first. Apply a small amount of glue to the nose of the tails, and spread it from one end of the slot to the other as you drive the well-fitted joint together.

Stand the bench up and place the top in position. Apply a few dots of glue to the pins and tails, and drive the parts together.

Finally, set the back in place and drive three or four 8d cut finish nails through it into the sides.

9. Apply the finish. The original of this piece is painted the barn red that's so common to country furniture. We finished the reproduction using an "antiquing kit," packaged and sold by the Bruning Paint Company. The finish is applied in two steps.

Paint the bucket bench red. When the paint is dry, apply the mahogany glaze. The idea is to brush or wipe the glaze over the paint. Wait a few minutes, then wipe it off. The glaze darkens the paint, and it collects in seams and depressions and corners and makes these areas even darker.

JOINERY DETAILS

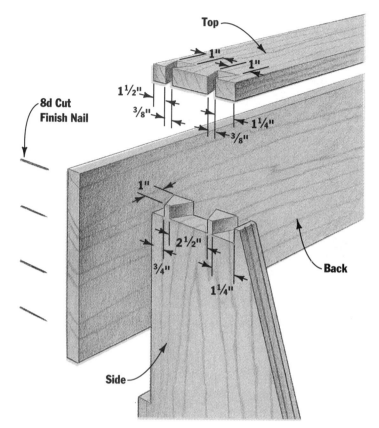

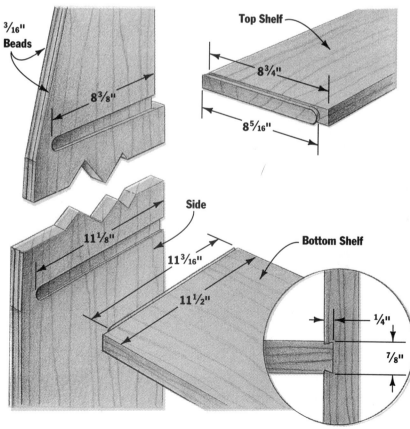

SHOP SMARTS

Making a Board

Laugh if you want, but there's more to "making a board" than lopping a 2-foot piece off a long 1 × 12. For best results in any furniture-making project, a board must be straight and flat. Its faces must be parallel to each other, and so must the edges. And those edges and faces must be at right angles to one another.

Take a look at that 2-foot 1 × 12.

It was kiln-dried to maybe 15 percent moisture content, but perhaps not even that dry. Then it was planed to a ³⁄₄-inch thickness and ripped to a width of 11¹⁄₄ inches. In the days between being kiln-dried and dressed at the sawmill and being crosscut in your shop, it swelled and shrank and swelled and shrank. It's probably cupped, maybe twisted. Are the edges straight and parallel? Square to the faces? Free of nicks and dents? Are the faces flat?

I didn't think so.

The ideal stock to use for any furniture project is stuff that's been kiln-dried especially for furniture making. That means it's been dried to about 6 to 8 percent moisture content. Sure, it may have rebounded some to a 10 to 12 percent moisture content. It may well be cupped and twisted. But it hasn't been "made into a board" yet. It's still rough-sawn, still truly an inch thick.

You may have kiln-dried furniture-making stock surfaced at the sawmill or lumberyard. But there's no guarantee the lumber will be flat and true days or weeks later, when you get around to working it. The wood will continue to swell and shrink with weather changes. As it does, it may bow or cup or twist ever so slightly.

You'll achieve the very best results if you surface the wood for your project as you make it. Don't mill all the stock for a chest of drawers in one day, then stretch the project's construction over the next several weeks. Mill the stock for a component, then make that component straightaway. Then mill more wood for the next component, and make that component.

To make a board, you need a table saw, a planer, and a jointer. They don't have to be commercial-shop scale. A 6-inch jointer with a

3-foot bed is completely satisfactory, as is a 10- to 12-inch portable planer.

The jointer does two things: It flattens boards and it straightens them. There isn't another power tool in the shop that will do these jobs, and these are critical to making boards. Unless you first flatten them on the jointer, the boards that emerge from your planer won't be true.

What a planer will do is make one side of a board parallel to another. If you feed a warped board through a planer, it will come out thinner but still warped. But if the stock is flat on one side, a planer will make the other side flat *and* parallel to the first face. The board will be true.

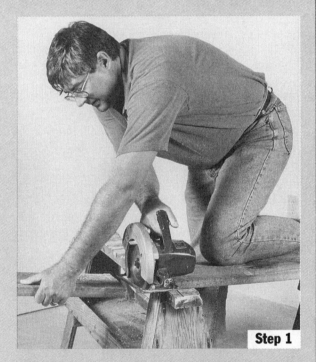

Step 1

1. Crosscut to rough length. Begin making a board by cutting it to rough size. As a general rule, rough size means 1 to 2 inches longer and ¹⁄₂ inch wider than final specifications. Don't cut pieces less than 12 inches long, though, because they are hazardous to joint. If your project calls for short pieces, gang them up so you can cut them from one longer piece after it's been surfaced.

Because you may be beginning with an 8-foot or longer board, you probably don't want to make

(continued)

MAKING EFFECTIVE USE OF STOCK

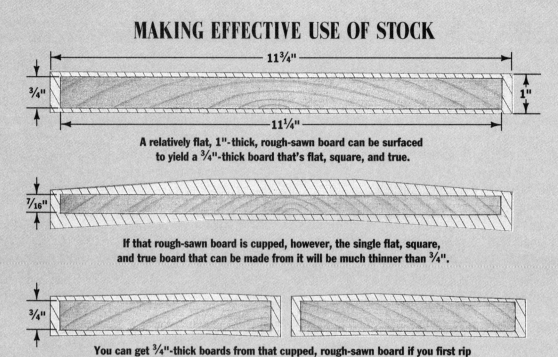

A relatively flat, 1"-thick, rough-sawn board can be surfaced
to yield a 3/4"-thick board that's flat, square, and true.

If that rough-sawn board is cupped, however, the single flat, square,
and true board that can be made from it will be much thinner than 3/4".

You can get 3/4"-thick boards from that cupped, rough-sawn board if you first rip
it in half (or thirds) and then joint and thickness-plane the resulting boards.

the rough crosscuts on the table saw. I use a circular saw. It's just fine for this work; the cut doesn't have to be perfectly square. If you have a radial arm saw or a chop saw, use that for rough crosscuts.

2. Rip the board to "jointer width." The second phase of rough-cutting is to rip the boards. Before flattening a board on the jointer,

Step 2

you have to reduce its width to something under the jointer's rated width—6 inches in the case of my old Delta. In many cases, the board will be sufficiently straight and flat to be ripped in the standard fashion, as shown in the Step 2 photo.

Cutting wood like this exposes new surfaces to the air, and that can lead to a little bit of wood movement. Some patient woodworkers sticker boards on a flat surface (stack them with spacers) for a few days after rough-cutting them, thus allowing them to achieve some sort of moisture equilibrium. In more real-world situations, you take the freshly cut boards directly to the jointer.

3. Joint one face of the board. The next step is to flatten one face, and you do this on the jointer. The 6-inch jointer shown in the Step 3 photo is fairly typical of home shops.

Tend to the machine first. Set the infeed table height so the jointer removes no more than 1/16 inch from the board per pass.

Examine the board next to determine which face you are going to flatten and which end of the board will lead the way over the jointer knives. To eliminate (or at least minimize) tear-out, orient the board so the grain descends toward the face

FLATTENING AND STRAIGHTENING STOCK

FACE JOINTING

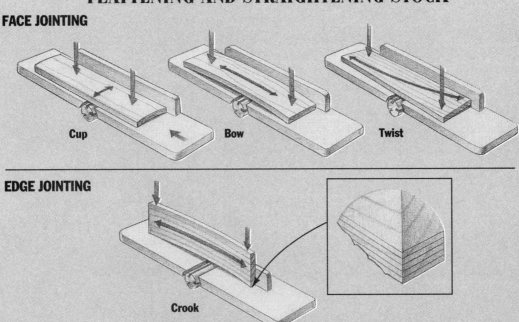

Cup   Bow   Twist

EDGE JOINTING

Crook

being surfaced. The board shown in the photos is something of an anomaly: it's darn flat as it is. Typically, a board has some measure of cup, bow, or twist that affects how you work it. Bear in mind that if the distortion is too severe, the board may be unusable.

If the board is cupped or bowed, you place the

Step 3

concave face down to prevent rocking. The twisted board is the toughest to flatten. Your inclination may be to ride the board across the jointer table on three corners, since it's stable this way. The result will be a tapered board. What you have to do is try to balance the board on its opposite corners, keeping it roughly level as you feed it. On the first few passes, the board will definitely be wobbly, but you have to balance the downward pressure you apply to keep the board level. Initially, material will be removed only from the ends or the edges of the face. But with each pass, more of the face should be pared by the knives and the board should become more stable on the jointer table.

Regardless of the nature of the board, the key in flattening the face is maintaining steady, even, downward pressure on the outfeed side as you advance the board across the cutter head. Obviously, the pressure has to be applied initially on the infeed side. But as the board's leading end advances about 12 inches past the knives, you should get your left hand on the outfeed side and concentrate the pressure there. If the board rises from the outfeed table even slightly at any point, you won't get a flat surface.

(continued)

AVOIDING TEAR-OUT

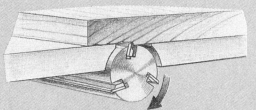

1. Cutting against the grain causes tear-out.

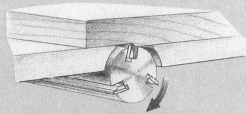

2. When jointing, orient the board so the grain runs "down" to the cutter head.

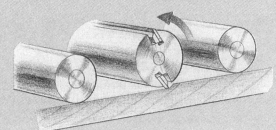

3. When planing, orient the board so the grain runs "up" to the cutter head.

The end of the board that LEADS the way across the jointer TRAILS going through the planer.

Step 4

Don't, however, lay a hand on the board and push steadily, allowing your hand to remain on the board as it passes over the cutter head. Not safe. Use push blocks, as shown in the Step 3 photo.

If you're working a rough-sawn board, keep machining the board until all the saw marks are gone. It'll be flat. If you're trying to flatten a previously planed board, it is harder to tell when to stop jointing. Try this: Scribble on the face you are jointing with a pencil. When the lines are gone, the board's flat.

4. Joint one edge. You do this so one edge is straight and square to the board's face. Obviously, you must orient the flat face against the jointer's fence. And the fence has to be square to the table.

As with the previous operation, maintain downward pressure on the outfeed side. But also press the stock firmly against the fence. Remember, too, to keep your hands off the area of the board that's directly over the cutter head. Keep working the edge until the jointer knives have cut the full length and width of the board.

If the board is slightly crowned, orient the concave edge down to prevent rocking.

5. Plane the board. This is a two-phase process. Run the flattened and jointed board through the thickness planer as many times as necessary to smooth the second face and make the second face parallel to the first (the first phase). Then continue to mill the board to reduce it to the desired thickness (the second phase).

Generally, the maximum depth of cut for a planer is $1/16$ inch. With pine, there shouldn't be problems with taking this much material off in one pass. Unlike a jointer, the planer's depth of cut must be reset after every pass.

For the first phase, smoothing and flattening the board's second face, run it through the planer with the jointed face down. Repeat this process until the top face is smooth.

Step 5

6. Rip the board to final width. When ripping the board, hold its jointed edge against the fence; the rough edge will be ripped parallel to the jointed edge.

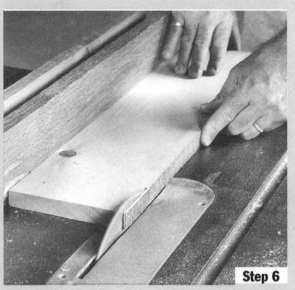

Step 6

For your own safety, stand to one side as you feed the board into the planer. Planers can and do kick boards back.

The next phase of the process is thicknessing, in which you plane the board down to the thickness you need. On the first thicknessing pass, send the board through the planer with the jointed face up. Lower the cutter head, and send the board through with the jointed face down. Continue this process, alternating board faces, until the piece is the necessary thickness. Taking material from both faces reduces the chance of the board's warping as you expose the inside of the board, which may have a slightly different moisture content.

Of course, you are seldom planing a single board. More typically, you'll be working a stack of boards that must all be the same thickness. Check through the stack and find the thickest board. Set the planer to remove $1/16$ inch or less from this board. Piece by piece, feed all the stock through. Some boards may not get planed at all the first time you run them through. That's okay.

After all the pieces have been through at the first setting, lower the cutter head, and run all the stock through again. The key to uniform final thickness is running all the boards through at each cutter-head setting before changing it.

7. Crosscut the board to its final length. Guide the workpiece with the miter gauge. Cut *both* ends of the board. After crosscutting the first end to square it and trim off any checking, measure and mark the final length. Then cut the second end. But before you make that *first* cut, know how much you can remove without shortening the board too much. Remember that woodbutcher's lament: "I cut it twice and it's *still* too short."

Step 7

DROP-LEAF KITCHEN TABLE

Drop-leaf tables tend to be formal. Walnut or cherry or mahogany. Cabriole legs. Rule-jointed leaves. Silky smooth finishes.

This country drop-leaf is a pleasant relief from that stuffiness. Made of pine, it has tapered legs, rudimentary joinery, and a painted finish. And it looks great! To me, it's a very good example of country woodworking.

Though it was probably built to be a kitchen table, we've been using it in our living room as a lamp table. Its nearly red finish provides a touch of just the right color to the room. It would make a great card table: Its light weight makes it easy to move around, and its utilitarian character says, "Go ahead and *use* me." In the nineteenth-century country home, a kind of card table is what it was. With the leaves down, it is small—only 18 × 39 inches. Thus it could be set out of the way when it wasn't being actively used. When it was needed—at mealtime, for example—even a child could carry it into the center of the room and prop open the leaves. Thus opened up, the top is nearly 40 inches square, big enough to accommodate four for a meal or a game of cards or Parcheesi.

This is a nice table project, especially for the woodworker who is still developing his or her skills. Because it isn't fancy, because its joinery is straightforward, it isn't difficult to build. Drop-leaf tables usually have rule joints between the top and the leaves, for example, but not this one. It does use drop-leaf table hinges, but not the rule joint, which is finicky to fit properly. You don't need a lot of expensive, high-quality material either. The original's tabletop, for example, has a huge knot evident, even through the finish.

These are more significant characteristics, to me, of country furniture's style than mere evidence of antiquity. I bring this up because it is a common practice in "reproducing" country furniture to simulate wear and age by barking the edges of the finished piece and sanding the finish away from the edges and from around knobs and pulls. Make it look old, you know. But no matter how well it is done, it lends a bogus quality to the completed piece. The paint is scuffed up, sure, and the edges are softened. But the surfaces are smooth and dead flat, the piece is square, the joints are solid and tight. There aren't repairs, or the odd nail

The reproduction table (*opposite*) lacks the patina and scars of the original (*above*), but it shares the original's simple grace.

CUTTING LIST

Piece	Number	Thickness	Width	Length	Material
Legs	4	$1^{1}/_{2}$"	$1^{1}/_{2}$"	$28^{3}/_{8}$"	pine
Short aprons	2	$^{3}/_{4}$"	$4^{1}/_{4}$"	13"	1-by pine
Long aprons	2	$^{3}/_{4}$"	$4^{1}/_{4}$"	32"	1-by pine
Leaf supports	2	$^{3}/_{4}$"	2"	18"	1-by pine
Top	1	$^{7}/_{8}$"	16"	39"	5/4 pine
Leaf board	2	$^{7}/_{8}$"	$6^{1}/_{4}$"	39"	5/4 pine
Leaf board	2	$^{7}/_{8}$"	$6^{1}/_{4}$"	36"	5/4 pine
Pivot pins	2	$^{5}/_{16}$" dia.		$1^{3}/_{8}$"	dowel
Pivot pins	2	$^{5}/_{16}$" dia.		1"	dowel

HARDWARE

2 pr. steel drop-leaf hinges, $1^{7}/_{16}$" × $3^{3}/_{16}$", with screws. Catalog number H-95 from Horton Brasses (203-635-4400).

6d cut finish nails

here and there, reinforcing a failed glue joint. Its antiquity is unabashedly ersatz.

I have to admit here that my responses to country furniture are frightfully schizoid. For me, a significant part of the charm of truly old country furniture pieces stems not simply from the way they've aged but also from the way they were built in the first place. It's the not-quite-tight joints, the not-quite-square frames, the not-quite-level tops. Some of you are nodding in agreement, and some of you are rolling your eyes and tapping your temples. But it's true. I look at the original drop-leaf table and I love it—dents, splits, rickety joints, and all.

At the same time, if you show me a new piece that has the proportions and design motifs, the construction and the colors, of some 150- to 200-year-old country piece, I'll probably like it, too. Built square and tight, using high-tech power tools and modern glues. It doesn't matter. If it has the proportions and design motifs and colors down, I'll like it. I won't care how it was made.

And yet, and yet . . . like a pinball caught between the bumpers, I go back and forth, back and forth.

When I built the reproduction of the drop-leaf, I refrained from trying to make it look old. I prepped the lumber to the best of my ability, making it flat and true. I crafted the joints as carefully as I know how, making them as tight as I could. But I stuck with the overt design features, idiosyncratic as they might be.

Here's an example.

In reproducing this table, it's entirely possible to make each leaf by gluing up two or three narrow boards. Nice flat, seamless panels. But the original wasn't done that way. Maybe cause he didn't have the ability to edge-glue stock into wide panels, or maybe because he feared that a single wide board would cup or warp, the original's builder combined two boards with a tongue-and-groove joint to form each leaf.

So I did the same. Except that—and here I go from one bumper to the other—over the years, that seam has opened up. Now it's a groove. And it's a striking element of the original's appearance. Maybe it'll strike you as goofy, but I like that groove-seam. I see it as a key aspect of this table's aesthetic.

Nevertheless, I made the tongue-and-groove joint just as tight as I could. If my table, like the original, lasts a hundred or more years, that same seam may open up into a groove, too. And I hope when it does, one of my great-grandchildren will like the table better that way. That's the essence of country furniture.

EXPLODED VIEW

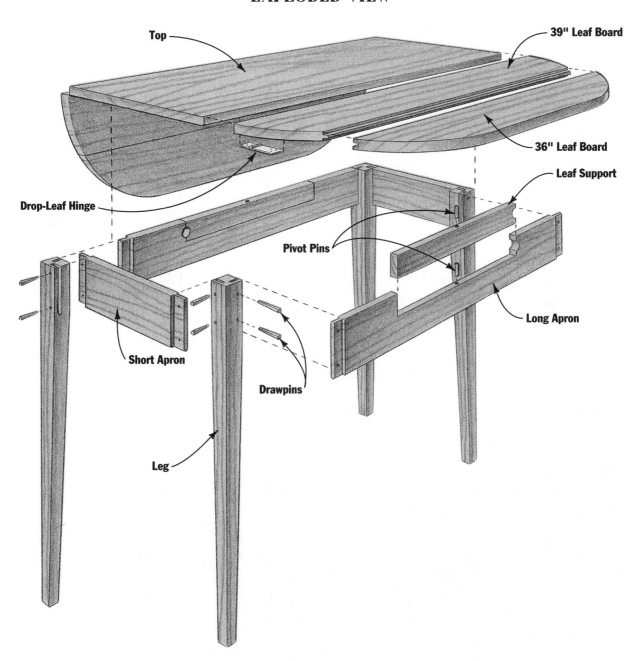

Top

39" Leaf Board

36" Leaf Board

Drop-Leaf Hinge

Leaf Support

Pivot Pins

Long Apron

Short Apron

Drawpins

Leg

---

1. Cut the legs, aprons, and leaf supports. To make the leg billets, rip eight 29-inch strips of 3/4 stock to about 1³⁄₄ inches wide. Face-glue them in pairs, forming the four billets. When the glue has dried and the clamps are off, scrape off the dried squeeze-out, then rip each billet to 1¹⁄₂ inches square.

Rip and crosscut stock for the aprons and leaf supports, as specified by the Cutting List.

2. Mortise the legs. All four legs are identical. Each has two 4¹⁄₄-inch-long mortises, which should be routed before the leg is tapered. Refer to the *Leg Layouts* for specific dimensions.

Cut the ¹⁄₄-inch-wide, 1-inch-deep mortises using a router (you can even use a fixed-base router for these mortises!) and a ¹⁄₄-inch straight bit. Refer to the *ShopSmarts* feature "Cutting Mortise-and-Tenon Joints" on page 83 for procedural tips.

PLAN VIEWS

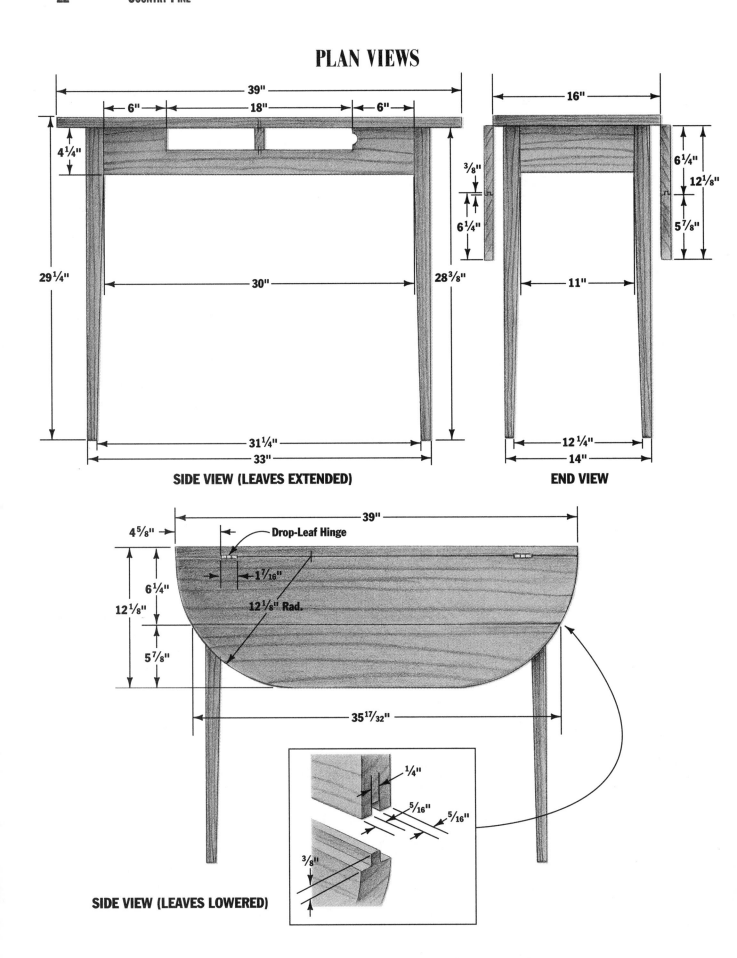

SIDE VIEW (LEAVES EXTENDED)

END VIEW

Drop-Leaf Hinge

12 1/8" Rad.

SIDE VIEW (LEAVES LOWERED)

PLAN VIEWS

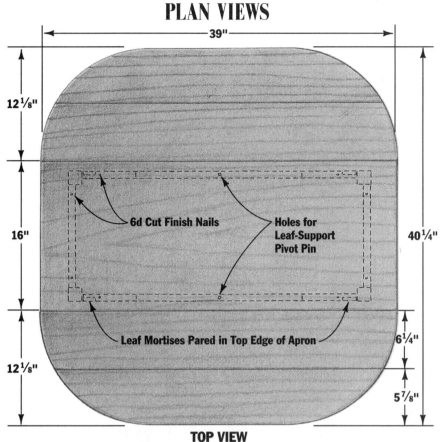

39"

12⅛"

16"

40¼"

12⅛"

6d Cut Finish Nails

Holes for
Leaf-Support
Pivot Pin

Leaf Mortises Pared in Top Edge of Apron

6¼"

5⅞"

TOP VIEW

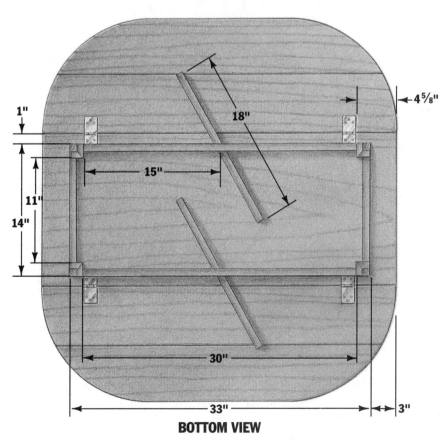

1"

18"

4⅝"

15"

11"

14"

30"

33"

3"

BOTTOM VIEW

3. Taper the legs. This task can be done on the table saw with a tapering jig. Details on the procedure can be found in the *ShopSmarts* feature "Tapering Legs on the Table Saw" on page 189.

The drawing *Leg Layouts* has all the pertinent dimensions. Lay out the taper on one leg, then use it to set up your tapering jig. To avoid confusion when tapering the legs, it's a good idea to mark the faces that must be tapered. The tapers begin 4¼ inches from the top. The footprint of each leg measures ⅞ inch square.

Cut one taper on each of the four legs, then reset the spindle of the toggle clamps, as necessary, and cut the second taper on each leg.

4. Tenon the aprons. The tenons that join the aprons to the legs are easily cut on the table saw using either a tenoning jig, described in the *ShopSmarts* feature "Cutting Mortise-and-Tenon Joints" on page 83, or a dado cutter. Note that these tenons extend the full width of the aprons; they aren't shouldered at the top and bottom. The procedure for using the tenoning jig is detailed in the *ShopSmarts* feature.

If you choose instead to use a dado cutter, set it up to make a ½- to ¾-inch-wide cut. Set the rip fence 1 inch from the outside of the cutter, and adjust the cutter height to something less than ¼ inch. The approach is to make two or more passes to cut each cheek of the tenon. Guide the workpiece with the miter gauge. The fence position prevents you from forming a tenon that's more than 1 inch long.

Before cutting the aprons, fine-tune the cutter height; cut a full tenon on a scrap of apron stock and test the fit in one of the mortises. When the height is set, cut the tenons on the aprons.

Since the end of the routed mortise is rounded, file the tenon edges to conform. Check the fit of the tenons in the mortises as you do this. Be sure to test assemble the entire leg-and-apron assembly; you probably will have to chamfer the end of at least one tenon going into each leg so it will clear the end of the other tenon going into the leg.

5. Notch the long aprons for the leaf supports. Begin by laying out the notches and the location of the finger hole. Refer to *Leg-to-Apron Joinery*. Bore the 1-inch-diameter hole, then cut the notch with a saber saw.

6. Bore the hinge-pin holes. Each leaf support and its pivot pins are trapped between the apron and the top. For the support to pivot properly, the four pivot holes—two in the support, one each in the top and the apron—have to be aligned and perpendicular. Drill the stopped holes in the supports and the aprons. All are 5/16 inch in diameter and 1/2 inch deep.

If you have a drill press, boring the holes in the support and the apron is relatively easy. Clamp a fence to the machine's table to locate the hole across the width of the workpiece. Then clamp the work to the fence, and drill. With a hand drill, use a doweling jig to position and guide the drill bit.

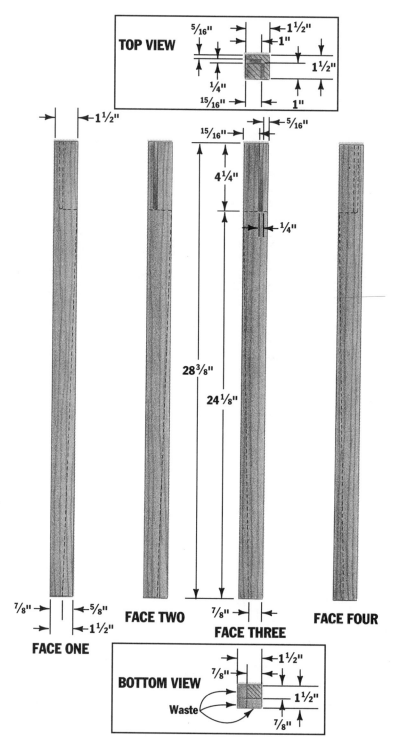

7. Assemble the legs and aprons. Sand the legs thoroughly to remove saw marks. Sand first with 80-grit paper. Brush or vacuum the dust from the work, then switch to 120-grit and sand again. Sand the aprons and leaf supports as well.

Spread glue lightly over the short-apron tenons and on the inside of the mortises for them. Assemble and clamp the subassemblies. After the glue sets—within an hour if you are using white or yellow glue—you can pull the clamps and then glue the long aprons to the legs. Clamp the assembly until the glue sets.

The Perfect Boring Tool

You might not instinctively think of the plunge router as a boring tool, but in some situations, it's the perfect one.

Take, for example, the pivot-pin holes needed in the leaf supports and apron of this table. The holes must be accurately positioned and perfectly perpendicular if the leaf supports are to pivot properly. Used in conjunction with the mortising fixture described in the *ShopSmarts* feature "Cutting Mortise-and-Tenon Joints" on page 83, the plunge router does an excellent job.

Secure the mortising fixture in your workbench vise. Mark the location for a test boring on a scrap of the working stock. Align this mark with the alignment line on the fixture, then clamp the test scrap in the fixture. Chuck the appropriate bit in the router. Adjust the depth stop to set the depth of the boring. Set the router on the fixture and adjust the edge guide so the hole will be where you want it. Attach stops to the fixture to keep the router from shifting. Turn on the router and plunge the bit into the stock.

If the hole is right where it needs to be, then the setup is right and you can bore the holes in the workpieces. Always keep the same face of the work against the back of the fixture. This will ensure that the holes align.

Finally, after the clamps have been removed, lock each joint with two drawpins, as shown in *Leg-to-Apron Joinery*. Fashion the drawpins from scraps of hardwood. To insert each drawpin, first drill a pilot hole, boring through the face of the leg and the tenon; there's no need to bore completely through the leg. Apply a bit of glue to the drawpin and drive it into the hole. After the glue cures, pare the pin flush.

While you have the glue out, glue a pivot pin into the pivot hole in each long apron.

8. Glue up the top and the leaf boards. The original's top is a single 16-inch-wide board, while each leaf is

LEG-TO-APRON JOINERY

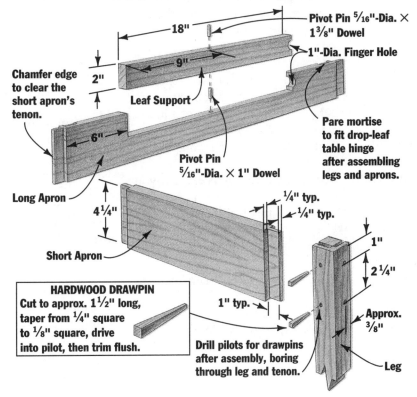

Pivot Pin $5/16$"-Dia. × $1 3/8$" Dowel

1"-Dia. Finger Hole

18"

9"

2"

Chamfer edge to clear the short apron's tenon.

Leaf Support

Pare mortise to fit drop-leaf table hinge after assembling legs and aprons.

6"

Long Apron

Pivot Pin $5/16$"-Dia. × 1" Dowel

$4 1/4$"

Short Apron

$1/4$" typ.

$1/4$" typ.

1"

$2 1/4$"

1" typ.

Approx. $3/8$"

Leg

HARDWOOD DRAWPIN
Cut to approx. $1 1/2$" long, taper from $1/4$" square to $1/8$" square, drive into pilot, then trim flush.

Drill pilots for drawpins after assembly, boring through leg and tenon.

made up of two 6¼-inch-wide boards joined (somewhat crudely) in a tongue-and-groove joint.

The boards making up the tabletop (including the leaves) should be resawed (or planed down) from 5/4 stock. Since it's unlikely that you'll find a single wide board for the top, glue up as many boards as necessary to create a panel for the top. If necessary (and it was for the table I built), glue up stock to form the leaf boards.

Scrape any dried glue squeeze-out from the panels. Sand them smooth and flat.

9. Cut the joinery on the leaf boards.
Each leaf is composed of two boards joined with a tongue-and-groove joint. The slot is cut in the edge of the longer of each pair of boards; the tongue, on the edge of the shorter.

If you have a tongue-and-groove bit assembly for your router, you can rout an appropriate joint quickly and easily. But if you use a ¼-inch slot cutter with a table-mounted router, you can rout a duplicate of the tongue-and-groove joint used in the original.

The depth of the slot should be ⅜ inch, but the typical slot cutter produces a ½-inch-deep slot. Use the router table's fence to limit the slot depth. Adjust the depth of cut to position the slot as close to the middle of the board's edge as you can. Cut the slots in two passes. After making the first pass, flip the board over and make a second pass. Though the slot may be slightly wider than ¼ inch, it will be centered on the edge.

After you've cut a slot in one edge of each board, reset the cutter to rout the tongues. Cut two rabbets to form the tongue. Make test cuts on a scrap to test the setting, and check the fit of the tongue formed in the grooves you've already cut. When you have the router properly adjusted, cut the tongues on the workpieces.

10. Assemble and shape the leaves.
Do you have the nerve to make up a joint that isn't perfectly square and tight? If you do, this is the place. Maybe you want to take a swipe at one shoulder of the groove with a block plane to ensure the joint won't close tightly.

At any rate, edge-glue the two boards making up each leaf.

After you've removed the clamps, scraped off any dried glue squeeze-out, and sanded the leaf, radius the corners. You can mark the cut line using a trammel, or you can make a pattern and trace it.

If you want a perfect edge on the leaves' curved corners, make a pattern of the exact radius you want. Use ¼-inch hardboard or ½-inch plywood for the pattern. Align it over the workpiece, and clamp both to the workbench, with the area to be cut extended off the bench top. Saw off the corner with a saber saw, keeping the blade ⅛ inch or so away from the pattern. With a router and a pattern bit, machine the edge. The bit's bearing will ride along the pattern, guiding the router, as the cutting edges trim the workpiece.

Use a saber saw to make the cut. Sand the cut edge smooth.

To capture the look of the original, toenail a 6d cut finish nail through the edge of the short-leaf board into the tongue-and-groove joint.

11. Attach the top.
The top is simply nailed to the leg-and-apron assembly. But before you do that, you must locate and bore the last two holes for the leaf-support pivots. And you need to install the drop-leaf table hinges before nailing down the top.

To locate the pivot holes, use dowel pins. Set the leaf supports in place, and insert one dowel pin each in their top pivot holes. Carefully align the top over the leg-and-apron assembly, then firmly press it onto the dowel pins, which will dimple the wood. On the original table, the pivot holes in the tabletop are through; you can see the pivot pins. So drill a through hole at each of the marked spots.

Now lay out the tabletop and the two leaves and install the drop-leaf hinges. These hinges should be surface-mounted, rather than being mortised into the wood. You do need to pare a recess into the edges of the tabletop and leaves for the hinge barrel, however. Screw the hinges to the tabletop.

Set the assembled top on the leg-and-apron assembly, and determine whether you will need to mortise the aprons for the hinge leaves. This was done on the original, and it was necessary on our reproduction, too. You just have to pare a recess whose depth equals the hinge-leaf thickness. Then, with the top in place, drill pilot holes for the 6d cut finish nails you'll use to fasten the top. Drive the nails.

Finally, insert the last two pivot pins. You don't want to glue the pins to both the leaf supports and the tabletop. So apply a dot of glue to the very top of the pin, insert the glue-free end in the hole, and drive it flush with the tabletop. The glue will bond it to the top.

12. Finish the table. The original table appears to have been finished with red milk paint. That means it isn't a vibrant red, but rather a rich red-brown. It also means the figure of the wood is subtly visible through the pigment.

I used the same finish on our reproduction, mixing and applying the milk paint as outlined in the *ShopSmarts* feature "Country Finishes" on page 305. After the last coat of milk paint dried, I applied a thinned coat of satin polyurethane. After that dried, I scuff-sanded it with 220-grit sandpaper and applied a full-strength coat of the polyurethane. The polyurethane darkened the color of the milk paint.

Before settling on the polyurethane, I experimented with several different "clear" sealers on

Use a router and edge guide to rout recesses in the tabletop and leaf edges for the drop-leaf table hinges. Lay out the locations of the hinges and the limits of the recesses. Cut one recess with a chisel, and when the hinge fits it perfectly, use it to set the router's bit height and edge-guide position. Then rout the other seven recesses, cutting by eye from mark to mark. Square the ends of each recess with a chisel.

scraps that I painted with the milk paint. Most of the options—boiled linseed oil, tung oil, brushing lacquer, polyurethane—*will* darken the paint color. I selected the polyurethane because it's a practical, durable surface that resists water marks and other hazards of use.

HANGING DISPLAY SHELF

This shelf is ample proof that it doesn't take a lot of embellishment to transform a rough, utilitarian design into something quite civilized. To me, it is classic country furniture. The piece is little more than three shelves trapped between two sides, yet it comes across as a light, pretty wall cabinet with a glass door.

Of course there is no door, no glass. It's just a shelf unit.

It's the face frame that produces the effect of a door. And the imagined door seems to transform the unit into a cabinet. The cornice molding under the top—a molding that mimics the face frame, I might add—contributes to the overall "cabinet" effect.

Overall, the shelf unit isn't particularly deep. Clearly, it was not intended as a bookshelf. Because it is fairly formal in appearance, it was surely meant for displaying valued items: perhaps the family's formal glassware or a treasured collection.

The thickness of the stock used in the piece also is important to its appearance. From whatever angle you

view the piece, it seems very light. Not delicate, but light. The proportions—the height and width in relation to the depth—play a significant role here. But so does the sophisticated balance achieved between the thicks and the thins. The face frame is a prominent element that's 2 inches wide, seen straight on. But the side extensions, the shelves, and the top are only 5/8 inch thick. Seen from an angle, it is clear that the face frame and the cornice molding are slender, thus achieving a good balance with the width of the sides and the thickness of the other parts.

It is, in sum, a sophisticated design, hardly what might be expected from a country woodworker.

This is a great weekend project. Take the plans into the shop Saturday morning. By nightfall, you can have the piece all assembled and ready for a finish. And depending upon the finish you choose, Sunday afternoon may be long enough to get that completed. Two coats of milk paint, for example, can be applied within a two-hour time frame.

Like the original (*above*), the reproduction shelf (*opposite*) is light in weight and appearance, the perfect showcase for your tchotchkes.

29

CUTTING LIST

Piece	Number	Thickness	Width	Length	Material
Sides	2	$5/8$"	$5^3/8$"	$33^5/8$"	1-by pine
Shelves	3	$5/8$"	$4^{15}/16$"	$22^1/2$"	1-by pine
Top	1	$5/8$"	$6^5/8$"	$24^7/8$"	1-by pine
Face frame stiles	2	$7/16$"	$1^7/8$"	$25^3/8$"	5/4 pine
Face frame rails	2	$7/16$"	2"	$23^1/4$"	5/4 pine
Back boards	3	$7/16$"	$5^7/8$"	$27^3/8$"	5/4 pine
Back board	1	$7/16$"	$5^5/8$"	$27^3/8$"	5/4 pine
Cornice molding	1	$7/16$"	$7/8$"	$24^1/4$"	5/4 pine
Cornice molding	2	$7/16$"	$7/8$"	$6^3/8$"	5/4 pine

HARDWARE
4d fine-cut headless brads
2 hanger plates, $9/16$" × 2", with screws

Now, unless you have a planer, you may be put off by those stock thicknesses I've just extolled. Don't be. Even a relatively inexperienced hobby woodworker can use his or her table saw to cut 1-by and 5/4 stock down to the thicknesses needed. The process is called resawing, and how to do it is detailed in the *ShopSmarts* feature titled "Resawing on the Table Saw" on page 112. It is safe, and it is easy. Even this stock preparation work can be accomplished in that self-same weekend.

To validate this claim, I built the shelf shown in one weekend, using wood I resawed on my 10-inch contractor's saw. (If you don't believe me . . . well, there's nothing I can do about it.)

Before I release you weekend woodworkers to get out there and tackle this project, there's one final aspect to the original that I want to tell you about. It's encouragement for those of you who worry about the accuracy of your work.

Here it is: The original is not square. Mind you, it looks great! But one side is $3/8$ inch longer than the other, and the distance from the top to the first shelf is $3/8$ inch greater on one side than on the other. The consequence is, if you hang the piece with the top level, the shelves aren't level. And if you level the shelves, the top's off.

But the point is: *It looks great!* It's what we call country woodworking. Do the best you can, and it'll all look great!

1. Prepare the stock. In the Cutting List, I've suggested taking the ⅝-inch-thick parts from standard 1-by stock, and the thinner parts from 5/4 stock. The rationale is that a single strip of 5/4 can yield two strips of $7/16$-inch-thick material. For example, two pieces of 5/4 pine cut to 6 × 28 inches should yield the four back boards needed.

The first step, then, is to cut the various parts to rough size. (Leave the boards for the molding and the face frame several inches overlong.) Then resaw the parts on the table saw to the thicknesses specified by the Cutting List. Follow the resawing procedure detailed in the *ShopSmarts* feature "Resawing on the Table Saw" on page 112.

After resawing the stock, sand away the saw marks with a belt sander. Rip and crosscut the sides, shelves, top, and back boards to their final dimensions. Leave the other parts at their rough dimensions.

EXPLODED VIEW

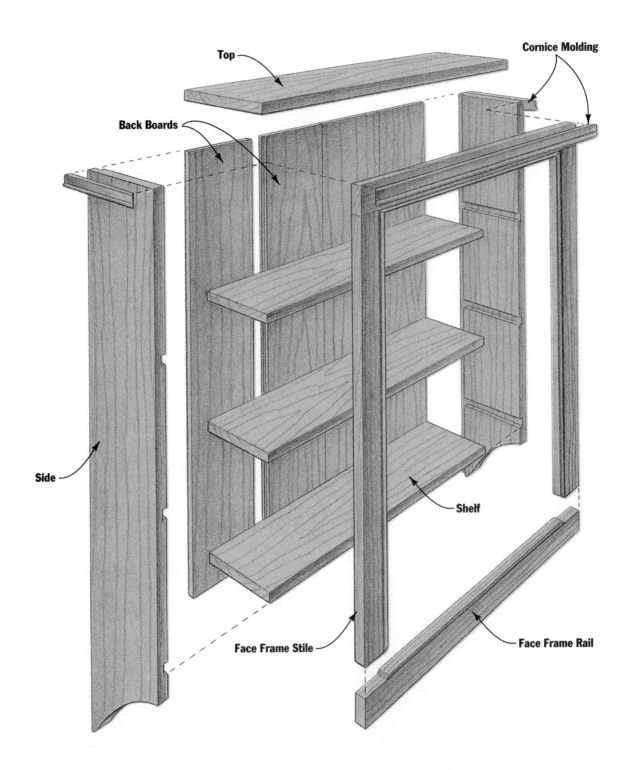

Top

Cornice Molding

Back Boards

Side

Shelf

Face Frame Stile

Face Frame Rail

PLAN VIEWS

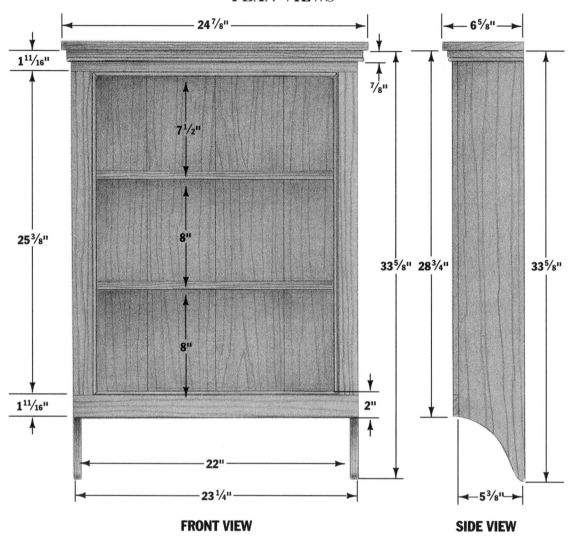

FRONT VIEW

SIDE VIEW

2. Cut the joinery. Lay out the dadoes on the sides. You can cut the dadoes and rabbets using a router and a $^5/_8$-inch straight bit. To ensure that your shelves are square and level, clamp the two sides edge to edge and rout each dado in both sides in a single pass of the router. Guide the router along a T-square or other straightedge clamped to the workpieces.

Smoothing resawed boards with a portable belt sander is quick and easy. Find a scrap strip a bit thinner than the resawed stock, and clamp it across the workbench, as shown. Instead of clamping the workpiece, you simply catch it against the strip. The belt sander can't shoot the workpiece across the shop because of the catch strip.

PLAN VIEWS

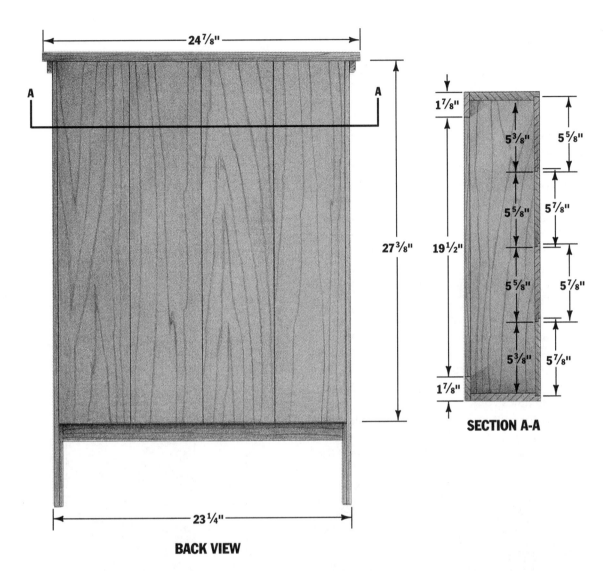

BACK VIEW

SECTION A-A

After the dadoes are done, mount an edge guide on the router and use it to guide the routing of the rabbet for the back. Although the back boards don't extend below the bottom shelf, the rabbets are plowed from one end to the other.

3. Cut the contour on the sides. Enlarge the pattern for the contour of the lower ends of the sides, and transfer the arc to the sides. Cut the contour with a saber saw, then saw the edges smooth.

4. Cut the shiplaps on the back boards. The back boards are shiplapped so that when they shrink, cracks won't open up that would reveal the wall behind the shelf. (This represents an alteration from the original. Its back is composed of a 17-inch-

wide board and a 5½-inch-wide board, which were simply butted edge to edge. There's now a considerable gap between them.)

A shiplap is an unglued edge joint formed by interlinking rabbets. You simply rout a rabbet along the edge of the back board, with a depth equal to half the board's thickness. Refer to *Section A-A* in the *Plan Views* for placement and dimensions of the cuts.

5. Assemble the shelf. With all the structural parts in readiness, you can glue and nail the piece together. Join the sides and shelves with glue and 4d (1½-inch-long) fine-cut headless brads. Glue and nail the top in place next. Finally, nail (don't glue) the back boards in place.

6. Rout the bead on the face frame parts and cornice molding. This is best done with a table-mounted router. Both beads are ¼-inch-diameter beads, but you must use two different bits to cut them. Use a standard edge-beading bit for the face frame, but use a so-called drawing-line beading bit (for example, Cascade's bit number C1119 or C1122) for the cornice molding (available from Cascade Tools, 800-235-0272). Set the bit height and the fence, then run the roughly sized parts along the fence, routing the bead.

7. Attach the face frame to the shelf. Rip the rails and stiles to the widths specified by the Cutting List. In the course of attaching these parts, you must miter and trim the bead for a perfect fit. Crosscut the rails so they extend from side to side, as shown in the *Front View*. Trim one end of each stile square, then miter just the bead from that end of each stile.

Set the top rail in place first, and hold a stile in position. Mark the rail for mitering and trimming. Do this on both ends of the top rail. Cut the miters on the table saw, then trim the excess bead from the rail with a handsaw. Attach the top rail with 4d fine-cut headless brads.

Now set the bottom rail in position and hold the stiles in place, as before. Mark, miter, and trim the bottom rail and the bottom ends of the stiles. Nail these parts to the shelf unit.

SIDE LAYOUT

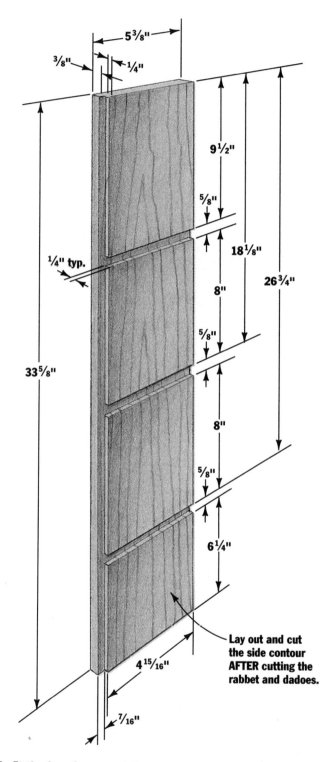

Lay out and cut the side contour AFTER cutting the rabbet and dadoes.

To fit the face frame, cut the two rails to length. Miter the bead on one end of a stile. Set the mitered stile in position over the end of the rail. With a marking knife, mark the rail's bead, as shown. Miter to the outside of the knife mark, and trim off the bead.

Resawing a Wide Board: Giving the Table Saw a Hand

Your table saw's depth-of-cut capacity may not be sufficient to cut completely through the wider parts like the top and the back boards. If this is the case, you can deal with these parts using—aawwk!—hand tools.

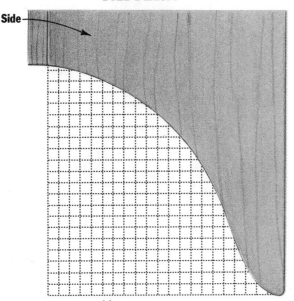

Separate the back boards with a handsaw guided by the table-sawn kerfs, as shown. The handsaw will likely produce a thinner kerf than the table saw, which means there will be a pronounced ridge down the center of each new—thinner—board. This is the problem with the top—a ridge that remains on the sawed face. Just plane this off with a block plane or a smoothing plane.

PATTERN

Side

1 Square = ¼"

8. Attach the cornice molding. Rip the cornice molding to its final width. Miter one end of each of the short side pieces, and nail them to the shelf unit. The square-cut ends can extend beyond the back of the unit, but the mitered ends must be perfectly positioned.

Fit the long molding strip between the ends. Miter one end, and hold the strip in place to mark the other end for length. Miter that end, and attach the molding to the case.

9. Apply a finish. The original has a crackled black paint. The crackled finish is popular, but it can be a trial to mimic. I opted simply to paint the shelf I made. The *ShopSmarts* feature "Country Finishes" on page 305 provides details on how to achieve the best paint job, from prime coat through final coat. Finally, I attached two hanger plates to the shelf's back so it could be hung on the wall.

STEP-BACK CUPBOARD

This pine step-back cupboard is a model country piece. The wood, the design, and the construction are remarkably unremarkable. The cupboard is strictly functional and very solid. It's the perfect big piece for a relative beginner to build.

The original is made of wide, fairly thick, hand-planed pine boards. Back when the original was built, 14- to 20-inch-wide pine boards were commonplace. As a consequence, none of the "panels" are glued up; they're all single boards. The thickness of the boards is a function of the planing process: Once they were smooth, the country woodworker quit planing them.

The design is aggressively plain. No molding, no fancy touches. Aside from chamfers on the door frames and some curves on the face frame stiles, the cupboard is free of embellishment. The original finish is gone. It's likely that it was painted outside as well as inside.

The case joinery is about as simple as it can get: The case is nailed together. And the face frame parts aren't even

connected to one another! Each is simply nailed to the case, independent of all the others. Nevertheless, the original cupboard is as sound and tight today as it was the day, more than 100 years ago, it was built.

The alterations we made in constructing a reproduction are minimal, largely dictated by material availability and contemporary woodworking conventions. The visible difference between the old piece and our new one is obvious from the photos. The old is soft and charming, the new is crisp and functional. The reproduction was made with wood of uniform thickness and with parallel edges; the assemblies are square; the chamfers and rounded edges are mechanically uniform. Much of the original's charm lies in its soft and subtle slouch.

All the more reason for a beginner not to be put off by the scale of the piece. Though large, it is simple to build. There's a minimum of parts, no drawers, very basic doors. Small imperfections contribute character.

The old cupboard (*above*) has been stripped of its original finish. When new, it looked like our painted reproduction (*opposite*).

EXPLODED VIEW—TOP CASE

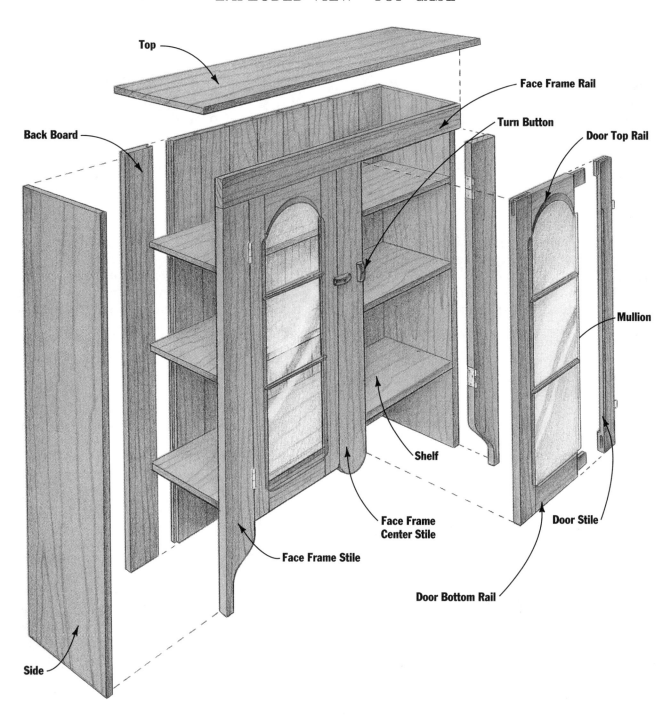

Top

Face Frame Rail

Turn Button

Door Top Rail

Back Board

Mullion

Shelf

Face Frame
Center Stile

Door Stile

Face Frame Stile

Door Bottom Rail

Side

BUILD THE BASE AND TOP CASE

1. Glue up the panels. Back when this cupboard was originally built, finding 14- to 20-inch-wide boards was no problem, so the case was constructed using individual wide boards.

For *you* to make many of the parts, you'll need to edge-glue narrow boards. Useful pointers on this process can be gleaned from the *ShopSmarts* features "Gluing Up Panels" and "Routing an Edge

EXPLODED VIEW—BASE

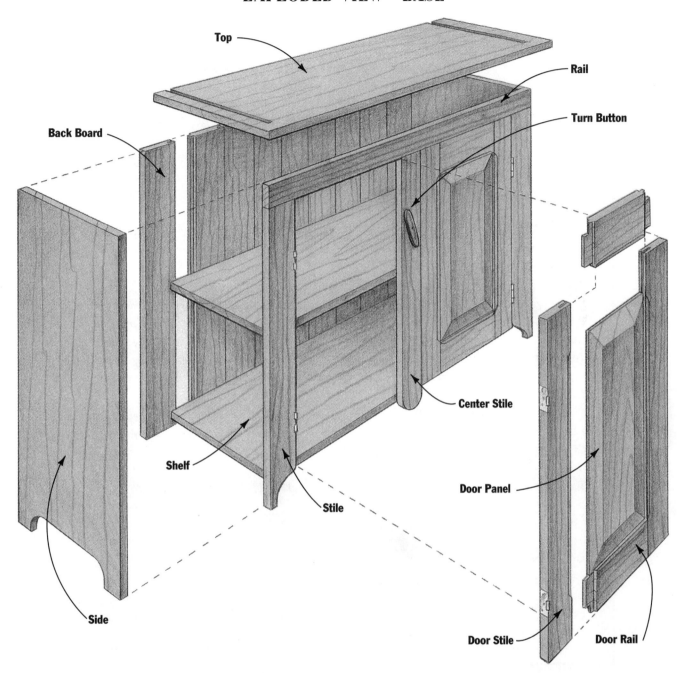

Top

Rail

Turn Button

Back Board

Center Stile

Shelf

Door Panel

Stile

Side

Door Stile

Door Rail

Joint" on pages 49 and 264, respectively. The Cutting List shows the sizes of the parts needed; glue up stock as needed to make parts of the sizes listed. At this time, make the base and top case sides, shelves, and tops.

2. Cut the feet. After the clamps are off the base sides, lay out the feet, as shown in the *Side Cutout Detail*, on the sides. Cut away the waste with a saber saw, and sand the cut edges smooth.

3. Rout stopped dadoes in the base's top. The top case's sides fit into these dadoes when the top case is set in place atop the base. Use a $3/4$-inch straight bit, and cut the dadoes $1/4$ inch deep. They should extend $11^3/8$ inches from the top case's back edge. Use a chisel to square the end of each dado.

4. Make the boards for the back. The back is made up of several boards, joined edge to edge with tongue-and-groove joints. In the original, only four

CUTTING LIST

Piece	Number	Thickness	Width	Length	Material
TOP CASE					
Sides	2	$3/4$"	$11^3/8$"	$48^1/4$"	1-by pine
Top	1	$3/4$"	$13^7/8$"	$50^1/2$"	1-by pine
Face frame rail	1	$3/4$"	$3^1/4$"	$45^1/2$"	1-by pine
Face frame stiles	2	$3/4$"	$4^1/4$"	$44^3/4$"	1-by pine
Face frame center stile	1	$3/4$"	$3^3/4$"	$36^3/8$"	1-by pine
Shelves	3	$3/4$"	$11^3/8$"	44"	1-by pine
Back	9	$3/4$"	$5^1/2$"	$48^3/4$"	1-by pine
TOP CASE DOORS					
Top rails	2	$3/4$"	$4^7/8$"	$16^1/2$"	1-by pine
Bottom rails	2	$3/4$"	$2^1/2$"	$14^7/8$"	1-by pine
Stiles	4	$3/4$"	$2^1/2$"	$34^1/4$"	1-by pine
Mullions	4	$3/4$"	$3/4$"	$12^1/4$"	1-by pine
Turn buttons	2	$3/4$"	$3/4$"	2"	1-by pine
BASE					
Sides	2	$3/4$"	$15^3/4$"	36"	1-by pine
Rail	1	$3/4$"	$2^1/2$"	$45^1/2$"	1-by pine
Stiles	2	$3/4$"	$4^1/4$"	$33^1/2$"	1-by pine
Center stile	1	$3/4$"	$3^3/4$"	$32^1/2$"	1-by pine
Top	1	$3/4$"	18"	50"	1-by pine
Shelves	2	$3/4$"	$15^3/4$"	44"	1-by pine
Back	9	$3/4$"	$5^1/2$"	$35^1/4$"	1-by pine
BASE DOORS					
Rails	4	$3/4$"	$4^1/4$"	$11^3/4$"	1-by pine
Stiles	4	$3/4$"	$3^3/4$"	$30^7/8$"	1-by pine
Panels	2	$3/4$"	$9^3/4$"	$23^1/8$"	1-by pine
Turn button	1	$3/4$"	$3/4$"	$5^3/4$"	1-by pine

HARDWARE

6d finish nails

6d cut finish nails

1 pc. glass, $10^3/8$" × $12^1/4$"

1 pc. glass, 10" × $12^1/4$"

1 pc. glass, $10^1/8$" × $12^1/4$"

4 pr. hinges, 2" × $1^1/2$"

3 brass roundhead screws, #8 × $1^1/4$" (for turn buttons)

wide boards were used. In our reproduction, we used nine. Rip and crosscut the stock to the sizes specified by the Cutting List.

Cut the tongues and grooves on the back pieces. Each piece gets a slot along one edge and a tongue along the other.

We used a ¼-inch slot cutter in a hand-held router to cut this joinery. Typically, a slot cutter produces a ½-inch-deep slot. Since you want it only ¼ inch deep, use the router's edge guide to limit how deep the bit cuts. Set the router's depth of cut to position the slot as close to the middle of the board's edge as you can. Cut the slots in two passes. After making the first pass, flip the board over and make a second pass in the same slot. Though the slot may be slightly wider than ¼ inch, it will be centered on the edge.

After you've cut a slot in one edge of each board, reset the cutter to rout the tongues. Each tongue is formed by cutting two rabbets: Rabbet the edge, turn the board over, and rabbet the same edge a second time. The ridge of wood left between the rabbets is the tongue. Make test cuts on a scrap to test the setting, and check the fit of the tongue

formed in the grooves you've already cut. When you have the router properly adjusted, cut the tongues on the workpieces.

5. Assemble the cases. The cases are assembled with cut nails. Glue won't contribute much strength, since the butt joints are all end grain to long grain. The nails will be sufficient. To prevent splitting, it is important to drill pilot holes for these nails.

The challenge here is to clamp or prop the panels in position while you drill the pilot holes and drive the nails. With a pencil and square, scribe lines across the sides for the shelves. Start with the top case; its parts are narrower and easier to work with. Stand the shelves and one side or edge on the floor. A couple of corner clamps can hold the shelves against the side while you drill and nail. Then add the second side. Finally, nail the case's top in place.

To nail the back boards in place, rest the top case across a pair of sawhorses. Trim the groove from the first board, and nail it in place. It should overlay both the top and the side. Be sure the top

PATTERNS AND DETAILS

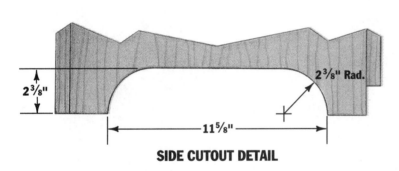

SIDE CUTOUT DETAIL

2³⁄₈"   11⁵⁄₈"   2³⁄₈" Rad.

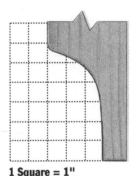

1 Square = 1"
TOP CASE STILE PATTERN

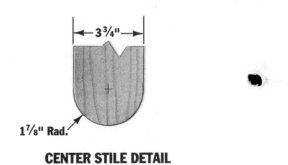

3¾"   1⁷⁄₈" Rad.

CENTER STILE DETAIL

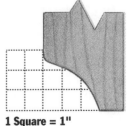

1 Square = 1"
BASE STILE PATTERN

PLAN VIEWS

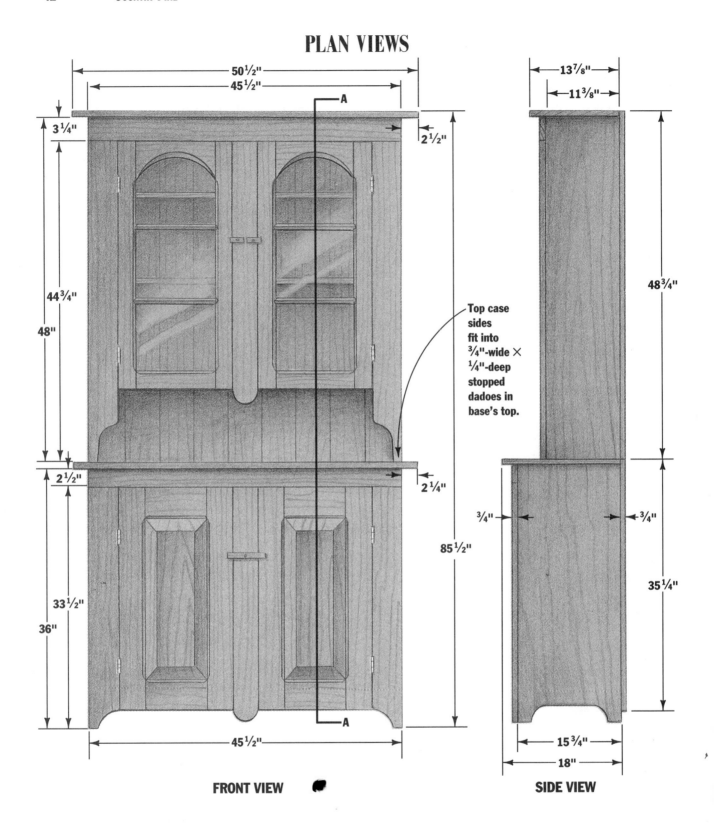

Top case sides fit into ³⁄₄"-wide × ¹⁄₄"-deep stopped dadoes in base's top.

50¹⁄₂"
45¹⁄₂"
3¹⁄₄"
2¹⁄₂"
44³⁄₄"
48"
2¹⁄₂"
2¹⁄₄"
85¹⁄₂"
33¹⁄₂"
36"
45¹⁄₂"

A

13⁷⁄₈"
11³⁄₈"
48³⁄₄"
³⁄₄"   ³⁄₄"
35¹⁄₄"
15³⁄₄"
18"

FRONT VIEW   **SIDE VIEW**

case is square when you nail down the board. Drive cut nails only through the back into the edge of the side and the top. Drive regular 6d finish nails through the shoulder of the board at the tongue, putting one nail into each shelf. Fit the next back board into place, and drive the finish nails along the tongue edge. Add the remaining boards in the same manner. The tongue must be trimmed from the last

PLAN VIEW

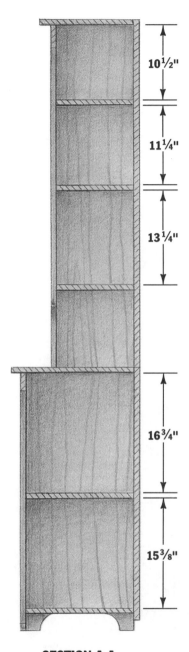

10½"

11¼"

13¼"

16¾"

15⅜"

SECTION A-A

Trying to nail loose boards together to form a case can also try your patience. Try this trick: Apply a couple of hand screws to each shelf, as shown here, so they'll stand on end. You can then rest a side across them and drive nails through it into the shelf ends.

6. Cut and install the face frames. The face frames on both the top case and the base are composed of three stiles and one rail. Interestingly, the parts are not joined to each other; rather, they are nailed to the case only.

Cut the parts to the sizes specified by the Cutting List. The center stiles are rounded on the lower end, as shown in the *Center Stile Detail*. The outside stiles have archlike contours on the lower ends. Enlarge the patterns for these contours, transfer them to the appropriate parts, and cut the contours with a saber saw. Sand the cut edges smooth.

Nail the parts to the cases using cut finish nails. Attach the rails first, driving a couple of nails through each end into the sides, and additional nails through the case tops into the rails. Then attach the stiles, nailing them to the sides and/or shelves. **Note:** The sides of the top case should project ¼ inch beyond the ends of the outer stiles so they can drop into the dadoes in the base's top.

board so its exposed edge will be flush. Use the cut nails to fasten it to the case side and top.

When the top case is completed, repeat the process to assemble the base.

BUILD THE BASE DOORS

1. Cut the door parts. Each base door has a raised panel that "floats" in a groove in the rails and stiles. The rails and stiles are joined with mortise-and-tenon joints. The inner edges of the door frame are embellished with stopped chamfers, which, to get the correct appearance at the inside corners, should be routed before assembly.

The base doors on our reproduction deviate from those on the original in a couple of particulars. The stock is not as thick as on the original, and the mortise-and-tenon joints are stopped rather than through. The net result of these changes is that the doors are easier to make.

Rip the door stock as required, and crosscut it to the sizes specified by the Cutting List. Lightly write the part name on each blank so you won't get the parts mixed up.

2. Cut the decorative chamfer. Begin by marking a "reference face" of each rail and stile (either the front or the back—it doesn't matter which, so long as you are consistent). Also mark the tenon shoulders on the rails. On the stiles, mark where the inside corners will be. The chamfer cuts should end at or just shy of these marks.

Now cut the decorative chamfer. Use a 30-degree

BASE DOOR CONSTRUCTION

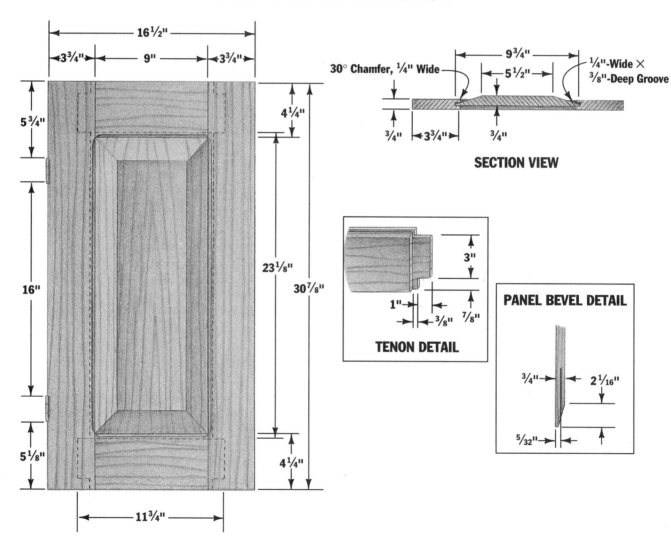

SECTION VIEW

TENON DETAIL

PANEL BEVEL DETAIL

chamfer bit if at all possible. Typically, chamfer bits are 45-degree, but CMT Tools (800-531-5559), Amana Tool (800-445-0077), and Eagle America (800-872-2511) are three manufacturers who make 30-degree chamfer bits. Begin the chamfer cut at one mark and carry it to the other. Be sure you don't cut the least bit beyond either mark, or you'll spoil the look of the finished door.

3. Groove the frame parts. Set up the router table to plow a $\frac{1}{4}$-inch-wide × $\frac{3}{8}$-inch-deep groove centered across the edge of both rails and stiles. You can make this cut using either a slot cutter or a straight bit. Groove just the inside edges of the frame parts.

4. Rout the mortises. The rails and stiles are joined with haunched mortise-and-tenon joints. The *ShopSmarts* feature "Cutting Mortise-and-Tenon Joints" on page 83 provides detailed information on routing mortises and cutting tenons on the table saw.

Rout the mortises first. They are the same width as the groove ($\frac{1}{4}$ inch) and are 3 inches long and $1\frac{3}{8}$ inches deep. Locate the mortises, as shown in *Base Door Construction*. The mortises are easy to rout using a $\frac{1}{4}$-inch upcut spiral bit and a plunge router.

5. Cut the tenons on the rails. These tenons are haunched, which is to say, they have an extension to one side that fills the short section of groove between the stile's end and the mortise. Follow the procedure outlined in the *ShopSmarts* feature "Cutting Mortise-and-Tenon Joints" on page 83 to cut the shoulders and cheeks of the tenons. Use the tenoning jig shown in the *ShopSmarts* feature. Next, form the haunch by trimming the tenon with a backsaw. Finally, use a file to round off the corners of the tenons so that they fit into the routed mortises.

Make Your Door Frames a Little Oversized

If a door opening is slightly large or slightly out-of-square, you've given yourself a margin for error.

Rip both the rails and stiles just a tad wider than specified and crosscut the stiles slightly long so the assembled frame will be $\frac{1}{16}$ to $\frac{1}{8}$ inch longer and wider than your specs call for. The final step is to trim the door, *not to the specified dimensions*, but to *fit*.

Making the frames slightly oversized can free you from some of the cares of woodworking, too. No more fumbling with cauls to protect the frame edges from clamp jaws. So what if you get a crease or two! The damage gets trimmed off.

---

6. Raise the panels. The panels are raised on the front only. They feature a straight bevel that has no fillet around the field. The bevel is irregular, but it averages $2\frac{1}{16}$ inches in width. Read through the *ShopSmarts* feature "Raising Panels" on page 140, and follow the directions given there to raise the panels.

Sand the bevels judiciously with a belt sander to remove the saw marks.

7. Assemble the base doors. Assemble the two doors without glue to test how everything fits. Disassemble the doors, and assuming no further adjusting is necessary, finish sand the separate parts. Then apply glue to the mortises and tenons (only) and assemble and clamp the doors. The panels should not be glued to the frames; they need to be free to expand and contract with seasonal humidity changes.

While the glue sets, turn to the top case doors.

BUILD THE TOP CASE DOORS

1. Cut the door parts. As with the base doors, the top case doors on our reproduction deviate from those on the original in stock thickness and in the particulars of the mortise-and-tenon joinery. The joint between stile and bottom rail is a haunched mortise-and-tenon, as in the base doors. But the one between top rail and stile is an open mortise-and-tenon, a joint that's often called a bridle joint or slip joint. To eliminate the need to shape the top pane of glass, the top rail has an expansive rabbet in it. Cutting both the rabbet and a strong conventional tenon is tough. The open mortise-and-tenon provides a very strong joint yet makes it a snap to cut the necessary rabbet.

GLAZED DOOR CONSTRUCTION

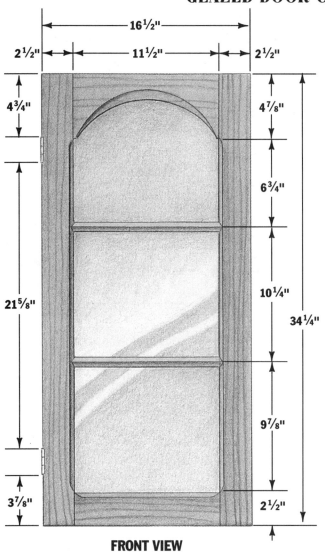

FRONT VIEW

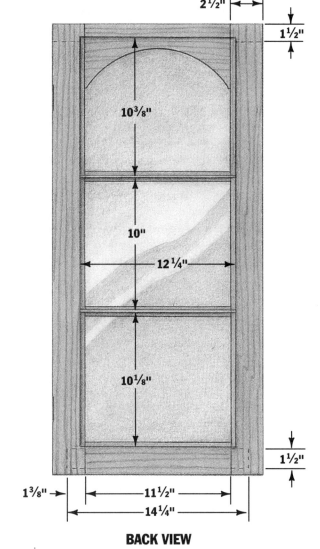

BACK VIEW

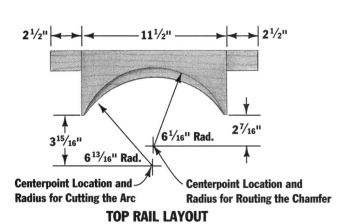

TOP RAIL LAYOUT

Centerpoint Location and Radius for Cutting the Arc

Centerpoint Location and Radius for Routing the Chamfer

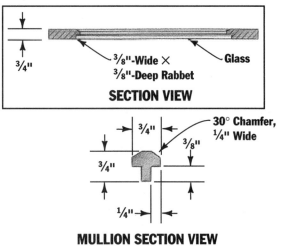

³⁄₈"-Wide × ³⁄₈"-Deep Rabbet

Glass

SECTION VIEW

30° Chamfer, ¹⁄₄" Wide

MULLION SECTION VIEW

To begin work on this pair of doors, rip the stock as required, and crosscut it to the sizes specified by the Cutting List. Lightly write the part name on each blank so you won't get the parts mixed up.

2. Chamfer the stiles, bottom rail, and mullions. As with the base doors, it's a good idea to do this first. Use a router and 30-degree chamfer bit. The chamfer should be 1/4 inch wide. As with the base doors, the chamfers are stopped at the inside corners of the frame, so you must mark these points on the workpieces and begin and end the cuts at these points.

3. Cut the bottom-rail-to-stile joinery. With a 1/4-inch upcut spiral bit and a plunge router, rout the mortises. Refer to the drawing *Glazed Door Construction* for the details of size and location. Cut the tenons on the table saw. Round the edges of the completed tenons with a file so they'll fit the mortises.

4. Cut the open mortise-and-tenon joint. This can be done entirely on the table saw. The tenon on each end of the top rail should be 1/4 inch thick and 2 1/2 inches wide. It should, at this point, be the full width of the rail. The mortise is nothing more than a 1/4-inch-wide, 1 1/2-inch-deep slot. Guide the workpiece with the tenoning jig. Set the blade height to 1 1/2 inches, and set the fence to create a 1/4-inch-wide shoulder. Make a pass with the reference face of the stile against the jig, then roll the stile and make a

pass with the reference face exposed. Make the same two passes on the other end of the stile. Now reset the fence and make passes to remove the remaining waste. Use a chisel to pare the bottom of the mortise smooth.

5. Cut the rabbet for the glass. On the stiles and bottom rail, this rabbet is 3/8 inch wide × 3/8 inch deep. Cut it with a straight bit in a table-mounted router. Mark the ends of the rabbets on the stiles; these are stopped. On the bottom rail, the rabbet is through.

On the mullions, the rabbet is 3/8 inch deep, but it is only 1/4 inch wide. Adjust the fence and rout the rabbets in these parts. Because these parts are so slender, it's a good idea to cut each rabbet in a series of passes, each new pass cutting only a small increment deeper than the previous one. Use double-sided carpet tape to attach a slim support strip to the outfeed side of the router table when cutting the second rabbet on each mullion.

On the top rail, the rabbet is much wider than 3/8 inch. Start by rabbeting these rails as you did the other pieces. Then move the fence farther away from the bit, and widen the rabbet. Be sure to feed the workpiece from right to left. Continue to widen the rabbet pass by pass. On the final pass or two, support the work by attaching a 3/8-inch-thick scrap to the router table with carpet tape.

6. Cut the arch and chamfer on the top rail. You *can* cut the arch with a saber saw, then form the chamfer with a file. But a trammel will allow you to do the job with your router.

Study the detail drawing *Top Rail Layout*, and note particularly the locations of the centerpoints used to cut and chamfer the rail's arc. Select a 2-foot-square piece of scrap, and clamp the workpiece to one end and a scrap to secure the router trammel's pivot to the other.

Attach the trammel to your router, and chuck a straight bit in the router. Adjust the trammel so the distance from the outside of the bit to the pivot is 6 13/16 inches; this is the radius of the cut. Cut the arc.

Routing the wide rabbet in the top rail is not difficult. Rout it in a series of passes, and after the first couple, stick a strip to the router table with carpet tape where it will support the rabbeted edge, keeping the rail square to the tabletop. On the last pass, shown here, the strip should be next to the fence.

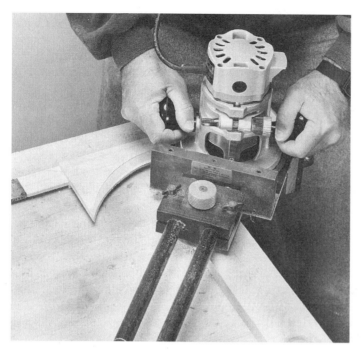

To form the chamfer, switch to a small panel-raising bit such as Bosch's number 85583M, which cuts a 9/16-inch-wide bevel. (For Bosch distributors, call S-B Power Tool Company at 919-636-4200.) Adjust the trammel to a 6¹/₁₆-inch radius. Be sure to move the pivot point, as indicated in the drawing. Make a very shallow cut initially, then increase the depth of cut until you have the chamfer looking just right along its top edge. You'll have a flat area along the bottom edge, which has to be worked by hand to blend it into the bevel.

When the first top rail is finished, switch workpieces and do the second. Then file the bevels of both to complete them.

7. Assemble the top case doors. Cope the ends of the mullions, as shown in the drawing *Glazed Door Construction*, so they fit between the stiles. This is hand work; use a coping saw to remove the bulk of the waste. To trim the cut and refine the fit, use a small file. Cope one end of each mullion first, and make sure it fits closely to the stile. Then carefully measure the required length and cope the other end.

Assemble the two doors without glue to test how everything fits. Disassemble the doors, and assuming no further adjusting is necessary, finish sand the separate parts. Then apply glue to the mortises and tenons and assemble and clamp the doors. After the glue has set and the clamps have been removed, use a chisel to square the corners of the rabbet.

ASSEMBLE THE CUPBOARD

1. Hang the doors. The doors are hung on 1½ × 2-inch hinges. The hinge positions are shown in the two door construction drawings. Pare mortises for the hinges in the door edges, and mount the hinges. Then, with the appropriate case resting on its back, set the door in place. Adjust the clearance between the door and top rail, then transfer the hinge locations to the side stiles. Pare hinge mortises in the stiles, then mount the doors. Plane each door stile as necessary so it will open and close.

Cut and shape the turn buttons, then attach them to the center stiles with screws, as shown in the *Front View*.

2. Apply a finish. A variety of finishes are appropriate for this piece. The original is painted a light blue inside and has a polyurethane varnish applied to the outside. Its original finish was probably paint, so we painted our reproduction. The outside has two coats of New England Red paint from Stulb Paint Company's Old Village line. The inside was painted in Cabinetmaker's Blue from the same line.

You probably have an appearance in mind, but if you don't, read the options outlined in the *ShopSmarts* feature "Country Finishes" on page 305. It will give you ideas and sketch out the techniques for applying three or four different finishes.

Whatever finish you use, remove the doors and hinges and turn buttons before applying it.

3. Glaze the top case doors. After the finish has dried, install the panes of glass in the top case doors. Use glazing points to secure the panes, then apply a fillet of glazing compound around the edges.

Remount the hinges, then the doors, then the turn buttons.

Gluing Up Panels

One of woodworking's fundamental procedures is gluing up. If ever you expect to make a project with components wider than 11 inches, you'll have a need to tackle and master it.

In fact, you might want to master gluing up, even if you do limit yourself to those projects with less-than-11-inch-wide components. The reason is: Those 1 × 12s you buy at the lumberyard are likely to cup (if they haven't before you pick them off the yard's stack). A good way to combat cupping is to edge-glue narrow boards to form wide ones.

Step 1

1. Arrange the boards. The first task is to set out the available boards and experiment with different combinations. A good-looking panel is the goal. You want to glue up boards that are compatible in figure, and you want to arrange the boards to conceal, as much as possible, the seams between boards. In the Step 1 photo, the three boards in the clamps are reasonably compatible with each other, while the board angled across them clearly is not. Since the needed panel can be created with just the three, that fourth board can be set aside for use in another project.

Note that none of the boards in the photo has been edge-jointed. Typically, I'll select the boards

for a panel, arrange them, then take them one-by-one to be jointed and ripped to width. Since I'm doing them one-by-one—it's only a couple steps from the glue-up table to the jointer and table saw—they don't get mixed up. Many woodworkers, however, mark the boards in some way so that they can stack them up, carry them to the machines for jointing and ripping, then return them to the original arrangement. Pick the approach you prefer.

When jointing a board's edges to prepare it for glue-up, just do your best to get them flat, smooth, and square to the faces. A lot of "tricks" are in circulation: Use biscuits for alignment and reinforcement, counsels one tipster. No biscuits, suggests another; use dowels (or splines) instead. Try planing a very slight dish into the edge from one end of the board to the other, urges yet another helpful woodworker. Then clamping the panel at the center will force the ends tightly together.

Most of these tricks are more trouble than they're worth. The fact is: Glue bonds smooth surfaces best. The smoother the surface, the better the bond. So joint that surface. (Or use the router edge-jointing technique explained in the *ShopSmarts* feature "Routing an Edge Joint" on page 264.)

2. Adjust the clamps and cauls. When the boards are ready for glue-up, pick a flat surface for doing the glue-up, and set out the clamps for the job. Use an odd number of clamps—three or five or seven, depending upon the length of the boards. For this panel I'm using a total of five, so I set out three. Adjust the jaws of each clamp so there's enough room for all the boards plus two cauls plus a finger or two of working space. Crank out the screw as far as it'll go as you do this. Adjust the clamps that will be placed on top of the boards, too.

The idea is to set the jaws so you can easily pick up a board, spread the glue, then drop it quickly into place on the clamp pipes. When the spread is done, three or four turns of a clamp's crank should apply pressure on the boards.

The cauls are optional, by the way. If the boards are wide enough, you can forego the

(continued)

Step 2

Step 3

cauls. The clamp jaws will mar the edges of the panel, of course, but you can rip the marks from the finished panel.

In this case, however, I am using cauls. Each is a scrap strip as long as the boards. This is the kind of caul to use. Only two strips are needed, regardless of the number of clamps you use, and they won't fall out of position while you tighten the individual clamps because each caul is supported by all the clamps. Fuss with two small cauls for each clamp during glue-up—that would be ten bitty scraps of wood in the glue-up shown—and the experience will consign you to an early grave.

3. Spread glue. Don't be too fussy about applying the glue. Just run a nice bead, as shown in the Step 3 photo, down the center of the edge. Applying glue to both mating edges is unnecessary, as is painting or spreading it over the entire edge. Run a bead on one edge of each joint. Rub the mating edges together. Not a long swipe, just a short shimmy. Then move the boards into the predetermined alignment and begin applying pressure.

The amount of time you have to get the joints assembled and the clamps applied—the so-called open assembly time—varies by glue. The hot hide glue that the makers of the country originals used gave them no more than five minutes to do the work. Liquid hide glue, the contemporary, no-heat-necessary version of that old, old adhesive,

allows up to a half-hour. The modern white and yellow glues that I use and that you probably use allow ten minutes.

If you are prepared, with the boards properly jointed and lined up, with the clamps set and the cauls at hand, if you don't dither, then ten minutes is more than enough time to glue and clamp three to six boards into a panel.

4. Tighten the center clamp first. The boards should be flat on the clamp pipe (or bar). As you tighten the clamp, get the boards flush right

Step 4

where they're on the clamp. Don't worry about the alignment out toward the ends. Focus for now on the center. Run your fingers back and forth on the joints, as I'm doing in the Step 4 photo, to be sure one board doesn't squirm out of alignment as the clamping pressure increases.

Step 5

5. Set the two clamps across the top of the panel. Drop them right onto the panel, so the pipes rest directly on the wood. Tighten them. As you tighten the clamps, make sure the boards are flush. If a board needs some coaxing, I loosen the clamp and tug up or down on the end of the board. I don't care if the end is out of whack, so long as the spot at the clamp I'm tightening comes flush. A last resort for me is the hammer-and-wood-block technique. (Set a wood block over the seam, and rap it sharply with a hammer.) When the boards are flush, tighten the clamp.

6. Tighten the end clamps. When the center three clamps are tight, work on the end clamps. As before, the goal is to get the boards flush and keep them that way as each clamp is tightened. By the time you get to the end clamps, it may take some serious coaxing to flush up the boards. Tugging on the ends usually won't work at this point, and hammering is more noisy than effective.

Bagging Black Stains

When water-based glues, like yellow and white glues, dribble onto pipe clamps, the result can be a dark stain on the workpiece. Sometimes the stain is superficial and sands away easily. Other times, it penetrates the wood.

Here's an easy way to avoid such stains. Lay a plastic trash bag—you probably have a few in the shop—over the clamps before setting the work in place; the glue won't stick to the plastic.

Set out the clamps. Spread the bag over them. Then set the boards in place. Before setting the topside clamps in place, pull the bag over the top of the panel. If the panel to be glued up is large, as is the one in the photo, you can slice the bag open.

Try this: Apply a metal-jawed clamp right on the joint to force the boards into alignment. (You should have crosscut the boards to a rough length, so any dents caused by the clamp will be trimmed off.) Tighten the end pipe clamp, then remove the alignment clamp.

(continued)

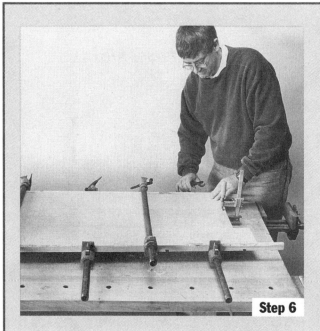

Step 6

The result of your glue application and the clamping pressure should be a fairly regular show of squeeze-out, as shown in the second Step 6 photo.

If there's no squeeze-out, this may indicate a glue-starved joint, not a good thing. The solution is not more clamp pressure. Too much pressure will simply crush the wood—especially since you're dealing here with pine. The solution may be to break down the assembly and reapply the glue. Pull the clamps quickly and see if the boards will separate. If you're lucky, they will, and you can apply a little more glue (don't overdo it, though). If the glue has set up and the boards won't separate, you may have to live with the joint. (Or wait for the glue to cure, rip it into boards, then reglue it.)

If, on the other hand, the squeeze-out comes in rivulets rather than tidy little beads, then you've applied too much glue. Now you've got a mess to clean up. Get a wet rag—not merely damp but wet—and scrub as much of the excess off the assembly as you can. You don't want the rivulets to dry on the wood.

How long should you leave the clamps on the panel? Depends on the glue you are using. Yellow glue, today's most commonly used woodworking glue, has a "closed assembly time" of 30 minutes. That means you can pull off the clamps after 30 minutes. Using white glue, the clamping time is an hour. With liquid hide glue, leave the clamps on 12 to 16 hours.

Glue continues to cure for a time, even after the clamps are removed. Those glues you are likely to use for these projects—white, yellow, and liquid hide—take a full day to cure or harden to full strength. Woodworking's rule of the gluey thumb says to let the panels cure overnight. Typically, you glue up one day, then pull off the clamps and work the panel the next.

7. Scrape off the dried glue. There's one last task to complete the glue-up: You must remove the dried squeeze-out, if you didn't wash it from the wood while it was still fresh. Even after they've cured, white and yellow glues will soften and clog sanding belts if you try to sand them. Paradoxically, the same glue is hard enough to dull the edges of your cutting tools—planer knives or chisels.

Use a paint scraper to remove the dried squeeze-out. Just pull it along the joint. The dried glue will break off, as you can see in the Step 7 photo. The panel is then ready to be sanded flat and smooth.

Step 6

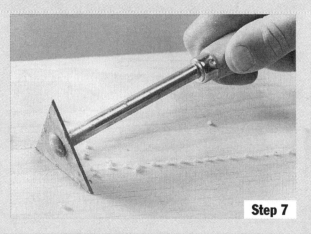

Step 7

Gluing Up Thin Stock

The Case of Drawers (page 103), the Stage Box (page 175), and some other projects call for parts made of ⅜-inch and ¼-inch stock. In some cases, the dimensions of the parts almost dictate that you glue up this thin stock. With standard clamps, this is pretty difficult.

So make your own clamps for the procedure. You may not use them often, but when you do need them, nothing else will do. The clamps can be fashioned from hardwood blocks, threaded rods, and a big handful of washers, hex nuts, and wing nuts. The drawing shows the dimensions and arrangement of hardware.

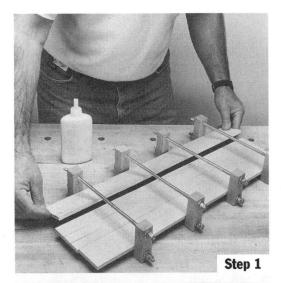

Step 1

1. Set the stock in the clamps. Stand the clamps on end. Back off the wing nuts to separate the blocks enough to accommodate the panel you want to create. Space the clamps evenly, and line up the clamps. Make sure the pieces of stock will fit.

Apply glue to the stock, just as if you were edge-gluing ¾-inch-thick boards. Set the boards in place, edge to edge.

2. Clamp the stock. Now tip each clamp, as shown in the Step 2 photo. The stock will be trapped between each clamp's twin threaded rods. This will force the boards flush with one another, keep them flat, and prevent the panel from cupping or bowing. Spin the two wing nuts on each clamp to tighten it. Finger-tight is tight enough.

Step 2

THREADED-ROD CLAMP

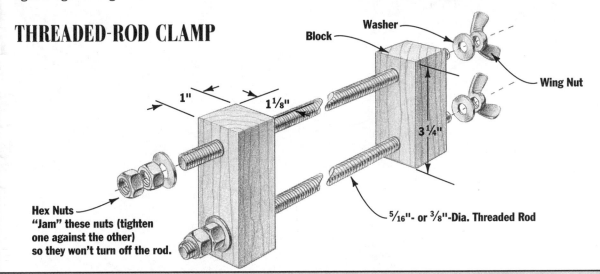

Block

Washer

Wing Nut

1"

1⅛"

3¼"

Hex Nuts
"Jam" these nuts (tighten one against the other) so they won't turn off the rod.

5⁄16"- or ⅜"-Dia. Threaded Rod

CANDLE BOXES

Boxes with sliding lids, such as these, are often called candle boxes. I imagine the boxes had innumerable uses in the rural American house of the 1800s, but the name candle box is the one that's stuck. If you scour antique stores, as I have over the last year, you'll see them in all sorts of sizes and proportions, everything from pencil-box sizes on up.

If in fact these boxes *were* candle boxes, as tradition would have it, the larger one would have held new candles. The smaller would have been for the stubs, which were saved for use in making new candles.

There is a sound rationale for the existence of the candle box. Since our highways and airports and shopping centers and even our backyards have been illuminated by dusk-to-dawn lights, we've been blinded to the night lives of our ancestors. A visit at dusk to a historical village like Virginia's Colonial Williamsburg will dilate your pupils. The denizens light candles and oil lamps at nightfall. No mercury vapor lamps flick on. No fluorescents or even candle-like incandescents light up. No flashlights shine through the darkness. Just real candles. As they burn, the wax melts away.

A new appreciation of the light levels our great-great-great-great-grand-parents lived in is in-

stilled. And this is true no matter where in the world they lived—Europe, Asia, Africa.

(Incidentally, the experience will throw a different light on the finishes applied to "colonial" furniture, too.)

Obviously, then, candles had considerable value. A lot of work went into their making, and without them, you just couldn't see after sunset. So people took care of the candles they had. A safe place for them was a candle box: The mice couldn't get at them to chew them up, and they wouldn't get misplaced or lost.

The two boxes shown below are typical of the genre. They featured sliding lids because that design eliminated the need for hardware. The large box has no metal in it at all. The sides and ends are assembled with dovetails. The bottom is attached with wooden pins. The smaller box, which is probably a more recent construction, is also dovetailed, but it has a few nails securing the bottom.

So the linchpin of the boxes is the dovetail joint. The dovetails in both boxes are through dovetails, hand-cut with large tails and small pins. The real trick with them is that the woodworker modified them to accommodate the lid groove. Without a bit of cheating, you can't rout them. So in the directions that follow, I'll explain how.

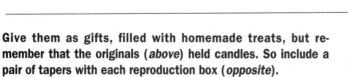

Give them as gifts, filled with homemade treats, but remember that the originals (*above*) held candles. So include a pair of tapers with each reproduction box (*opposite*).

CUTTING LIST

LARGE BOX

Piece	Number	Thickness	Width	Length	Material
Sides	2	$5/8$"	$6^{13}/16$"	$17^1/4$"	pine
Closed end	1	$5/8$"	$6^{13}/16$"	$9^1/2$"	pine
Open end	1	$5/8$"	$6^{13}/16$"	$9^1/2$"	pine
Lid-groove strip	2	$5/8$"	$11/16$"	$17^1/4$"	pine
Lid-groove strip	1	$5/8$"	$11/16$"	$9^1/2$"	pine
Bottom	1	$5/8$"	$8^1/4$"	16"	pine
Lid	1	$5/8$"	$8^{13}/16$"	$16^{15}/16$"	pine
Pegs	12	$3/16$"	$3/16$"	1"	hardwood

SMALL BOX

Piece	Number	Thickness	Width	Length	Material
Sides	2	$7/16$"	$2^7/8$"	$8^3/8$"	pine
Closed end	1	$7/16$"	$2^7/8$"	$6^7/16$"	pine
Open end	1	$7/16$"	$2^7/8$"	$6^7/16$"	pine
Lid-groove strip	1	$7/16$"	$9/16$"	$6^7/16$"	pine
Lid-groove strip	2	$7/16$"	$9/16$"	$8^3/8$"	pine
Bottom	1	$5/16$"	$6^7/16$"	$8^3/8$"	pine
Lid	1	$7/16$"	$6^1/4$"	$8^3/16$"	pine

HARDWARE
1" headless cut brads

With the proper dovetail jig, routing through dovetails isn't difficult. There are three different types of through dovetail jigs on the market:

- The Leigh jig and Porter-Cable's Omnijig have movable guide fingers that you adjust to produce the size and spacing of dovetails that you want. (Leigh Industries: 800-663-8932; Porter-Cable: 901-668-8600)
- Keller templates are fixed in size and spacing but can be repositioned on the workpiece between cuts to alter the size and spacing of the dovetails. (Keller & Company: 707-763-9336)
- The Incra and Jointech jigs are router-table accessories that guide the workpiece; you shift the fence in distinct increments for each pass to control the size and spacing of the dovetails.

All of these jigs are expensive, so you won't buy one just to make a couple of candle boxes. But the candle boxes are good initial projects if you do get such a jig. And thereafter, you'll use the jig in building lots of other projects.

We don't much use candles anymore, though they've gotten comparatively cheap. And typically—not always, I know from experience, but typically—our homes are rodent-free. So building wooden boxes to conserve candles isn't a high priority. But without trying too hard, I'll bet you come up with enough practical uses for such boxes to warrant building a half-dozen. I'm building several right now to package modest-sized Christmas presents for favored relatives.

I'll probably toss a couple of candles inside with the gift, just for the sake of tradition.

EXPLODED VIEW—LARGE BOX

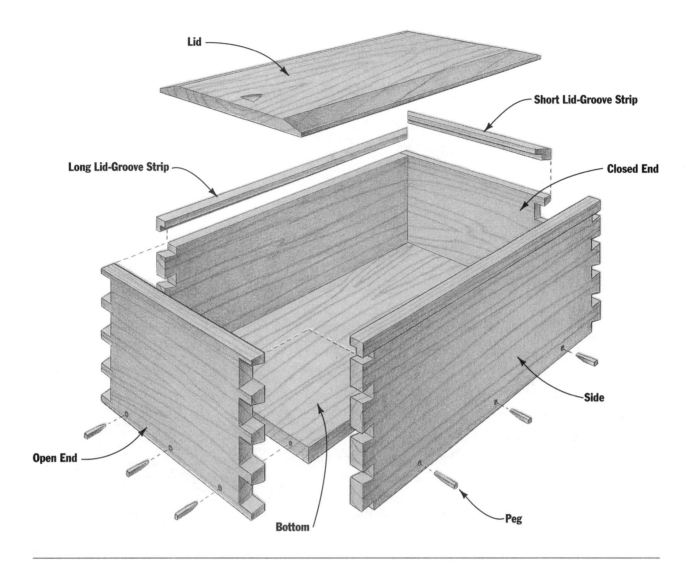

Lid

Short Lid-Groove Strip

Long Lid-Groove Strip

Closed End

Side

Open End

Bottom

Peg

---

1. Prepare the stock. All the parts in the small box come from $7/16$-inch stock, except the bottom, which is only $5/16$ inch thick. The parts for the large box are cut from $5/8$-inch stock.

Resaw and plane stock to the necessary thickness. Tips on thicknessing stock can be found in the *ShopSmarts* features "Making a Board" on page 13 and "Resawing on the Table Saw" on page 112. Useful tips on planing very thin stock are included with the directions for the Case of Drawers (page 103).

Rip the parts to width next. You can crosscut the lids, bottoms, and groove strips to the dimensions specified by the Cutting List. The sides and ends can be crosscut but should be left a couple of inches too long until you've cut and fitted dovetails on a test piece. With some jigs, you can't trim the parts to final length until after the dovetails are routed.

2. Set up the jig for dovetailing. All the through-dovetail jigs require the use of two different bits. One is a dovetail bit, used to rout the tails. The other is a straight bit, used to rout the pins. (If the world were an ideal place, you'd have two routers, one for each bit. Failing that, you'll have to switch bits.)

Adjust the jig as necessary to establish the spacing depicted in the drawings. Using scrap material as a workpiece, cut the tails. Usually this is a matter of feeding the router into the appropriate slots, just as when cutting half-blind dovetails.

PLAN VIEWS—LARGE BOX

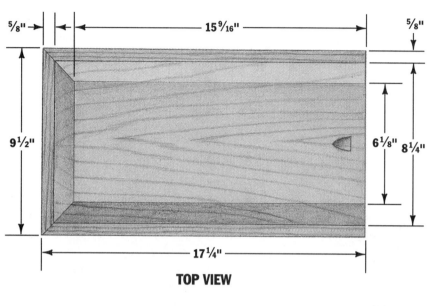

5/8" → **15 9/16"** **5/8"**

9 1/2" **6 1/8"** **8 1/4"**

17 1/4"

TOP VIEW

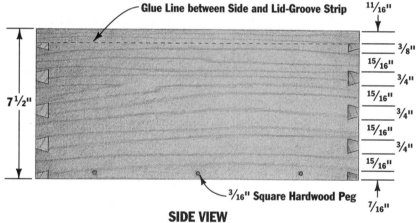

Glue Line between Side and Lid-Groove Strip

11/16"

3/8"

15/16"

3/4"

15/16"

3/4"

15/16"

3/4"

15/16"

7 1/2"

3/16" Square Hardwood Peg

7/16"

SIDE VIEW

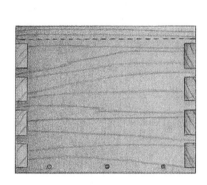

CLOSED END VIEW

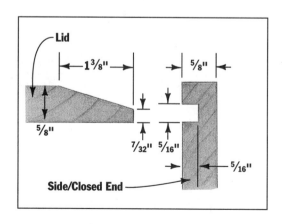

Lid

1 3/8" **5/8"**

5/8"

7/32" **5/16"**

5/16"

Side/Closed End

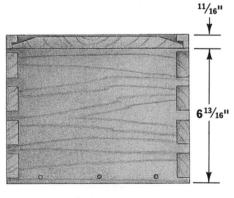

11/16"

6 13/16"

OPEN END VIEW

Here's how through dovetails are routed with Porter-Cable's Omnijig. The size of the slots (and thus the pins) is fixed. But the width of the tails (and thus the distance between the pins) can be varied by moving the forklike fingers that form the Omnijig's adjustable template. To rout the tails, the template is set forward on the jig. To rout the pins, the template is shifted back. To set up, then, you "lay out the dovetails" by positioning the fingers. For the large candle box, I spaced them to produce four tails in each joint.

The first step (*top left*) is to rout the slots in all the tailboards (the candle-box sides). You use a ³/₄-inch 14-degree dovetail bit with a ⁵/₈-inch template guide for this. A scrap board is clamped to the top of the jig, beneath the template. The workpiece is clamped in the front of the jig, tight against the scrap. The tails are routed by guiding the router into each fork. The fork is matched to

the template guide, so there's no side-to-side movement possible. The width of the slot routed matches the diameter of the dovetail bit.

The second step is to rout the pinboards. Switch to a ⁹/₁₆-inch straight bit, but keep the ⁵/₈-inch template guide. Clamp a pinboard (the candle-box end) in the front position. Shift the template to the back position. Now there's room for side-to-side movement between the template fingers. Rout out the waste between the pins (*top right*). To prevent chip-out along the bottom edge of the cut, make a very shallow first pass, just skimming the bit along the surface of the workpiece.

Next, cut the pins. Clamp the pinboard in place. Reset the jig as necessary. With adjustable jigs, this is usually a matter of repositioning the template. With the Keller, you actually use a different template. Whatever is necessary for your jig, do it. Change bits, adjust the depth of cut as necessary, and rout.

Assemble your test joint and assess the fit. Fine-tune the fit by adjusting the jig and router as specified by your dovetail jig's manual.

3. Rout the dovetails. When the jig is properly set up, as proven by a tightly fitted sample joint, do the dovetails on the workpieces. Trim the sides and ends to that length. Rout the tails on the sides. Then switch over and rout the pins on the two ends.

The finished pins (*above*) are perfectly sized and positioned to fit the slots previously cut in the tailboards.

PLAN VIEWS—SMALL BOX

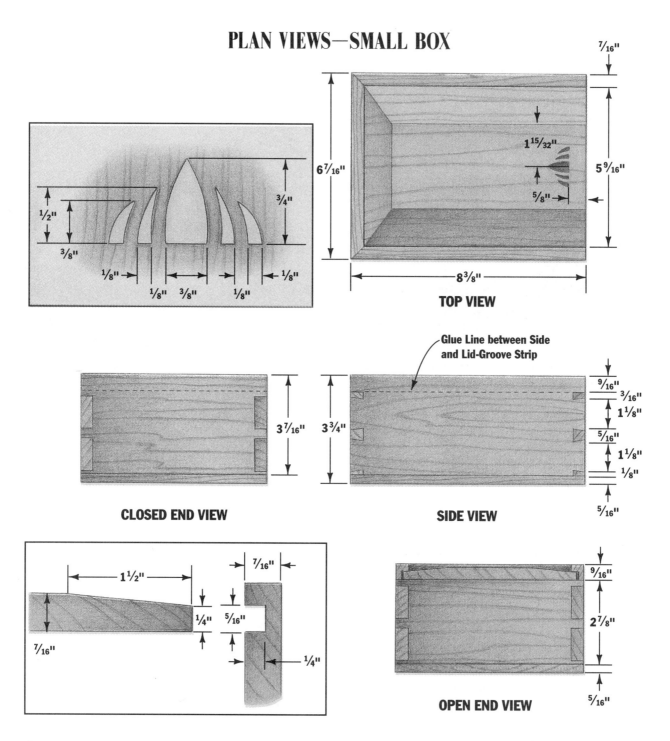

TOP VIEW

CLOSED END VIEW

Glue Line between Side and Lid-Groove Strip

SIDE VIEW

OPEN END VIEW

4. Glue the lid-groove strips to the sides and closed end. This is a simple edge-gluing procedure. But first . . .

Assemble the sides and ends without glue, and mark the top edge of all four parts. Label the mates to each joint, too, so that later you can reassemble the box just the way you've got it now.

With the parts labeled, go ahead and glue the groove strips to the top edge of both sides and one of the ends. See the top photo on the opposite page.

5. Rout the lid groove. After the glue has cured and the clamps have been removed, scrape off any dried squeeze-out and sand the sides and closed end. Rout the panel groove, as shown in the *Plan Views*. Do this on the router table, using a straight bit. Just plow the groove through from end to end.

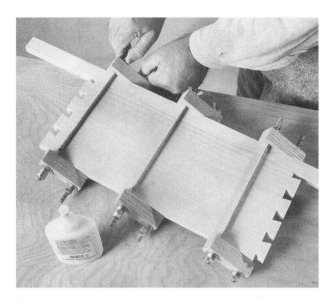

You can use the special shop-made threaded-rod clamps shown in the *ShopSmarts* feature "Gluing Up Panels" on page 49 to clamp the parts. It's not a bad idea to let the strips run a bit longer than the pieces to which they are glued. You can trim them as you assemble the box.

6. Assemble the box. The first task here is to trim the parts to their final dimensions if you had to rout overlong tails and pins.

Miter the ends of the glued-on groove strip, forming miter joints between the closed end and the

To close the dovetail joint, you have to put the clamp pressure on the outer surfaces of the tailboards. Hold scraps against the candle-box sides—clear of the pins, as shown here—and apply the clamps to them.

sides. The ends of the strip at the box's open end remain square-cut.

Apply glue to the joints, and assemble the sides and ends.

The bottom of the small box overlays the sides and ends, and it is nailed in place with 1-inch headless cut brads.

The bottom of the large box fits inside the sides and ends. It is secured with small wooden pegs. Whittle the pegs, as shown in the *Exploded View*. Set the bottom in position, and drill pilot holes for the pegs. Apply a dot of glue to a peg, and drive it into its pilot hole. Trim each peg almost flush, and sand them all smooth. (Typically, wooden pegs stand a bit proud; if you run a finger across the surface, you'll feel them.)

7. Bevel the lid to fit. You *can* bevel the lid on the table saw, but it takes only a minute or so to do this job with a block plane or smoothing plane. It will give your box more of a handcrafted look if you hand plane the bevels. Rough out the bevels along the sides and across the end.

Periodically, stop your work and test the fit of the lid to the box. You want the lid to slide smoothly but without rattling in its grooves. Keep in mind the kind of finish you will use. If you plan to paint or varnish the box, you can make the fit a bit looser to accommodate the layer or two of finish you will ultimately apply.

8. Chisel the thumb depression. Each lid has a small depression chiseled near the open end so it can be slid open with a thumb or finger. On the large box, the depression is shaped a lot like a thumbprint and is about $1/4$ inch deep. On the small box, this feature is a more elaborate, five-part carving. Refer to the detail drawing in the *Plan Views*, and lay out the design on the lid. Pare the depressions with a small gouge (or if you don't have a gouge, with a narrow chisel).

9. Apply a finish. In keeping with the originals, I used a clear finish on the small box and grain-painted the large box. The product I used on the small box was a brushing lacquer called Deft.

General information on applying these finishes can be found in the *ShopSmarts* feature "Country Finishes" on page 305.

HALF-ROUND TABLE

This little table is a honey. I took the original home to measure it and work on sketches. I took my eye off it for just a second . . . really, it was just a blink. And—that quick!—my wife had it placed against the wall in the family room with a basket arrangement on it.

I don't know how, exactly, to account for this response. I bought it from a Lancaster County, Pennsylvania, "picker." (A picker is a kind of scout in the antiques and collectibles hierarchy. He or she scours society's rural eddies for stuff that antique dealers want but don't have time to scout out themselves. Pickers buy for cheap, and sell to dealers for dear.) People like this table instantly. Women in the office. Guys in the shop. And of course my wife.

It's not like it's pristine. The legs are beat up from 150 years of shin kicking. The edge of the top is riddled with little holes. It's never had a finish applied.

But the universal response is: "Hey, I really like that. That's pretty neat."

So here it is. As a woodworking project, it's got a couple of interesting challenges, but it's small enough and simple enough to make in just a couple of evenings, using a modest amount of material. Among the challenges are tapering the

legs and cutting the double mortise-and-tenon joint that joins the two aprons.

An unusual aspect of the table is that the legs are pine. The conventional wisdom is that pine is unsuitable for legs because it is weak and brittle. The country woodworker might have made a table or pie safe or other piece of furniture almost entirely of pine but have used poplar for the legs. This table's legs are pine. They're nicked and battered, and one's got a bit of a bow to it. But they are still sound.

Another quirk is that the tabletop is made up of two separate boards. They aren't glued together, though at one spot, a nail has been driven through the edge of one into the other. I wouldn't recommend this as the way to build this table, though it has worked well for more than 150 years. It sufficed, probably, because of its utilitarian purpose. The holes that riddled the top's edge appear to be thumbtack holes. This suggests that the top was covered with a piece of oilcloth, which was thumbtacked in place. This was a common practice among the rural Pennsylvania Dutch. As I say, very utilitarian.

We took a little extra care in the making of our reproduction, so the table is attractive as well as utilitarian.

Making the legs

As they age, the legs and aprons of this reproduction table (*opposite*) will darken to match those of the 150-year-old original (*above*).

EXPLODED VIEW

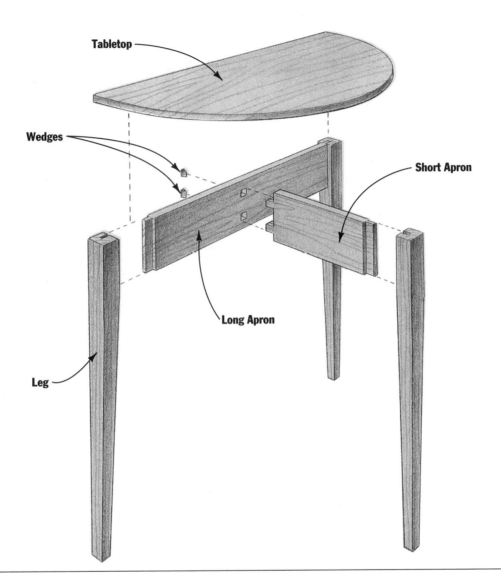

Tabletop

Wedges

Short Apron

Long Apron

Leg

CUTTING LIST

Piece	Number	Thickness	Width	Length	Material
Legs	3	$1\frac{3}{4}$"	$1\frac{3}{4}$"	28"	8/4 pine
Long apron	1	1"	5"	$28\frac{3}{4}$"	5/4 pine
Short apron	1	1"	5"	$13\frac{1}{4}$"	5/4 pine
Wedges	2	$\frac{1}{8}$"	$\frac{3}{4}$"	1"	hardwood
Tabletop	1	$\frac{7}{8}$"	$17\frac{1}{2}$"	$35\frac{7}{8}$"	5/4 pine

HARDWARE
6d cut finish nails

involves a bit of materials problem solving. Finding a piece of 1¾-inch-thick white pine is a lot less easy than buying 1-by pine. You can laminate two lengths of 5/4, forming a roughly 2-inch-square billet. There is a glue line, but the legs thus made are workable. Another option is to buy furniture-grade 8/4 white pine lumber, from a vendor selling hardwoods, which is what we did.

The original table has 1-inch-thick aprons and a ⅞-inch-thick top. The drawings show the dimensions of this original. You can use straight 1-by pine for the aprons and top with only a few alterations, primarily in the dimensions of the mortises and tenons. Although it was a little more work, we resawed 5/4 stock for the aprons and top so we could hold to the dimensions of the original. Using slightly thinner stock may seem like a minor deviation, but it can have rather dramatic visual impact. I just wanted to avoid tinkering with something that really worked.

Everyone likes what they see in the original! *Let's not change a thing.*

1. Cut the legs and aprons. To make the leg billets, rip six 28-inch strips of 5/4 stock to 2 inches wide. Face-glue them in pairs, forming the three leg billets. When the glue has dried and the clamps are off, rip each billet to 1¾ inches square and sand away all the saw marks.

Rip and crosscut stock for the aprons, as specified by the Cutting List. To achieve the 1-inch thickness needed, you can plane the stock with a planer or resaw the stock on the table saw. If you need to resaw, refer to the *ShopSmarts* feature "Resawing on the Table Saw" on page 112 for the

LEG LAYOUTS

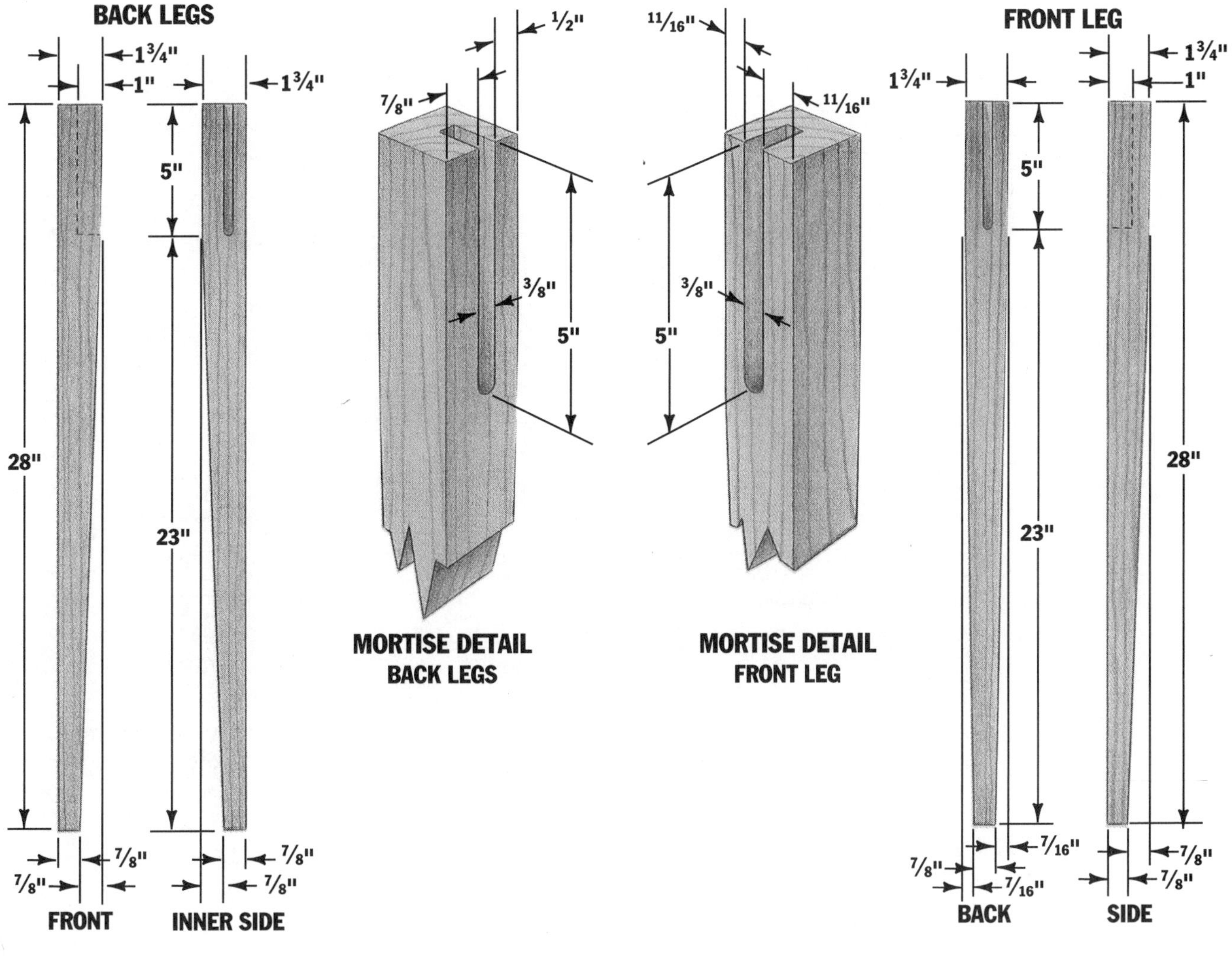

BACK LEGS

1¾" 1" 1¾"

5"

28"

23"

7/8" 7/8" 7/8" 7/8"

FRONT **INNER SIDE**

MORTISE DETAIL
BACK LEGS

½" ⅞" 3/8" 5" 5"

MORTISE DETAIL
FRONT LEG

11/16" 11/16" 3/8" 5" 5"

FRONT LEG

1¾" 1¾" 1" 5"

28"

23"

7/16" 7/8" 7/8" 7/16" 7/8"

BACK **SIDE**

PLAN VIEWS

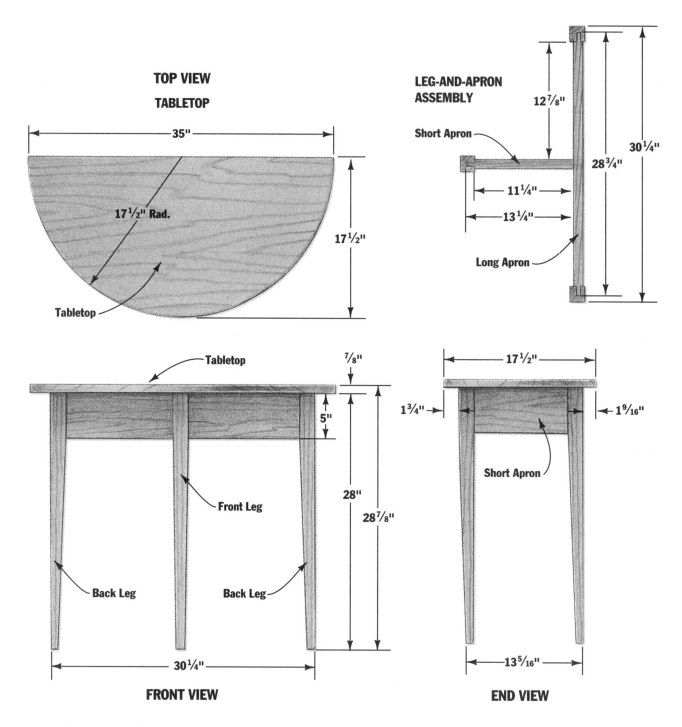

TOP VIEW
TABLETOP

35"

17½" Rad.

17½"

Tabletop

LEG-AND-APRON ASSEMBLY

12⁷⁄₈"

Short Apron

30¼"

28¾"

11¼"

13¼"

Long Apron

7⁄₈"

Tabletop

5"

Front Leg

28"

28⁷⁄₈"

Back Leg

Back Leg

30¼"

FRONT VIEW

17½"

1¾"

1⁹⁄₁₆"

Short Apron

13⁵⁄₁₆"

END VIEW

procedure. Typically, you only need to skim about ¹⁄₁₆ to ³⁄₁₆ inch from 5/4 stock. Sand the aprons to remove saw marks.

2. Mortise the legs. Each leg has one 5-inch-long mortise, which should be routed before the leg is tapered. Note that the front leg mortise is posi-

tioned slightly differently from the back leg mortises. And remember that the two back legs are mirror images, not duplicates. Refer to *Leg Layouts* for specific dimensions. And label each leg so you won't get them mixed up when tapering them.

Cut the mortises using a router (you can even use a fixed-base router for these mortises!) and a

PLAN VIEWS

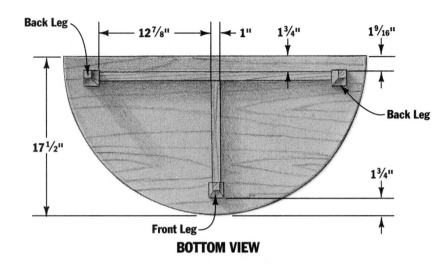

Back Leg

12⁷/₈"   1"   1³/₄"   1⁹/₁₆"

Back Leg

17¹/₂"

1³/₄"

Front Leg

BOTTOM VIEW

Long Apron

BACK VIEW

³/₈-inch straight bit. Refer to the *ShopSmarts* feature "Cutting Mortise-and-Tenon Joints" on page 83 for procedural tips.

3. Taper the legs. This task can be done on the table saw with a tapering jig. Details on the procedure can be found in the *ShopSmarts* feature "Tapering Legs on the Table Saw" on page 189.

Leg Layouts shows all the pertinent dimensions. Mark the faces of the legs that must be tapered. Note that the two back legs have two adjoining faces tapered, while the front leg has three faces tapered. The tapers all begin 5 inches from the top. The footprint of each leg measures ⁷/₈ inch square.

4. Tenon the aprons. The tenons that join the aprons to the legs are easily cut on the table saw. Note that these tenons extend the full width of the aprons; they aren't shouldered at the top and bottom.

Use the tenoning jig shown in the *ShopSmarts* feature "Cutting Mortise-and-Tenon Joints" on page 83 to cut the tenons on the table saw. The feature details the setup and cutting sequence.

Next, cut the double tenons on the short apron, shown in *Apron Layouts*. Adjust the table saw blade height to the thickness of the aprons. Stand the apron on end, and guide it with the miter gauge. Cut to the waste side of each layout line. Clean the

APRON LAYOUTS

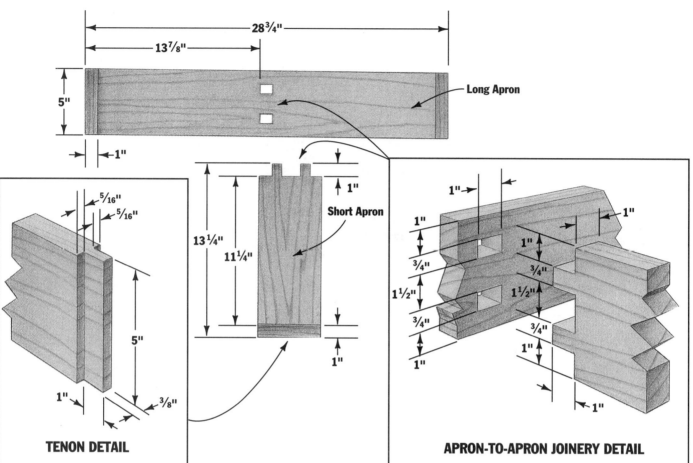

Long Apron

5"

28¾"

13⅞"

1"

Short Apron

13¼"

11¼"

1"

1"

TENON DETAIL

5/16"

5/16"

5"

1"

3/8"

APRON-TO-APRON JOINERY DETAIL

1"

1"

1"

1"

¾"

¾"

1½"

1½"

¾"

¾"

1"

1"

1"

1"

waste from between the two tenons with repeated cuts. Complete the tenons by setting the apron on edge and cutting away the waste.

Finally, kerf the two tenons for wedges that will lock these tenons in the mortises.

5. Mortise the long apron. The locations of the two through mortises are shown in *Apron Layouts*. For the most accurate fit, use the double tenons on the short apron to lay out the mortises, rather than measuring and marking. Scribe a line across the long apron 12⅞ inches from the shoulder of one of the leg tenons. Line up the short apron so the ends of the double tenons are against the long apron at the line. Use a marking knife or a very sharp pencil to trace around the tenons.

With a drill, rough out the mortises. Be sure you don't touch the layout lines. Use a chisel to square the mortises, paring up to the layout lines. Test the fit of the tenons, and pare the mortises as required to achieve a perfect fit.

You'll get a more accurate fit by using the tenons cut on the short apron to lay out and position the mortises on the long apron than you would by laying them out from the plans with a ruler. Hold the short apron against the long apron, as shown, and scribe around the tenons. Just be sure to cut *inside* the lines.

Trammel Routing with a Pivot Base

To cut this tabletop, you need to anchor the trammel's pivot at the very edge of the workpiece. Using a pivot base allows you to accomplish this easily.

Typically, a trammel pivot base is used when you don't want to sink the pivot into the workpiece, leaving a hole. You attach the pivot base to the workpiece with double-sided tape. The base can be as formal as a square of acrylic plastic or as ephemeral as a scrap of wood. The former you'd use again and again. The latter you'd roust out of the scrap bin, use once, then toss. You tape the base to the workpiece, sink the pivot into it, make the cut, then pry the base off the workpiece. The pivot hasn't marred the workpiece.

In the case of this semicircular tabletop, you attach the pivot base to the tabletop with carpet tape (the type with adhesive on both sides), positioning it so it overhangs the edge. Sink the pivot into the scrap, and make the cut.

Incidentally, because the cut here begins and ends at the edge of the workpiece, you can make it safely and effectively with a fixed-base router.

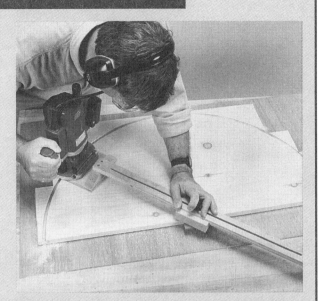

To protect the benchtop, lay the glued-up tabletop on an expendable piece of plywood. Attach the pivot base at the edge of the tabletop with double-sided carpet tape, then set the router and trammel in place. Rout the arc. Note how we economized on lumber in gluing up the tabletop.

6. Assemble the legs and aprons. Start with the aprons. From a scrap of some hard wood, whittle a couple of wedges to drive into the kerfs in the tenons after the aprons are assembled.

Spread glue lightly over the double tenons and on the inside of the through mortises. Join the two aprons. Carefully drive the wedges into the kerfs in the tenons.

Now glue the legs in place. Make sure the legs are square to the aprons. Clamp them until the glue sets.

7. Cut and attach the top. Like the aprons, the boards making up the tabletop should be resawed (or planed down) from 5/4 stock. Glue up as many boards as are necessary to create a panel

$17\frac{1}{2}$ inches wide. Sand the finished panel, then cut the semicircular shape with a router and trammel.

Position the tabletop on the leg-and-apron assembly, as shown in the *Plan Views*. Drive 6d cut finish nails through the top into the aprons.

8. Finish the table. The original table was never finished, except for the top, which was painted flat black on the top and edges. That gave us a precedent to follow. We painted the top flat black and left the legs and aprons unfinished. It will take years for the legs and aprons on the reproduction to develop the dark patina of the original, but the table still does look good.

QUEBEC BONNET CUPBOARD

Never heard of a *bonnetière?* Neither had I, before I began investigating this country original. The dealer who let me measure and photograph it apparently hadn't either: She told me it was a jelly cupboard.

But a *bonnetière* is almost certainly what it is. That translates to "bonnet cupboard."

The cupboard first knocked my eye out in an antique store in Massachusetts. Its size and particularly its moldings were unusual to me, and very appealing. Oh, and its vivid red paint made something of an impression, too. A good six months later, I saw it again, this time in a store in New Hampshire. The dealer (who operated both stores, incidentally) said it was made in Quebec.

The sort of impact this cabinet has on you depends upon whether you see it in black-and-white or full color. In these two photos, what gives it impact is its design, its conformation. The cupboard is nicely proportioned and marvelously trimmed. But if you were to see it in color, its vibrant red paint would make the first impact.

Proof? A neighbor of mine here in Pennsylvania remembered seeing this very cabinet. She had been in Massachusetts during the same summer I was, in the same touristy town. And what stuck in her mind about the town was the antiques store that had "the beautiful red cabinet!"

In drawing the plans and building our reproduction, the trim presented the biggest challenge. A search through a good half-dozen router-bit catalogs didn't yield a single bit that would produce any of the various profiles I needed. Then I paged through the catalogs again, looking at *sections* of bit profiles. I thought about what I'd get if I were to turn the routed profile upside down, or tip it slightly. Then I began to find bits that would do. The drawing *Profiles* should explain for you, step by step, just how to reproduce the moldings.

But I still didn't really know what this cabinet would have been called by its maker. Or what, if anything, was *Quebecois* about it? So I began looking for books about Canadian country furniture.

It turns out that the French-Canadian furniture built in Montreal and Quebec City is a subset of French Provincial furniture, the style produced in Normandy, Brittany, and other provinces of France remote from Paris.

Our reproduction (*opposite*), faithful but for the evidence of wear and age (*above*), is used not for bonnets, but for linens and bedclothes.

CUTTING LIST

Piece	Number	Thickness	Width	Length	Material
Sides	2	$3/4$"	$18^1/_2$"	$61^1/_2$"	1-by pine
Top	1	$3/4$"	$17^{15}/_{16}$"	26"	1-by pine
Bottom	1	$3/4$"	$16^7/_{16}$"	$25^1/_4$"	1-by pine
Shelves	4	$3/4$"	$16^7/_{16}$"	$25^1/_4$"	1-by pine
Back boards	6	$3/4$"	$7^1/_2$"	$25^1/_4$"	1-by pine
Back boards	2	$3/4$"	$9^1/_4$"	$25^1/_4$"	1-by pine
Top face frame rail	1	$3/4$"	$4^1/_4$"	$25^1/_4$"	1-by pine
Bottom face frame rail	1	$3/4$"	$3^1/_4$"	$25^1/_4$"	1-by pine
Face frame hinge stile	1	$3/4$"	$3^1/_2$"	56"	1-by pine
Face frame latch stile	1	$3/4$"	3"	56"	1-by pine
Base sides	2	1"	$5^1/_8$"	$18^1/_2$"	5/4 pine
Base molding	2	1"	$1^5/_8$"	$18^1/_2$"	5/4 pine*
Base front	1	1"	$5^1/_8$"	$27^1/_8$"	5/4 pine
Base back	1	1"	$5^1/_8$"	26"	5/4 pine
Door hinge stile	1	$3/4$"	$4^3/_8$"	$53^7/_8$"	1-by pine
Door latch stile	1	$3/4$"	$4^1/_4$"	$53^7/_8$"	1-by pine
Door top rail	1	$3/4$"	$4^5/_8$"	$13^1/_4$"	1-by pine
Door middle rail	1	$3/4$"	$4^1/_4$"	$13^1/_4$"	1-by pine
Door bottom rail	1	$3/4$"	$4^1/_2$"	$13^1/_4$"	1-by pine
Door top panel	1	$1/2$"	$10^7/_8$"	$18^1/_4$"	1-by pine
Door bottom panel	1	$1/2$"	$10^7/_8$"	$23^3/_4$"	1-by pine
Turn button	1	$1/4$"	$5/8$"	$1^3/_8$"	pine
Face frame surround molding	2	1"	$1^5/_8$"	$59^{13}/_{16}$"	5/4 pine*
Face frame surround molding	2	1"	$1^5/_8$"	$25^1/_4$"	5/4 pine*
Crown fascia body	1	$5/8$"	$1^1/_2$"	$27^1/_4$"	1-by pine
Crown fascia body	2	$5/8$"	$1^1/_2$"	$20^1/_4$"	1-by pine
Crown fascia molding	2	1"	$1^5/_8$"	$20^1/_4$"	5/4 pine*
Crown bed molding	2	$9/_{16}$"	$1^5/_8$"	$20^1/_4$"	molding
Crown bed molding	1	$9/_{16}$"	$1^5/_8$"	$30^7/_8$"	molding
Crown cap	2	1"	$2^7/_{16}$"	$20^1/_4$"	5/4 pine
Crown cap	1	1"	$1^5/_{16}$"	$30^7/_8$"	5/4 pine

HARDWARE

8d finish nails
6d finish nails
4d finish nails
1 pr. butt hinges, $2^1/_2$" × $1^1/_2$"
1 wooden knob, $1^3/_8$" dia.
6 flathead wood screws, #8 × $1^1/_4$"
1 brass roundhead screw, #6 × 1" (for turn button)

*The profile is routed on strips of 5/4 pine stock, dimensioned as specified here. Then the molding is ripped to the final widths and thicknesses specified by the text.

EXPLODED VIEW

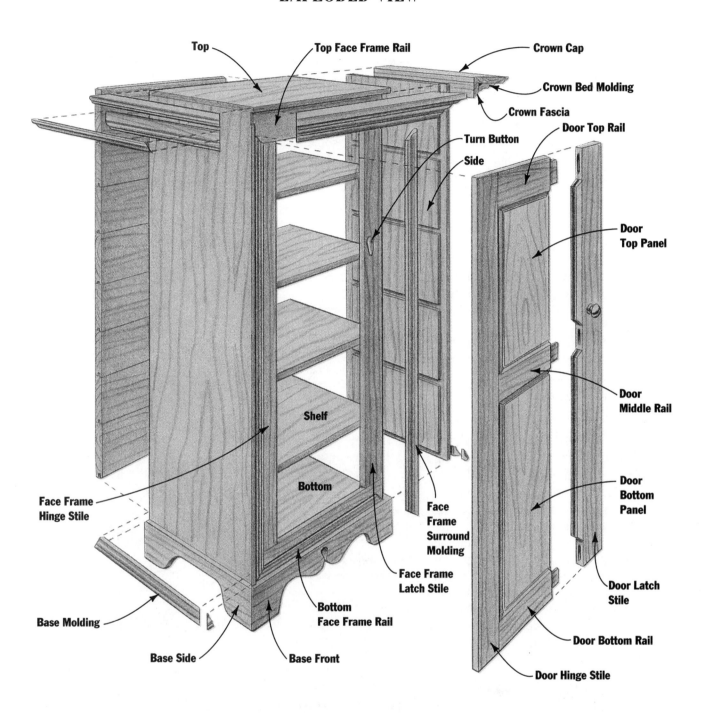

Top

Top Face Frame Rail

Crown Cap

Crown Bed Molding

Crown Fascia

Door Top Rail

Turn Button

Side

Door Top Panel

Door Middle Rail

Shelf

Door Bottom Panel

Face Frame Hinge Stile

Bottom

Face Frame Surround Molding

Face Frame Latch Stile

Door Latch Stile

Base Molding

Bottom Face Frame Rail

Door Bottom Rail

Base Side

Base Front

Door Hinge Stile

The eventual ouster of the French by the British altered the stylistic influences. Woodworkers from England, Scotland, and New England migrated into Canada, bringing their own ideas and styles. The character of the ornamentation changed considerably, especially by the time this bonnet cupboard was built.

The *bonnetière* is a French Provincial furniture form that emerged in the late seventeenth century and continued to be built through the nineteenth century. It is a fairly tall, narrow cupboard with a single door that was for storing the elaborate high bonnets worn by women in Normandy and Brittany. In Canada, this type of cupboard was nearly always used as a general wardrobe, rather than, as in France, a bonnet cupboard exclusively. This particular cupboard may have been used as a washstand as well as a wardrobe. A basin, soap dish, and other toilet articles would have been placed on one of the shelves, and a mirror would have hung on the inside of the door.

Though this cupboard lacks either the diamond-point panels or the scrolled rails and panels that were typical of French Provincial cupboards and armoires, I suspect that's simply a result of its being a later piece, one dating to the mid- or late nineteenth century, well after the French influence had waned. But it has the prominent cornice characteristic of French-Canadian furniture. Typically, a molded cornice would have been made in three separate parts. That's the case with this cupboard.

So its lineage is interesting. But you wouldn't build it for that reason alone. You'd build it, as we did, because it's an unusual piece, robust and handsome. Practical, too. Even if you paint it something other than red.

BUILD THE CASE

1. Glue up the side, shelf, top, and bottom panels. The dimensions of these basic case parts are given in the Cutting List. Tips on gluing up are found in the *ShopSmarts* feature "Gluing Up Panels" on page 49. The sides should be free of prominent defects, but because the top, bottom, and shelves are not on display, you can use the knottier lumber for those parts.

2. Lay out the sides and cut the joinery. Study the *Side Layout*. Note that the shelves are dadoed into the sides. The bottom, back boards, and face frame are set into rabbets in the sides. And, though it isn't joinery, the front edges of the sides are nosed. Because of the size of the side panels, these cuts are easiest to perform with a router. Nose the sides first. Use an edge guide to control the cut. Then switch to a straight bit and cut the rabbets and dadoes. Use that edge guide to control the rabbeting cuts, and a straightedge to control the dadoing cuts.

3. Make the back boards. The back is made up of six 1 × 8s and two 1 × 10s, joined edge to edge with tongue-and-groove joints. Crosscut the stock to the sizes specified by the Cutting List. Cut the tongues and grooves on all the 1 × 8 pieces. Each piece gets a slot along one edge and a tongue along the other. The bottom piece, a 1 × 10, has a tongue along the top edge, but the bottom edge

SIDE LAYOUT

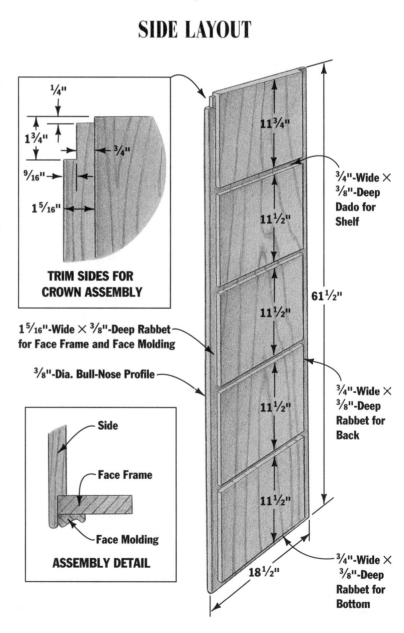

TRIM SIDES FOR CROWN ASSEMBLY

1⁵⁄₁₆"-Wide × ³⁄₈"-Deep Rabbet for Face Frame and Face Molding

³⁄₈"-Dia. Bull-Nose Profile

Side

Face Frame

Face Molding

ASSEMBLY DETAIL

11³⁄₄"

11¹⁄₂"

11¹⁄₂"

11¹⁄₂"

11¹⁄₂"

61¹⁄₂"

18¹⁄₂"

³⁄₄"-Wide × ³⁄₈"-Deep Dado for Shelf

³⁄₄"-Wide × ³⁄₈"-Deep Rabbet for Back

³⁄₄"-Wide × ³⁄₈"-Deep Rabbet for Bottom

¹⁄₄"

1³⁄₄"

⁹⁄₁₆"

1⁵⁄₁₆"

³⁄₄"

Line Up Those Dadoes!

You can ensure that the dadoes in the sides will align across the case if you lay the panels side by side and rout the dadoes in both of them at the same time. Align the panels with tops and bottoms flush. Use a long straight-edge to guide the router.

is left square. The top board gets a groove in its bottom edge. As you install the boards, you'll probably need to trim this top board to fit.

4. Make the face frame. Rip and crosscut the rails and stiles to the dimensions given by the Cutting List. (To ensure a good fit, you may want to make the face frame 1/8 to 1/4 inch wider and longer than specified; you can trim the assembled frame for a perfect fit.)

The rails and stiles are joined with mortise-and-tenon joints, as shown in *Face Frame Joinery Detail* of the *Plan Views*. Use the approach presented in the *ShopSmarts* feature "Cutting Mortise-and-Tenon Joints" on page 83 to make the joints. Then assemble the face frame.

5. Assemble the case. Start with the sides, shelves, and bottom. Join these parts with glue and nails. Countersink the nails.

Install the back boards next, nailing them to the sides and shelves. Don't use glue. Start at the bottom and work toward the top. The top board should have to be trimmed a little to fit. (**Note:** When nailing the back boards, try to support the case in such a way that the nosing doesn't get dented. If you simply rest the case—nosing down—across a couple of sawhorses, it could happen.)

Finally, trim and fit the face frame to the case. Nail it to the sides and shelves. Countersink the nails. Putty all the exposed nailheads, on the sides as well as the front.

CONSTRUCT THE BASE

1. Cut the parts. The base assembly is a separate unit that is attached to the case with screws. Begin making it by cutting the base back to the dimensions specified by the Cutting List. Cut the front and sides several inches longer than specified so that you can miter them to their final lengths during assembly. Trim the back to the shape shown in *Section B-B* of the *Plan Views*.

2. Rout the molded edges on the sides. The decorative profile along the top edges of the base sides is, in the original, an integral part of those side pieces. Because of the configuration of the bit, however, the profile must be routed as a separate molding. After routing the molding, you can trim and glue it to the base sides.

We used an architectural molding bit, catalog number 175-0205 from Eagle America (800-872-2511). To rout the molding, follow the sequence in *Fascia and Base Profile*.

Glue a strip of the molding to the top edge of each of the base sides. Apply clamps cautiously to the molding so that it won't be

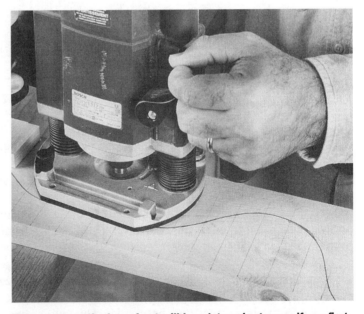

The cutout on the base front will be a lot easier to saw if you first drill a 1-inch-diameter hole at the center of the contour. This gives you the option of starting at the center of the contour and sawing out, or starting at the edge and sawing in. Using a plunge router and a 1-inch-diameter bit will produce a clean hole square to the face. And it will produce a perfect shape, one you couldn't duplicate with a saber saw.

PLAN VIEWS

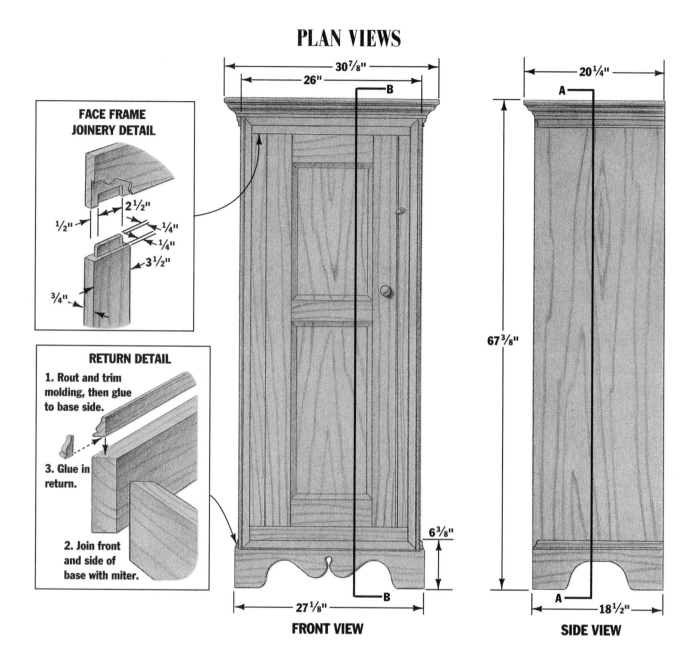

FACE FRAME JOINERY DETAIL

2 1/2"
1/2" 1/4" 1/4" 3 1/2" 3/4"

RETURN DETAIL

1. Rout and trim molding, then glue to base side.

3. Glue in return.

2. Join front and side of base with miter.

30 7/8"
26"
B

67 3/8"
20 1/4"
A

6 3/8"

27 1/8" B

FRONT VIEW

18 1/2" A

SIDE VIEW

marred. Save leftover scraps of the molding to make returns, which are fitted to the base after it's joined to the case.

3. Cut the base profile. Enlarge the patterns for the front and side base cutouts. Transfer the contours to the base front and base sides. Cut the contour with a band saw or saber saw. Sand the cut edges smooth and straight.

4. Assemble the base and attach it to the case. Miter both ends of the base front, reducing the piece to the length specified by the Cutting List.

Miter one end of each side. Then assemble the front, sides, and back with glue and nails.

With the case standing on its head, set the base in place, line it up carefully, then drive several screws through it into the case bottom. Position the screws carefully so they won't break through the bottom board.

Complete the base installation by gluing returns to the molded profile on the base sides. To make a return, miter a scrap of the molded profile, then crosscut the molding to get a wedge-shaped bit of molding. Glue it into the wedge-shaped gap formed by the mitered profile on the base and the case side.

PLAN VIEWS

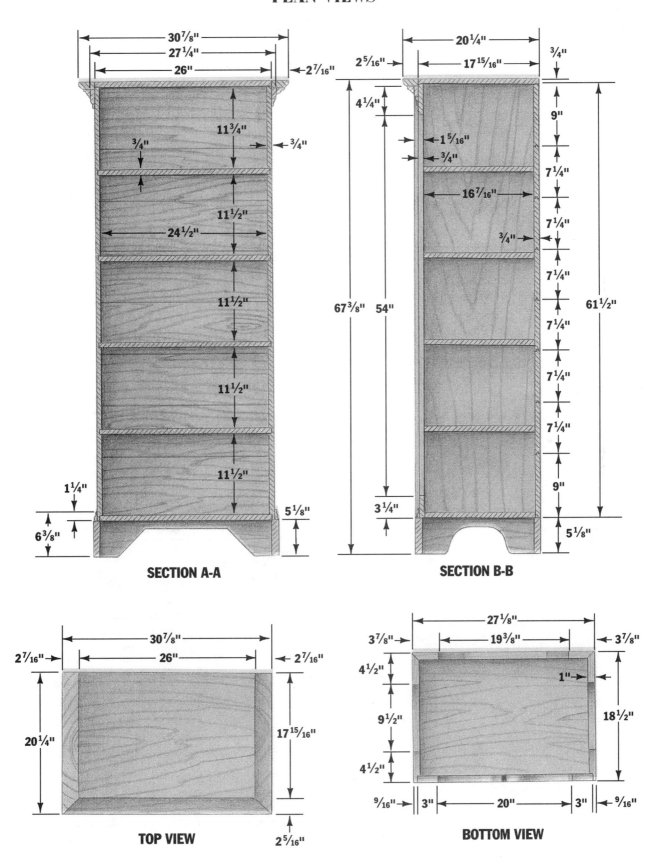

SECTION A-A

SECTION B-B

TOP VIEW

BOTTOM VIEW

PATTERNS

FRONT

5³/₈"

3⁷/₈" ← 19³/₈" → 3⁷/₈"

27¹/₈"

SIDE BASE PATTERN

1 Square = ¹/₂"

C_L

FRONT BASE PATTERN

1 Square = ¹/₂"

SIDE

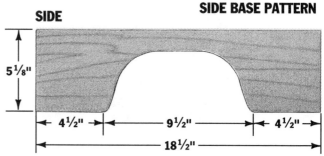

5¹/₈"

4¹/₂" ← 9¹/₂" → 4¹/₂"

18¹/₂"

PROFILES

CROWN MOLDING ASSEMBLY

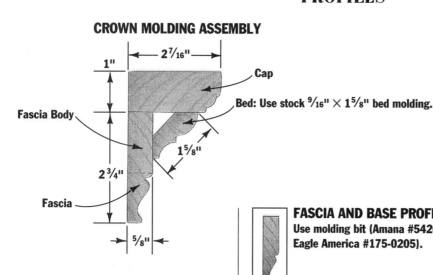

2⁷/₁₆"

1"

Cap

Fascia Body

Bed: Use stock ⁹/₁₆" × 1⁵/₈" bed molding.

1⁵/₈"

2³/₄"

Fascia

5/₈"

CAP PROFILE

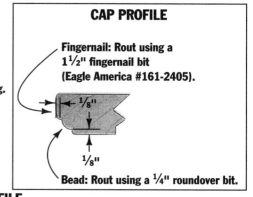

Fingernail: Rout using a
1¹/₂" fingernail bit
(Eagle America #161-2405).

¹/₈"

¹/₈"

Bead: Rout using a ¹/₄" roundover bit.

FASCIA AND BASE PROFILE
Use molding bit (Amana #54204;
Eagle America #175-0205).

11/₁₆"

1. Rout profile on 5/4 stock.

2. Bevel back at 15° to
thickness shown.

3. Rip at points indicated,
reducing width to 1¹/₄".

4. Sand bead form onto
molding; glue to fascia body.

FACE MOLDING
Use molding bit
(Amana #54204;
Eagle America #175-0205).

5/₈"

1. Rout profile on 5/4 stock.

2. Bevel back at 15° to
thickness shown.

3. Rip at points indicated,
reducing width to 1¹/₈".

4. Sand bead form onto
molding.

STICKING PROFILE
Use French Provincial bit
(Eagle America #174-2815;
Freud #99-008).

1. Rout basic profile using
only a portion of the bit.

2. Round-over the
shoulder with sandpaper.

3. Cut a slot for the panel.

DOOR CONSTRUCTION

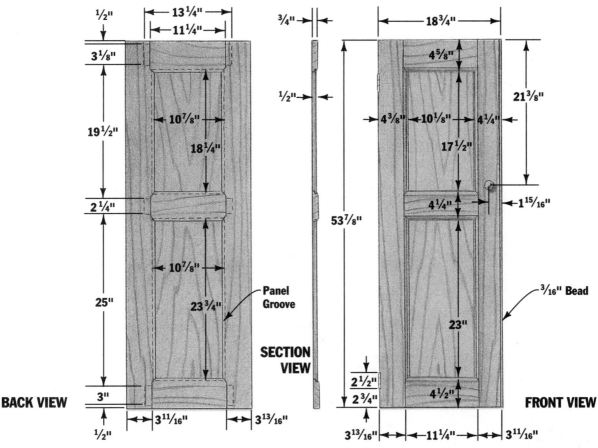

BACK VIEW

SECTION VIEW

FRONT VIEW

¾" Bead

Panel Groove

BUILD THE DOOR

1. Cut the rails and stiles; glue up the panels. The dimensions for these parts are on the Cutting List. Rip and crosscut the stock for the rails and stiles. Before glue-up, the stock for the panels must be resawed or planed to a ½-inch thickness. After reducing the stock to the necessary thickness, rip and crosscut it, then glue up the panels. Procedural tips are in the *ShopSmarts* feature "Gluing Up Panels" on page 49.

2. Cut the sticking on the rails and stiles. The sticking is the decorative profile cut on the inside edges of the rails and stiles. Typically, these days, it's cut on the workpiece at the same time as the groove for the panel; one cutter makes both cuts. But the profile used here requires a different angle of attack. Do the job on the router table, as indicated in the *Sticking Profile*.

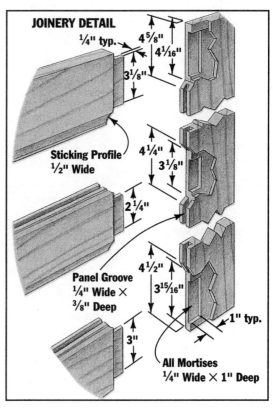

JOINERY DETAIL

¼" typ.   4⅝"   4¹⁄₁₆"   3⅛"

Sticking Profile ½" Wide

4¼"   3⅛"

2¼"

Panel Groove ¼" Wide × ⅜" Deep

4½"   3¹⁵⁄₁₆"

3"   1" typ.

All Mortises ¼" Wide × 1" Deep

Before mitering the sticking on the door rails, assemble the rails and stiles without glue. Mark on the stiles where the rails intersect, as shown. You can use a marking knife for this, but I used a mechanical pencil, which produces a very fine line. The line on the rail establishes the $1/2$-inch sticking width and also marks the base of the miter.

Cut the miters on the table saw. Tilt the blade to 45 degrees, then raise it to just under $1/2$ inch. Guide the workpiece with the miter gauge, and nibble at the miter, bringing the cut to within $1/16$ inch or $1/32$ inch of the mark. Then set the rails aside and cut the stiles.

Miter and trim the stiles using the same table saw setup. Miter a bit shy of the marks. To trim the sticking, make repeated cuts, as shown, working from miter to miter (or from the miter to the end of the stile). In this photo, the vertical lines are extensions of the initial layout marks. The angled lines are simply reference marks, reminding me in which direction the miter should be cut. After the waste is roughed away on the table saw, use a chisel to refine the joint. Pare the base of the cut flat. Test assemble the parts, and pare the miters as necessary to perfect the joints.

The basic cut is made with a portion of the so-called French Provincial bit. We used a bit provided by Eagle America (catalog number 174-2815). Adjust the bit height to just capture the full bead. Set the fence to limit the depth of the cut to 3/16 inch. Cut the full length of one edge of both stiles and the top and bottom rails. Cut the full length of *both* edges of the middle rail.

To create the roundover at the shoulder, break the edge with a few passes with a block plane. Then sand the edge.

Finally, rout the 3/16-inch bead along the edge of the latch stile.

3. Cut the joinery. The rails and stiles are joined by mortise-and-tenon joints. The panels float in a groove cut in the rails and stiles. Plow the groove first, then do the mortise-and-tenon joints.

The groove extends the full length of the rails and stiles. It can be cut with a slot cutter or straight bit on the router table, or on the table saw.

The dimensions and locations of the mortises and the tenons are shown in the *Joinery Detail* of *Door Construction*. Details on routing mortises and sawing tenons can be found in the *ShopSmarts* feature "Cutting Mortise-and-Tenon Joints" on page 83. When you rout the mortises, be sure to account for the material that will be cut away to complete the joinery. Make the mortises 1 9/16 inches deep.

To complete the joinery, the sticking profile must be mitered and trimmed away where the rails and stiles come together. On the stiles, lay out the areas that need to be trimmed away. Cut the miters first, doing this on the table saw. Tilt the blade to 45 degrees, and set the height to cut just through the profile. Make the miter cuts on all the rails and on the stiles. The waste on the stiles can be trimmed away with repeated table saw cuts, with a saber saw, or with a coping saw. Use a chisel to trim the cut surfaces and refine the fit of the joints.

4. Rabbet the panels. You have 1/2-inch-thick panels and frame parts with a 1/4-inch-wide groove in them for the panels. Rabbet or undercut the back edges of the panels. Make the rabbet about 7/16 inch wide. Don't reduce the panel thickness at the edge too much, or the panels will rattle in the grooves.

5. Assemble the door. Do this without glue first to give the joints a final fit-test. Then, following any necessary adjustments, glue the frame parts together. First glue all the rails into one stile. Then slip the panels into place and glue the second stile to the assembly. Don't glue the panels, of course.

6. Hang the door. Use 2 1/2-inch butt hinges, mortised into the hinge stile and the face frame. Install the wooden knob and the turn button.

TRIM OUT THE CABINET

1. Make the face frame surround and crown fascia moldings. The profile of these moldings is the same as that on the base sides. It is routed in the same sequence, using the same bits. (See Step 2 under "Construct the Base" on page 75.) The lengths required are specified by the Cutting List, but it's a good idea to make the moldings longer to begin with, and to make several extras.

2. Make the crown cap. Cut 5/4 stock to the dimensions specified by the Cutting List. The profile combines a quarter-round bead and a so-called fingernail. Rout the bead first, using a 1/4-inch roundover bit in a table-mounted router. Remove the bit's bearing and use the fence to guide and control the cut. Make the flat above the bead wide enough that it won't be removed when you rout the fingernail.

Switch to a 1 1/2-inch fingernail bit to rout the remaining section of the profile.

3. Buy the crown bed. Because this molding profile is so close to a stock architectural molding, I opted to use stock molding. You can buy it at your local building-supply center.

4. Install the crown. Begin by trimming the bull-nosing from the cupboard sides to accommodate the fascia body, which backs the crown bed molding. The most reliable approach is to simply hold a length of the fascia body to the front of the cupboard, then mark the extent of the trimming necessary.

After the trimming is done, proceed to fit and miter the crown cap. Edge-glue the front piece to the front edge of the top, since it parallels the grain

Let Those Moldings Run Wild

Let the side moldings run "wild" when you install them. That is, if a molding is longer than the side is wide, let the extra length extend past the back edge. After all the molding is installed, trim the overlong strips flush with the back edge using a backsaw.

direction of the top. The side pieces shouldn't be glued along their full lengths. Instead, apply a 2- or 3-inch-long bead of glue, beginning at the miters. Toenail the back ends to the top. This approach accommodates the expansion and contraction of the sides; the glue will hold the molding firmly at the miter, but the nails at the back will give a bit as the side moves.

Add the fascia body next. Along the front, the body can be glued and nailed in place. Use 4d finish nails. Along the sides, the fascia body can be glued for a few inches at the front edge, but in the middle and at the back, it should only be nailed (no glue). Miters join the front piece to the side pieces.

The fascia molding is applied along the sides only; there is none on the front. The molding is square-cut at the back, coped at the front. You can either cope the molding with a coping saw, finishing up with a round file, or else miter the molding and glue in a return. As with the previous elements of the crown, glue the fascia to the sides only near the front, and nail it in the middle and back.

Add the crown bed last. Fit and miter the molding pieces. As you install the molding, apply glue to the miters.

5. Install the face frame surround. This is the last of the trim. Cut the lengths of trim to fit, mitering the ends. Nail it in place.

APPLY THE FINISH

The finish *has* to be red paint. We used an oil paint manufactured by the Stulb Company and sold under the Old Village label. Rittenhouse Red is the hue. See the *ShopSmarts* feature "Country Finishes" on page 305 for painting tips.

Cutting Mortise-and-Tenon Joints

The mortise-and-tenon is woodworking's essential frame joint. The basic elements are the mortise, which is a hole—round, square, or rectangular—and the tenon, which is a tongue cut on the end of the joining member to fit the mortise. Once assembled with glue or pegs, the mortise-and-tenon joint resists all four types of stress: tension, compression, shear, and racking. And it does it better than any other type of joint.

Mortising

The main advantages of the router for mortising include the smoothness of its finished cuts and the accuracy of placement and sizing that's possible. The only disadvantage that comes to mind is the limited reach of the router bit. A narrow, deep mortise—$\frac{1}{4}$ inch wide × $1\frac{3}{4}$ inches or more deep, for example—is problematic for a router. (The longest $\frac{1}{4}$-inch straight bit I've come across is a $2\frac{7}{8}$-inch-long two-flute bit made by Amana, number 45211. Call Amana Tool at 800-445-0077 for the name of a dealer.) The joints in these projects, be assured, have been scaled with this limitation in mind.

To rout a mortise, the first thing you must do is cobble up a mortising fixture to hold the workpiece. The fixture shown in the drawing below is perfect. It looks a lot like a wooden miter box. The fixture is clamped in a vise, and the workpiece is set in the open-ended box and clamped to the back. The router is supported by the fixture's back and side, and the edge guide references the outer face of the side. Stops screwed to the side fix the length of the mortise.

In dimensioning a fixture for your project, space the side and back far enough apart to give broad support to the router. When assembling the fixture, make sure the top edges are square to the faces of the side and back, so the mortise will be square to the workpiece edge.

1. Set up the fixture. Use a workpiece with the mortise laid out and with an alignment line scribed across the mortise's width. Clamp the workpiece in place, with the workpiece line aligned with one marked across the side and back.

Set the router in place and plunge the bit—with the router switched *off,* of course—to the workpiece. Adjust the edge guide.

MORTISING FIXTURE

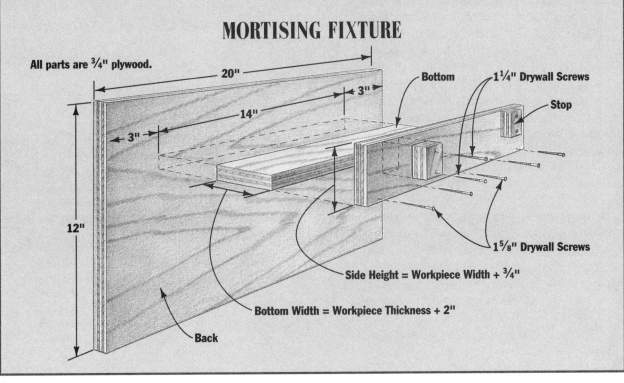

All parts are $\frac{3}{4}$" plywood.

20"

3"

14"

3"

Bottom

1$\frac{1}{4}$" Drywall Screws

Stop

12"

1$\frac{5}{8}$" Drywall Screws

Side Height = Workpiece Width + $\frac{3}{4}$"

Bottom Width = Workpiece Thickness + 2"

Back

(continued)

Move the router so the bit is aligned at one end of the mortise. Place a stop block against the tip of the edge guide, and attach it to the side with a couple of drywall screws.

Move the router to the other end of the mortise, and attach the second stop to the side.

As long as you line up the workpiece and the fixture alignment marks, every mortise will be consistently placed and sized.

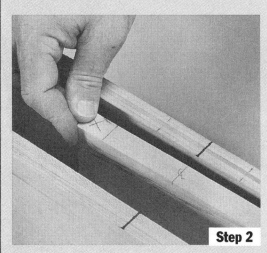

Step 2

2. Clamp the workpiece in the mortising fixture. When using the fixture, you need to mark only the midpoint of each mortise on the workpiece, as shown in the Step 2 photo. Line up that mark with the fixture's alignment mark, and the mortise will be the right size and in the right place. (The "X" under my thumb, by the way, indicates an inch of waste that will be trimmed *after* assembly. This waste provides some extra meat to the mortise's end wall, preventing me from inadvertently breaking out the end grain when pushing a tenon into the mortise.)

3. Rout the mortise. With the workpiece clamped in the fixture, and with the router all set up, rout the mortise. Note in the first Step 3 photo that even though the workpiece extends beyond the end of the fixture, the two clamps you see are sufficient to secure it.

Plunge-cut the ends of the mortise first. Doing this ensures that the ends of the

SETTING UP MORTISING FIXTURE

1. Set the workpiece in the trough, and line up the mark on it with the mark on the fixture.

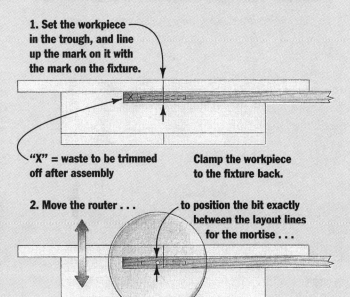

"X" = waste to be trimmed off after assembly

Clamp the workpiece to the fixture back.

2. Move the router . . . to position the bit exactly between the layout lines for the mortise . . .

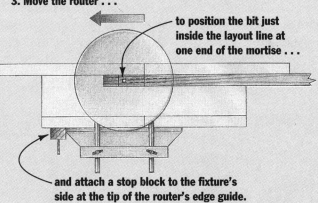

then lock down the edge guide.

3. Move the router . . . to position the bit just inside the layout line at one end of the mortise . . .

and attach a stop block to the fixture's side at the tip of the router's edge guide.

4. Move the router . . . to position the bit just inside the layout line at the other end of the mortise . . .

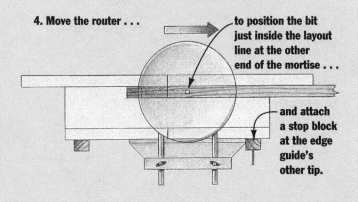

and attach a stop block at the edge guide's other tip.

Step 3

mortise will be vertical. Then rout out the waste between the ends in a series of passes.

When you cut, be sure you feed the router in the right direction, the one that uses the force of the bit rotation to pull the guide against the work. To do this, you've got to retract the bit between cutting passes. So I push the router to make the cutting pass, then retract the bit clear of the work and pull the router back. Then I replunge the bit for another cutting pass.

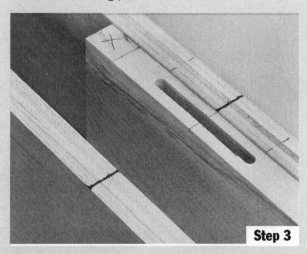

Step 3

The finished mortise is clean and true. Note the length of the mortise in relation to the end points ticked in pencil on the fixture, as well as the midpoint marked on the fixture and on the stile.

To do the mortise on the other end of this workpiece, you merely have to pull the clamps and slide the piece through the trough until the appropriate marks line up. Then reclamp it, and rout.

When routing a mortise that's open on one end, as is often the case with leg-and-apron constructions, you need only one stop.

Tenoning

There are lots of ways to cut tenons, but the following approach is slick and easy. You use a shop-made tenoning jig (designed by my friend and colleague, Bob Moran) on your table saw.

In brief, the sequence is this: Cut the shoulders on the table saw. Then set the tenoning jig on the saw table, adjust the rip fence to position the cut, clamp the workpiece in the jig, and cut the cheeks.

Tenons are typically cut after the mortises. Therefore, you need to adjust the tenon's thickness to fit the mortises. To set up, you cut a test tenon and see how it fits the mortise. Ideally, you'll have made this first tenon a bit too thick, so subsequent adjustments will thin it to the perfect fit.

(And remember that with many of today's glues, it's a good idea to "leave room for the glue." In other words, don't make the joint too tight.)

Let's look at the tenoning jig first. The drawing on page 86 should make clear how it's constructed.

Unlike jigs that straddle the rip fence, this one has no side-to-side play because it rides *against* the fence. Its broad, flat base prevents it from tipping when you're cutting the cheeks on a long piece of stock. Two well-placed handles make it easy to control the jig and keep both hands well away from the blade. Toggle clamps hold the stock securely yet allow fast workpiece changeover.

Although you can't use the table saw's blade guard, Bob incorporated a chip deflector in the design. That, coupled with the two-handed feed technique, makes this jig as safe as a tenoning jig can be. Nevertheless, exercise caution when using it.

Here's the tenon-cutting sequence:

1. Cut the shoulders first. Clean, accurate, square shoulder cuts are important for final appearance and to add to strength. Cut them a hair's breadth overdeep. To govern the tenon length, use the rip fence. Measure from the fence to the outside of the blade—that's the tenon length. Set the workpiece against the miter gauge, and butt the end against the fence. Push the miter gauge to make the cut.

(continued)

2. Set the blade height for the cheek cuts. Only after you've made all the shoulder cuts should you change the table saw setup to cut the cheeks. The first step is to set the blade height. Use the

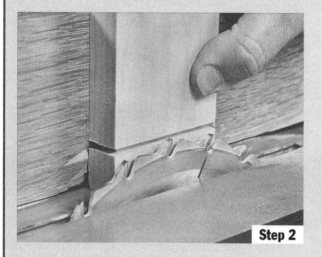

Step 2

workpiece. Hold it next to the blade, as shown in the Step 2 photo, and crank the blade up until its highest tooth is aligned with the shoulder kerf. Any higher and the blade will kerf the tenon's shoulder during the cheek cut. Such kerfs would be evident on the rail after the parts are assembled.

3. Position the tenoning jig for the cheek cuts. Move the fence back, and set the tenoning jig on the saw table. Move the jig into position over the blade, and adjust the rip fence. I prefer to make the cheek cut on the side of the workpiece that's against the jig. Therefore, I make the coarse fence setting, as shown in the Step 3 photo, by measuring from the jig to the outside of the blade with a metal rule. (One reason I make the cut where I do is so that, should the jig drift from the fence, the blade would gouge the waste, not the tenon itself.)

TENONING JIG

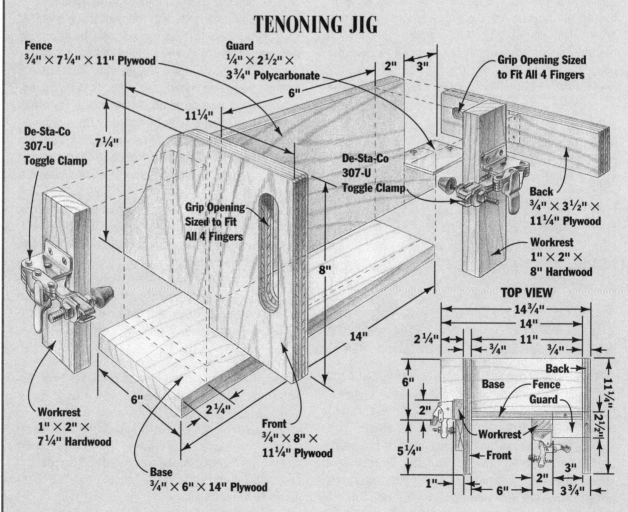

Fence
3/4" × 7 1/4" × 11" Plywood

Guard
1/4" × 2 1/2" × 3 3/4" Polycarbonate

Grip Opening Sized to Fit All 4 Fingers

De-Sta-Co 307-U Toggle Clamp

De-Sta-Co 307-U Toggle Clamp

Grip Opening Sized to Fit All 4 Fingers

Back
3/4" × 3 1/2" × 11 1/4" Plywood

Workrest
1" × 2" × 8" Hardwood

Workrest
1" × 2" × 7 1/4" Hardwood

Front
3/4" × 8" × 11 1/4" Plywood

Base
3/4" × 6" × 14" Plywood

TOP VIEW

Back

Base   Fence

Guard

Workrest

Front

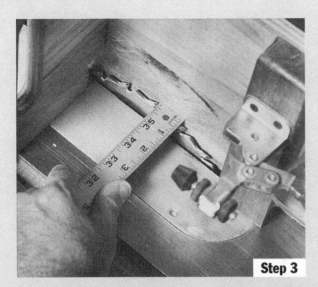

Step 3

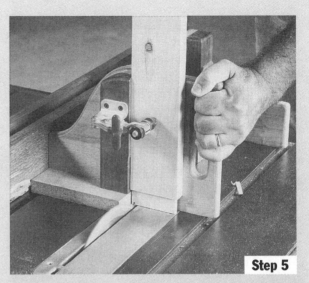

Step 5

The fine fence setting is made after cutting the cheeks on a test piece and seeing how it fits in the mortise. Just remember to trim both cheeks each time you adjust the fence, so the tenon remains centered on the workpiece.

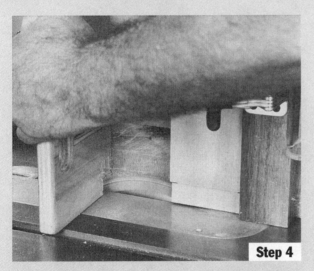

Step 4

4. Cut the cheeks. Cutting the cheeks is a matter of standing the workpiece on end in the jig, locking it there with the toggle clamp, and feeding it into the blade. Use both hands to advance the jig. After cutting the first cheek, simply unlock the clamp, rotate the workpiece 180 degrees, and re-lock the clamp. Then make the second cut.

5. Make the edge cuts. The last task is nipping the tenons to their final width. This isn't *always* done, but if edge cuts are necessary, the tenoning jig has a separate fence on the front for this. As you do for the cheek cuts, stand the workpiece on end, and lock it to the jig with the toggle clamp. That way the workpiece won't shift out of position, and you have both hands free to guide the jig.

The jig is constructed so that the edge of the front fence is flush with the jig's side. If you are forming tenons with shoulders of a consistent width all around, you don't even need to reset the rip fence for the edge cuts. Pop the workpiece into the front position, snap the clamp, and make the cut. It will be the same width as the cheek cuts.

With the mortise routed and the tenon cut, you are all ready to assemble the joint. But there's one last hitch. The ends of the routed mortise are rounded. The edges of the sawed tenon are square. I use a file to break the tenon's edges. A lick or two on each edge is all it takes with pine.

And you'll have a perfect fit.

Step 5

CANDLE SHELF

Candle shelves are in the same category as pipe boxes. Both are popular "smalls." They don't require a lot of material or take a lot of time to make. They don't eat up space in the home. And they are attractive accents in a country home.

But you may ask, in this day and age, what practical use are they?

Where I live, 20 miles out of town, with a small orchard on one side and hay and small-grain fields on the other, a candle shelf comes in handy four or seven times a year. That's how often the power goes out, and when it goes, it's out an hour or two—or so it seems when we sit in the dark. That's when we get a taste of the life our ancestors lived. And we appreciate some of the little tricks they came up with to "improve" candlelight.

A candle shelf is one of those tricks.

Can you picture the movie scene where the characters pick their way through the dark by candlelight? They always hold that candle high, don't they? Why? Because when you hold the candle high, the light seems to penetrate the gloom better. (Experiment sometime; you'll see.) Thus, one of the tricks of living by candlelight is positioning the candle up off the table or chest, up on the wall.

On the candle shelf. Oh, those who could afford it had polished metal candle sconces to enhance the candlelight, but not our country woodworker.

The fellow who cobbled up this candle shelf had to make do with a wooden piece. It does have some advantages. With its high back and arch-topped sides, the shelf provides some protection for the candle, preventing it from being knocked over and shielding the flame from drafts. Too, the back shields the wall from the flame's heat and soot.

What's odd about this candle shelf, to me, is that it's painted a very dark color.

That oddity didn't register at first, since the shelf was the perfect little project I was looking for. Just a few, small pieces of wood, a dozen or so brads, is all it would take to make it, I thought. And the form is nice, too. Not overly sculpted. It would look good in the country home. Seems to be genuine; it has seen a lot of use. The hanging hole is notched from its contact with the nail on which it hung, and the shelf itself still has wax caked in the corners.

Later, after I gave the *use* of candle shelves some thought, I realized that the dark color of this specimen would have just swallowed up candlelight. So when I made a copy, I painted it a light color, a traditional golden mustard. Then I

The original candle shelf (*above*) was strictly utilitarian. Festooned with holiday garlands, my reproduction (*opposite*) is strictly for decoration.

EXPLODED VIEW

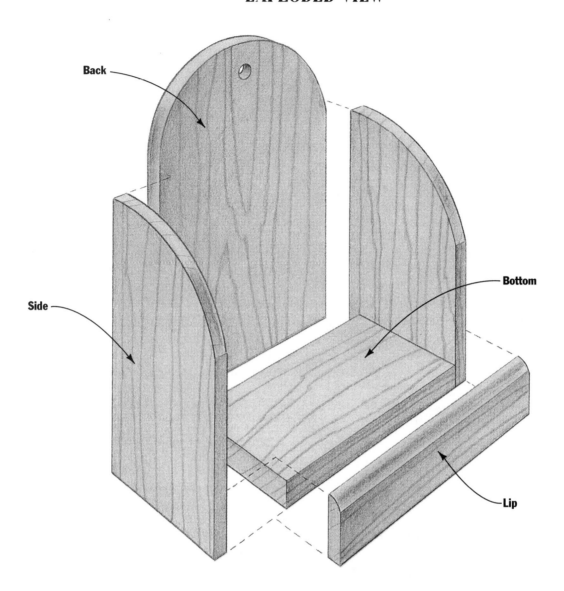

Back

Side

Bottom

Lip

CUTTING LIST

Piece	Number	Thickness	Width	Length	Material
Back	1	$^1/_2$"	$6^7/_8$"	$11^1/_4$"	pine
Bottom	1	$^3/_4$"	$6^7/_8$"	$3^9/_{16}$"	1-by pine
Sides	2	$^7/_{16}$"	$4^1/_{16}$"	8"	pine
Lip	1	$^1/_2$"	$1^5/_8$"	$7^3/_4$"	pine

HARDWARE
$1^1/_2$" headless cut brads

compared the light cast by a candle in my new shelf with that cast by a candle in the country original. There's a difference, and so the mystery remains.

The candle shelf is one of those one-evening projects. (This just may account for its popularity.)

No gluing up is required. You simply resaw a few small boards, cut a few arcs with your router, then nail the shelf together. You'll even have time to apply a couple of coats of milk paint. And then catch the sports and weather on the 11 o'clock news.

---

1. Cut the parts. It's not unlikely that you'll find all the stock you need for this project in your scrap bin. The largest piece, at $6\frac{7}{8}$ inches × $11\frac{1}{4}$ inches, is the back. That's just the size that gets saved but seldom used.

Rip and crosscut the parts to rough size, then resaw (or plane) the back, sides, and lip to the thicknesses specified by the Cutting List. Sand the sawed surfaces smooth. The bottom is the only piece that's a standard thickness.

2. Shape the back and sides. The tops of the sides and back are embellished with arching contours. The back is easily cut using a router and trammel. The cutting radius is barely larger than the radius of the typical router's baseplate, so the pivot

point is very close to the edge of the router. Sink the pivot into what will be the back of the workpiece.

The sides also can be cut with a router and trammel, but the radius and orientation of the arc are such that the trammel pivot must be off the work. It's easier to cut with a saber saw and sand the edges. Scribe the cut line using a layout bow. To do this, mark the three layout points indicated on the *Side Layout*. Adjust the layout bow to the arc that spans all three points. Set it on the workpiece and scribe along the bow with a pencil. Then cut to the line.

The most difficult part about routing the candle-shelf back is securing the workpiece. Clamps would probably be in the way of any trammel, so capture the workpiece between a bench stop and your vise's dog. Either hang the area to be cut off the workbench edge, as shown here, or sandwich a scrap board beneath the work to protect the bench top from the bit. Note that you can do this task with a fixed-base router.

SIDE LAYOUT

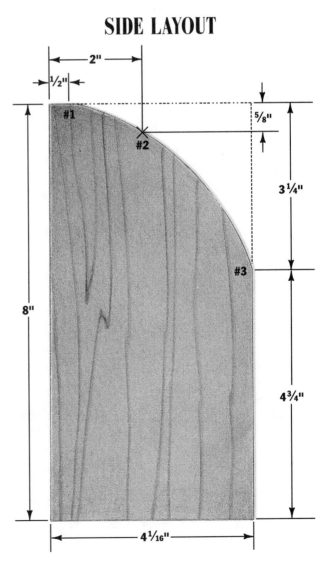

PLAN VIEWS

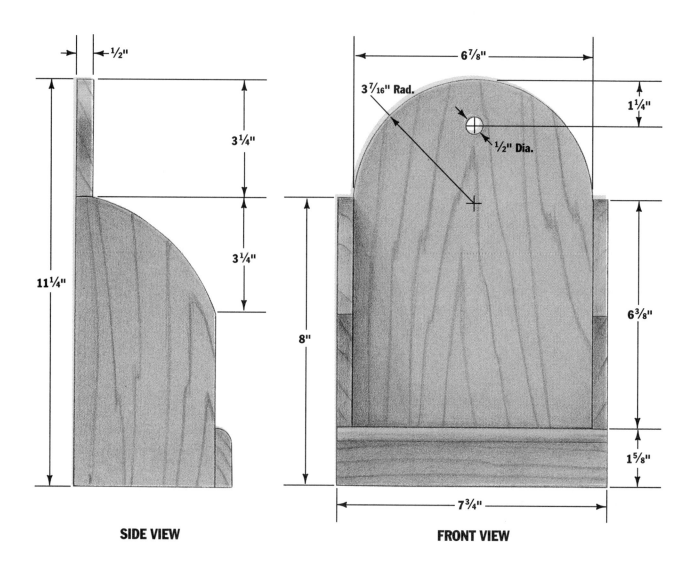

½"

3¼"

3¼"

11¼"

SIDE VIEW

6⅞"

3 7/16" Rad.

1¼"

½" Dia.

8"

6⅜"

1⅝"

7¾"

FRONT VIEW

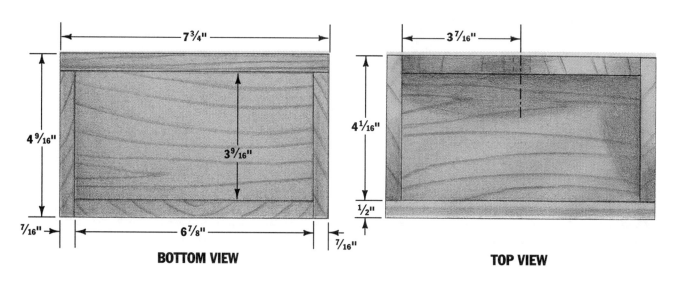

7¾"

4 9/16"

3 9/16"

7/16"

6⅞"

7/16"

BOTTOM VIEW

3 7/16"

4 1/16"

½"

TOP VIEW

Laying Out Curves

A layout bow is a terrific little gizmo for laying out curves. It is like a miniature arrow-shooting bow. You adjust the bow's curvature to the arc that pleases you, set it on the workpiece, and scribe along it with a pencil or layout knife.

The details of making a bow are these. Select a ¼-inch-thick ripping, and square the ends. (The length can range from 12 to 18 inches on up to several feet; let the job suggest an appropriate length.) With a coping saw, cut a ½-inch-long kerf into each end, as shown in the drawing. Knot a string and catch it in one of the kerfs. Extend the string to the other kerf, catch it there, and pull it tight, causing the ripping to bow.

To hold the bow at any particular arc, simply loop the string's free end around the bow's edge and through the kerf, as shown. A couple of loops should keep it from slipping.

You can make a "keeper" if you want, but each bow is so easy to make, you can toss it when you're done with your layout. Next time you have need of it, make another.

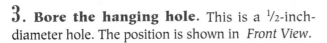

3. Bore the hanging hole. This is a ½-inch-diameter hole. The position is shown in *Front View*.

4. Round-over the lip. On the original, this roundover is clearly hand-formed. You can duplicate the character of the original by forming the profile with a spokeshave or even a rasp.

If you do use a router, use a roundover bit with a cutting radius larger than ½ inch, so you get more of a thumbnail effect than a roundover. I used a ⅝-inch cutter in a table-mounted router and guided the workpiece along the fence to make the cut.

5. Assemble the shelf. Nail the parts together with cut brads. You may find it advisable to drill pilot holes, depending upon the size and style of brads you use. So-called headless brads don't need pilots, and they are unobtrusive in the finished piece, even if you don't countersink them. Traditional cut brads, on the other hand, are pretty thick and can split thin pine easily. They are pretty difficult to hide in the finished piece, but in a project like this, you don't necessarily want to hide them. The fasteners are evident in the original.

6. Apply a finish. In choosing a finish for your candle shelf, remember that a light color will reflect light more effectively than a dark one. Pine is a light-colored wood, of course, so a natural finish (or no finish at all) is a good choice. I used paint on the reproduction shown.

Useful information on choosing and applying a finish can be found in the *ShopSmarts* feature "Country Finishes" on page 305.

Here is evidence of the tribulations of using cut nails. The candle shelf on the right was made with so-called headless cut brads, some of which lie on the bench in front of it. The brads are long and slender; they don't need pilot holes. The candle shelf on the left was assembled with traditional cut brads, which often do need pilot holes. The split in the side could have been avoided by drilling a pilot for it and by orienting the brad *with* the grain, rather than across it.

DRY SINK

This is a great project because it works on different levels for different woodworkers. For a guy like me, who sometimes talks a better joint than he crafts, the project is simple enough and straightforward enough to be built in a week or so. And for a woodworker like my friend Rob, who for several years made his living as a furniture maker but now works at a desk job, it's a pleasant two-day change-of-pace project.

Moreover, it rounds out the collection. Without a dry sink, no collection of country furniture projects could be complete. The name may be something of a country furniture fraud, but the form isn't. And the form is practical and attractive even today.

More often than not, a dry sink gets incorporated into a living room setting, with the sink festooned with colorful houseplants. But other uses are possible. Consider that one former owner of the original used it as a changing table. Her bare-bunned baby couldn't roll away when lying in the sink. And the area beneath was perfect for stowing diapers and baby's sundries.

The original apparently hails from Pennsylvania's Bucks County. It is in good condition, considering that it was built around 1830, a good 165 years ago. Back then, it would have

been called a bucket bench. If you flip to the Open Bucket Bench project (page 7), you can read how bucket benches were used. And you'll probably see how this piece evolved from that earlier version. A board added to the front kept splashes and spills from overflowing onto the floor. This splashguard turned the top of the bench into a basin. Later, when indoor plumbing put the concept of a "sink" into American heads, this basin that had neither faucet nor drain became known as a dry sink. But that was at least a generation after this piece was built.

In the years since its creation, the original has undergone some modifications. The most obvious is the finish. There's no doubt that it was painted. Less obvious is that the doors aren't original.

My guess is that the doors are old and represent a marriage of two old, abused pieces of furniture. The doors on the dry sink were broken or rotted. Whatever piece the doors came from was unsalvageable. So the doors were trimmed a smidge—there's a bead along the right-hand door's hinge edge, but not along the left-hand door's—and fitted to the dry sink. Serious collectors typically regard this sort of marriage as fraudulent, but it seems to be pretty pragmatic to me. One usable piece is better than two unusable ones. (And really

In today's living room, the newly built piece (*opposite*) is called a dry sink. When the original (*above*) was built, it was called a bucket bench.

CUTTING LIST

Piece	Number	Thickness	Width	Length	Material
Sides	2	1"	15"	30¾"	5/4 pine
Top/Bottom	2	1"	15"	34"	5/4 pine
Shelf	1	¾"	15"	34"	1-by pine
Front splashguard	1	1"	6¾"	36"	5/4 pine
Back splashguard	1	¾"	6¾"	36"	1-by pine
Stiles	2	¾"	3¼"	24"	1-by pine
Back boards	2	¾"	9¼"	20¾"	1-by pine
Back boards	2	¾"	9¼"	24"	1-by pine
Door rails	4	¾"	2¾"	12⁵⁄₁₆"	1-by pine
Door stiles	4	¾"	2¾"	21⁵⁄₈"	1-by pine
Door panels	2	½"	10⁵⁄₁₆"	17⅛"	pine

HARDWARE

2 pr. butt hinges, 2" × 1½"

1 brass hook, 1¾" long, with brass eye screw. Catalog number 4415 from Paxton Hardware (410-592-8505).

1 Victorian-style spring latch, 2¾" × 1¼". Catalog number 4353 from Paxton Hardware.

6d cut finish nails

serious collectors probably wouldn't be interested in this piece anyway.)

Well, such issues are neither here nor there for the woodworker interested in *building* what is probably too dear to *buy*. The issue for us is: What's involved in building it? For the beginner, the most difficult elements are the doors, with their mortise-and-tenon joints. Boards need to be glued up to form sufficiently wide pieces for the sides and shelves, but all the case joints are nailed butt joints. So the doors are the challenge. But by using the appropriate jigs and fixtures with a table saw and a router, even a beginner should have no trouble making them.

The dry sink's simplicity turns out to be an attraction even for woodworkers with journeyman's skills. For Rob Yoder, the former pro who built the reproduction, the project was an opportunity to make something attractive for his own home without committing a whole lot of precious time to the job. He even used hand tools for many of the operations, including preparing the stock. Yet it took him only a few hours of pressure-free work, spread over two or three days, to complete the piece, ready for a finish.

Successful completion in two or three days? That's a good project.

---

1. Cut and glue up the case parts. As you can see from the Cutting List, the case has parts in two thicknesses. The sides, the front splashguard, and the top and bottom are cut from 1-inch stock, while the shelf, all the back parts, and the stiles are cut from ¾-inch stock. If you buy from a country sawmill, you may find boards 15 inches wide, but

most of us have to glue up narrow stock to achieve such widths. The *ShopSmarts* feature "Gluing Up Panels" on page 49 details how to do this.

Crosscut, rip, and joint the individual boards as necessary to make the case parts. Glue up stock to form the sides, top, and bottom. Set the clamped panels aside to cure.

EXPLODED VIEW

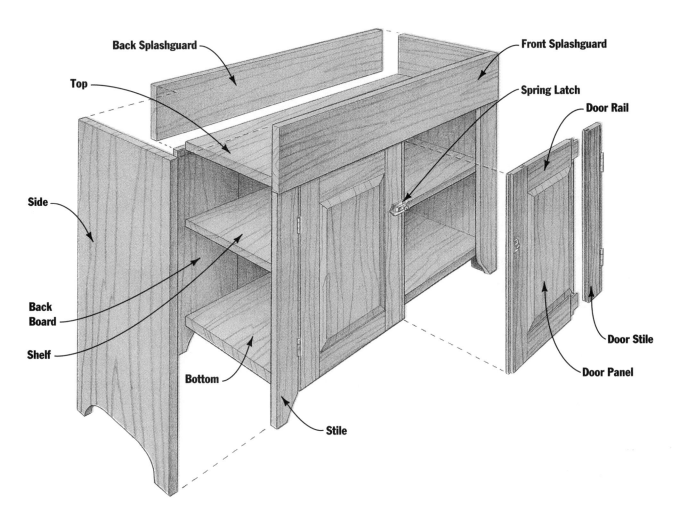

Back Splashguard

Top

Front Splashguard

Spring Latch

Door Rail

Side

Back Board

Shelf

Bottom

Stile

Door Stile

Door Panel

2. Cut the joinery on the back boards. To keep seams between back boards from opening up, they are assembled edge to edge with tongue-and-groove joints. The shorter two back boards each have a tongue on one edge and a groove on the other. The longer two boards are machined on one edge only; one board has a tongue, the other has a groove.

These can be cut with a router and slot cutter. See the photo on page 99. Cut the grooves first. One pass on each board should clean out the groove. *Remember:* Groove one edge of the two short boards, and one edge of only one long board.

To form the tongues, reduce the cut depth, but no more than $1/16$ inch, so the tongues are just a skosh shorter than the groove is deep. Form a tongue on the two short boards and the second of the long boards (the one that wasn't grooved).

3. Cut the door parts. If the glued-up panels are still curing, move ahead with the project by making the doors next. Cut the rails and stiles

To Thickness or Not to Thickness

If you use standard lumberyard stock, you may find that the 5/4 stock is really $1\frac{3}{16}$ inches thick, not 1 inch. If you have a planer, you can, of course, mill the stock to the specified thickness. But you don't need to worry much about that extra $3/16$ inch on this project. Just use the boards as they are.

Back when the original was built, the country woodworker had to hand plane his stock. It was a lot of work, and he'd quit planing just as soon as the boards were flat and square.

PLAN VIEWS

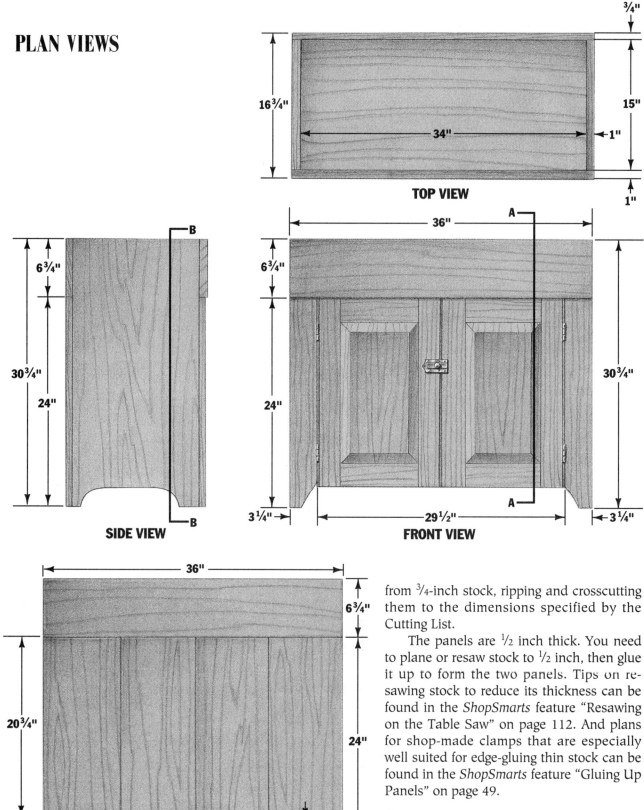

TOP VIEW

16³/₄"   15"   34"   ³/₄"   1"   1"

6³/₄"   30³/₄"   24"

SIDE VIEW

B   B

36"   6³/₄"   30³/₄"   24"   29¹/₂"   3¹/₄"   3¹/₄"

A   A

FRONT VIEW

36"   6³/₄"   20³/₄"   24"   3¹/₄"

1¹/₂"   1³/₄"   9¹/₄"   8¹⁵/₁₆"   8¹⁵/₁₆"   8⁷/₈"

BACK VIEW

from ³/₄-inch stock, ripping and crosscutting them to the dimensions specified by the Cutting List.

The panels are ¹/₂ inch thick. You need to plane or resaw stock to ¹/₂ inch, then glue it up to form the two panels. Tips on re-sawing stock to reduce its thickness can be found in the *ShopSmarts* feature "Resawing on the Table Saw" on page 112. And plans for shop-made clamps that are especially well suited for edge-gluing thin stock can be found in the *ShopSmarts* feature "Gluing Up Panels" on page 49.

4. Cut the joinery. As shown in *Door Construction*, the door frames are assembled with mortise-and-tenon joints. The panels float in a ¹/₄-inch-wide × ¹/₂-inch-deep groove plowed in the frame members.

PLAN VIEWS

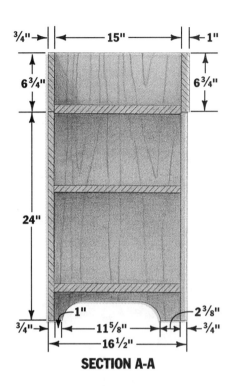

SECTION A-A

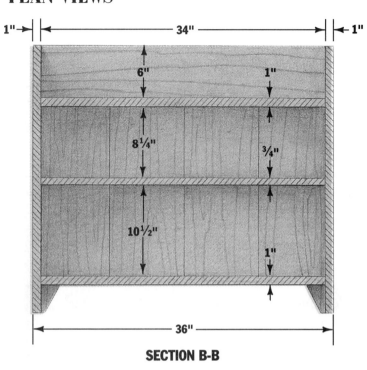

SECTION B-B

Cut the grooves first, doing your best to center each across the thickness of the stock. You can do this on the table saw, as you did with the tongue-and-groove joinery, or with a router and slot cutter. Plow

Not every router's edge guide will accommodate a slot cutter, so when you want to produce a slot less than ½ inch deep, the edge guide is no help. Here's a solution: Make your own job-specific guide and bond it to the router baseplate with double-sided carpet tape. The guide shown was cut from a scrap of ¾-inch plywood, using a hole saw.

the groove from end to end on all the rails and stiles.

Do the mortises and tenons next, using the approach shown in the *ShopSmarts* feature "Cutting Mortise-and-Tenon Joints" on page 83. The mortises, of course, are contained within the panel groove. The tenons are haunched. Cut the haunch either with the workpiece in the tenoning jig's edge-cutting position or by using a backsaw.

5. Raise the door panels. The original's bevels were formed, of course, with a hand plane. The distinct line between the bevel and the raised field was essentially removed by aggressive sanding, and the result is a panel that appears to be very soft.

For the machine-oriented, raising the panels is a simple table saw operation. The whys and hows can be found on page 140 in yet another *ShopSmarts* feature, called, appropriately enough, "Raising Panels." The bevels on the dry sink's door panels are about 1⅝ inches wide. Cut the bevels, then sand them to round the transition from bevel to field.

6. Assemble the doors. Begin assembling each door by gluing its rails into one of its stiles. Insert the panel into its groove without gluing it, then glue the second stile in place. Make sure the door stays square and flat as you apply clamps. While the glue cures, turn back to the case.

7. Cut the contours on the sides and stiles. Remove the clamps, scrape off any dried squeeze-out, then sand the sides smooth and reasonably flat. If necessary, trim the sides to their final dimensions.

Next, enlarge the patterns for the cutouts that form the dry sink's feet. Transfer the longer pattern to the sides, and cut the contour with a saber saw. Sand the cut edge smooth. In like manner, enlarge the stile contour, transfer it to the stile ends, and cut it.

8. Assemble the case. The shelf, top, and bottom must still be cleaned up and sanded. If necessary, trim them to their final dimensions.

Assembling the case is a hammer-and-nail proposition, but because the shanks of the cut nails are pretty hefty, it's a good idea to drill pilot holes for them. Nail the sides to the top, bottom, and shelf. Then attach the back splashguard, which should be flush with the tops of the sides. It should overlap only a portion of the top board.

Do the back boards next. Butt the long grooved board against the splashguard's bottom edge, position it flush with the side, and nail it to the side, top, shelf, and bottom. Install the two short boards next, and add the long board with the tongue last.

Trim the long back boards, as shown in the *Back View*. Lay out the cuts, and make them with a saber saw.

Finally, turn the case over and attach the front splashguard and the stiles.

DOOR CONSTRUCTION

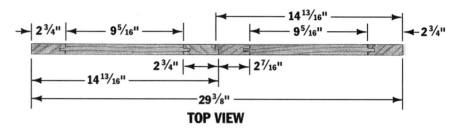

TOP VIEW

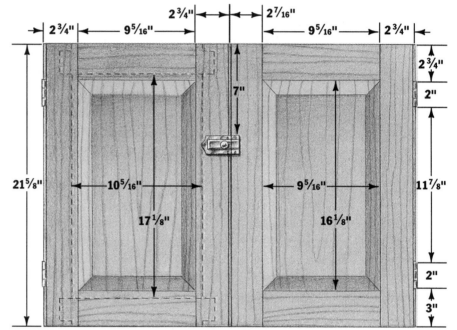

FRONT VIEW

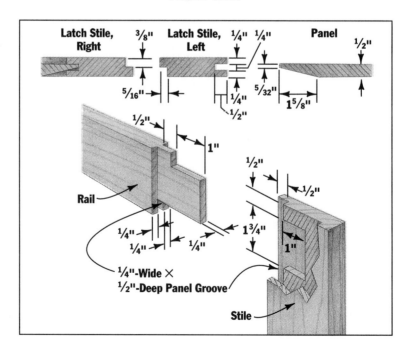

9. Hang the doors. Remove the clamps from the doors, scrape and sand them, and, if necessary, trim them square.

Before the doors can be hung, the shiplap has to be cut along the latch edges of the doors. The rabbet that must be cut into each door is $^5/_{16}$ inch wide and $^3/_8$ inch deep. The router will probably produce the cleanest cut, but the job can be done on the table saw. Just be sure you cut the rabbet into the back edge of the left-hand door and the front edge of the right-hand door.

With the case resting on its back across a couple of sawhorses, the doors can now be set into the door opening. Trim the doors if necessary to fit them. Then lay out the hinge locations on both the doors and the case.

Now that the doors fit, you can rout the $^3/_{16}$-inch bead along the hinge stiles, as well as the $^1/_8$-inch bead along the latch stile of the left-hand door. Bits to cut these beads are available from Cascade Tools (800-235-0272).

Cut the hinge mortises in the case stiles and in the doors. Screw the hinges to the case, then to the doors. Close the right-hand door and install the hook and eye screw that latch it. Close the left-hand door and install the spring latch.

10. Apply a finish. Although the dry sink surely was painted originally, it is one of the myriad pieces that fell victim to the Grim Stripper several decades ago. As it exists today, it is an aged, dark honey color.

In keeping with that appearance, we colored our reproduction with Wood-Kote's cherry gel stain. After the stain dried, we applied a sanding sealer,

While cutting hinge mortises might be seen as a router's job, it is really a lot easier and less problematic to pare them with a chisel. Hold the hinge leaf in position against the stile, and cut around it with a marking knife. Deepen these cuts with the chisel, then pare, as shown, until a recess of the appropriate depth has been created.

then a thin application of a very dark gel stain as a glaze. The glaze coat is wiped on and almost immediately wiped off. Very little remains on the surface, but what does remain darkens the color. The glaze also collects in seams and in corners, simulating the dirt accumulation that stems from age and use. Finally the project was sealed a second time with the sanding sealer.

Read the *ShopSmarts* feature "Country Finishes" on page 305 for more suggestions.

PATTERNS

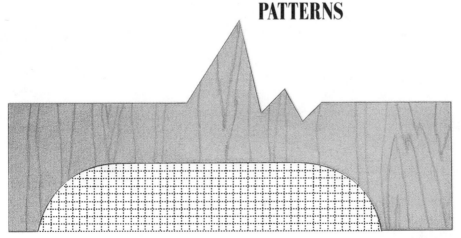

1 Square = $^1/_4$"

SIDE

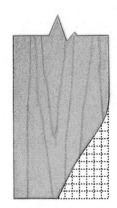

1 Square = $^1/_4$"

STILE

CASE OF DRAWERS

"Case of drawers" is a genus of practical country furniture. Characterized by an unobtrusive case filled with lots of drawers, familiar species in this genus are spool cabinets, seed chests, apothecary chests, and tool chests. Is it their practicality that makes these pieces so seductive? They're so precise and orderly, almost delicate, compared to chests of drawers. Everyone can come up with several ways to use one.

The original of this project is presently in my kitchen, providing out-of-sight storage for all sorts of little odds and ends. My wife wants one for her jewelry. Nine drawers, enhanced with dividers and dressed for the job in velvet. And I see at least one being useful in the shop: nine drawers for small tools and for screws and brads and other small fasteners and hardware items. The reproduction is in my office, organizing paper clips, pens and pencils, tape, note pads and index cards, loose change, film, and similar treasures.

I call this a "case of drawers" because I don't know what its original use was. One colleague

strongly suspects it was a tool chest. The dealer from whom I bought it hadn't a clue.

I purchased the original in Maine, though that's not an indication of where it was built. While it seemed to be simply made, closer examination in my workshop revealed a surprise or two. The case, which in the antique shop's dim light appeared to be mitered, is in fact dovetailed. (Okay, okay. So how did I miss *that*? I'll try to explain presently.) The nice beveled back panel is a replacement. And at least two of the drawers are replacements, too.

The top and sides of the case have a reddish-brown finish, likely the original. Seems to be a thin paint—milk paint, perhaps. The front edges of the case and the drawer fronts were refinished with a walnutty-brown stain, surely by the same cobbler who replaced the back and the two drawers.

Since complete and absolute originality is not as important here as it might be to a *serious* collector or museum curator, these surprises were not unpleasant ones. It's fun, actually, to study a piece and figure out how it's put together and to work out

Since the original (*above*) probably was part of a woodworker's tool chest, it is fitting that the reproduction (*opposite*) should land in a woodworking shop.

CUTTING LIST

Piece	Number	Thickness	Width	Length	Material
Case top/bottom	2	$1/2$"	$6 1/8$"	$32 1/8$"	pine
Case sides	2	$1/2$"	$6 1/8$"	$8 3/8$"	pine
Face trim, top/bottom	2	$1/2$"	$3/4$"	$32 1/8$"	pine
Face trim, sides	2	$1/2$"	$3/4$"	$8 5/8$"	pine
Case back	1	$3/4$"	$8 5/8$"	$32 1/8$"	pine
Horizontal partitions	2	$3/8$"	$6 5/16$"	$31 3/8$"	pine
Vertical partitions	3	$3/8$"	$6 5/16$"	$2 1/4$"	pine
Vertical partitions	2	$3/8$"	$6 5/16$"	$2 1/2$"	pine
Vertical partition	1	$3/8$"	$6 5/16$"	$2 7/8$"	pine
Top-tier drawer fronts	4	$1/2$"	2"	$7 7/16$"*	pine
Top-tier drawer sides	8	$3/8$"	2"	$6 1/16$"	pine
Top-tier drawer backs	4	$3/8$"	$1 7/8$"	$6 11/16$"	pine
Top-tier drawer bottoms	4	$1/8$"	$5 3/4$"	$6 3/4$"	pine
Middle-tier drawer fronts	3	$1/2$"	$2 1/4$"	$10 1/16$"*	pine
Middle-tier drawer sides	6	$3/8$"	$2 1/4$"	$6 1/16$"	pine
Middle-tier drawer backs	3	$3/8$"	$2 1/8$"	$9 5/16$"	pine
Middle-tier drawer bottoms	3	$1/8$"	$5 3/4$"	$9 3/8$"	pine
Bottom-tier drawer fronts	2	$1/2$"	$2 5/8$"	$15 5/16$"*	pine
Bottom-tier drawer sides	4	$3/8$"	$2 5/8$"	$6 1/16$"	pine
Bottom-tier drawer backs	2	$3/8$"	$2 1/2$"	$14 9/16$"	pine
Bottom-tier drawer bottoms	2	$1/8$"	$5 3/4$"	$14 5/8$"	pine

HARDWARE

1" brads

13 brass pulls, $1/2$" dia. × $1/2$" high, with integral screw. Item H-42, Desk Interior Knob, from Horton Brasses (203-635-4400).

*See Steps 1 and 2 under "Build the Drawers" on page 109 before cutting the drawer fronts. The dimensions listed here are the final lengths. You need to start with fronts that are about $1/2$" longer.

a way to reproduce it. Having a mystery or two to puzzle over adds to the enjoyment. Of course, in this instance, the repairs were obvious; no one was trying to conceal them and thus portray the case of drawers as completely original.

The design and construction of this case of drawers is quite sophisticated. The proportions are elegant, almost delicate.

Depth is given to the front of the bank by arranging elements in three different planes. The case sides, top, and bottom provide a frame for the pattern of drawers. Because these parts are nosed, the frame

has more shape. The various horizontal and vertical partitions are recessed $3/16$ inch from the surrounding frame. These parts, too, are nosed, lending more richness than simple flat-edged partitions would. Recessed $1/8$ inch deeper are the faces of the drawers.

The small brass pulls add a fillip to the grid design. Each of the four top drawers has a single pull centered on its face. Each of the two bottom drawers has two pulls, and they fall directly below the top ones. Syncopating this rhythm are the five pulls on the three middle-tier drawers. The outer drawers have two pulls each. The center drawer, though the

EXPLODED VIEW

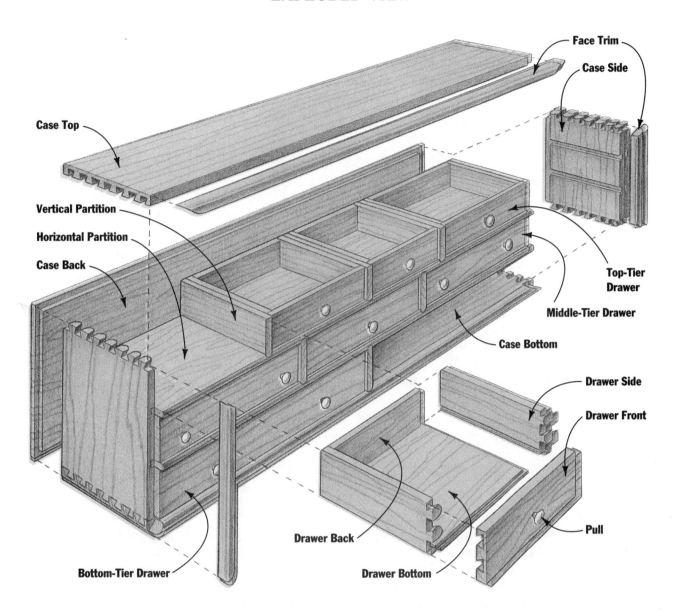

same size, has but a single pull: It falls dead-center on the bank, aligned with the vertical partitions above and below.

Even the back is attractive. Rather than an unplaned plank, the back is handsomely beveled. So the case doesn't need to keep its back to the wall. The entire piece is presentable.

Is this much ado about relatively little? I don't think so. It reflects the refined design of better country furniture pieces. They may be country, but that doesn't mean they lack elegance and refinement.

The polish carries from the design into the con-struction. Though the case is dovetailed, for example, the front edges of the sides, top, and bottom are mitered. One hundred fifty years ago, dovetails were simply utilitarian joinery, not an element to be shown off. In this case, the dovetails were shrouded under coats of paint and hidden behind false joints. The camouflage works, as far as I'm concerned.

Though this may be a utilitarian piece, it's extra-ordinarily versatile. Its attractiveness enhances that versatility. It works in the kitchen or the office as well as it does in the dressing room or shop. Wherever you place it, it'll attract attention. Positive attention.

PLAN VIEWS

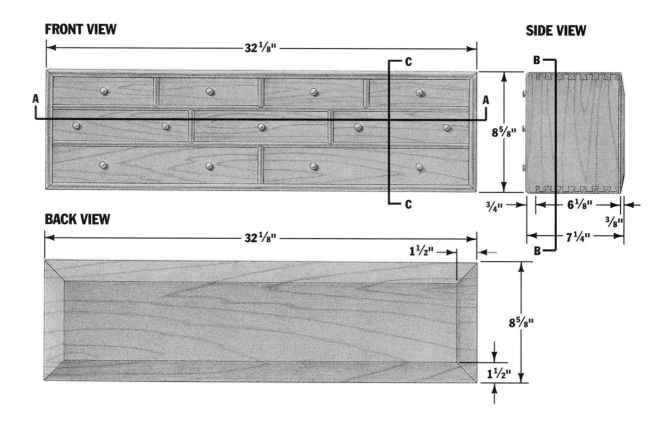

FRONT VIEW

32 1/8"

C

A

A

8 5/8"

C

SIDE VIEW

B

3/4"   6 1/8"

3/8"

7 1/4"

B

BACK VIEW

32 1/8"

1 1/2"

8 5/8"

1 1/2"

BUILD THE CASE

1. Cut the case parts. These parts include the top and bottom, the sides, the four face-trim pieces, the back, and all the partitions. Only the back is cut from standard 3/4-inch material. All the rest of the parts come from 3/8-inch and 1/2-inch stock. Resaw and plane stock to the necessary thicknesses, then rip and crosscut the parts to the dimensions specified by the Cutting List. Don't, however, crosscut the vertical partitions yet; it will be safer and easier to nose them *before* they're cut into short pieces. Tips on thicknessing stock can be found in the *ShopSmarts* features "Making a Board" and "Resawing on the Table Saw" on pages 13 and 112, respectively.

2. Rout the case joinery. The sides, top, and bottom are joined by half-blind dovetails. The horizontal partitions are housed in shallow dadoes routed in the sides. The back sets into a rabbet routed into the sides.

Cut the case dovetails first. This is done with a router, a 1/2-inch 14-degree dovetail bit, a 7/16-inch template guide, and a commonplace dovetail jig. Refer to the *ShopSmarts* feature "Routing Dovetails" on page 232 for an explanation of the basic procedure. The case top and bottom are the "socket pieces" and thus are placed in the top of the dovetail jig. The sides are the "tail pieces" and are clamped in the front of the jig. Rout the dovetails.

Rout the 3/8-inch-wide, 1/8-inch-deep dadoes for the horizontal partitions next. These can be routed through, from front and back. Finally, rout the 3/8-inch-wide, 1/8-inch-deep rabbet for the back.

3. Nose and install the face trim. The woodworker who crafted the original case of drawers hand cut the dovetails, so it was relatively easy for him to incorporate the miters at the front edges of the case. Routing the dovetails instead makes it

PLAN VIEWS

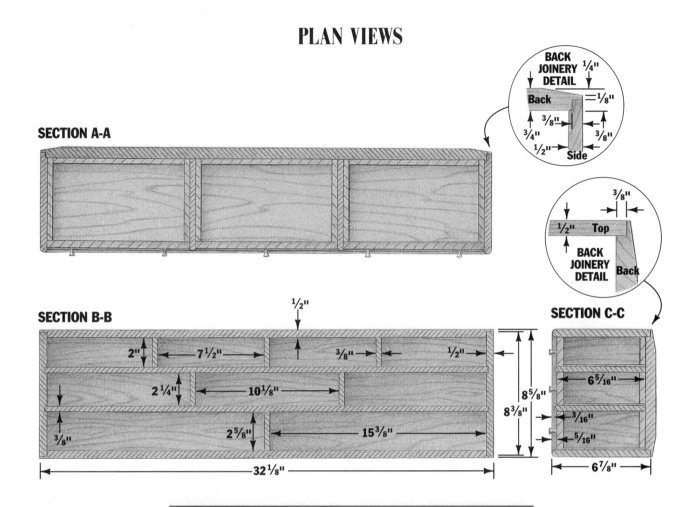

SECTION A-A

BACK JOINERY DETAIL
1/4"
Back
1/8"
3/8"
3/4"
1/2"
Side
3/8"

BACK JOINERY DETAIL
3/8"
1/2" Top
Back

SECTION B-B

1/2"
2"
7 1/2"
3/8"
1/2"
2 1/4"
10 1/8"
3/8"
2 5/8"
15 3/8"
32 1/8"

SECTION C-C

8 5/8"
8 3/8"
6 5/16"
3/16"
5/16"
6 7/8"

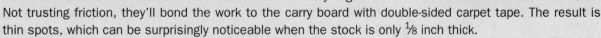

Planing Thin Stock

The typical home-shop planer isn't really designed to plane stock to less than 1/2 inch. The planer *can* do it, but it needs some help in the form of a "carry board" or "planer board."

A carry board would be any flat board with parallel faces that's longer and wider than the workpiece. It carries the workpiece through the planer, and its thickness bolsters that of the workpiece. Just lay the workpiece on the carry board and feed both into the planer. Usually, there's enough pressure from the feed roller and enough friction between the two boards for the two to emerge from the planer together. But even if they don't, even if the carry board stalls and the workpiece emerges alone, you'll be okay. The carry board will have done its job, and your workpiece will be properly planed.

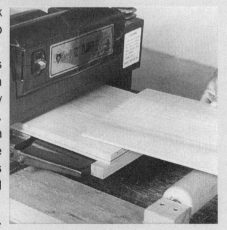

Some woodworkers feel the two boards need to stay together. Not trusting friction, they'll bond the work to the carry board with double-sided carpet tape. The result is thin spots, which can be surprisingly noticeable when the stock is only 1/8 inch thick.

An alternative, shown in the photo, is a planer board. This is simply a carry board with a cleat attached across the bottom. The cleat catches against the infeed table and holds the board in a fixed position. In effect, the board is an auxiliary feed bed. You just lay the work on the board and it is fed through the planer.

CASE JOINERY

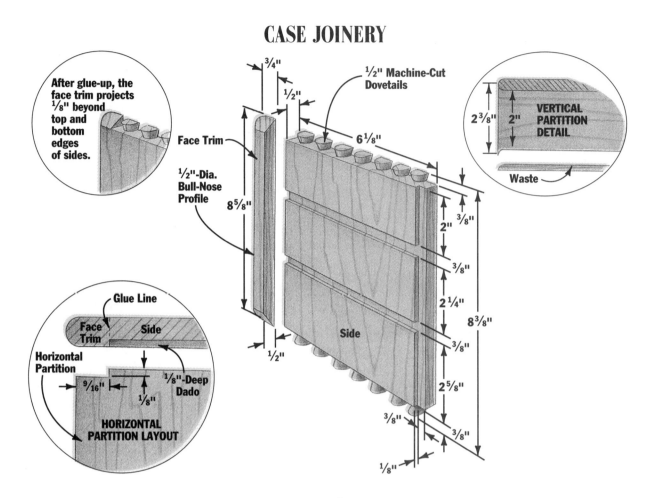

After glue-up, the face trim projects ¹/₈" beyond top and bottom edges of sides.

Face Trim

¹/₂"-Dia. Bull-Nose Profile

8⁵/₈"

¾"

¹/₂"

¹/₂" Machine-Cut Dovetails

6¹/₈"

VERTICAL PARTITION DETAIL

2³/₈"   2"

Waste

2"

³/₈"

³/₈"

2¹/₄"

8³/₈"

³/₈"

2⁵/₈"

Side

¹/₂"

³/₈"

³/₈"

¹/₈"

Glue Line

Face Trim

Side

Horizontal Partition

⁹/₁₆"

¹/₈"

¹/₈"-Deep Dado

HORIZONTAL PARTITION LAYOUT

considerably less easy to include the miter detail. The use of this face trim allows you to keep the miters.

Nose the trim pieces, using either a ¹/₂-inch bull-nose bit or a ¹/₄-inch roundover bit in a table-mounted router. Assemble the sides, top, and bottom without glue, and fit and miter the trim. Mark the trim and the case parts so you can properly align the two. Disassemble the case, and edge-glue each trim piece to the appropriate case part.

Roundover Nosing

You can nose the case parts with a roundover bit if you do it on the router table. Use the router table fence (instead of the bit's pilot bearing) to guide and control the cut. If you try it with a hand-held router, you depend on the pilot bearing to guide the cut. But after the first pass, the bit's pilot bearing won't have a surface to reference on the second pass. The result? Gouged work. With the bit and fence set, you can zip through all the parts in short order.

4. Shape the back panel. The back is beveled around the exposed face to create a raised field and present a more attractive appearance. The bevels are about 1¹/₄ to 1¹/₂ inches wide and can be produced on the router table using a panel-raising bit or on the table saw.

After the bevels are cut and sanded smooth, cut the rabbet around the inside edge that allows the back to set into the case while still overlapping the back edges of the case.

5. Prepare the partitions. Begin by nosing the front edges of the partitions with either a ³/₈-inch bull-nose bit or a ³/₁₆-inch roundover bit in a table-mounted router.

To fit the dadoes in the sides, the horizontal partitions must be notched to accommodate the un-dadoed face trim. The notch should be ⁹/₁₆ inch × ¹/₈ inch. Cut each a little undersized, and fit it

Put away the coping saw and round file! This trick makes it easy to cope the vertical partitions on the router table. After the router table is set up, attach a 3/16-inch-thick outfeed support to the fence with double-sided carpet tape. This will ensure you get a straight cut along the partition's edge. Feed the workpiece along the fence, stopping at the very tip.

to the appropriate side dado. File the notch as necessary to get a tight fit against the trim.

Now crosscut and cope the vertical partitions; crosscut these parts to the lengths specified by the Cutting List. Next, trim the partitions to reduce their height and to cope their leading edges so they blend into the horizontal partitions. This is done quickly and easily using a table-mounted router and a 3/8-inch straight bit. Set the fence to expose only half

the bit, then feed the partition along the fence, trimming 3/16 inch from the edge. Stop the cut at the front edge of the partition.

6. Assemble the case. The case is held together with glue and selectively used 1-inch brads. Join the vertical and horizontal partitions first. Carefully lay out the locations of the verticals on the horizontals. Glue and nail the verticals to the horizontals. (If you use cut brads, it's okay to drive the brads flush with the wood surface, but leave the ends exposed. If you use wire brads, set them and putty over them before applying a finish.)

Spread glue on the dovetails and in the dadoes. Join a side and the top. Fit the partition subassembly in place. Add the bottom, then the second side. Drive brads through the top and bottom into the vertical partitions.

Set the back in place, and drive brads through the back into the case edges and also through the case into the back.

BUILD THE DRAWERS

1. Cut the parts. All of the drawers are constructed in the same way. The fronts are 1/2-inch stock, the sides and backs are 3/8-inch stock, and the bottoms are 1/8 inch. The fronts and sides are joined with machine-cut half-blind dovetails. The backs fit between the sides and are nailed in place. The bottoms fit into half-dovetail grooves routed in the sides and fronts.

Resaw and plane stock to the required thicknesses. Rip and crosscut all the drawer parts but the fronts and bottoms to the dimensions specified by the Cutting List. There are lots of parts, so it's important to clearly label each piece. Before crosscutting the fronts, test the dovetailing setup to determine how much longer than final length you must make the fronts. (See the next step.) The bottoms should be cut to fit during assembly, so hold that stock for later.

2. Rout the dovetails. The drawer fronts go in the top of the jig; the drawer sides, in the front of the jig. The router setup is the same as that used for the case dovetails. The procedure is the same, too, but the setup of the jig is slightly different. The typical dovetail jig isn't really designed to deal with thin stock, such as that used in these drawers. (The fronts are 1/2 inch thick, and the sides are 3/8 inch thick.) When the tails are right, the sockets are too deep. When the sockets are right, the tails are vestigial. What you have to do is cut the drawer fronts somewhat long, rout the dovetails with too-deep sockets, then trim the fronts to their final length.

To set up the jig, shift the template back so the "comb" tips are flush with the drawer side. This setup yields tails with a bit of a flat but with satisfactory thickness. The sockets in the drawer front will be too deep (with my jig, $\frac{1}{4}$ inch too deep). Trim the excess from the front after the dovetails are routed, taking an equal amount of stock off each end. To confirm how much you need to add to the length of each drawer front, rout a couple of test joints on scraps of the working stock.

To reiterate:
- Do your test joint.
- Determine how much to add to the length of each front.
- Crosscut the drawer fronts to their interim length.
- Rout all the dovetails.
- Trim all the drawer fronts to finished length.

Bear in mind that machine-cut $\frac{1}{2}$-inch dovetails extend $\frac{7}{8}$ inch from center to center. Because of this, the top- and middle-tier drawers won't both begin and end with an even half-pin because of the widths of the parts; however, this won't effect the strength of the joints. The bottom drawers are just the right size to begin and end with a half-pin.

3. Cut the joinery for the bottoms. The bottoms, as noted, are held in a kind of half-dovetail rabbet routed along the bottom edges of the sides and fronts. The cut is made on the router table with a dovetail bit. Set the bit to project just $\frac{1}{8}$ inch above the tabletop. Set the fence so the bit just grazes the workpiece, creating the sort of cut shown in *Drawer Construction*. Make a cut along the bottom inside edge of every drawer front and side.

4. Assemble the drawers. The dovetail is a strong joint and needs only a little glue to secure it. Spread the glue on mating surfaces with a small brush, and press the front and sides together. Clamp each drawer until the glue sets. Set the back in place, and drive a couple of brads through each side into it.

5. Fit and install the bottoms. Now it's time to rip and crosscut the bottoms. The bottoms are oriented so their grain runs from drawer side to drawer side. Thus, to cut the bottoms to length (the dimension from drawer front to drawer back), you rip them. As you rip each one, you need to bevel the edge at 14 degrees so it fits tightly into the half-dovetail rabbet cut in the drawer front. Rip all the bottoms.

Crosscut the bottoms next, doing it with the saw blade tilted to 14 degrees. Cut one end of the

Adjust the template position so the "comb" tips are just flush with the side's outer surface. This will yield a satisfactory tail, as you can see. But when you assemble the dovetails, you'll discover that instead of being flush, the front overhangs the side, as shown. The solution is to measure the amount the front projects past the side, then add twice that to the length of each drawer front. Rout the dovetails, then trim the fronts to finished size.

bottom, then turn it over and cut the other end. Don't just cut the bottoms to some tape-measure dimension; the joinery doesn't allow much margin for error. Cut each one to fit a drawer, and glue it in place as soon as it fits.

The bottoms are secured by slipping them into place from the back and gluing them to the drawer fronts only. This approach allows the bottom to swell and shrink freely without knocking the drawer apart.

6. Fit each drawer to the case. Do this one by one, planing or sanding the back, sides, and top edges as necessary to refine how the drawer fits the case and how easily it can be opened and closed. If the fits are sufficiently close, you may want to mark on each drawer where it goes in the bank.

7. Install the pulls. Lay out the pull locations. Drill a pilot hole for each pull, being careful to avoid drilling all the way through the drawer front. Turn a pull into each pilot hole.

DRAWER CONSTRUCTION

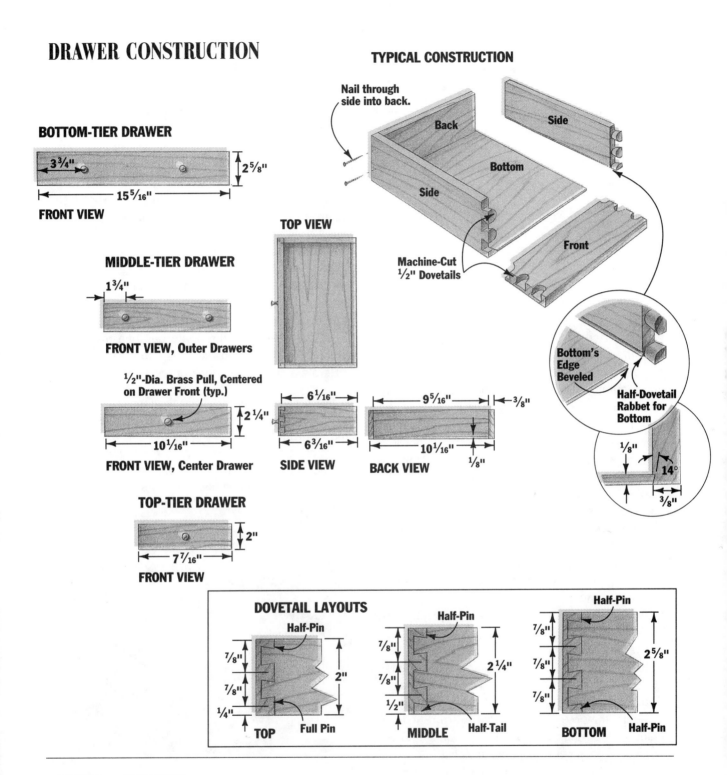

BOTTOM-TIER DRAWER

3 3/4"   2 5/8"

15 5/16"

FRONT VIEW

MIDDLE-TIER DRAWER

1 3/4"

FRONT VIEW, Outer Drawers

1/2"-Dia. Brass Pull, Centered on Drawer Front (typ.)

2 1/4"

10 1/16"

FRONT VIEW, Center Drawer

TOP-TIER DRAWER

2"

7 7/16"

FRONT VIEW

TOP VIEW

TYPICAL CONSTRUCTION

Nail through side into back.

Back

Side

Bottom

Side

Front

Machine-Cut 1/2" Dovetails

Bottom's Edge Beveled

Half-Dovetail Rabbet for Bottom

1/8"   14°

3/8"

6 1/16"

6 3/16"

SIDE VIEW

9 5/16"   3/8"

10 1/16"   1/8"

BACK VIEW

DOVETAIL LAYOUTS

Half-Pin

7/8"

7/8"   2"

1/4"   Full Pin

TOP

Half-Pin

7/8"

7/8"   2 1/4"

1/2"   Half-Tail

MIDDLE

Half-Pin

7/8"

7/8"   2 5/8"

7/8"   Half-Pin

BOTTOM

APPLY A FINISH

Based on the finish on the case of the original case of drawers, I opted for reddish-brown milk paint for the reproduction. Because it lacks body, milk paint is somewhat transparent: The texture of the wood's grain will show through it. And because it is quite flat, I opted to wipe on a coat of boiled linseed oil to protect the milk paint and give it some sheen.

Details of applying milk paint, as well as other finishes, can be found in the *ShopSmarts* feature "Country Finishes" on page 305.

Resawing on the Table Saw

A number of this book's projects call for ¹/₂-inch stock, ³/₈-inch stock, or ¹/₄-inch stock. Some need ⁹/₁₆-, ⁷/₁₆-, even ⁵/₁₆-inch stock. These aren't standard thicknesses. You can't just run to the lumberyard and buy pine stock that's any thinner than ³/₄ inch.

Where do you get this stock? You make it, using a process called *resawing*.

All you need is a table saw—the typical 10-inch home-shop variety works just fine—with a decent rip blade. A shop-made device called a featherboard (or sometimes a fingerboard) is a desirable safety accessory. In brief, what you do is stand the board on edge and feed it along the fence into the blade, thus cutting it into two thinner pieces. If the board's width is less than the maximum cutting depth of the blade, that's all there is to it. If it's wider, but not more than twice the maximum cutting depth, resaw it in two passes, making a cut into each edge. If the board is wider still, make the two resawing passes, then use a handsaw to complete the cut. This doesn't take long, and with the two kerfs to guide the handsaw, the cut should be accurate.

If you own a thickness planer, you can plane standard-thickness stock thinner. But if that entails removing much more than ¹/₈ inch, the process wastes a lot of wood. Far better is to saw the stock thinner.

Being mindful of some details can help you achieve better results in resawing.

First, use a rip blade, as I said, preferably one with no more than 24 teeth. Combination blades generally lack the gullet depth needed to carry away the amount of waste created by resawing. As a result, they overheat and then warp. But a rip blade is designed to do jobs like resawing and will produce a good cut without complaining.

Second, use that featherboard—the drawing shows the layout of the one I've used for resawing for years. Clamp it to the saw table on the infeed side, as shown in the photos. Get it as close to the blade as you can without having the featherboard actually overlap the blade and pinch it. The fingers should bear against the workpiece, holding the stock firmly against the rip fence and preventing it from being kicked back. I use two C-clamps on the featherboard and haven't had any trouble with it twisting out of position.

Third, start with as thick a board as possible. Resawing creates a whole new surface, exposing the interior of the wood to the air. Previously buried cells are suddenly free to absorb or release moisture. The upshot is: Newly resawed boards usually warp. You must allow for it, being prepared to joint and thickness-plane. If the board isn't thick enough to begin with, you won't have enough material to be able to flatten the new boards.

Fourth, make sure the board has one truly flat face and two straight edges, square to the flat side.

Here's a step-by-step look at resawing.

1. Set up the table saw. Set the fence to cut the desired thickness plus ¹/₁₆ inch—this will give you a little extra stock for cleaning up the cut. Assuming it's going to take only two cuts to resaw the board, set the blade height to just over half the board's width. Clamp the featherboard to the saw table.

Step 2

2. Make the first cut. To do this, set the board's flat face against the fence. Feed it into the blade with a push stick or push block. Even though the blade is buried in the wood for most of the cut, keep both hands away from the blade area. The featherboard will keep the board against the fence for most of the cut. In the Step 2 photo the workpiece is almost completely past the blade. Note the position of the featherboard vis-à-vis the blade.

If the saw bogs down significantly when the workpiece is fed into it, stop the saw and reduce the depth of cut by 50 percent. With pine, this shouldn't be a factor, though with hardwoods, it could be. If you do have to reduce the depth of cut, you'll have to make multiple passes to resaw each board. Make two passes with the blade at a given setting before increasing the depth of cut.

Step 4

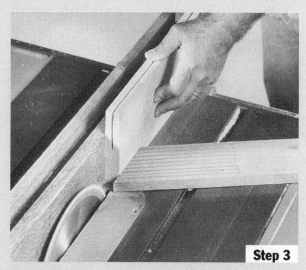

Step 3

3. Make the second cut. Flip the stock end for end, so you can set the same face of the stock against the fence, but now with the other edge down. In the Step 3 photo the second pass is just beginning. The kerf made on the first pass is up. The work is engaged by the featherboard and is just being pushed into the blade with a foam-bottomed push block.

4. Sand the new boards. Even the best blade may not do a perfect job. In the Step 4 photo I've got a burn mark from the blade, the blade's usual scuff marks, and a slight ridge left where the two passes overlapped. But the new faces will clean up easily on a jointer or planer. Even a belt sander will do the job. Because of the stiffness of the circular blade, the resawed surface should be nearly flat and parallel to the face that references the rip fence.

If you're edge-gluing resawed boards, glue them together before you smooth them.

By resawing you can economically create the thin stock you need for the Case of Drawers (page 103), the Stage Box (page 175), and those other projects that need $1/2$-inch or $1/4$-inch stock. From a single 1-by, you can produce two pieces of $1/4$-inch stock. From a 5/4 board, you can make two $3/8$-inch boards.

FEATHERBOARD LAYOUT

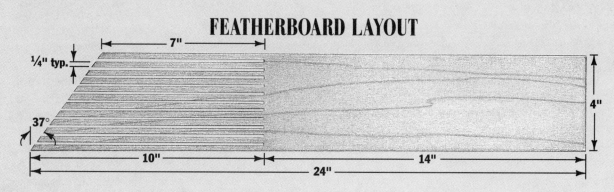

$1/4$" typ.

7"

4"

37°

10"

14"

24"

TOOL TRAYS

These tool trays were intended to be shop projects, meaning country items that would grace the shop. I figured on using them to carry tools from shop to repair to spruce-up, and back again.

You know where I'm going with this. To get a small tray to carry my tools, I had to make two. The first one I made usually has dried flowers or some such in it. It holds a foliage display beside the fireplace or on the kitchen counter, or it serves as a centerpiece on the table. I've seen a tray similar to the large one being used as a holder for magazines, though I have **not** had to compete for the use of *that* reproduction.

I have only good guesses as to what these particular trays were used for originally. No definite information. Scour antique galleries and flea markets, and you'll see dozens of variations on the form. Often, they are billed as knife boxes or trays—carriers for eating utensils.

Only the smaller of these was so used, I am sure. Though it seems a bit rough and rustic for keeping the eating utensils, it nevertheless is the right size. I can picture a woodworker knocking together leftovers from a large project to make a little something for the house. The only embellishments were the slightly curved handle contour and the bevel around the bottom. Not fancy, but a step above strictly utilitarian. And it was painted.

The other tray is way too big to be a knife tray. It was a tradesman's tool carrier, I am sure, filled with a selection of tools to take to a repair or a construction project. Or perhaps it was a huckster's carrier. He'd fill it with an assortment of fruits or vegetables, for example, to carry from his wagon to your doorstep. What pictures come to your mind? In any case, this tray doesn't appear to have been finished. It's simply colored by age.

Both trays are easy to make. Making two, or even three or four, is no big deal. If your experience is limited, either tray is a good learning project.

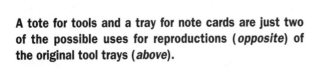

A tote for tools and a tray for note cards are just two of the possible uses for reproductions (*opposite*) of the original tool trays (*above*).

EXPLODED VIEW

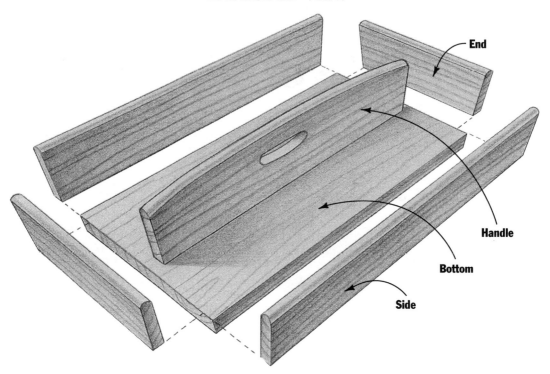

End

Handle

Bottom

Side

CUTTING LIST

SMALL TRAY

Piece	Number	Thickness	Width	Length	Material
Sides	2	$\frac{7}{8}$"	$3\frac{5}{16}$"	17"	5/4 pine
Ends	2	$\frac{7}{8}$"	$3\frac{5}{16}$"	$7\frac{3}{4}$"	5/4 pine
Bottom	1	$\frac{7}{8}$"	$10\frac{1}{2}$"	18"	5/4 pine
Handle	1	$\frac{7}{8}$"	$6\frac{7}{8}$"	$15\frac{1}{4}$"	5/4 pine

HARDWARE
7d cut finish nails

LARGE TRAY

Piece	Number	Thickness	Width	Length	Material
Sides	2	$\frac{7}{8}$"	$4\frac{17}{32}$"	$30\frac{1}{2}$"	5/4 pine
Ends	2	$\frac{7}{8}$"	$4\frac{17}{32}$"	$13\frac{11}{32}$"	5/4 pine
Bottom	1	$\frac{7}{8}$"	$13\frac{9}{32}$"	$28\frac{7}{16}$"	5/4 pine
Handle	1	$\frac{7}{8}$"	$5\frac{3}{4}$"	$28\frac{23}{32}$"	5/4 pine

HARDWARE
8d cut finish nails

Neither requires a lot of material, and neither takes more than a few hours to make. But you'll pick up or hone skills that'll be useful on a whole range of other projects.

The disparity in appearance between newly constructed items and the old originals is especially pronounced in these two projects. I nailed together a copy of the small tray one afternoon, and it just wasn't appealing to me. The edges were too square and regular compared to the original. I had rounded-over the handle edges with a router and bit, and those edges were too smooth and regular. So I took rasp in hand and worked the corners and the edges.

Because they take little time to build and require only a small amount of wood, either one is a good project for experimentation with aging techniques. One result of my experiments is that I do have reproductions of these trays in my home shop, as well as in my home.

BUILD THE SMALL TRAY

1. Cut the parts. If you are aiming to produce a true copy, use 5/4 pine for this project, and resaw or plane the stock to the $\frac{7}{8}$-inch thickness specified by the Cutting List. If you have to resaw and belt-sand all the stock (if you don't have a planer, in other words), you can save yourself a bit of work by leaving the bottom piece at the 5/4-stock's typical $1\frac{1}{16}$-inch thickness.

But consider that at $\frac{7}{8}$ inch, the thickness of the stock used in the original seems a bit heavy. You might save yourself some work by building the small tray using 1-by stock. You'll have to alter the lengths of the ends and the handle if you do this.

2. Bevel the bottom. This is done most easily on the router table. Use a standard 45-degree chamfer bit, but set the fence to guide the cut, rather than relying on the bit's pilot bearing.

PLAN VIEWS—SMALL TRAY

TOP VIEW

3$\frac{7}{16}$"

7$\frac{3}{4}$" 9$\frac{1}{2}$" 10$\frac{1}{2}$"

3$\frac{7}{16}$"

15$\frac{1}{4}$"
17"
18"

SIDE VIEW

7$\frac{3}{4}$"

$\frac{7}{16}$" 3$\frac{5}{16}$"
4$\frac{3}{16}$"
$\frac{7}{8}$"
$\frac{7}{16}$"

END VIEW

6$\frac{7}{8}$"

3. Nail together the sides, ends, and bottom. Use 7d cut finish nails, and drill pilot holes for them so you won't split the wood. The sides overlap the ends. After the sides and ends are joined, lay the bottom in position and nail it.

4. Make the handle. This is the most time-consuming part of this project, but it isn't difficult.

Trim the handle to length, set it into the tray, and scribe along the top of the ends on the handle. Lay out the handgrip and the contour of the handle's top edge, as shown in *Handle Layout—Small Tray*.

Form the handgrip hole by boring 1-inch-diameter holes at each end and then sawing out the waste between them with a saber saw. Use a half-round file to smooth the edges as much as possible. Cut the top-edge contour with the saber saw, and file this edge as smooth as you can.

With a roundover bit in a table-mounted router, round the handle's top edges as well as the edges of the handgrip hole. The radius of the bit can be $^1/_4$ inch or $^3/_8$ inch, whatever suits you. You may want to work the edges a bit with the file, to introduce a little irregularity into the profile left by the router bit.

5. Attach the handle. Slip the handle into the tray, and adjust its position so it is upright and

equidistant from the sides. Drill pilot holes and drive nails through the ends into the handle.

Templates Breed Regularity

You can produce the perfect handle shape by making a template of the handle. Use a piece of hardboard, medium-density fiberboard (MDF), or void-free plywood. Study the handle layout drawings, and set up a router with a trammel to rout the various arcs in the handle's contour. After the template is finished, trace it onto the handle board. Cut just shy of the lines with a saber saw. Then temporarily fasten the template to the workpiece, and trim the workpiece flush to the template with a router and flush-trimmer or a pattern bit.

A second, more sensible option is to remember that this is a humble country project. The original's contour is irregular. And if the contour of your reproduction is, too, so much the better. The country woodworker who built the original did it strictly with hand tools. No templates. No spindle sanders.

HANDLE LAYOUT—SMALL TRAY

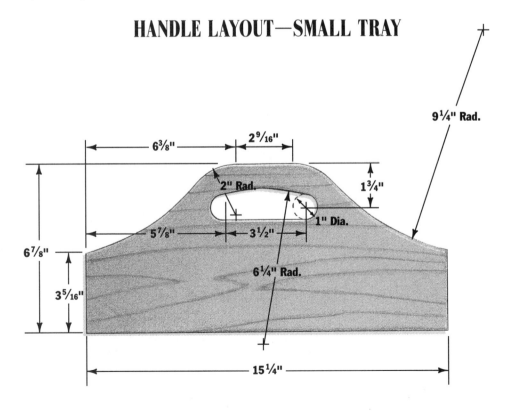

6. Apply a finish. The outside of the original was painted blue, but curiously, the two compartments were not painted at all. There's a distinct line on the handle that's level with the top edges of the sides and ends. The exposed area was painted, but not down into the compartments. Perhaps it was an economy—don't waste paint on surfaces that aren't visible when the tray compartments are full.

I painted the entire tray, including the compartments and the bottom, with two coats of green milk paint. But before I did, I worked the edges with a rasp and a file to soften them and introduce some irregularity to the project's contours. Then I painted it.

After the paint was dry, I worked the edges some more. And I did the typical distressing stuff—whacked a couple edges with a square-edged steel bar to dent them, beat on one end with stuff, stuck it with a screwdriver and a blunt rod, and just generally kicked it around the shop. I even pushed it back and forth on a rough-edged concrete step to thoroughly scuff the bottom. Then I wiped some dark maroon glaze on it, let it set for a few minutes, and wiped most of it off again. The little bit that collected in depressions and seams makes the piece look dirty and thus old.

BUILD THE LARGE TRAY

1. Cut the parts to rough size. As with the small tray, the large tray is built of 7/8-inch-thick stock. Rip and crosscut the stock to rough size, then resaw or plane it to the specified thickness.

2. Glue up the bottom. Edge-glue two or three boards to form the bottom. Tips on the process can be found in the *ShopSmarts* feature "Gluing Up Panels" on page 49. After the glue has set, remove the clamps, scrape off any dried glue squeeze-out, then sand the bottom.

Don't trim the bottom to its final size yet. That is done during assembly.

3. Miter and bevel the sides and ends. Because this tray is joined with butt joints rather than miter joints, you do not need to grapple with compound miters, which can be tricky to cut and assemble. It's a good country solution. The critical angle is 13 degrees.

First, tilt the table saw blade to 13 degrees, and rip bevels on the edges of each side and end.

Next, rout a thumbnail profile along the top edge of the four parts using a 1-inch or larger thumbnail bit in a table-mounted router.

Finally, miter both ends of each part. Set the table saw miter gauge to 13 degrees, and cut the workpieces.

4. Assemble the tray. Nail the sides and ends together using 8d cut finish nails. To avoid splitting the wood, drill pilot holes.

Trim the bottom to size next. With the table saw

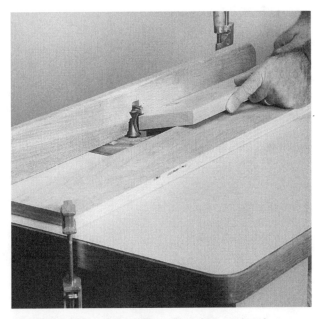

To rout the fingernail profile on the sides and ends, use two fences. The router table fence guides the workpiece. Align this fence so it is flush with the deepest part of the bit's cutting edge. The second fence—a scrap of 1-by stock—supports the workpiece at an angle. Place it as shown, and position it to tip the workpiece just enough that its beveled edge is flat against the router table fence. Make sure the support fence is parallel to the guide fence and that the clamps securing it don't interfere with the workpiece movement.

blade tilted to 13 degrees, rip a bevel on one long edge and across one end. Set the frame atop the bottom, and align it flush with the bottom's just-beveled side and end. Mark the bottom's remaining

PLAN VIEWS—LARGE TRAY

TOP VIEW

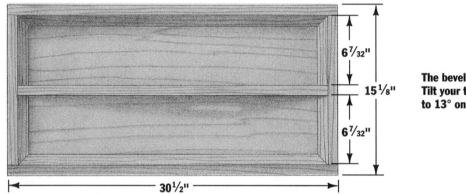

6 7/32"

15 1/8"

6 7/32"

30 1/2"

**The bevel angle is 13°.
Tilt your table saw's blade
to 13° on the scale.**

SIDE VIEW

END VIEW

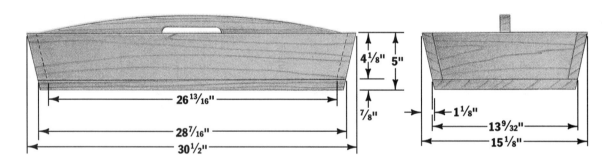

4 1/8"   5"

7/8"

26 13/16"

28 7/16"

30 1/2"

1 1/8"

13 9/32"

15 1/8"

HANDLE LAYOUT—LARGE TRAY

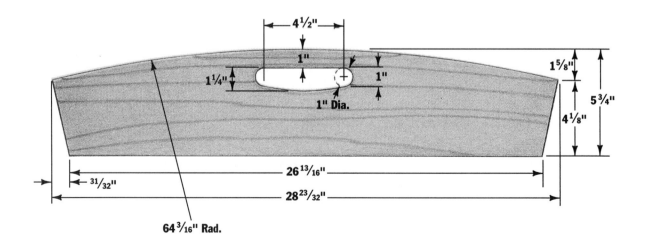

4 1/2"

1"

1 1/4"

1"

1" Dia.

1 5/8"

5 3/4"

4 1/8"

26 13/16"

31/32"

28 23/32"

64 3/16" Rad.

side and end for trimming by scribing along the outside face of the frame. With the blade still tilted to 13 degrees, bevel these edges.

Set the bottom back on the frame, and line it up. Drill pilot holes, and nail the bottom to the frame.

5. Make the handle. Rip and crosscut the handle about an inch wider and as much as 6 inches longer than what is specified by the Cutting List. With a router and a very long trammel, rout the handle arc, as shown in the photo below. Then rout the fingernail profile on the curved edge.

Now trim the handle to length, mitering the ends at 13 degrees. Set the handle into the tray, and determine how much must be ripped from it. Rip the handle as necessary.

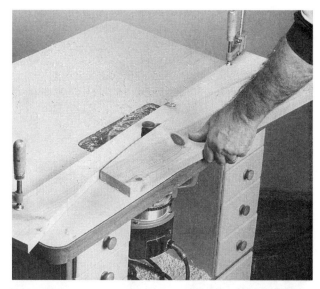

The best way to control the workpiece when routing the fingernail profile on the handle is with a curved fence. The fence arc need not be perfect, as you can see. Just lay the handle on a scrap board, trace the arc, and cut it with a saber saw. (This will work so long as the handle's curve is the arc of a circle, cut using a trammel.)

The handle's arc is cut with a lonnnngggg trammel. Clamp a 2 × 4 (or other scrap board) across the workbench, much as shown. Drive a screw through the trammel arm—which in this case is a 3-inch-wide strip of ¼-inch plywood—into the scrap. Align the workpiece parallel to the scrap, with the edge to be cut extending beyond the end of the bench. Clamp it at one end only. Cut from the workpiece's end to the top of the arc. When half the arc is thus cut, move the clamps to the workpiece's other end and cut the second half.

Finally, lay out the handgrip opening. Form the handgrip hole by boring 1-inch-diameter holes at each end and then sawing out the waste between them with a saber saw. Use a half-round file to smooth the edges as much as possible. With a ¼- to ⅜-inch roundover bit in a table-mounted router, round the edges of the handgrip hole.

6. Attach the handle. Set the handle into place, as shown in the *Plan Views—Large Tray*. Drill pilot holes, and drive 8d cut finish nails through the ends into the handle.

7. Apply a finish. The original of the large tray appears to be finished only with the grime of the decades. It appears not to have been varnished or painted.

The finish you apply depends upon the use you have in mind and, of course, your personal tastes and finish preferences. The *ShopSmarts* feature "Country Finishes" on page 305 provides step-by-step sequences for applying milk paint, regular latex or oil-based paints, and stains.

SCHOOLMASTER'S DESK

I love furniture with a story.

Oh, I don't mean how the piece was a great bargain down at the local K-Wal. "Well, yup. I needed something to put the TV on. Ugh-ly? Well, yup. But I couldn't beat the price."

That's no story at all.

No, I like the kinds of stories that people tell about who owned a piece, or how it was used, or who built it, or where it came from. Maybe you are the same way.

The context in which I will always view this slope-top desk was provided by the note that came with it. The note is cryptic and enigmatic. Written in a sprawling, aged hand, it says:

"F. N. Liesmann

"January 25th, 1967

"Grand Pa used the desk from 1880 till 1885 when he taught English and German in the John Harris school corner Race and Paxton St.

"[H]ad it refinished By Mr. Burk of Hughesville brought it back today[.] Grand Pa came to Harrisburg Pa august 3, 1865 maried Anna Mary Ripper May 24th 1868, died June 6th 1917 Mamma died Feb 19th 1920."

The note came in an envelope. On it is written, "[T]he desk refinish January 25th 1967 by Mr. Burk of Hughesville, Pa re did the Book Case too[.]"

These few words tell a lot, and suggest more. The desk is well over 100 years old. Was it new in 1880? We don't know; the note doesn't say. It was owned, and apparently valued, by the Liesmann family at least 80 of those years. Mr. Liesmann, author of the note, was of the third generation. Did it pass to a fourth? We don't know that either. When Mr. Liesmann had it refinished, was it because he thought it looked shabby? Did he "fix it up" to keep? Or to sell? Another mystery. But we *do* know that he didn't just set it out for the trashman. He reinvested in it.

The dealer from whom I bought the original desk was very proud of the note, because it validated the antiquity of the desk. So often, the buyer has to take the age of a piece on faith. You look at the hardware, at elements of the design, and at the character of the woodworking and the joinery to establish an age. Here was documentary evidence.

But there's so much more I want to know about the desk

The original desk (*above*) was used by an 1880s schoolmaster, but the reproduction (*opposite*) serves a progeny's pupil.

CUTTING LIST

Piece	Number	Thickness	Width	Length	Material
Front legs	2	$1\,^3/_4$"	$1\,^3/_4$"	$26\,^{15}/_{16}$"	8/4 pine
Back legs	2	$1\,^3/_4$"	$1\,^3/_4$"	$29\,^1/_2$"	8/4 pine
Front apron	1	$^3/_4$"	$4\,^{13}/_{16}$"	$32\,^3/_4$"	1-by pine
Back apron	1	$^3/_4$"	$7\,^7/_8$"	$32\,^3/_4$"	1-by pine
Side aprons	2	$^3/_4$"	$7\,^7/_8$"	$22\,^1/_2$"	1-by pine
Bottom	1	$^3/_4$"	$22\,^1/_2$"	$32\,^3/_4$"	1-by pine
Top	1	$^3/_4$"	$6\,^3/_4$"	$35\,^3/_8$"	1-by pine
Top stiles	2	$^3/_4$"	5"	$18\,^1/_8$"	1-by pine
Gallery back	1	$^9/_{16}$"	$3\,^1/_8$"	$35\,^1/_4$"	pine
Gallery ends	2	$^9/_{16}$"	$2\,^3/_8$"	6"	pine
Lid	1	$^3/_4$"	$18\,^1/_8$"	$22\,^3/_4$"	1-by pine
Breadboard ends	2	$^3/_4$"	$1\,^1/_4$"	$18\,^1/_8$"	1-by pine

HARDWARE

6d cut finish nails

1 pr. butt hinges, 2" × $1\,^1/_2$"

(not to mention the family). The note raises more questions than it answers. Where and when was the desk made? What finish was on it? How did Grandpa come to possess it? Did he have to provide his own desk? Or did the school provide it, and he bought it when he left the John Harris School? See the mysteries I'm thinking about here?

When I first looked at the desk, of course, I wasn't expecting the puzzle I got. I was attracted to an appealing project. The slope-top form of desk was used in homes and business places throughout the eighteenth and nineteenth centuries. Everyone with an interest in country-style furniture has seen a lap desk, a standing desk, or a writing desk that's very close to this schoolmaster's desk. It would be a good addition to the collection.

Moreover, I was attracted to a simple project. The construction of this piece is almost primitive. No effort was made, for example, to create compartments inside the well. Perhaps the elementary level of the joinery is best seen in the lid's breadboard ends. In most old pieces, the breadboard ends were joined to the main panel with a sliding dovetail, a dado and tongue, or several mortise-and-tenon joints. Here, the breadboard ends are simply nailed

in place. It's fairly remarkable to me that they are still firmly attached.

As I looked over the old desk, it was clear it had been used hard. Nails were driven into joints here and there, even the mortise-and-tenon joints. The lock that once secured the lid was gone. Inside, the wood is stained where a bottle of ink clearly was stored and used. But I found no evidence that anyone had carved their initials into the desk.

One aspect of the design and construction that escaped me initially is its height. When I use the desk, even sitting in an atypically low chair that I have, I can't get my knees under it. I sit beside it. And each time I do, I think about Grandpa Liesmann, before a class in the John Harris School back in 1884, all those years ago. Did he not sit at his desk? Was it taller then, a standing desk perhaps? Well, it *is* an attractive and useful desk as it is now. I wouldn't change it. I like it the way it is.

And if I had answers to all my questions about the desk, about Grandpa Liesmann, his wife and children, and about their children, would I be happier about the desk's story? Probably not. I think I like it just the way it is. A puzzle to think about whenever I see the desk.

EXPLODED VIEW

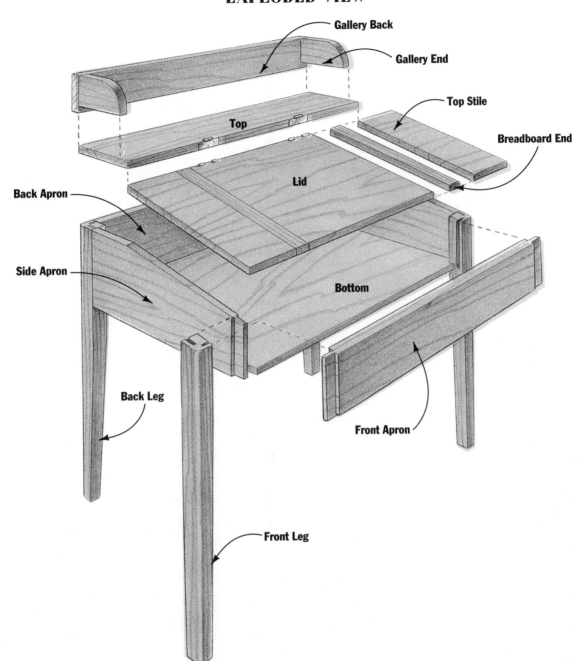

1. Make the leg blanks. The legs will be the first parts to be worked. If you've got access to clear, straight-grained, *flat* 8/4 pine, you can joint, plane, and rip the leg blanks from it.

Lacking 8/4 stock, you can glue-laminate two pieces of 5/4 stock or three pieces of 1-by stock for each blank. After the glue has cured, scrape off dried squeeze-out, and joint, plane, and rip the blanks to the necessary thickness and width.

2. Glue up the lid and bottom. The dimensions for these parts are specified by the Cutting List. Both are sufficiently wide that you'll undoubtedly have to edge-glue several narrow boards to form each. A step-by-step sequence showing how to do this is presented in the *ShopSmarts* feature "Gluing Up Panels" on page 49. Once the panels are clamped, they can be set aside and you can move on to the other tasks. When the time comes to install them, they'll be ready.

PLAN VIEWS

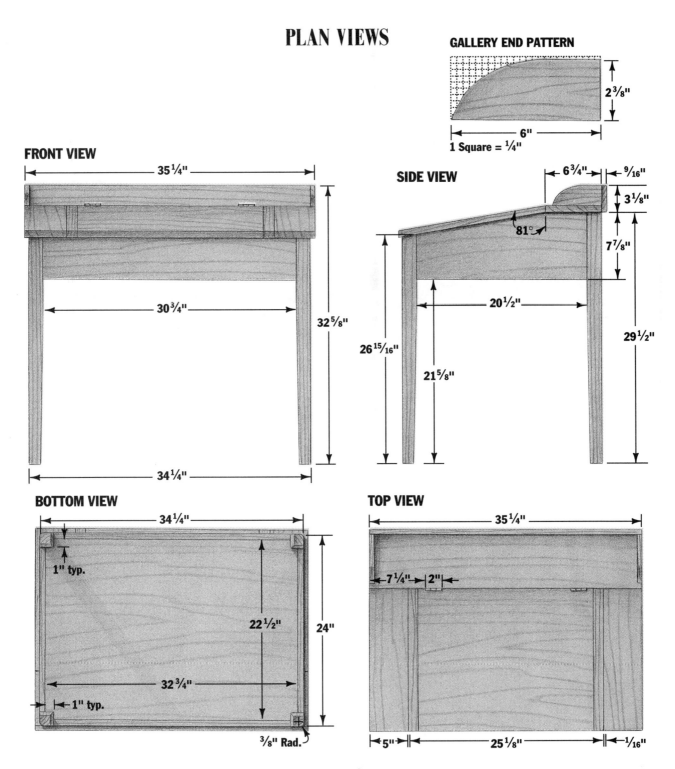

GALLERY END PATTERN

2³⁄₈"

6"

1 Square = ¹⁄₄"

FRONT VIEW

35¹⁄₄"

30³⁄₄"

32⁵⁄₈"

34¹⁄₄"

SIDE VIEW

6³⁄₄"

⁹⁄₁₆"

3¹⁄₈"

81°

7⁷⁄₈"

20¹⁄₂"

29¹⁄₂"

26¹⁵⁄₁₆"

21⁵⁄₈"

BOTTOM VIEW

34¹⁄₄"

1" typ.

22¹⁄₂"

24"

32³⁄₄"

1" typ.

³⁄₈" Rad.

TOP VIEW

35¹⁄₄"

7¹⁄₄"

2"

5"

25¹⁄₈"

¹⁄₁₆"

3. **Rout the mortises in the legs.** The dimensions for the necessary mortises are shown in *Leg Layouts*. Use the type of mortising fixture shown in the *ShopSmarts* feature "Cutting Mortise-and-Tenon Joints" on page 83 to hold each leg while you rout its mortises. Follow the sequence detailed in the *ShopSmarts* feature to rout the mortises.

4. **Taper the legs.** The desk's legs are tapered on the two adjoining inner faces. The taper extends from the bottom of the aprons to the foot. Though the front and back legs are different lengths, the tapers are exactly the same (the back legs' extra length is above the tapers). The straight outside corner of each leg is rounded-over.

Laminate Four Leg Blanks at One Time

Glue-laminating requires lots of clamps. Each roughly 30-inch leg blank, for example, should be clamped with five hand screws minimum.

With five pipe clamps, however, you should be able to do the blanks for all four legs during a single glue-up.

Set out three clamps on the bench top, with their jaws spread to accommodate all four legs plus a couple of cauls. Leg by leg, glue up the stock and set it in the clamps. To prevent the blanks from being bonded to each other inadvertently, wind a plastic trash bag over and under the individual blanks, separating one from another. Fit the cauls in place last.

Tighten the middle clamp first. Set two more clamps in place atop the stack, as shown, and tighten them. Tighten the two end clamps last. Give each clamp's screw a final turn, then set the whole shebang aside.

After the glue has dried and cured, break down the package, removing the clamps and separating the individual blanks. Each should part cleanly from its neighbor.

LEG LAYOUTS

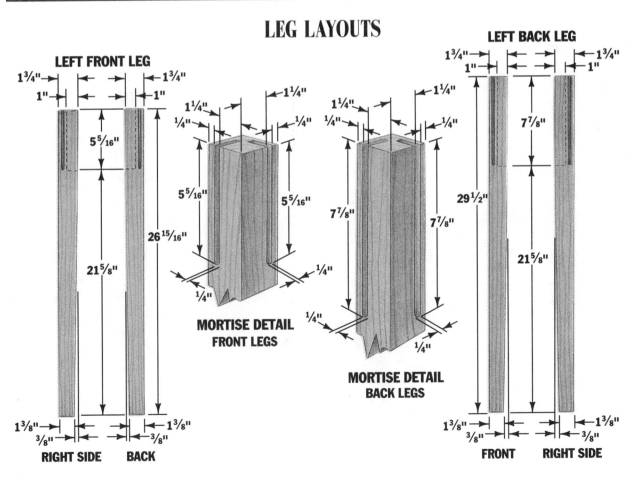

LEFT FRONT LEG

1³/₄" 1³/₄"
1" 1"
5⁵/₁₆"
26¹⁵/₁₆"
21⁵/₈"
1³/₈" 1³/₈"
³/₈" ³/₈"
RIGHT SIDE   BACK

1¹/₄" 1¹/₄"
¹/₄" ¹/₄"
5⁵/₁₆" 5⁵/₁₆"
¹/₄" ¹/₄"
MORTISE DETAIL
FRONT LEGS

1¹/₄" 1¹/₄"
¹/₄" ¹/₄"
7⁷/₈" 7⁷/₈"
¹/₄"
¹/₄"
MORTISE DETAIL
BACK LEGS

LEFT BACK LEG

1³/₄" 1³/₄"
1" 1"
7⁷/₈"
29¹/₂"
21⁵/₈"
1³/₈" 1³/₈"
³/₈" ³/₈"
FRONT   RIGHT SIDE

Although tapers can be cut on a jointer or router table, I'd suggest doing these on the table saw. Use the approach shown in the *ShopSmarts* feature "Tapering Legs on the Table Saw" on page 189. Taper two faces of each leg.

Round-over what will be the outside corner of each leg. Use a 3/8-inch-radius roundover bit in a table-mounted router.

Finally, sand each leg smooth.

5. Make the aprons. Cut the aprons to the dimensions specified by the Cutting List. Eventually, you'll need to cut tapers on the side aprons, but hold off on this operation until after the tenons are cut.

The tenon dimensions are shown in *Apron Layouts*. Ordinarily, I would say to cut tenons on the table saw using the tenoning jig. But the back and sides are a bit wide for that jig. So cut these tenons using a dado cutter or on the router table using a large-diameter straight bit.

Set it so the depth of cut is 1/4 inch. Position the fence so the maximum width of cut is 1 inch. Guide the workpiece with a miter gauge or sled. A pass made with the apron end butted against the fence will produce the tenon's shoulder and cut part of the

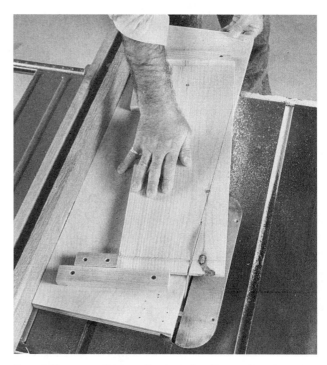

To cut the apron tapers, the tapering jig needs only to be set up with the stop and positioning blocks. You can safely hold the workpiece in place on the jig with your hand while you feed the jig across the saw table.

APRON LAYOUTS

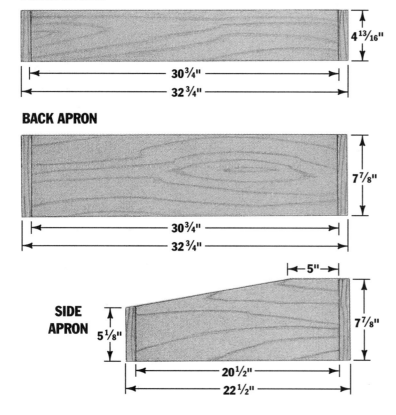

FRONT APRON

4 13/16"

30 3/4"

32 3/4"

BACK APRON

7 7/8"

30 3/4"

32 3/4"

SIDE APRON

5"

5 1/8"

7 7/8"

20 1/2"

22 1/2"

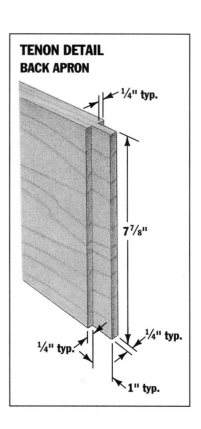

**TENON DETAIL
BACK APRON**

1/4" typ.

7 7/8"

1/4" typ.

1/4" typ.

1" typ.

cheek. A second pass made with the end pulled away from the fence will clean the remainder of the cheek. Roll the workpiece over, and cut the tenon's second cheek in the same way.

Cut a test tenon on a scrap of the apron stock and fit it to one of the already-cut mortises. When the setup is right, cut all the tenons. Round the bottom edge of each tenon with a file so it conforms to the shape of the routed mortises.

Before beginning to assemble the desk, taper the side aprons. Lay out the taper, as shown in *Apron Layouts*. Cut the aprons on the table saw, using the tapering jig shown in the *ShopSmarts* feature "Tapering Legs on the Table Saw" on page 189.

6. Assemble the desk's frame. The first operation is to joint the legs and aprons. Spread glue on the tenons and in the mortises, then assemble the joints and clamp the unit with pipe clamps.

After the glue has set and the clamps are off, drill a hole into each joint for a "drawpin." The pins can be located somewhat roughly, about 3/8 inch from the seam between leg and apron and approximately midway between the top and bottom of the tenon.

Cut drawpins from 5/16-inch dowel, and whittle a bit of taper on one edge to ease insertion. Put a dot of glue on each pin and drive it into place. Use a chisel to pare the end flush.

Complete the framework by trimming the tops of the front legs. Use a backsaw or panel saw.

7. Fit and install the bottom. The bottom panel is glued up. Sand it smooth and flat, then rip and crosscut it to the final dimensions. It will have to be notched at the corners to accommodate the legs.

The bottom is nailed in place. With the desk resting on its back, fit the bottom in place, making sure it's flush with the edges of the aprons. Drill pilot holes and drive 6d cut finish nails through the aprons into the bottom. Sink the nailheads and putty them over.

8. Attach the top. The top consists of three pieces—the top proper and two pieces I call stiles, which abut the top and flank the lid. Cut these parts to the dimensions specified by the Cutting List. The ends of the stiles must be beveled, as shown in *Side View*.

Lay these parts in place and fasten them with 6d cut finish nails. Drill pilot holes for the nails to avoid splitting the wood. Sink the nailheads and putty them over.

9. Make and attach the gallery. The gallery is the "fence" around the top of the desk. It's made of 9/16-inch stock. The back piece is butted against the top's back edge, and the ends are set atop the top.

Resaw or plane stock to the required thickness, and sand it smooth and flat. Rip and crosscut the back piece to fit. Hold it in place and drive nails through it into the top. Shape the ends, as shown in *Gallery End Pattern* in the *Plan Views*. Set them in place, and drive nails through the back into them. Drive a nail through the lower segment of the curved edge into the desktop. Drill pilot holes for these nails, of course. Countersink the nails and cover the heads with wood putty.

10. Attach the lid. The main section of the lid assembly is glued up. Sand it smooth and flat, then rip and crosscut it to the final dimensions. Cut the breadboard ends.

The usual approach with breadboard ends is to join them to the main panel with a sliding dovetail or mortise-and-tenon joints. In this case, the joinery is much simpler: the nailed butt joint. Butt the end against the panel, drill pilot holes, and drive nails. Countersink the nails and cover them with wood putty.

The lid is hinged to the top's edge, as indicated in the *Plan Views* drawings. Lay out the hinge locations. Pare mortises for the hinges, and install them.

11. Apply the finish. When I got the desk, it was finished with a clear varnish. But I think it unlikely that the desk originally was finished with anything other than paint.

Nevertheless, I decided to mimic the finish on the desk when I got it. So we stained the desk with Miniwax stain, choosing the hue called Colonial Maple. I applied the stain over a still-wet coat of McCloskey's Stain Controller, as described in the *ShopSmarts* feature "Country Finishes" on page 305. After the second coat of the stain had dried, I finished the finish with a coat of polyurethane paste varnish.

POST-AND-PANEL CHEST

This is a blanket chest with a difference. It's relatively small—less than 4 feet long. It has no drawers, and it has no till inside. But it is very attractive and eminently suitable for storing extra blankets and bedding or out-of-season clothing.

In its serviceability, this blanket chest is like most others of the genre. What makes it different is its construction. Instead of being of the familiar six-board construction style, it is of the frame-and-panel style.

Frame-and-panel construction is one of the best ways to accommodate wood movement. Wide boards used to form a chest like this would shrink and expand considerably with changes in temperature and humidity. I suspect, however, that the builder of this chest was less concerned with wood movement than with appearance.

Here's why: In a simple chest with an overlaid lid, such as this one, wood movement doesn't matter a whole lot. The chest would change height slightly during the course of seasons, but there aren't major cross-grain joints to be racked. It's in a cabinet with drawers and a flush door that this wood movement causes problems.

The builder probably just liked the appearance of frame-and-panel constructions. Certainly this chest is more distinctive than an unembellished six-board chest. It attracted me immediately, even in a large and *very* cluttered antique store. The color—a yellow ochre—and the condition of the original paint job contribute to its eye-catching appeal.

As a furniture-making project, the chest is more challenging than that six-board chest, but not at all beyond the capacity of the hobby woodworker.

Too handsome to be hidden in the bedroom, the reproduction (*opposite*) of the original old chest (*above*) can serve usefully in the living room.

CUTTING LIST

Piece	Number	Thickness	Width	Length	Material
Posts	4	$2^3/_{16}$"	$2^3/_{16}$"	$25^3/_4$"	1-by pine
Rails	3	$^3/_4$"	4"	$37^5/_8$"	1-by pine
Bottom back rail	1	$^3/_4$"	6"	$37^5/_8$"	1-by pine
End rails	4	$^3/_4$"	4"	$16^7/_8$"	1-by pine
Stile	1	$^3/_4$"	$3^3/_4$"	$14^1/_2$"	1-by pine
Front panels	2	$^5/_8$"	$12^3/_4$"	$16^7/_{16}$"	1-by pine
End panels	2	$^5/_8$"	$12^3/_4$"	$15^1/_8$"	1-by pine
Back panel	1	$^5/_8$"	$10^3/_4$"	$35^7/_8$"	1-by pine
Batten	1	$^1/_2$"	4"	$17^1/_8$"	1-by pine
Lid prop	1	$^1/_2$"	$4^1/_4$"	$17^3/_4$"	1-by pine
Bottom	1	$^3/_4$"	$17^1/_4$"	38"	1-by pine
Pins	18	$^1/_4$"	$^1/_4$"	1"	hardwood
Lid	1	$^3/_4$"	$18^{13}/_{16}$"	$41^1/_2$"	1-by pine
Lid molding	2	$^7/_8$"	$1^1/_4$"	$19^{11}/_{16}$"	5/4 pine
Lid molding	1	$^7/_8$"	$1^1/_4$"	$41^1/_2$"	5/4 pine

HARDWARE

1 pr. hinges, $1^3/_4$" × $1^1/_4$"

1 half-mortise lock: $^9/_{16}$" × $3^1/_8$"selvedge, $1^3/_8$" backset. Catalog number 4448 from Paxton Hardware (410-592-8505).

1 escutcheon, $1^1/_8$" × $1^5/_8$". Catalog number 248 from Paxton Hardware.

6d cut finish nails

BUILD THE CHEST

1. Glue up the chest's panels. To make the chest, a number of panels, including the bottom and all the raised panels, must be glued up from narrow boards. To save some time, glue up these panels first, then work on the legs and frame parts while the glue in them sets. The dimensions of these panels are given in the Cutting List. Tips on gluing up are found in the *ShopSmarts* feature "Gluing Up Panels" on page 49.

The bottom is made of standard 1-by pine, but the stock for the panels must be resawed or planed to a $^5/_8$-inch thickness. After thicknessing the stock, rip and crosscut it, then glue up the panels.

Because the bottom is not on display, you can use fairly knotty lumber for it. The raised panels in the original do have a few knots, and the same is true of our reproduction. You have to suit yourself on this matter in your reproduction.

2. Mortise and slot the posts. The original chest's posts are turned on the bottoms to form feet. Primarily because of this turning, I believe, the original's builder used a hardwood for the posts, not pine. Pine simply isn't a good turning wood.

You have an option here. We made a chest using pine for the posts but gave them tapered rather than turned feet. Except for the foot portion, our reproduction posts are identical to the originals.

EXPLODED VIEW

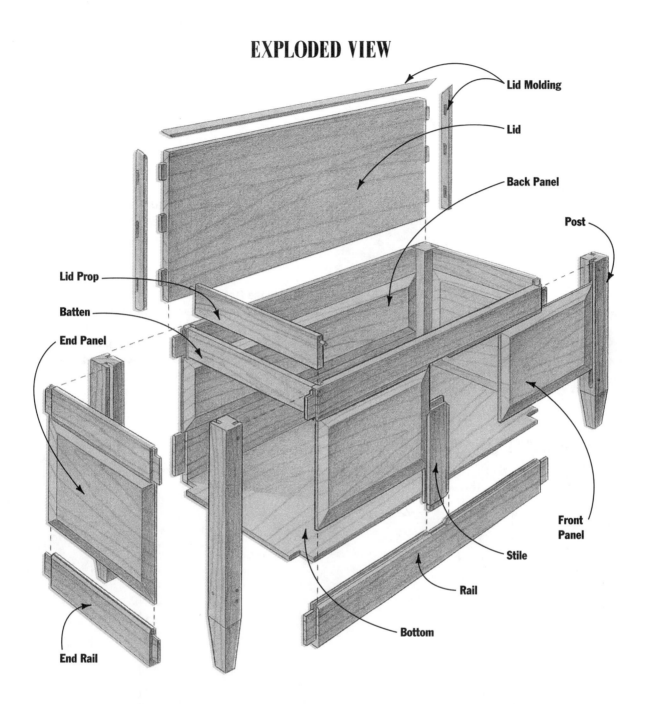

Lid Molding

Lid

Back Panel

Post

Lid Prop

Batten

End Panel

Front Panel

Stile

Rail

Bottom

End Rail

Choose your stock and prepare the post blanks. If necessary, glue up several thicknesses of 1-by stock to form the blanks.

Lay out the mortises and slots following the drawing *Post Layouts*. Rout the mortises using a plunge router equipped with an edge guide and the longest ¼-inch straight bit you can lay your hands on. Secure the posts in the shop-made fixture shown in the *ShopSmarts* feature "Cutting Mortise-and-Tenon Joints" on page 83. You'll find the details on setting up and routing mortises there.

Use the same edge guide–equipped router and

the same bit to rout the panel slot, which extends from the lower mortise to the top of the post.

3. Turn (or taper) the feet on the posts. If you plan to turn the feet on your chest's posts, do it now. Follow the *Turned Foot Layout* detail of the *Plan Views*.

On the other hand, if you are going to taper the post bottoms to form feet, do that now. Consult the *ShopSmarts* feature "Tapering Legs on the Table Saw" on page 189. Lay out the taper on one post, and use it to set up the taper jig. Cut the tapers.

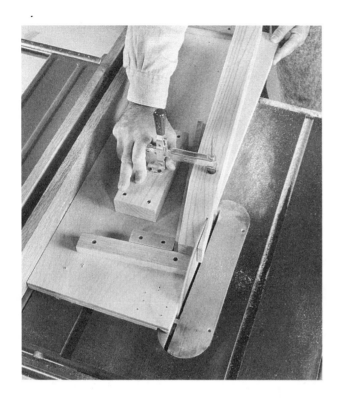

4. Cut the chest rails and stile. The chest's framework has several rails, but only one stile. All are cut from 1-by stock. Rip and crosscut the stock to the dimensions specified by the Cutting List.

5. Cut the joinery on the rails and stile. Study the drawing *Frame and Panel Layouts*. All of these frame parts are tenoned, and the front rails are mortised for the stile. In addition, all are slotted for the raised panels. All but the back rails are given a decorative bevel. Particularly note that the joinery cuts are offset, which is to say, closer to the back edge than the front.

Tapering the feet on the chest posts is not a whole lot different than tapering table legs. This is the same jig I used to taper legs for the Drop-Leaf Kitchen Table (page 19) and the Splay-Leg Table (page 183), but with the stop and positioning blocks located to accommodate the chest posts. Because of the orientation of the post and the short cut, only one toggle clamp is necessary.

POST LAYOUTS

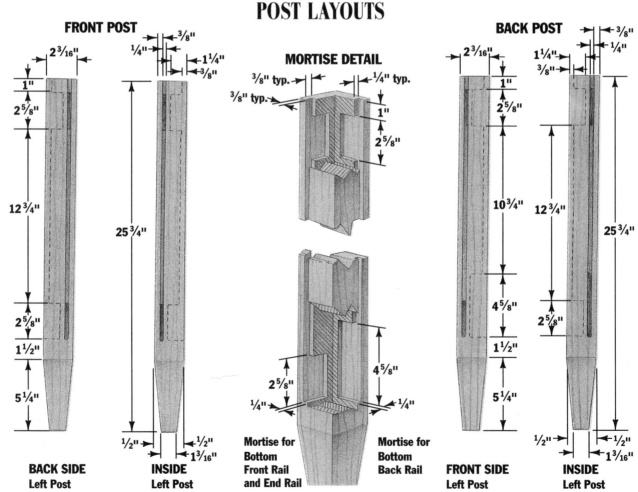

PLAN VIEWS

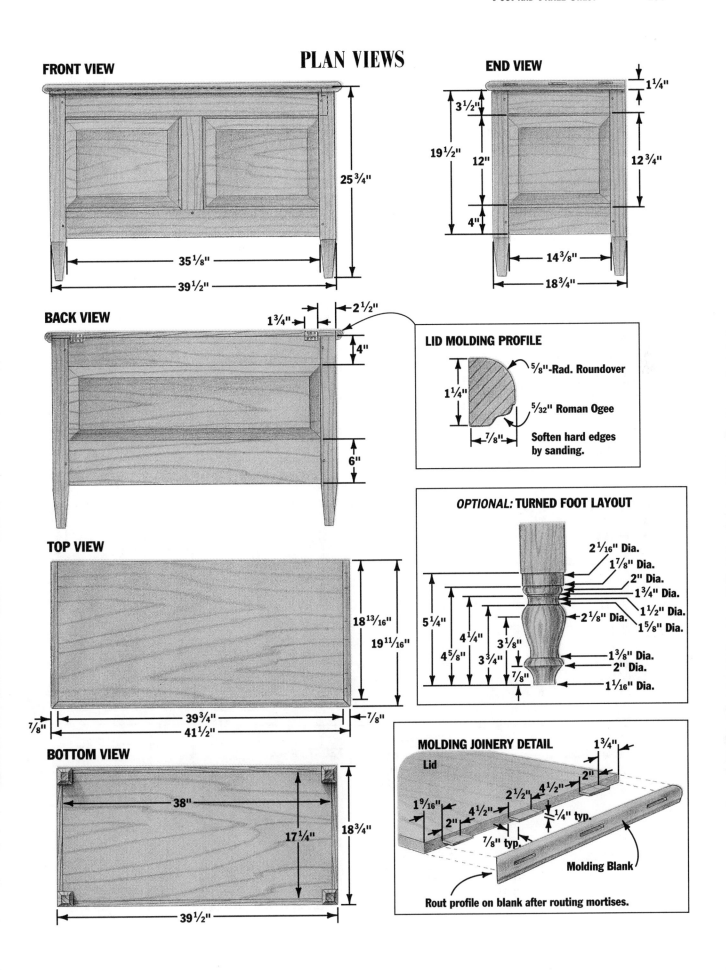

FRONT VIEW

25³/₄"

35¹/₈"

39¹/₂"

END VIEW

1¹/₄"

3¹/₂"

19¹/₂"

12"

12³/₄"

4"

14³/₈"

18³/₄"

BACK VIEW

2¹/₂"

1³/₄"

4"

6"

LID MOLDING PROFILE

⁵/₈"-Rad. Roundover

1¹/₄"

⁵/₃₂" Roman Ogee

⁷/₈"

Soften hard edges
by sanding.

TOP VIEW

18¹³/₁₆"

19¹¹/₁₆"

7/8"   39³/₄"   ⁷/₈"

41¹/₂"

OPTIONAL: TURNED FOOT LAYOUT

2¹/₁₆" Dia.

1⁷/₈" Dia.

2" Dia.

1³/₄" Dia.

1¹/₂" Dia.

2¹/₈" Dia.

1⁵/₈" Dia.

5¹/₄"

4¹/₄"

4⁵/₈"

3¹/₈"

3³/₄"

1³/₈" Dia.

2" Dia.

⁷/₈"

1¹/₁₆" Dia.

BOTTOM VIEW

38"

17¹/₄"

18³/₄"

39¹/₂"

MOLDING JOINERY DETAIL

Lid

1³/₄"

1⁹/₁₆"

2"

4¹/₂"

2¹/₂"

4¹/₂"

2"

¹/₄" typ.

⁷/₈" typ.

Molding Blank

Rout profile on blank after routing mortises.

Begin by cutting the panel slot and bevel profile on the rails and stile. Do the slot, then the bevel. Both cuts can be done on the table saw or with a router, whichever you prefer. Make the cuts on one edge of each rail but on both edges of the stile.

The lone stile is joined to the two front rails by mortise-and-tenon joints. Rout the mortises in the front rails using the plunge router and an edge guide. Secure the rails in the type of fixture used in mortising the posts. Note that the mortises are "in" the panel slot.

Cut the tenons on the frame parts next. Do this on the table saw, using the tenoning jig shown in the *ShopSmarts* feature "Cutting Mortise-and-Tenon Joints" on page 83. Remember that the tenons are

offset, so you should cut one cheek of each tenon, then readjust the rip fence to cut the second cheek on each. The tenon edges can be trimmed as necessary on the table saw with the tenoning jig.

To complete the joinery, the bevel and slot must be mitered and trimmed away where the front rails and the stile come together. On the rails, lay out the areas that need to be trimmed away. Cut the miters first, doing this on the table saw. Tilt the blade to 45 degrees, and set the height to cut just to the bottom of the slot. Make the miter cuts on both rails and on the stile. The waste on the rails can be trimmed away with repeated table saw cuts, with a saber saw, or with a coping saw. Use a chisel to trim the cut surfaces and refine the fit of the joints.

FRAME AND PANEL LAYOUTS

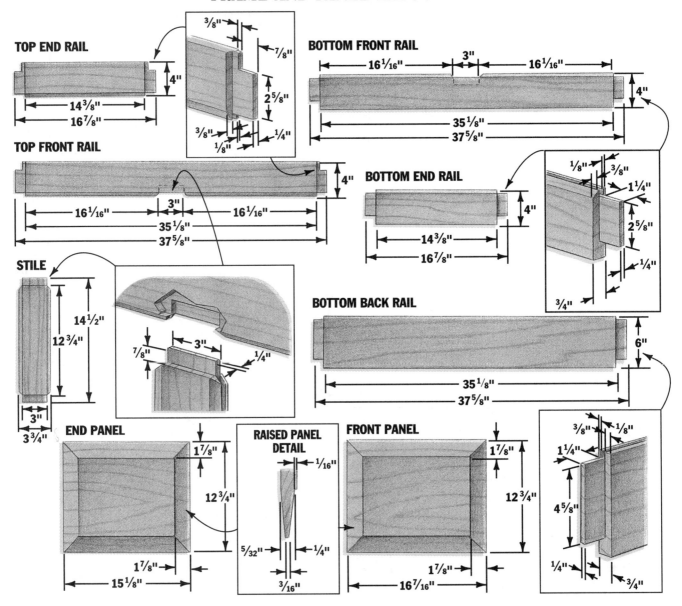

LID PROP DETAIL

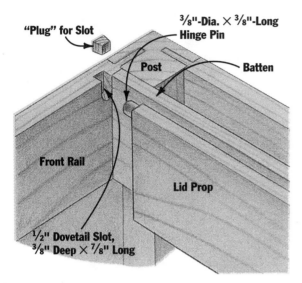

"Plug" for Slot

$3/8$"-Dia. $\times$ $3/8$"-Long Hinge Pin

Post

Batten

Front Rail

Lid Prop

$1/2$" Dovetail Slot, $3/8$" Deep $\times$ $7/8$" Long

---

6. Prepare the lid prop. The lid prop in this chest looks like the hinged top for a till. A till is a small compartment that was often incorporated into six-board chests. Its lid would double as a prop to keep the chest lid open. Holding the chest lid open with one hand, you'd lift the till lid, then lower the chest lid until it rested against a corner of the till lid. The odd thing is that this chest doesn't appear to have ever had a till. It just has the till's lid. So I call it a lid prop.

Resaw or plane two pieces of stock to a $1/2$-inch thickness for the batten and the prop. Cut these pieces to the sizes specified by the Cutting List. To complete the prop, cut a $3/8 \times 4$-inch notch in each end of it. Then file the tab left at each end into a $3/8$-inch-diameter hinge pin.

You could drill hinge pin holes in the front and back top rails, but the builder of this chest cut a dovetail slot into these parts instead. This allowed him to assemble the chest, then drop the prop into place, securing it with a short scrap planed to fit the slot. With a router and $1/2$-inch dovetail bit, rout the slots, as shown in the *Lid Prop Detail*. Finally, cut a short strip to plug the open ends of the slot after the prop is in place.

7. Raise the panels. This is a table saw task, given the design of the panels. In the assembled chest, the raised field of these panels is recessed $1/8$ inch below the surface of the frame members. To achieve this, the angle of each panel's bevels must be shallow, more shallow than that produced by the typical panel-raising router bit. The back of each

---

Fitting the Panels to the Slots

To ensure that the panels fit the panel slots properly, make several test cuts on scraps of the panel stock.

Before cutting the front of the panels, "capture" the setup on a couple of scrap pieces. Save them to use in testing the setup used to cut the panel backs. As you switch to the panel back setup—altering the tilt of the blade and the position of the fence—use the scraps to test the setup. Cut the first scrap and check its fit in the slot cut in the rails. If the fit is perfect, go ahead and cut the panels themselves. If it's loose or tight, adjust the setup, then make a test cut on the second scrap and check its fit in the slot. Keep adjusting and testing until you do have that perfect fit.

---

panel is also raised, ever so slightly, to fit the panel to the slot in the frame members.

A complete explanation of how to raise panels on the table saw is given in the *ShopSmarts* feature "Raising Panels" on page 140.

Assuming the panels have been glued up and the glue has cured, scrape off any dried squeeze-out and sand the panels. Set the rip fence $1^7/8$ inches from the outside of the blade, and set the blade height to $1/16$ inch for the shoulder cuts. The shoulder cut defines the raised field of the panel and creates a fillet around it. Make these cuts on the front of each panel.

Attach a support panel to the rip fence and adjust its position for the bevel cuts, as outlined in the *ShopSmarts* feature. See the *Raised Panel Detail* of the drawing *Frame and Panel Layouts* for guidance in setting the blade height and tilt for the front and back bevels. Cut all the panel fronts, then alter the setup and do the panel backs.

Sand the bevels to remove saw marks.

8. Assemble the chest. Do this in stages, beginning with the back and the front. Join the back posts, the back rails, and the back panel without glue to check out how everything fits. If it's okay, reassemble it with glue. If it isn't okay, do whatever is necessary to make it okay; then glue it together.

Secure each mortise-and-tenon joint with a single pin. Drill a $1/4$-inch-diameter, $3/4$-inch-deep

You can lay out the post notches in the bottom with a rule, but it's more accurate to lay them out to fit. Set one long edge of the bottom against the posts (*left*). Mark that edge at each post. Then shift the workpiece, and mark an end edge. Shift the panel again and do the second long edge. After a final shift of the panel, you can mark the second end. Extend the marks with a square, then cut the notches with a saber saw or backsaw (*right*).

hole through the face of the post into the joint. It should be roughly ³⁄₈ inch from the joint's shoulder and in the middle of the tenon.

To make the pins, cut a strip of ¹⁄₄-inch-square hardwood, and crosscut it into 1-inch-long pieces. Whittle a bit of taper on one end of a pin, put a dot of glue on it, then drive it into a hole. Repeat this process until you've pinned all the joints. After the glue dries, you can pare the pins flush.

Repeat the entire process to assemble the chest front. Attach the front posts, rails, stile, and panels. Pin all the mortise-and-tenon joints.

The third stage is to join the front and back subassemblies with the end rails and panels. Check how everything fits, then assemble the parts with glue. Pin the mortise-and-tenon joints.

9. Fit and install the chest bottom. The bottom panel should already be glued up. Sand it smooth and flat. Then rip and crosscut the panel to the final dimensions.

It will have to be notched at the corners to accommodate the posts. For the best fit, set the panel against the posts, as shown in the top left photo, and mark the bottom at the posts with a pencil or knife. Cut the notches.

The bottom is nailed in place. With the chest resting on its back, fit the bottom in place, making sure it's flush to the edges of the bottom rails. Drill pilot holes, and hammer 6d cut finish nails through the bottom rails into the bottom. (Roll the chest over to nail through the back rail.) Sink the nailheads and putty them over.

MAKE THE LID

1. Tenon the lid. The lid panel must be glued up from narrow boards. Its dimensions are given in the Cutting List. Tips on gluing up are found in the *ShopSmarts* feature "Gluing Up Panels" on page 49.

After the clamps are off, the squeeze-out has been scraped off, and the panel has been sanded smooth and flat, cut the tenons that join the lid and molding. The positions and sizes of the tenons are shown in the *Molding Joinery Detail* of the *Plan Views*. Form the cheeks of the tenons by cutting wide rabbets across the ends of the lid with a dado cutter in the table saw or with a bottom-cutting bit in a router. Use a coping saw or saber saw to trim the waste from between the three individual tenons, and clean up, if necessary, with a chisel or file.

2. Make the lid molding. Rip three blanks to the dimensions specified by the Cutting List, but crosscut them several inches longer than specified. Before routing the profile on the blanks, mortise the two pieces for the lid ends. To lay out the mortises, butt the molding blank against the ends of the tenons and scribe around the tenons. (Position the blank so it extends beyond the lid at both ends, not just the end to be mitered.) Rout the mortises with a plunge router and a straight bit. Hold the blank in the same sort of fixture used to hold the posts for mortising. Square the ends of the mortises with a chisel.

After the mortise-and-tenon joints are satisfactorily fitted, rout the profile. This is best done on the router table. Use a $5/8$-inch roundover bit to shape the top edge of the molding. Then use a $5/32$-inch Roman ogee bit to shape the bottom edge.

3. Apply the lid molding. Fit the end moldings in place first, to mark the miters. Cut the miters and glue the moldings in place. Set the front molding against the tips of the end moldings and mark it for mitering. Miter the molding, and glue it in place. Finally, trim the ends of the end moldings flush with the back edge of the lid. Use a backsaw.

4. Install the lid and lock. Set the lid in place. Install the hinges; you can set the hinges in mortises if you like, but that wasn't done on the original.

Finally, rout the mortise for the lock and install the lock in its mortise, and attach the catch to the lid. Remove the hardware to ready the chest for finishing.

The lid molding installed across each lid end doubles as a breadboard end to help keep the lid flat. It is installed using mortise-and-tenon joints, as shown. When you glue it in place, apply glue to the end of the miter to keep that joint closed, and apply glue to the tenons. But don't spread glue where the molding's long grain abuts the lid's end grain.

FINISH THE CHEST

The original chest is painted a yellow-ochre color. We painted our reproduction with pumpkin milk paint. No, the pumpkin isn't a special additive, it's the color. A step-by-step sequence for applying milk paint can be found in the *ShopSmarts* feature "Country Finishes" on page 305.

We applied only a single coat of the paint, and we didn't seal the knots. The result is a transparent finish that gives the chest distinct color but allows the figure and texture and character of the pine to show through.

To add some durability to the finish, and to lend some sheen to the finish, we applied a coat of wiping polyurethane varnish. This deepened the color somewhat.

Raising Panels

In building reproductions of this collection's country originals, the table saw came to the fore as the ideal machine for raising panels. Perhaps you're accustomed to using the router to raise panels. The projects here don't fit within the boundaries the router sets up.

Those boundaries include limits on the width and angle of the straight bevels that the router bit cuts. What the router does that the table saw can't is mill coves and ogees and other profiles to raise a panel. But those profiles are irrelevant for this collection of projects. To make these country projects, what you need to be able to do is cut bevels of varying widths and angles.

And that's what the table saw does best.

Step by step, here's how to raise a straight-beveled panel that has a fillet or step between the bevel and the field. I use my 10-inch contractor's saw, set up with CMT's 110-500 combination blade. (CMT Tools: 800-531-5559) I don't fuss with any jigs. I just attach a 5- to 6-inch-high plywood facing to the rip fence to help support the panel. This is about twice the height of the wooden facing that's usually attached to the fence.

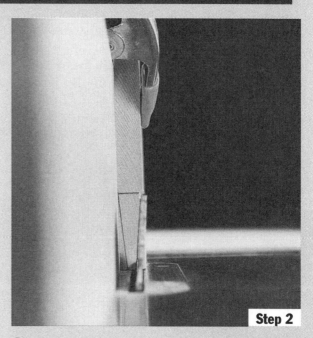

Step 2

2. Set up the saw for the bevel cuts. To cut the bevel, you must position the rip fence where the blade will tilt *away* from it. With most saws, this means the fence must be shifted to the left side of the blade. Consequently, the plywood facing must be attached to the right side of the fence.

The best way to set the blade for the bevel cuts is to line it up against the layout of the desired bevel. Draw the layout on the edge of the workpiece, as shown in the Step 2 photo. Raise the blade to the height of the fillet cut, and tilt it to align with the layout. (The panel in the photos is for the Post-and-Panel Chest [page 131], which is beveled on both faces.) To do this, stand the panel directly behind the blade. If you need to, clamp the workpiece to the fence with a spring clamp 'til you get the blade tilted. Sight across the blade to the layout. Don't worry about the angle on the saw's indicator; just keep your eye on the blade and the layout.

Step 1

1. Kerf the panel to form the fillet. The fillet is usually about $^1/_{16}$ inch high, so set the blade only that high. Set the rip fence to the width of the bevel by measuring from the fence to the *outside* of the blade. Kerf the panel parallel to all four edges.

3. Make the bevel cuts. With the table saw set (blade at the correct height and the correct angle, facing attached to the right side of the fence), cut the bevels.

When I make these cuts, I stand beside the saw, so I am behind the fence rather than at one end of it. I can pull the workpiece against the fence and slide it

Step 3

from right to left, making the cut, as shown in the first Step 3 photo. Though not very high, the facing is high enough that with my thumbs braced against the back of it, my fingers are out of the blade's way. And I make the facing long enough that it fully backs the workpiece until its trailing end clears the blade.

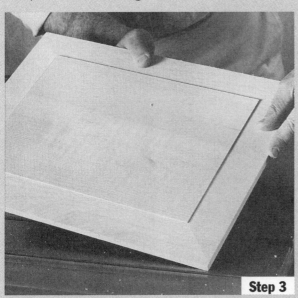

Step 3

The freshly sawed panel still needs scraping and sanding to remove planer marks and saw marks. But to this point, the job has gone quickly and the results are crisp and consistent.

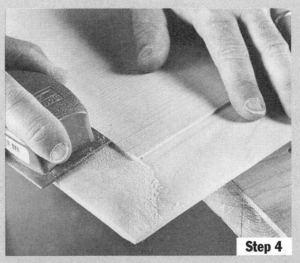

Step 4

4. Sand the bevels. To do a good job of sanding right up to the fillet, you have to hand sand, in my opinion. Lately, I've taken to using Sandvik's metal hand-sanding plates for the initial work. Using a medium-grit plate, you can quickly rub out the saw marks, working right up against the fillet. Then switch to sandpaper on a hand-sanding block to ready the panel for assembly and finishing.

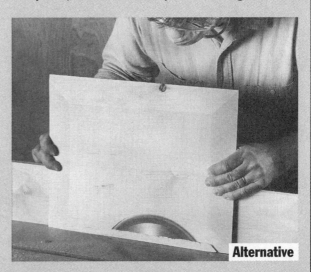

Alternative

Alternative. A panel without a fillet around the field, such as those used in the Step-Back Cupboard (page 37) and the Dry Sink (page 95), can be cut in one fewer step: Scribe the bevel layout on the edge of the workpiece, set the blade, and cut. The initial sanding can be done quickly with a belt sander.

SIDE TABLE

A mass of contradictions is what this handsome little side table is. On the one hand, it seems to support conventional woodworking wisdom, while on the other, it seems to fly directly in its face. What it really is is a wonderful example of country woodworking. Practical and sensible.

Though built of pine, this little table has hardwood legs. In this it supports a bit of woodworking's conventional wisdom. That bit of CW is that pine makes weak, easily broken legs. "You want sturdy legs, don't make 'em of pine" runs the line.

The country woodworkers of the eighteenth and nineteenth centuries often used several different woods in a project. Usually, very practical considerations dictated where a "secondary" wood would be used. Pine doesn't turn well, so the turned drawer pulls aren't pine. Pine is pretty brittle for use in slender legs, so a hardwood is substituted. With a coat of paint on them, all woods look pretty much the same.

(I can't help but point out, however, that while the CW line has truth in it, it is nevertheless also true that lots of country tables have pine legs. Three tables in this book have fairly slender pine legs, and each table has been in use for well over 100 years. It is easily as likely that this table's builder happened to have 8/4 maple but no 8/4 pine. *That's* a pretty practical consideration!)

Where the table diverges from woodworking's current CW is in its construction. A lot of woodworkers will argue that the lack of a rail above the drawer weakens the structure. The drawer rail becomes a fulcrum; the feet want to wiggle, and particularly to pinch in toward one another. Because there's no top rail, there's nothing to prevent this.

A woodworking friend of mine feels exactly this way. He believes this table has been cut down, not by trimming the feet, but by trimming the tops of the legs *and* removing the top drawer rail. He says the table is about an inch-and-a-half lower than what's typical, and that strengthens his conviction.

I don't agree with him. Sure, the top's been replaced, maybe even recently, though with old wood. I can envision the old table with a top that's split, warped, and gouged, just boogered beyond easy restoration. And I can envision some bloke—surely the same one who stripped the paint from the table and varnished it—replacing that beat-up top. But I just can't visualize a reason for cutting down the upper part of the leg-and-apron structure.

This slender pine table reproduction (*opposite*) with sturdy maple legs, accented with hardwood pulls, can be a side table, a lamp table, even a household desk.

CUTTING LIST

Piece	Number	Thickness	Width	Length	Material
Legs	4	$1\frac{3}{4}$"	$1\frac{3}{4}$"	$26\frac{3}{4}$"	hardwood
Back apron	1	$\frac{3}{4}$"	$4\frac{5}{8}$"	$28\frac{7}{8}$"	1-by pine
End aprons	2	$\frac{3}{4}$"	$4\frac{5}{8}$"	$18\frac{7}{8}$"	1-by pine
Drawer rail	1	$1\frac{1}{8}$"	$1\frac{1}{4}$"	$28\frac{1}{8}$"	5/4 pine
Drawer runners	2	$\frac{3}{4}$"	$1\frac{3}{8}$"	$17\frac{3}{8}$"	1-by pine
Drawer guides	2	$\frac{3}{4}$"	$\frac{3}{4}$"	16"	1-by pine
Drawer front	1	$\frac{3}{4}$"	$3\frac{5}{16}$"	$25\frac{15}{16}$"	1-by pine
Drawer sides	2	$\frac{3}{4}$"	$3\frac{5}{16}$"	$18\frac{1}{8}$"	1-by pine
Drawer back	1	$\frac{3}{4}$"	$2\frac{11}{16}$"	$24\frac{7}{16}$"	1-by pine
Drawer bottom	1	$\frac{5}{8}$"	$17\frac{1}{4}$"	$25\frac{3}{16}$"	1-by pine
Pulls	2	2"	2"	$1\frac{1}{16}$"	hardwood
Tabletop	1	$\frac{3}{4}$"	$25\frac{1}{4}$"	36"	1-by pine
Tabletop clips	6	$\frac{5}{8}$"	$1\frac{1}{2}$"	$1\frac{1}{8}$"	1-by pine

HARDWARE

4d cut finish nails

2 flathead wood screws, #10 × $1\frac{3}{4}$" (for drawer pulls)

6 flathead wood screws, #8 × $1\frac{1}{4}$" (for tabletop clips)

Optional: 2 maple pulls, 2" dia., with screws. Catalog number WK-3 from Horton Brasses (203-635-4400).

Of course, the main reason I don't buy the argument is that I've seen other old tables with similar construction. In the end, regardless of how you feel about the construction, theoretically speaking, you have to admit that it's held up pretty well.

And you'll agree, I'm sure, that it looks good. Atypically low though it may be, the height is satisfactory for use as a side or occasional table or a bedside table. It doesn't *look* too low, and it hasn't *felt* too low in anyplace we've used it around the house. Certainly, the overall proportions are pleasing. While no element of the table is particularly remarkable, the sum is, to me, distinctive. It was in a very cluttered tableau that I first saw it, and my eye went directly to it.

Its appearance may just be another of its contradictions. It's practical and sensible, and in an undefinable way, very comely.

MAKE THE TABLE FRAME

1. **Cut the leg blanks, aprons, and drawer rail.** The dimensions of these parts are specified by the Cutting List. All are cut from different stock: the aprons from standard 1-by pine, the rail from 5/4 pine, the legs from 10/4 stock. The legs of the original are hardwood, not pine; I'd suggest you use poplar, maple, birch, or some other blond hardwood (we used maple).

2. **Lay out and rout the mortises in the legs.** It is always easiest to cut mortises in legs *before* they are tapered or shaped in any way. As you can see in the drawing *Leg-to-Apron Joinery*, the drawer rail joins the front legs in a double-tenon joint, while the back and end aprons join the legs in single-tenon joints.

Using plywood odds and ends and a few drywall screws, construct a mortising trough like that

EXPLODED VIEW

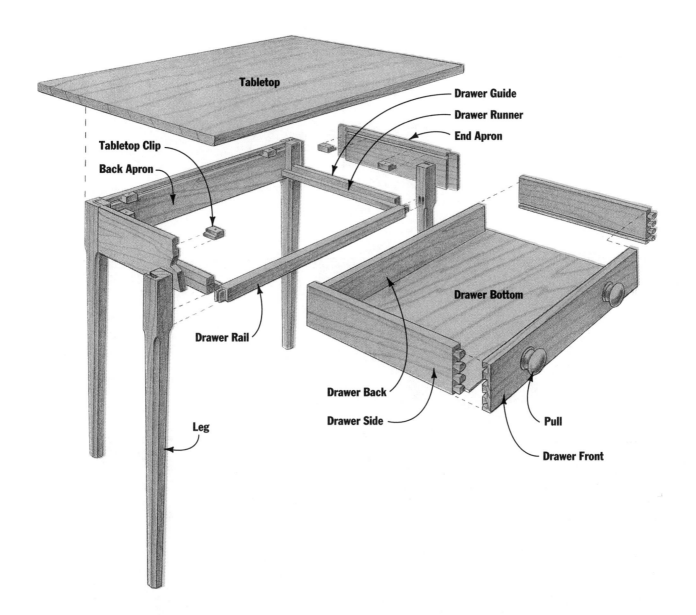

Tabletop

Drawer Guide

Drawer Runner

End Apron

Tabletop Clip

Back Apron

Drawer Bottom

Drawer Rail

Drawer Back

Drawer Side

Leg

Pull

Drawer Front

shown in the *ShopSmarts* feature "Cutting Mortise-and-Tenon Joints" on page 83. Tailor the fixture's dimensions as necessary to accommodate the legs.

As outlined in the *ShopSmarts* feature, set up your plunge router with its edge guide and a ¼-inch straight bit to rout the apron mortises. Position the fixture's stops to control the length of the apron mortises. All the apron mortises are the same length. After all are routed, change the stop positions to do the double-mortises for the drawer rail. Set the edge guide for routing the first mortise in each pair, and

rout this mortise in each of the front legs. Then reposition the edge guide and rout the second mortise in the pair.

3. Taper the legs. What is unusual about this table's legs is that they are tapered from top to bottom: There's no untapered segment. Do the job on the table saw, as outlined in the *ShopSmarts* feature "Tapering Legs on the Table Saw" on page 189.

After the legs are tapered, sand away the saw marks.

LEG-TO-APRON JOINERY

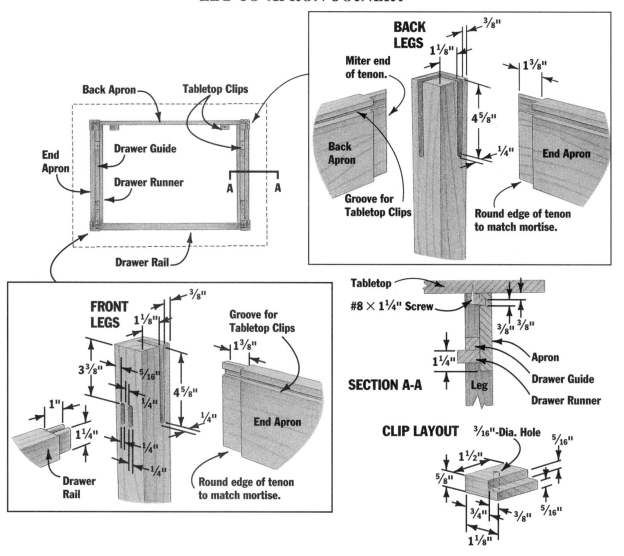

SECTION A-A

CLIP LAYOUT

4. Rout the leg chamfers. This is surprisingly easy to do. On each leg, mark the end of the chamfers—4⅝ inches down from the top. (The original country woodworker scribed a line around the legs with a scratch awl, a line still visible.) Chuck a 45-degree chamfer bit in a table-mounted router. Use a starting pin as a fulcrum and lever a leg to the spinning bit, then let the bit's pilot bearing guide the cut to the leg's foot. Rout all the chamfers in this manner.

In routing the chamfers on the table legs, the bit's pilot bearing controls the cut. But a starting pin enables you to maintain control at the beginning of the cut, in that instant between the bit's initial contact with the work and the work's firm contact with the pilot bearing. Rest the work against the starting pin, then lever it into the bit.

LEG LAYOUTS

TAPER THE LEG

FRONT/BACK   SIDE   **CHAMFER THE TAPERED LEG**

Rout mortises
BEFORE tapering.

$4\frac{5}{8}$"

$26\frac{3}{4}$"

$22\frac{1}{8}$"

$\frac{3}{8}$" $\frac{3}{8}$" $\frac{3}{8}$" $\frac{3}{8}$" $\frac{7}{16}$"

$\frac{3}{8}$" $\frac{3}{8}$"

$1\frac{3}{4}$" $1\frac{3}{4}$"   1"

5. Cut tenons on the aprons and the drawer rail. Because the legs are tapered from end to end, the shoulders of the tenons on the aprons and the drawer rail must be angled very slightly, only 1 degree off square. And because of the angle, you should cut the tenons using a dado cutter.

To begin the tenoning process, cut this angle on the ends of the aprons and the drawer rail. At the same time, cut the angle on one end of a 12- to 16-inch-long scrap of 1 × 6 stock (or something close to that size). This scrap will be used as a pusher in cutting the inner cheeks of the drawer rail's double tenons.

Before you change to the dado cutter, cut the inner cheeks on the drawer rail. Adjust the depth of cut to 1 inch, and position the rip fence $\frac{7}{16}$ inch from the blade. Stand the rail on end, back it with the pusher, and guide it along the fence, making the first cut. Spin the rail around and roll the pusher over, then make the second cut. Repeat the sequence on the other end of the rail. If necessary, reposition the fence and make an additional pass at each end of the rail to remove any waste remaining in the gap just formed.

Switch from the saw blade to the dado cutter. Adjust the depth of cut to just $\frac{1}{4}$ inch. Position the rip fence 1 inch from the *outside* of the cutter. Lay the drawer rail flat on the saw table, with its end butted against the fence. Guiding the workpiece with the miter guide, make a first pass. Back the rail away from the fence and make a second cut, completing the first outer cheek. Repeat the process to

Cutting the inner cheeks of the drawer rail's double tenons may sound tricky, but it's really easy. Take a look! With the saw blade and rip fence properly adjusted, you stand the rail on end. Press the rail against the fence, and simultaneously advance it toward the blade with the pusher you made when crosscutting the rail and the aprons (*left*). As they clear the blade, tip the rail and pusher away from you, which lifts them up and off the blade (*center*). Spin the rail 180 degrees and turn the pusher over. Now the rail is tilting ever so slightly away from you but is firmly backed by the pusher. Make the second pass (*right*).

PLAN VIEWS

TOP VIEW

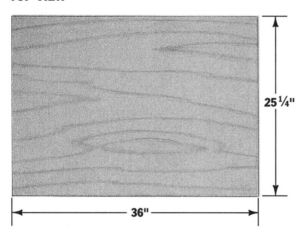

25¼"

36"

FRONT VIEW

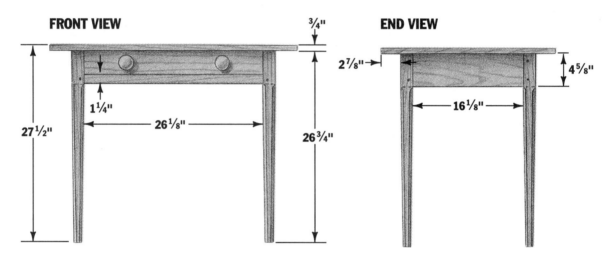

¾"

1¼"

26⅛"

27½"

26¾"

END VIEW

2⅞"

4⅝"

16⅛"

cut a cheek on the other end of the rail. Then re-adjust the miter gauge as necessary to cut the second cheek on each end of the rail.

Use the same approach to cut the tenons on the ends of the aprons. You do have to reposition the fence because the apron tenons are slightly longer than the rail tenons.

6. Assemble the legs, aprons, and rail. A couple of little jobs remain before the framework can be glued together. A groove must be plowed along the inside of the aprons. The wooden clips that secure the tabletop to the framework—eventually—engage this groove. Use a ⅜-inch straight bit on a table-mounted router to cut the groove. As shown in *Leg-to-Apron Joinery,* the groove *can* be plowed from end to end, though you may want to make it a stopped groove so it won't cut into the tenons.

The second little job is to round-over the edges of the tenons as necessary to fit them to their respective mortises. Use a file for this. And miter the ends of the tenons that go into the back legs, as shown in *Leg-to-Apron Joinery.*

After fitting everything together satisfactorily in a dry run, sand all the parts. Then glue up the aprons, rail, and legs.

7. Cut and install the drawer runners and guides. Even as the glue sets, you can be cutting and fitting the drawer runners and drawer guides. The basic dimensions are given by the Cutting List. The runners must be notched to accommodate the legs.

Glue and clamp the guides to the end aprons first. After the clamps are off the guides, glue the runners to the aprons.

PLAN VIEWS

BOTTOM VIEW

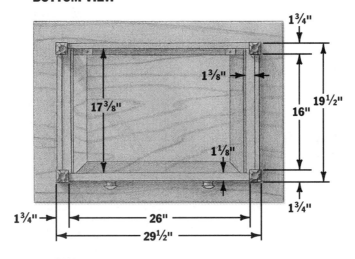

BACK VIEW

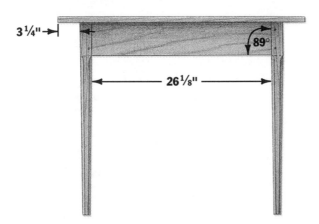

MAKE THE DRAWER

1. Cut the drawer parts. Rip and crosscut the front, sides, and back for the drawer. Rip and crosscut enough stock to form the bottom, then resaw or plane it to the required thickness. The dimensions of these parts are specified by the Cutting List.

2. Rout the dovetails. The front and sides are joined by half-blind dovetails. In the original, of course, the dovetails were hand cut. For our reproduction, we cut them with a router. Use a ½-inch 14-degree dovetail bit and a dovetail jig. The specifics of setting up and using such a jig are laid out in the *ShopSmarts* feature "Routing Dovetails" on page 232.

3. Plow the groove for the bottom. As shown in *Drawer Construction*, the bottom is housed in a ⅜-inch-wide × ⅜-inch-deep groove routed in the sides and front. Cut the groove with a ⅜-inch straight bit in a table-mounted router.

4. Make the bottom. Edge-glue the stock planed for the bottom, forming a panel of the necessary size. Since the panel is ⅝ inch thick while the groove for it is only ⅜ inch wide, the bottom must be beveled around three sides to reduce the thickness at the edges. You can do this, as did the original country woodworker, with a hand plane. Or you can do it on the table saw or router table.

DRAWER CONSTRUCTION

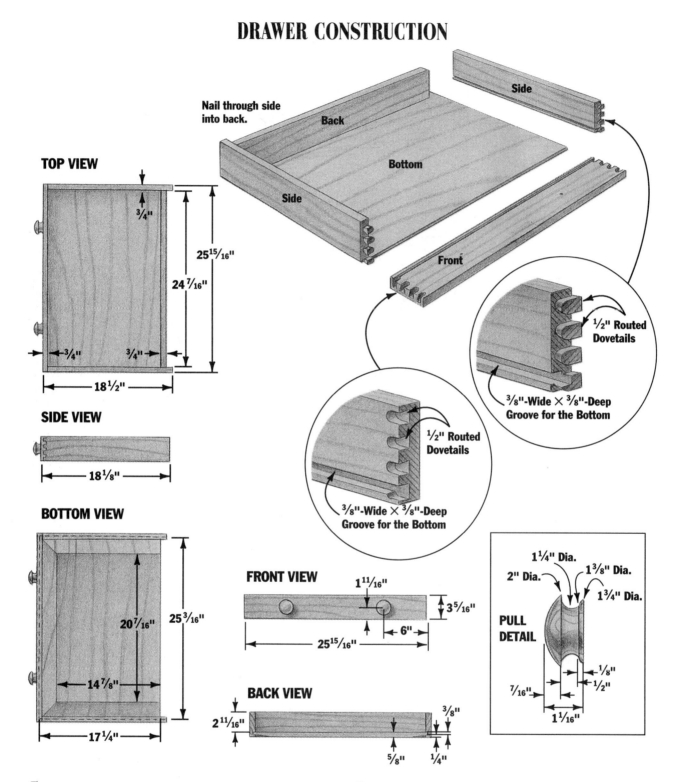

Nail through side into back.

Back

Side

Bottom

Side

Front

TOP VIEW

3/4"

25 15/16"

24 7/16"

3/4"   3/4"

18 1/2"

SIDE VIEW

18 1/8"

BOTTOM VIEW

20 7/16"   25 3/16"

14 7/8"

17 1/4"

1/2" Routed Dovetails

3/8"-Wide × 3/8"-Deep Groove for the Bottom

1/2" Routed Dovetails

3/8"-Wide × 3/8"-Deep Groove for the Bottom

FRONT VIEW

1 11/16"

3 5/16"

6"

25 15/16"

BACK VIEW

2 11/16"

3/8"

5/8"   1/4"

PULL DETAIL

1 1/4" Dia.

2" Dia.   1 3/8" Dia.

1 3/4" Dia.

1/8"

7/16"   1/2"

1 1/16"

5. Assemble the drawer. With the joinery cut and the parts sanded, proceed with assembly. Glue the sides to the front. Slide the bottom into its groove. Fit the back in place and drive two or three nails through each side into it. Drive a couple of nails through the bottom into the back to keep it in place.

6. Install the pulls. The pulls on the original table were turned from a moderately dark hardwood—possibly walnut. Walnut—or any hardwood, for that matter—turns a lot easier than pine. And as finished, the darker hue of the pulls contrasts nicely with the rest of the table.

We turned pulls to match those on the original and attached them to the drawer front with #10 × 1¾-inch flathead wood screws. The *Pull Detail* in the *Drawer Construction* drawing shows the profile. You're not a turner? The Cutting List includes a source for wooden pulls that are a close approximation of the originals.

7. Fit the drawer to the table. In an ideal workshop, the drawer will slip right into the table without binding, without rattling. If your shop should turn out to be less than ideal, and the drawer is too tight, don't fret. Plane or sand the tight drawer as necessary to fit it to the table. Should the drawer be unacceptably loose, you'll have to make another.

MAKE THE TOP

1. Glue up the boards for the top. The original table's top is made up of only two boards, one more than 13 inches wide. The boards have dried over the years and cupped, giving the tabletop two fairly substantial hollows. If you select your stock judiciously and glue up narrow boards to form the tabletop, you shouldn't have this problem.

Tips on preparing the stock and gluing up panels can be found in the *ShopSmarts* feature "Gluing Up Panels" on page 49.

After the clamps are off the panel, scrape off any dried glue squeeze-out, and sand the top smooth and flat.

2. Make the tabletop clips. All the clips can be taken from a single scrap about 5 × 6 inches. Plane the scrap to the required thickness, then cut a ⅜-inch-wide × 5/16-inch-deep rabbet across both ends of it. Rip the piece into three 1½-inch-wide strips, then nip the clips from the strips. Drill a 3/16-inch-diameter hole through each clip.

3. Install the top. Set the tabletop on the workbench, good side down, and position the leg-and-apron assembly on it. Fit the clips in place, and drive a screw through each into the tabletop.

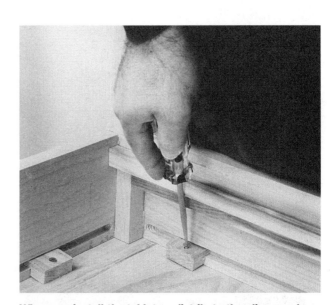

When you install the tabletop, distribute the clips evenly. Note that the clips fit at a slight angle. Getting the screws driven in the clips on the sides is a bit awkward because of the drawer runners, but it can be done with a screwdriver.

This mounting approach keeps the top securely in place, yet allows it to expand and contract without damaging either the top or the leg-and-apron assembly.

FINISH THE TABLE

There's no way to know how this table was originally finished, though it surely was painted. When I bought it, the original had a fairly fresh clear finish.

We stuck with the original as it exists now and finished our reproduction with several coats of Deft, a semi-gloss brushing lacquer. Deft is easy to apply, meaning it dries quickly (within a couple of hours). You can apply three or four coats of this finish to the table in a single day. The fumes are super-potent, however, so apply it only in a well-ventilated workspace. The resulting finish is attractive and reasonably durable.

CORNER CUPBOARD

The corner cupboard is among the archetypical projects for those who favor country furniture styles. It isn't contemporary at all. It's a piece you always picture in an early-American home but seldom in a twentieth-century one.

Why is this? One reason is because most of the early-American homes had 9- to 10-foot ceilings. There are gorgeous old corner cupboards out there. You can buy one. But you may not be able to fit it in a house with 8-foot ceilings. Does it mean you shouldn't build one for your contemporary home? Of course not. It just means you have to find plans for one of the correct scale.

And do I have some plans for you! This pine cupboard is a wonderful example of the genre. The original was built around 1840 in western Maryland. It seems big and commodious— which a corner cupboard should be—and, though made of pine, it is attractive.

My guess is that the Marylander who built the original faced constraints not unlike those that today's hobby workworker faces. He didn't have a lot of space in the shop for assembling a mammoth cabinet, and producing the veneered, sculpted, heavily ornamented designs of the period were beyond his skills (and tool assortment).

So, although it is big, it is

manageable. The cupboard is in two pieces. The top, which frames the glazed doors, is merely set upon the base. This construction makes it easier to build. The longest board required—remember that these boards had to be hand planed to the required thickness and flatness—is just over 4 feet. And the base can be assembled and moved aside before the top is built.

The design circumvents heavy sculpting and rococo carving. Depth is conveyed through the use of raised surfaces—the drawer front and door frames. The moldings are simple but effective.

For today's woodworkers, there are a number of attractive aspects to this cupboard. One is that, despite its apparent mass, it will fit comfortably into a contemporary house with its 8-foot ceilings. The cupboard is a fraction under $7\frac{1}{2}$ feet tall. Although wide, the cupboard is surprisingly shallow. This means you can display the treasured family china—it won't be lost in the shadows at the back of a deep cabinet. (It also means that this cupboard will fit tightly into out-of-square corners, regardless of whether the corner is wider or narrower than 90 degrees.)

Another appealing aspect is the easy-to-reproduce design flourishes: the waist molding, the crown molding,

The original corner cupboard (*above*) was built to showcase the family's treasured china, though in today's version (*opposite*), most any collection might be displayed.

EXPLODED VIEW—TOP CASE

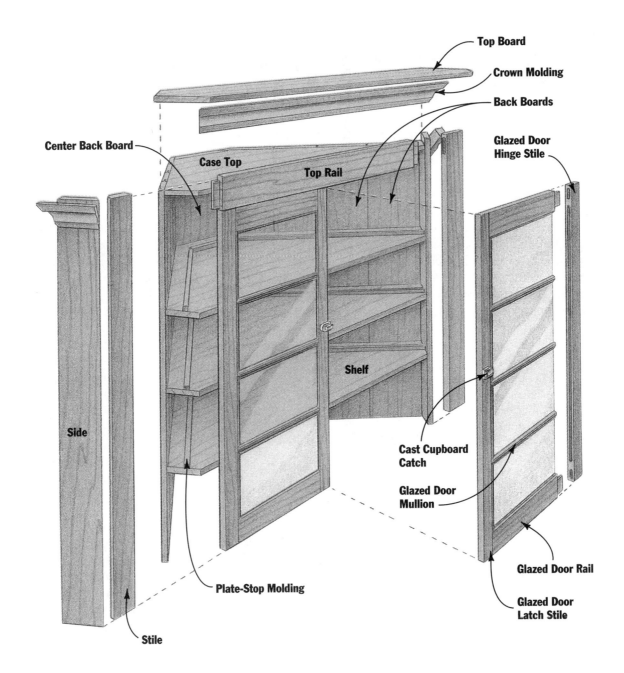

Top Board

Crown Molding

Back Boards

Glazed Door Hinge Stile

Center Back Board

Case Top

Top Rail

Side

Shelf

Cast Cupboard Catch

Glazed Door Mullion

Plate-Stop Molding

Stile

Glazed Door Rail

Glazed Door Latch Stile

the small raised panels flanking the central drawer, the bevel-edged doors. You do need a few 5/4 boards to supplement the usual 1-by pine stock, but 5/4 stock is pretty widely available. And you do need some stock that's been planed to $5/8$- and $1/2$-inch thicknesses. (If you don't have a planer—and how many of us do?—you can usually get a lumber dealer to mill the stock for a modest fee. You can also resaw lumber to the thickness you need.)

Some clear pine—pricey as it is—is in order for this project. All the exposed parts should be knot- and defect-free stock. Through judicious layout, you may be able to extract suitable pieces from #2 common stock. But don't count on getting all the parts this way, unless you have a lot of boards and are willing to generate a lot of waste. The shelves and back boards can be #2 common: Knots and defects in these parts will be concealed beneath a coat of paint.

EXPLODED VIEW—BASE

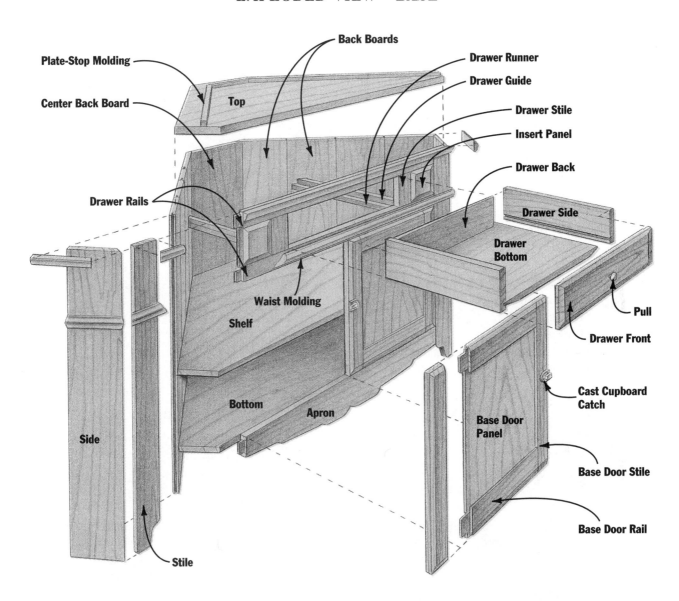

Plate-Stop Molding

Back Boards

Drawer Runner

Drawer Guide

Center Back Board

Top

Drawer Stile

Insert Panel

Drawer Back

Drawer Side

Drawer Rails

Drawer Bottom

Waist Molding

Shelf

Pull

Drawer Front

Side

Bottom

Apron

Base Door Panel

Cast Cupboard Catch

Base Door Stile

Stile

Base Door Rail

BUILD THE CASES

1. Cut the shelves. Begin the construction process with the shelves. There are seven altogether, including the case top and the base top and bottom. Except for thickness, all are identical. The top and bottom shelves in the base are made of 5/4 stock, which is usually 1⅛ inches thick. The others are 1-by pine, which is ¾ inch thick. Refer to *Shelf Layout* for the dimensions.

Glue up panels for the shelves. When the clamps are off, trim the panels to the dimensions specified by the Cutting List. Then lay out and cut the panels to the required shape.

A plate-stop molding is nailed to four of the shelves; one of the four is the base top, a 1¹⁄₁₆-inch-thick shelf. The molding position is shown in the layout drawing. (The molding allows you to stand

CUTTING LIST

Piece	Number	Thickness	Width	Length	Material
BASE					
Top/Bottom	2	$1^1/_{16}$"	$19^5/_8$"	$51^5/_8$"	5/4 pine
Plate-stop molding	1	$1/_2$"	$1/_2$"	$8^7/_{16}$"	1-by pine
Plate-stop molding	2	$1/_2$"	$1/_2$"	$24^1/_2$"	1-by pine
Shelf	1	$3/_4$"	$19^5/_8$"	$51^5/_8$"	1-by pine
Stiles	2	$3/_4$"	$3^7/_8$"	37"	1-by pine
Drawer rails	2	$3/_4$"	$2^1/_2$"	$38^7/_8$"	1-by pine
Drawer stiles	2	$3/_4$"	$2^1/_2$"	7"	1-by pine
Insert panels	2	$7/_8$"	$5^3/_4$"	$5^3/_4$"	5/4 pine
Apron	1	$3/_4$"	4"	$38^7/_8$"	1-by pine
Sides	2	$3/_4$"	6"	37"	1-by pine
Center back board	1	$3/_4$"	$10^3/_4$"	37"	1-by pine
Back boards	8	$3/_4$"	$7^1/_4$"	33"	1-by pine
Drawer runners	2	$3/_4$"	$1^1/_2$"	$15^1/_2$"	1-by pine
Drawer guides	2	$3/_4$"	$7/_8$"	$15^1/_2$"	1-by pine
Waist molding	2	$1/_2$"	$1^1/_2$"	45"	1-by pine
Waist molding	4	$1/_2$"	$1^1/_2$"	7"	1-by pine
TOP CASE					
Case top	1	$3/_4$"	$19^5/_8$"	$51^5/_8$"	1-by pine
Shelves	3	$3/_4$"	$19^5/_8$"	$51^5/_8$"	1-by pine
Plate-stop molding	3	$1/_2$"	$1/_2$"	$8^7/_{16}$"	1-by pine
Plate-stop molding	6	$1/_2$"	$1/_2$"	$24^1/_2$"	1-by pine
Top rail	1	$3/_4$"	$4^7/_8$"	$38^7/_8$"	1-by pine
Stiles	2	$3/_4$"	$3^7/_8$"	$51^3/_8$"	1-by pine
Sides	2	$3/_4$"	6"	$51^3/_8$"	1-by pine
Center back board	1	$3/_4$"	$10^3/_4$"	50"	1-by pine
Back boards	8	$3/_4$"	$7^1/_4$"	50"	1-by pine
Crown molding	1	$3/_4$"	$5^1/_{16}$"	48"	1-by pine
Crown molding	2	$3/_4$"	$5^1/_{16}$"	9"	1-by pine
Top board	1	$3/_4$"	$8^3/_4$"	$61^1/_8$"	1-by pine

dishes on edge, leaning them against the cupboard back.) It is easiest to install the molding before the cupboard is assembled. Rip it to the $1/_2 \times 1/_2$-inch dimension, then crosscut and miter the pieces to fit. Use glue and 1-inch cut brads to install the molding.

2. Make the back boards. The back has three facets. The center section is a single wide board, while the flanking sections are made up of tongue-and-groove 1 × 8s. Rip and crosscut the stock to the sizes specified by the Cutting List.

As you can see from the *Top View* and the horizontal sections, the center back board is beveled along both edges so the back boards flanking it can overlap it. Bevel the edges of the center back boards for both the base and top cases. The broad face of each must be $10^3/_4$ inches wide.

Cut the tongues and grooves on all the other back pieces. Each piece gets a slot along one edge, and a tongue along the other.

Piece	Number	Thickness	Width	Length	Material
DRAWER					
Front	1	$7/8$"	$4^{15}/16$"	$21^3/4$"	5/4 pine
Sides	2	$5/8$"	$4^{15}/16$"	$15^7/16$"	1-by pine
Back	1	$5/8$"	$4^3/8$"	$20^1/2$"	1-by pine
Bottom	1	$1/2$"	$15^7/16$"	21"	1-by pine
BASE DOORS					
Rails	4	$7/8$"	$2^7/8$"	$15^5/8$"	5/4 pine
Stiles	4	$7/8$"	$2^7/8$"	$21^1/8$"	5/4 pine
Panels	2	$5/8$"	$13^5/8$"	$16^3/8$"	1-by pine
Turn button	1	$3/4$"	$3/4$"	$2^1/4$"	pine
GLAZED DOORS					
Rails	4	$7/8$"	3"	$16^1/4$"	5/4 pine
Hinge stiles	2	$7/8$"	$2^3/4$"	$46^3/8$"	5/4 pine
Latch stiles	2	$7/8$"	$1^7/8$"	$46^3/8$"	5/4 pine
Mullions	6	$5/8$"	$7/8$"	$14^1/4$"	1-by pine
Turn button	1	$3/4$"	$3/4$"	$2^1/4$"	pine

HARDWARE

1" cut brads

6d cut finish nails

4d cut finish nails

2 pr. hinges, $1^1/2$" × $1^1/4$" (for base doors)

2 pr. hinges, $1^3/4$" × 1" (for glazed doors)

1 cast cupboard catch (for base doors), $1^3/8$" × 2", brass. Catalog number B03.03 from Garrett Wade Inc. (800-221-2942).

1 cast cupboard catch (for glazed doors), $1^3/8$" × 2", brass. Catalog number B03.02 from Garrett Wade.

1 cast plain knob, 1" dia., with integral screw. Catalog number A39.05 from Garrett Wade.

12 brass flathead wood screws, #4 × $1/2$"

2 roundhead wood screws, #8 × $1^1/2$" (for turn buttons)

8 pcs. glass, 10" × 14"

Glazing points, as needed

Glazing compound, as needed

3. Cut the face frame parts. The face frame for the base is composed of two stiles, two drawer stiles, two drawer rails, two insert panels, and the apron. The face frame for the top case has two stiles but only a single rail. Although the sides are not strictly face frame parts, this is a good time to cut them, too.

The insert panels are $7/8$ inch thick. Plane or resaw 5/4 stock to make these two pieces. Tips on resawing can be found in the *ShopSmarts* feature "Resawing on the Table Saw" on page 112. Crosscut the properly thicknessed stock to the size specified by the Cutting List.

The rest of the parts are cut from 1-by stock. Rip and crosscut these parts to the sizes specified by the Cutting List.

As you rip the stiles for the top and base face frames, bevel the edges that join the sides at 20 degrees. Bevel one edge of each side piece at the same 20-degree angle.

PLAN VIEWS

FRONT VIEW

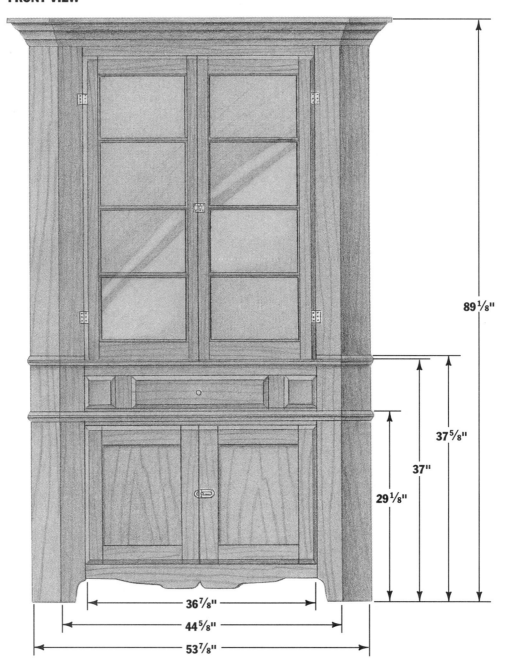

89 1/8"

37 5/8"

37"

29 1/8"

36 7/8"

44 5/8"

53 7/8"

4. Shape the insert panels. The insert panels are raised on the table saw, then a tongue is cut around the four edges. This tongue fits into a groove you'll cut in the stiles and rails, holding the panels in place yet allowing them some freedom to expand and contract with humidity changes.

The bevel surrounding the raised field is $^5/_8$ inch wide on the finished panel. Lay out the bevel on one edge of a scrap of the panel stock, and use the layout to set the angle of the saw blade.

The tongue can be cut with a straight bit in the table-mounted router. Set the bit and fence to form a $^1/_4 \times {}^3/_8$-inch rabbet around the back face of the panels. Reset the bit and fence to cut a similar rabbet around the beveled front face.

Finish sand the panels.

5. Cut the joinery. The face frame parts are joined in mortise-and-tenon joints. As previously noted, the insert panels float in grooves cut in the

PLAN VIEWS

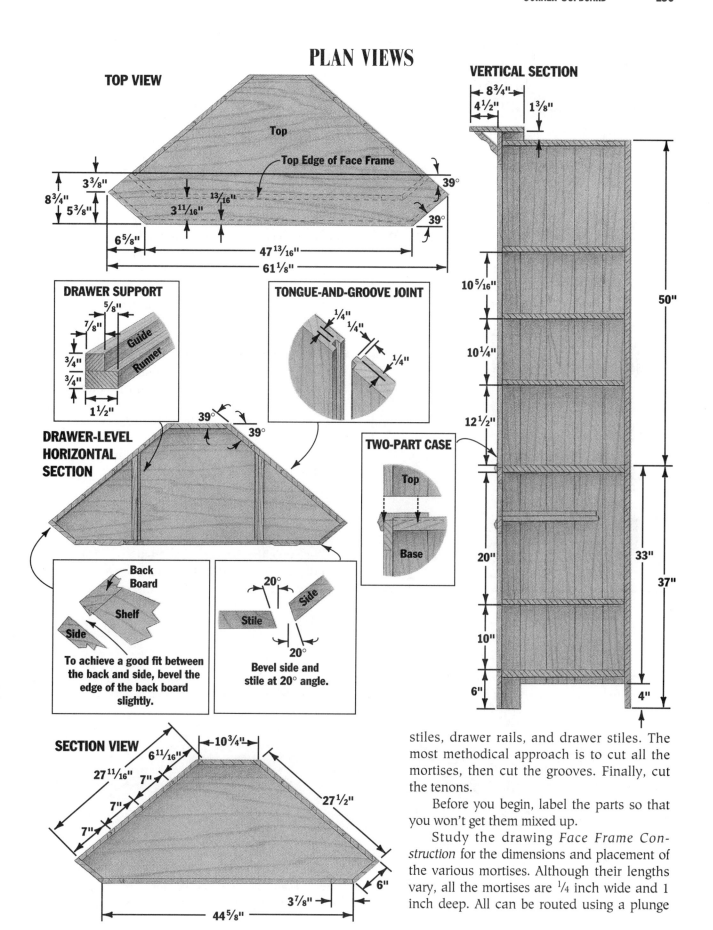

TOP VIEW

Top

Top Edge of Face Frame

3³⁄₈"
8³⁄₄"
5³⁄₈"
13⁄₁₆"
3¹¹⁄₁₆"
39°
39°
6⁵⁄₈"
47¹³⁄₁₆"
61¹⁄₈"

VERTICAL SECTION

8³⁄₄"
4¹⁄₂"
1³⁄₈"
10⁵⁄₁₆"
10¹⁄₄"
12¹⁄₂"
20"
10"
6"
50"
33"
37"
4"

DRAWER SUPPORT

⁵⁄₈"
⁷⁄₈"
Guide
Runner
³⁄₄"
³⁄₄"
1¹⁄₂"

TONGUE-AND-GROOVE JOINT

¹⁄₄"
¹⁄₄"
¹⁄₄"

DRAWER-LEVEL HORIZONTAL SECTION

39°
39°

TWO-PART CASE

Top
Base

Back Board
Shelf
Side

To achieve a good fit between the back and side, bevel the edge of the back board slightly.

20°
20°
Stile
Side
Bevel side and stile at 20° angle.

SECTION VIEW

10³⁄₄"
6¹¹⁄₁₆"
27¹¹⁄₁₆"
7"
7"
7"
27¹⁄₂"
6"
3⁷⁄₈"
44⁵⁄₈"

stiles, drawer rails, and drawer stiles. The most methodical approach is to cut all the mortises, then cut the grooves. Finally, cut the tenons.

Before you begin, label the parts so that you won't get them mixed up.

Study the drawing *Face Frame Construction* for the dimensions and placement of the various mortises. Although their lengths vary, all the mortises are ¹⁄₄ inch wide and 1 inch deep. All can be routed using a plunge

Amazing Obtuse Bevel Cut Trick

No table saw arbor tilts more than 45 degrees. Cutting a 51-degree bevel, as required for the back of the Corner Cupboard, thus can't be done with the board flat on the saw table.

Try this! Instead of feeding the workpiece on edge along the fence, keep the board down on the table. Just elevate one edge slightly, as shown in the photo, by setting a scrap strip beside the fence. A strip 1 inch thick will tip the workpiece enough to give you the required 51-degree bevel if the blade is tilted to 45 degrees.

router equipped with an edge guide and the shop-made fixture shown in the *ShopSmarts* feature "Cutting Mortise-and-Tenon Joints" on page 83.

The grooves for the insert panels can be routed using a $^1/_4$-inch straight bit in a table-mounted router. The grooves are $^3/_8$ inch deep. On the stiles, the groove extends between the drawer rail mortises. On the drawer rails, it extends from the mortises to the ends of the rails. On the drawer stiles, it extends from end to end. Cut the grooves.

The tenons are cut on the table saw using the tenoning jig shown in the *ShopSmarts* feature on the mortise-and-tenon joint. Trim the individual tenons to the widths specified in the *Face Frame Construction* drawing. Use a file to round the edges of the tenons, fitting them to the mortises.

Finish sand the frame parts.

6. Cut the apron's contour. Enlarge the patterns shown in *Patterns and Profiles* for the apron and for the stiles' foot ends. Transfer the contours to the appropriate parts and cut as close to the line as you can with a saber saw. Sand the edges.

7. Assemble the face frames. Before gluing the face frames together, assemble the parts without glue to make sure everything fits properly.

Assemble the top face frame. As you apply the clamps, check the assembly with a square to ensure that it is square and stays square.

Assemble the drawer rails and drawer stiles next. Be judicious in spreading the glue, so you avoid getting any in the grooves for the insert panels. Slip

SHELF LAYOUT

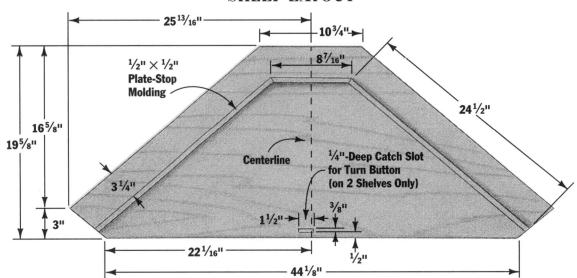

FACE FRAME CONSTRUCTION

TOP FACE FRAME

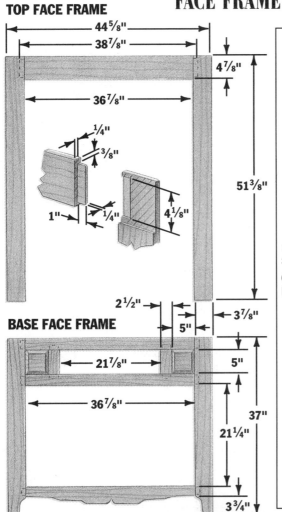

BASE FACE FRAME

BASE FACE FRAME JOINERY

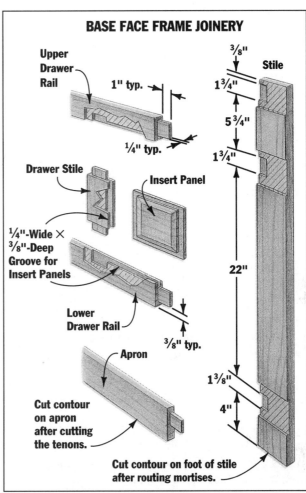

Upper Drawer Rail

1" typ.

¹⁄₄" typ.

Drawer Stile

Insert Panel

¹⁄₄"-Wide × ³⁄₈"-Deep Groove for Insert Panels

Lower Drawer Rail

³⁄₈" typ.

Apron

Cut contour on apron after cutting the tenons.

Cut contour on foot of stile after routing mortises.

Stile

³⁄₈"
1³⁄₄"
5³⁄₄"
1³⁄₄"
22"
1³⁄₈"
4"

Tongue Nailing without Pain

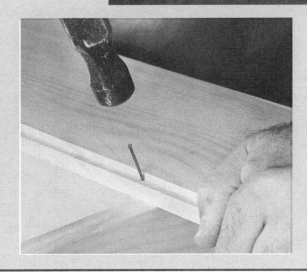

The traditional technique for fastening down tongue-and-groove material is to drive 6d finish nails through the shoulder of the board at the tongue. You then fit the next board into place and drive the finish nails along its tongue edge. Use this approach to nail the back boards in place. The first and last boards will have to be face-nailed, of course. The last board installed on each side of the back—the one overlapping the center back board—should be beveled, as indicated in the section views.

PATTERNS AND PROFILES

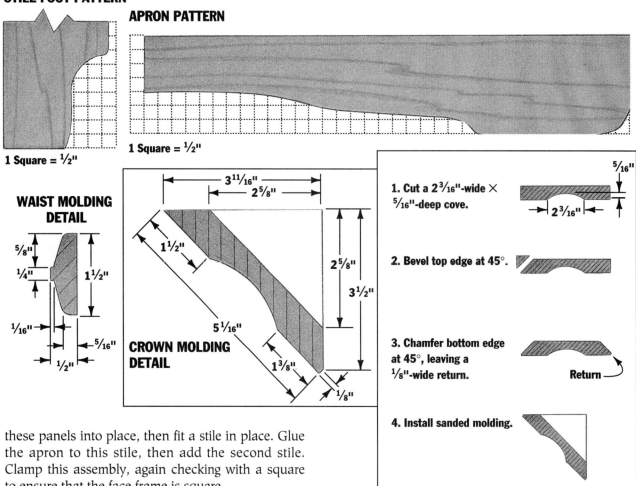

STILE FOOT PATTERN

1 Square = ½"

APRON PATTERN

1 Square = ½"

WAIST MOLDING DETAIL

⁵⁄₈" ¼" 1½" ¹⁄₁₆" ⁵⁄₁₆" ½"

CROWN MOLDING DETAIL

3¹¹⁄₁₆" 2⁵⁄₈" 1½" 5¹⁄₁₆" 1³⁄₈" ⅛" 2⁵⁄₈" 3½"

1. Cut a 2³⁄₁₆"-wide × ⁵⁄₁₆"-deep cove. ⁵⁄₁₆" 2³⁄₁₆"

2. Bevel top edge at 45°.

3. Chamfer bottom edge at 45°, leaving a ⅛"-wide return.   Return

4. Install sanded molding.

these panels into place, then fit a stile in place. Glue the apron to this stile, then add the second stile. Clamp this assembly, again checking with a square to ensure that the face frame is square.

Clean up any glue squeeze-out with a wet rag as quickly as you can, rather than waiting for it to dry. After the clamps are off, touch-up sand the frames.

8. Assemble the base case. The cases are assembled largely with 6d cut finish nails. On the front of the cupboard, the nails are countersunk and puttied over. (With cut nails, it's a good idea to drill pilot holes to prevent the wood from splitting.)

The top and bottom shelves are made of 5/4 stock. Position the parts carefully. The top shelf (which is the 5/4 shelf with the plate-stop molding) should protrude ¼ inch above the top edges of the back and face frame. The top case, which has no bottom, thus drops around the base's top shelf and is held in position without fasteners. Similarly, the bottom shelf must be positioned so it projects about ¼ inch above the apron's top edge; it thus serves as a stop for the base doors.

Begin assembling the base case by nailing the center back board to the shelves. You may need some

help to get started. A helper can hold the shelves while you position the center back board and drive the nails. Once these parts are assembled, you can lay the case on its back to install the face frame. The sides are added next. Finally, you roll the case over and nail the tongue-and-groove back boards in place.

Align the face frame carefully before nailing it down. Make sure the case is square. While glue isn't necessary for most of this assembly, it's important to apply glue to the beveled edge joint between the stiles and sides. Clamp the sides tight to the stiles while you nail the side to the shelves.

9. Assemble the top case. The process is pretty much the same as that for the base. The top case has no bottom; the lowest shelf is 12½ inches above the bottom of the stiles. The top edges of all the back boards are flush with the top shelf, but the face frame rises 1³⁄₈ inches above it, as shown in *Vertical Section*. Position the shelves carefully, since they are intended to align with the mullions of the glazed doors. A misalignment will spoil the effect.

Nail the center back board to the shelves. Lay this assembly on its back and apply the face frame. Nail through the frame into the shelves, then countersink and putty over the nails. Glue the sides to the edges of the stiles, and nail them to the shelves as well. Roll the case over and attach the remaining back boards.

10. Cut and install the top board. This is the visual, not structural, top to the cupboard. It is nailed to the top edges of the face frame and sides, and the crown molding is nailed to it, as well as the case. The layout of this part is shown in the *Top View*. Lay out and cut the top.

To install the top, position it as indicated in the *Top View*, and drive nails through the board into the edges of the face frame and sides.

11. Make the crown molding. The crown molding is a remarkably simple embellishment. It's one of the few moldings you'll ever make on the table saw with nothing more than a standard saw blade. No molding head, just a saw blade.

The molding features a $5/16$-inch-deep cove set off by a $1\frac{1}{2}$-inch-wide flat and a $1\frac{3}{8}$-inch-wide flat. The lower edge has a small return, which offsets the edge from the case by about $1/8$ inch, creating a subtle shadow line to emphasize the crown.

Creating the molding is a simple three-step operation. Begin by cutting the cove into a $5\frac{1}{16}$-inch-wide board. The *ShopSmarts* feature "Coving on the Table Saw" on page 170 provides details on the process. When the cove is cut to the proper depth and width, bevel the top edge at 45 degrees, as shown in *Crown Molding Detail*. Reset the fence and chamfer the molding's lower edge, creating the return in the process. Scrape or sand the molding to remove all traces of saw marks.

12. Install the crown molding. Begin this process by nailing some triangular-section blocking between the top and case. It should have two $2\frac{5}{8}$-inch-wide faces and one $3\frac{11}{16}$-inch-wide face. Be sure this blocking provides adequate backing for the molding while allowing it to seat tightly against the top and case. Assuming it does, nail several pieces of it in place; you don't need to install continuous strips.

Before attacking the molding itself, check out "The Trick Is in the Miter" on page 164. There you'll find tips on making the miter cuts on the table saw.

Crosscut three pieces of molding. The lengths specified for the molding in the Cutting List allow plenty of excess. You'll trim each to final length as you miter and install it.

Begin at the cupboard's left side. Miter the side crown molding and one end of the front crown molding. Check the fit of the miter joint. If it is satisfactory, install the side piece. Don't worry about its length; you can saw it flush with the cupboard back after it's nailed in place. Align the lower corner of the miter with the front edge of the cabinet. Drive nails through the side molding and into the cupboard.

Now hold the front crown molding in place and mark it for length. Miter it. Apply glue to the mitered surfaces, and put the front molding against the side molding. Nail it into place. Then fit the right side molding to the cupboard, marking and trimming the end as you did the left side molding. Nail it into place.

13. Make the waist moldings. The waist moldings extend from side to side across the middle of the cupboard, just above and below the drawer. The lower molding is purely decorative, but the upper molding both conceals the seam between the cupboard's base and top and serves to trap the top between itself and the protruding top shelf.

With the right router bit—a straight-bevel panel raiser—the moldings are easy to make. To get just the right width of cut, guide the cut with the router-table fence. Use the bit to chamfer the edges of the molding strip, leaving a $1/4$-inch-wide ridge. Break the edges of the shoulders with sandpaper, then finish sand the moldings.

For best results, use clear stock. For safety's sake, use a blank that's got as much girth as possible. After routing the profile, rip the required $1/2$-inch-thick molding from the strip. Keep the profile to the outside of the table saw blade as you do this.

14. Install the waist moldings. The waist moldings are simply nailed to the case with 1-inch cut brads (not the familiar wire brads).

Fit and miter the lower molding, and nail it in place, as shown in the *Front View*. Position the upper molding so that, in conjunction with the top shelf, it forms a channel into which the top case fits. When fitting this molding, mark the door opening and trim away the upper bevel, leaving the central ridge and lower bevel. Install this molding strip so its trimmed edge is flush with the top of the base face frame.

The Trick Is in the Miter

The trick to installing the crown molding is in the mitering. Make the cuts on the table saw, using the miter gauge to guide the molding. Be sure to always set the stock in the miter gauge as it will be installed, but upside down. That is, hold the molding in the miter gauge at the angle at which it will be installed. Put the bevel that abuts the case side against the miter gauge, and put the bevel that abuts the top against the table.

Note that the Corner Cupboard's crown molding is so big that you'll need to attach a tall facing to the miter gauge to support it, as shown in the photos. Your table saw probably won't have sufficient depth of cut to cut completely through the molding. Make the table-saw cut as deep as you can, then finish with a handsaw.

Pivot the miter gauge head 20 degrees off square. Note that you can pivot the miter gauge head to either the right or the left of the 90-degree mark. For these outside corners, always pivot the head *away from the blade*. For the first cut, place the gauge in the slot to the left of the blade. Place the molding in the gauge, and grasp it firmly so it doesn't slip. Cut the first miter.

The second cut miters the adjoining piece of molding. Switch the miter gauge to the right-hand slot, and swing the head away from the blade, setting it 20 degrees off square. Make the miter cut. Put the two pieces of molding in place against the case side to check the fit of the joint.

MAKE THE DRAWER

1. Cut the drawer supports. The drawer construction begins with the drawer supports. Made up of the runners and guides, the supports extend from the face frame to the back. Cut the runners and guides to the sizes specified by the Cutting List.

2. Install the supports. Glue the guides to the runners, as shown in the drawer support detail of *Drawer-Level Horizontal Section*. Check the measurement from the face frame to the case back, then cut the supports to the proper length, mitering the ends in the process. Nail through the face frame and the back into the supports to secure them. Make sure they are level and square to the face of the case.

3. Cut the drawer parts. The Cutting List specifies the sizes. The front is made from $7/8$-inch-thick stock, the sides and back from $5/8$-inch-thick stock,

and the bottom from $1/2$-inch-thick stock. If you have a planer, you can mill stock to these thicknesses easily. If you don't have a planer, you can resaw stock, described in the *ShopSmarts* feature "Resawing on the Table Saw" on page 112.

Glue up the bottom panel.

4. Build the drawer. Cut the bevel around the drawer front on the table saw. The process is exactly like that for raising panels, and tips on doing that are found in the *ShopSmarts* feature "Raising Panels" on page 140. Lay out the desired bevel on the end of a drawer front, and use the layout to set up the table saw, as explained in the *ShopSmarts* feature.

Readjust the blade and fence settings to bevel the bottom. Because the bevel width is greater, you'll have to raise the blade, too. The fence needs to be closer to the blade, so the cut tapers the

DRAWER CONSTRUCTION

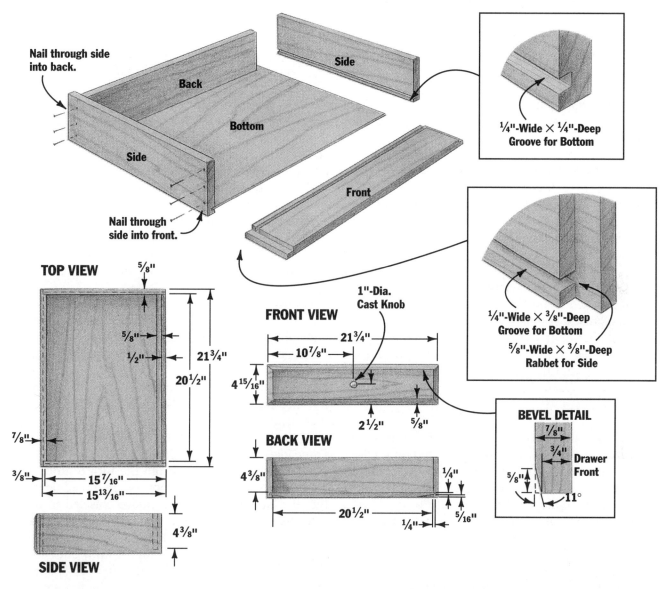

Nail through side into back.

Nail through side into front.

Back

Side

Bottom

Side

Front

¼"-Wide × ¼"-Deep Groove for Bottom

¼"-Wide × ³⁄₈"-Deep Groove for Bottom

⁵⁄₈"-Wide × ³⁄₈"-Deep Rabbet for Side

TOP VIEW

⁵⁄₈"
⁵⁄₈"
½"
21³⁄₄"
20½"
⁷⁄₈"
³⁄₈"
15⁷⁄₁₆"
15¹³⁄₁₆"

SIDE VIEW

4³⁄₈"

1"-Dia. Cast Knob

FRONT VIEW

21³⁄₄"
10⁷⁄₈"
4¹⁵⁄₁₆"
2½"
⁵⁄₈"

BACK VIEW

4³⁄₈"
20½"
¼"
⁵⁄₁₆"
¼"

BEVEL DETAIL

⁷⁄₈"
¾"
Drawer Front
⁵⁄₈"
11°

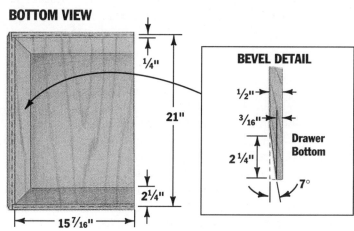

BOTTOM VIEW

¼"
21"
2¼"
15⁷⁄₁₆"

BEVEL DETAIL

½"
³⁄₁₆"
Drawer Bottom
2¼"
7°

bottom from a full thickness down to ³⁄₁₆ inch.

The joinery is straightforward. Plow a groove in the sides and the front for the bottom. In the sides, the groove is ¼ inch deep, but in the front it is ³⁄₈ inch deep. Rabbet the front for the sides. This rabbet is ⁵⁄₈ inch wide and ³⁄₈ inch deep.

Assemble the drawer with 4d cut finish nails. Install the cast knob.

5. Fit the drawer to the case. Once the drawer is assembled, fit it to the case. Plane the drawer surfaces as necessary to achieve a satisfactory fit.

MAKE THE BASE DOORS

1. Cut the parts. The Cutting List specifies the sizes. As with the drawer, none of the door parts are $^3/_4$ inch thick. The frame parts are $^7/_8$ inch thick, so they must be resawed (or planed down) from 5/4 stock. The door panels must be glued up from $^5/_8$-inch stock resawed (or planed down) from 1-by stock.

2. Groove the rails and stiles. The panel "floats" in a $^3/_8$-inch-wide × $^1/_2$-inch-deep groove in the rails and stiles. Cut this groove on the table saw with a dado cutter, or on the router table with a straight bit. The groove is centered across the edge of the stock.

3. Cut the mortises and tenons. The mortises can be routed using the same jig used for the face frame mortises. You need a $^3/_8$-inch straight bit.

Cut the tenons on the table saw, using your tenoning jig. After the tenons are formed, use a backsaw to trim the haunches. File the corners of the tenons, rounding them so the tenons will fit the routed mortises.

4. Shape the panels. After the two panels are glued up and trimmed to size, you need only raise them. The bevels surrounding the raised field are roughly $2^1/_2$ inches wide. They have no fillet between them and the field. Because of the bevel width, and because there is no fillet, it is easiest to raise the panels on the table saw.

Position the rip fence where the blade will tilt *away* from it. Raise the blade as high as you can, and tilt it. Set the fence so that at the table surface, the fence is $^5/_{16}$ inch away from the inside of the blade. This setting should produce the proper bevel. If a test cut proves the setup, cut the panels.

Sand or scrape away all saw marks.

5. Assemble the doors. As a test, assemble the doors without glue. Make any adjustments to the joints that may be necessary to fit the parts and square the doors. Finish sand all the parts. Then glue up the assembly. Glue the tenons into the mortises, but don't glue the panels in the grooves; they must be free to move a little.

When the clamps are off the doors, cut the bevels on the hinge stiles and both rails (the latch stile is NOT beveled). These bevels are the same as those on the drawer front and the insert panels.

6. Hang the doors. The first step is to ensure that they fit comfortably within the door opening. You need about $^1/_{16}$ inch of clearance all around. Plane the edges of the doors as necessary to achieve the clearance.

The hinges are mortised into both the doors and the face frame. Use a chisel to pare the mortises, then install the hinges.

Attach the catch to the doors as shown in the *Front View* in *Base Door Construction*. To keep the doors closed, you must install the turn button on the inside of the left-hand door. When turned down, the turn button catches the groove chiseled in the middle shelf and keeps the left door closed. Latching the right door to the left keeps *it* closed. Notch the end of the turn button with a backsaw, then round the edges with a file and sandpaper. Drill a pilot hole, and install the turn button with a #8 × 1$^1/_2$-inch roundhead wood screw.

MAKE THE GLAZED DOORS

1. Cut the parts. The Cutting List specifies the sizes. As with the base doors, the frame parts are $^7/_8$ inch thick, so they must be resawed (or planed down) from 5/4 stock.

2. Stick the rails, stiles, and mullions. The sticking is the decorative profile; here it is a simple bevel. Use a small panel-raising bit—we used Bosch's number 85583M bit in a table-mounted router. (For Bosch distributors, call S-B Power Tool Company at 919-636-4200.)

Adjust the fence to set the width of cut at $^7/_{16}$ inch. Rout the profile on one edge of each rail and stile and both edges of each mullion. The cut can be made from end to end. You want a $^1/_{16}$-inch fillet between the bevel and the flat at the glass.

BASE DOOR CONSTRUCTION

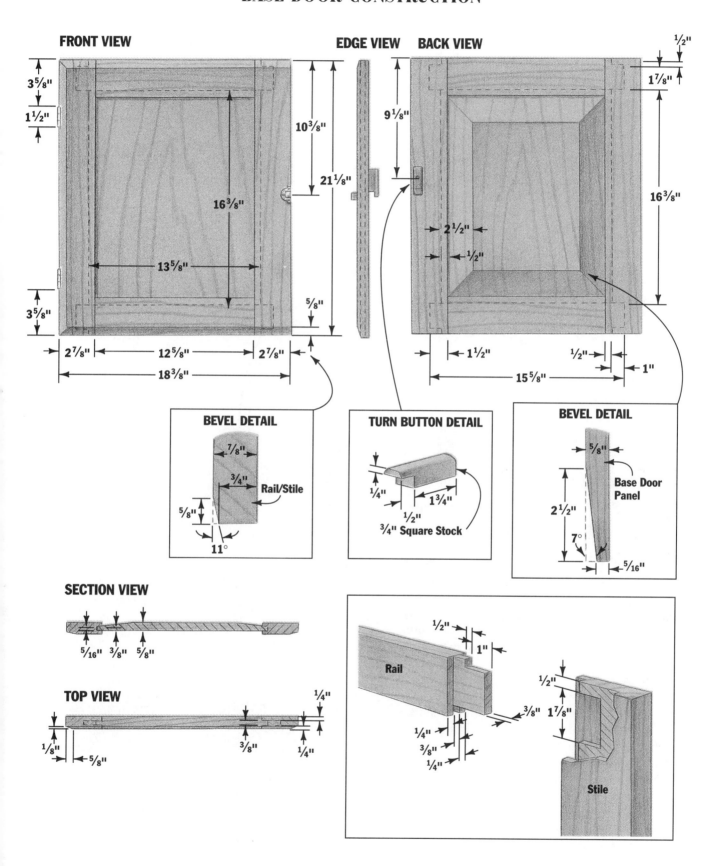

GLAZED DOOR CONSTRUCTION

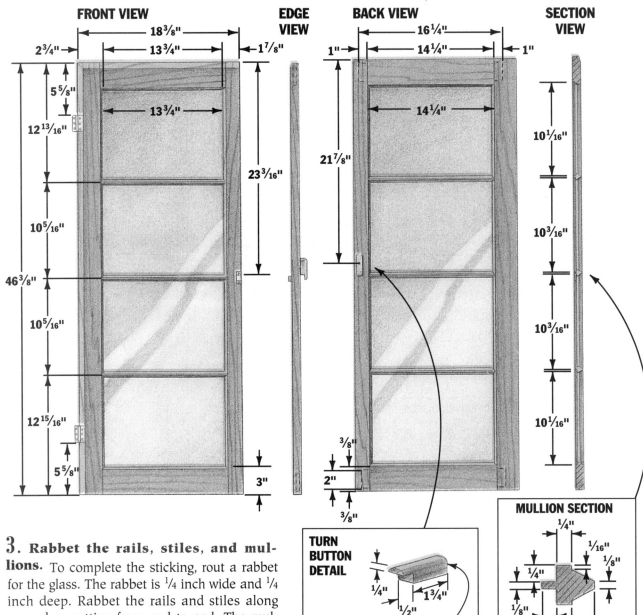

FRONT VIEW EDGE VIEW BACK VIEW SECTION VIEW

MULLION SECTION

TURN BUTTON DETAIL

3/4" Square Stock

3. Rabbet the rails, stiles, and mullions. To complete the sticking, rout a rabbet for the glass. The rabbet is $\frac{1}{4}$ inch wide and $\frac{1}{4}$ inch deep. Rabbet the rails and stiles along one edge, cutting from end to end. The mullions are rabbeted along two edges, again from end to end.

4. Cut the mortises and tenons. To join the rails and stiles in mortise-and-tenon joints, the tenon shoulders on the rails must be coped to conform to the sticking on the stiles *or* the sticking must be trimmed away where the rail abuts the stile. The latter approach is easier here.

The first step is to rout the mortises. Make them $1\frac{1}{4}$ inches deep; after the sticking is trimmed away, they'll be 1 inch deep.

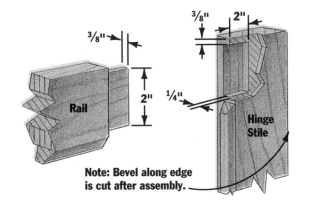

Rail

Hinge Stile

Note: Bevel along edge is cut after assembly.

Determine where the rails will intersect the stiles, and miter just the decorative sticking with a backsaw. Then trim the sticking away from the end of the rail to the miter cut, as shown in *Glazed Door Construction*.

The tenons are cut on the table saw in the usual way, but there's an extra step needed. The tenons should be 1 inch long. Make the shoulder cuts on the rails. Then miter the sticking. This can be done by tilting the blade to 45 degrees and guiding the workpiece with the miter gauge. Make the cheek cuts, and finally trim back the top and bottom edges and round off the tenons to fit the mortises.

5. Assemble the doors. Before you can actually assemble the doors, you have to cope the ends of the mullions. Because you have no tenon to work around, and because the mullions are so slender, this is not difficult to do. The challenge is to achieve

the proper fit without over-shortening any of the workpieces.

Use a coping saw to make the basic cut, and refine it as necessary with a small file. Cope one end of each mullion. Assemble the rails and stiles, and measure and mark the lengths required for the mullions. Mark and cut the mullions to length, coping the second end of each.

When you are finished, everything should fit together easily and accurately. Glue up the doors.

When the clamps are off the doors, cut the bevels on the hinge stile and the top rail (the bottom rail and latch stile are NOT beveled). The bevels are the same as those on the base doors.

6. Hang the doors. Ensure that the doors fit within the door opening with about 1/16 inch of clearance all around. Plane the edges of the doors as necessary to achieve the clearance.

The hinges on the glazed doors are butts, but they are surface-mounted. Installing them is a simple matter with the case lying on its back and the doors shimmed into position. Lay the hinges on the doors, make sure they're aligned, then drill pilot holes and drive the screws.

Attach the catch to the doors as shown in the *Front View* in *Glazed Door Construction*. Make and install a duplicate of the turn button used on the left-hand base door.

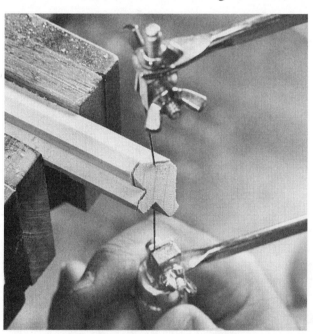

Coping a mullion is simple in concept, but it may take a little practice. Miter one end of the mullion stock. Holding the coping saw (or fret saw, shown here) at right angles to the run of the stock, cut along the arris between the molded surface and the mitered surface. If you stay on that arris—and that's pretty tough to do—you should have a perfect fit. If you find the arris hard to see, darken it by rubbing it with the side of a pencil's lead.

FINISH THE CUPBOARD

The original cupboard was finished inside and out with a red-brown milk paint. Our reproduction, as you can see in the cover photo, is painted blue, with the interior painted off-white. We used ordinary latex paint and had it tinted to the particular hue we wanted.

You may want to mimic the original and use

milk paint. Or you may have some other appearance in mind. Tips on applying several different finishes can be found in the *ShopSmarts* feature "Country Finishes" on page 305.

After the cupboard is finished, install the glass in the upper doors. Use glazing points to secure each pane, then apply glazing compound.

Coving on the Table Saw

The country woodworkers who built the originals shown in this furniture collection created cove moldings with a hand plane. Some contemporary woodworkers still do it that way, but there's usually less toil involved if you use the table saw or router to do the job.

To do it with a router—table-mounted only, please—you need one of two or three different router bits designed for the purpose. The bits leave a smooth surface, almost eliminating the need to sand, but there's a limited size range available.

The coves on our reproductions were cut on the table saw. This seems to be the most direct and versatile way to do it. You don't need a special cutter—a standard rip or combination blade does the job. To cut a cove, you simply guide the workpiece across the blade at an angle somewhere between 0 and 90 degrees. As shown in the drawing, this approach yields a wide variety of cove contours. And if you use a smaller-diameter blade—say, one from your 7$\frac{1}{4}$-inch circular saw—you can get another range of contours.

Cutting a cove on the table saw is as easy as 1-2-3. Use a ripping blade or a combination blade in the saw. Get both the miter gauge and the rip fence off the saw table.

To use as fences, you need two straight pieces of hardwood as long as the diagonal dimension of your saw's table. You need deep-throated clamps to secure these fences to the saw table. You need a parallel rule, which you can make (see "Parallel Rule" on page 173), to determine the angle at which to set the fences. Finally, you need a couple of jointer-type push blocks.

1. Set the blade height. Sketch the approximate cove profile you want on the end of a 2-foot length of the working stock. This will be your test piece. Lay it on the saw table, as shown in the Step 1 photo, and adjust the blade height to line up the highest tooth with the deepest part of the profile.

THE EFFECT OF FEED ANGLE

Blade is perpendicular to table in every case.

Fence Clamped across Saw Table

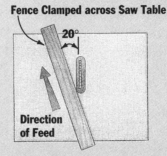

20°

Direction of Feed

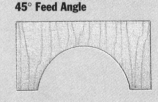

20° Feed Angle

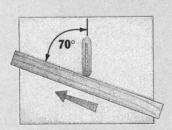

45°

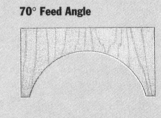

45° Feed Angle

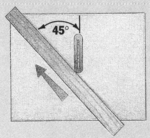

70°

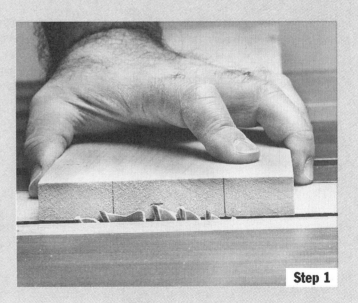

70° Feed Angle

Step 1

2. Find the fence angle. Adjust your shop-made parallel rule to the width of the desired cove. Set the rule on the saw table, straddling the blade as shown in the Step 2 photo, and slide the rule through an arc around the blade. What you want is the position at which both straightedges touch the blade simultaneously. It helps to move the blade by hand, so you can be sure the saw teeth are barely grazing the rule on both the infeed and outfeed sides.

Step 3

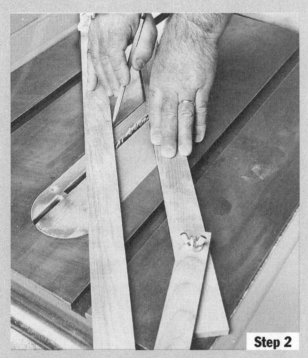

Step 2

When you've found the angle, scribe along the inside edge of each straightedge onto the saw table. If a pencil line doesn't show up, use a china marker. If your cove arcs from edge to edge, these are the marks to which you line up your fences.

3. Offset the layout lines to position the fences. In most cases, you need to offset the fences somewhat to accommodate a workpiece that's wider than the cove itself.

The Corner Cupboard is a good example. The working stock for the crown molding is more than 5 inches wide, but the cove is only $2^3/_{16}$ inches wide. There's a $1^1/_2$-inch-wide shoulder on one

side of the cove and a $1^3/_8$-inch-wide shoulder on the other. You have to offset the layout lines so you know where to position the fence.

To offset them, readjust the parallel rule by adding the width of one shoulder to the width of the cove. Align one straightedge with the layout line on the outfeed side of the blade. Scribe along the inside edge of the other straightedge, creating a fence line on the infeed side of the table.

4. Clamp the fence to the saw table. Set the first fence board on the line and clamp it securely to the saw table. Crank the blade down below the saw table. Place the sample workpiece against the fence, directly over the blade. Set the second fence against the sample, as shown in the Step 4 photo, and clamp it to the saw table. Be sure you position the clamps where they won't interfere with the movement of the work. Slide the workpiece through the channel to ensure that it moves freely, but without chattering from side to side.

(Okay. You *can* make the cut with a single fence, *so long as it is on the infeed side of the saw blade.* Otherwise, the blade will tend to pull

(continued)

Step 4

cove. You make lots of passes, nibbling away to form the profile.

Raise the blade so it projects $1/8$ inch above the saw table—no more than that!—and make the first cut. Use jointer-type push blocks, if you have them, to feed the workpiece. While you do need to provide downward pressure on the work at the same time you are advancing it, you shouldn't lay your hands on the work directly over the blade. (You wouldn't do that in jointing a board; don't do it here either.)

The danger in not applying enough downward pressure and in making too aggressive a cut—one with the blade set too high—is that the work will ride up on the blade. That's kickback position. The teeth will grab the work and throw it at you. So be very judicious in your cuts, and keep the pressure on.

After the first pass, raise the blade another $1/8$ inch. Make a second pass. Raise the blade another $1/8$ inch and make another pass. Just repeat the process again and again until you are just a skosh under the final depth. Raise the blade only $1/16$ inch for the final pass. This will yield a smoother surface, and that will reduce the amount of sanding you have to do.

the work away from the fence, and it may just throw it in your face! It is a lot safer to use two fences, as I've shown here.)

Now you are ready to cut.

5. Cut the cove. Even though it is your table saw, on which you are used to making cuts in single, dynamic passes, you have to work slowly to cut a

6. Sand the cove. It definitely will need sanding. If you can get a curved scraper into the cove, you can remove the saw marks more quickly with it.

Step 5

Step 6

Parallel Rule

One of the essential measuring devices you need to cut coves is the parallel rule. It is easy to make. You need only four strips of hardwood and four stove bolts, washers, and wing nuts.

1. **Cut the parts to size.** Cut the parts to the dimensions shown in the drawing *Parallel Rule Plan*. Use a stable, straight-grained hardwood so the rule will remain straight and true.

2. **Drill the holes.** The most important process in making the parallel rule is drilling the bolt holes. For the jig to work properly, the holes on each arm must be the same distance apart. The holes on each straightedge must be the same distance from the guiding, or outside, edge.

First, tape or clamp each pair of parts together, face to face, before you drill. Second, clamp a fence to your drill press table at the appropriate distance from the bit. This will place the holes an equal distance from one edge.

If you don't have a drill press, drill only one set of holes after taping the pairs together. Then remove the tape and flip one piece end-for-end. Now the hole in one piece can serve as a guide for drilling the remaining hole in the second piece. Make sure the edges that were paired the first time the pieces were taped together are the edges that are paired the second time. Then drill the remaining holes. Take care not to skew the holes.

Separate the pairs. Countersink the holes in the straightedges.

3. **Assemble the rule.** Bolt the pieces together with stove bolts and wing nuts. Spread the straightedges as wide as possible. Measure between them at their ends and at several other points to make sure they are parallel. Double-check at several other settings, too. If the two straightedges don't remain parallel at all settings, remake the rule.

PARALLEL RULE PLAN

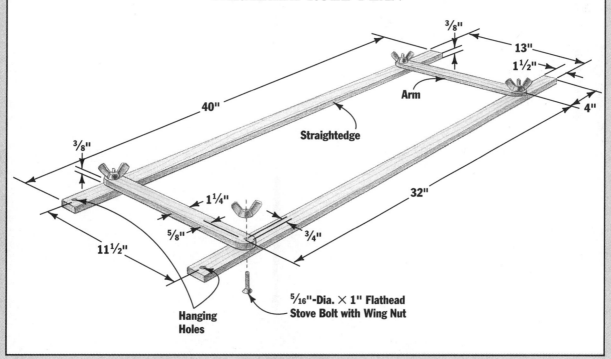

$\frac{3}{8}$"

13"

$1\frac{1}{2}$"

Arm

40"

4"

Straightedge

$\frac{3}{8}$"

$1\frac{1}{4}$"

32"

$\frac{5}{8}$"

$\frac{3}{4}$"

$11\frac{1}{2}$"

Hanging Holes

$\frac{5}{16}$"-Dia. × 1" Flathead Stove Bolt with Wing Nut

STAGE BOX

At first—and even second and third—glance, this box is a mystery. You *do* glance at the box more than once, because it is perversely intriguing.

Is that because it is so different from the typical small chest?

In size, it resembles a document box. But the single drawer, located at the top of the box, is in the wrong place. There's no lift lid either. Although there's clearly a compartment beneath the drawer, there's no obvious access to it. The box has a handle on top, so it must be something that's carried around.

Though roughly made and finished in a lusterless gray, it's attractive. The joinery isn't flawless. Even the dovetails are nailed. (Why would a woodworker *nail* dovetails?) It has an air of complete practicality about it. But it has an elegance to it, too. The handle, though primitive, is a wonderful handwrought curve, installed—inadvertently, I would guess—on a slight skew across the top. Personalizing the box are two large, crudely carved initials: A.K.

Even the name—stage box—doesn't immediately expose it. Today "stage" first connotes the performing arts and not, as it might have in the eighteenth and nineteenth centuries, public transit. What the stage box is is the forerunner of today's attaché case. In his stage box, the driver of a stage coach or freight wagon kept fares, bills of lading, and other business papers. Perhaps his own personal valuables were stashed in it, too.

The drawer has two compartments and a lock. Locking the drawer effectively bars access to the box's contents, since to get to the space beneath the drawer, you have to remove the drawer completely. The practicality of the drawer's position is that only a single lock is needed, not an insignificant consideration when manufactured locks were expensive and difficult to come by.

The nails in the dovetails are a practical measure as well. Both driver and stage box would be out in the weather. A good downpour would soak them both, and a soaking would dissolve hide glue pretty quickly. Thus a glued stage box is a short-lived, insecure stage box. Hence the nails.

The stage box is a swell accent project. It's unusual and attractive, with the added benefit of being practical.

If you do tackle the project, be aware that you need to resaw or plane almost all the material to ½ inch or less in thickness.

Also be aware that you have to either hand cut the dovetails or rout them with a commercial jig for cutting through dovetails. Those devices meeting the need include the Leigh jig, Porter-

The original stage box (*above*) held a teamster's bills of lading, but the reproduction (*opposite*) can hold household bills and accounts.

175

CUTTING LIST

Piece	Number	Thickness	Width	Length	Material
Ends	2	$1/2$"	6"	8"	pine
Front	1	$1/2$"	3"	16"	pine
Back	1	$1/2$"	6"	16"	pine
Top	1	$1/2$"	8"	16"	pine
Bottom	1	$1/4$"	8"	16"	pine
Drawer supports	2	$1/4$"	1"	7"	pine
Drawer front	1	$3/4$"	$3^1/2$"	$15^5/8$"	pine
Drawer sides	2	$1/4$"	$2^{11}/16$"	$7^3/8$"	pine
Drawer back/divider	2	$1/4$"	$2^{11}/16$"	$14^3/8$"	pine
Drawer bottom	1	$1/4$"	$7^3/8$"	$14^7/8$"	pine*

HARDWARE

$1/2$" × 18-gauge wire brads

2d cut brads

1 lock (for drawer)

1 handwrought handle with matching staples†

1 brass pull, $1/2$" dia. × $1/2$" high, with integral screw. Item H-42, Desk Interior Knob, from Horton Brasses (203-635-4400).

*The drawer bottom can be formed of two or more separate boards without edge-gluing them.

† See "Making the Handle" on page 180.

Cable's Omnijig, Keller templates, and the incremental positioning jigs like the Jointech or Incra jig.

Finally, you have to confront the handle. The handle is an important part of the box. Without it, the box just wouldn't be as interesting. But it isn't something you can pick up at the hardware store or buy out of a catalog. The only way you'll get one is to get involved with blacksmithing, either by making it yourself or by finding a blacksmith to make it for you. At the same time he or she makes the handle, have the smith make a couple of staples to secure it to the box. Failing that, you can use either the largest bail-type handle you can find or simply forgo the handle.

1. Cut the box parts. The ends, top, front, and back are cut from $1/2$-inch-thick stock, while the bottom is $1/4$-inch-thick stock. Resaw or plane boards to the required thicknesses, then rip and crosscut the parts to the dimensions specified by the Cutting List.

2. Rout the dovetails. The ends are joined to the front and back by through dovetails. On the original, the hand-cut dovetails are irregular in size and spacing. The dovetails aren't all that difficult to cut by hand, and hand cutting them will enhance your stage box.

But as I already admitted, the dovetails in our reproduction were machine-cut. A number of different through-dovetail jigs are on the market. Whatever jig you use will have step-by-step instructions specific to it. (We used the through-dovetail template for Porter-Cable's Omnijig.) Typically, the jig's template has fingers that regulate the movement of the template guide–equipped router. The fingers can be moved to adjust the spacing between tails. You use a dovetail bit to cut the tails, then switch to a straight bit to rout the pins.

Because the spacing of the dovetails joining the ends and the back is different from that of the dove-

EXPLODED VIEW

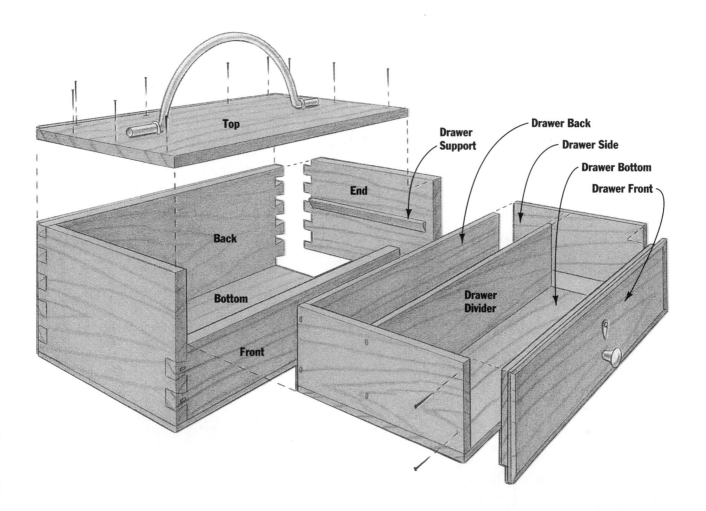

tails joining the ends and the front, you have to rout the joints separately.

Set the finger spacing for the back dovetails first. Rout the tails on both ends of the back board using a 3/4-inch dovetail bit. Switch to the appropriate straight bit, and make any adjustments that might be required by your jig when shifting from tail cutting to pin cutting. Then rout the pins on the back edges of the ends.

Set the finger spacing for the front dovetails next. Rout the tails on both ends of the front. Then switch bits and rout the pins on the front edges of the ends.

3. Assemble the box without its top. Once the dovetails are cut, assemble the ends, front, and back without glue, and lay out the positions of the drawer supports. Knock the box apart, and make and attach the supports to the ends.

The supports can be quickly hand planed from a couple of 7-inch strips of 1/4 × 1-inch stock. But you may choose to tilt the blade of your table saw about 10 degrees, and rip a couple of wedge-shaped strips. Attach the supports with 1/2-inch wire brads or nails (no glue).

Apply glue to the pins and tails, and join the front and back to the ends. Lay the bottom in place and nail it with cut brads. (Not at all like wire brads, cut brads are so thick you'll wonder why they're called brads.) Since the stock is thin, you'll need to drill pilot holes to avoid splitting the wood.

After the bottom is secure, drill pilot holes and drive a brad through each tail into the pinboard.

4. Cut the drawer parts. The drawer front is the thickest piece in the entire box and can be cut from a standard 1-by board. The sides, back, divider, and bottom are all ¼ inch thick. To economize, you can resaw 1-by stock for these parts. Each 1-by board should yield two pieces of the required thickness. Plane or sand the resawed stock to smooth it, then rip and crosscut the parts to the dimensions specified by the Cutting List. It isn't necessary to have a one-piece bottom, by the way; use two or three narrow strips for it if that's easier (it was for the builder of the original).

5. Make the drawer front. The front is rabbeted around all four edges, as shown in *Drawer Construction*. This can be done quickly and easily on the table saw or router table.

For decoration, the front is slightly beveled around the edges of its face. Do this with a few licks of a block plane.

PLAN VIEWS

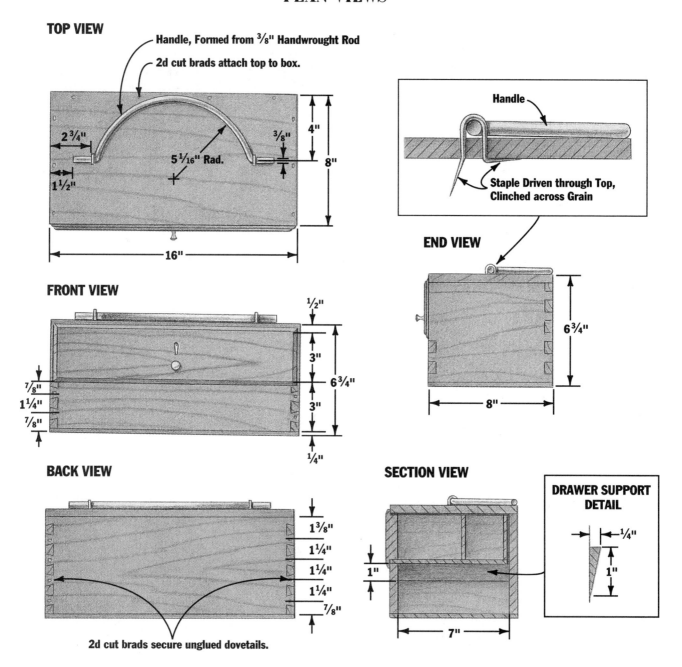

TOP VIEW

Handle, Formed from ⅜" Handwrought Rod

2d cut brads attach top to box.

2¾"

5 1/16" Rad.

⅜"

4"

8"

1½"

16"

FRONT VIEW

½"

3"

3"

6¾"

⅞"

1¼"

⅞"

¼"

BACK VIEW

1⅜"

1¼"

1¼"

1¼"

⅞"

2d cut brads secure unglued dovetails.

Handle

Staple Driven through Top, Clinched across Grain

END VIEW

6¾"

8"

SECTION VIEW

1"

7"

DRAWER SUPPORT DETAIL

¼"

1"

Finally, *with the lock in hand,* lay out and cut the mortise it requires. For the sake of appearance, position the lock so the keyhole is in the center of the drawer. With some lock models, this may cause the lock itself to be slightly offset, but that's okay. We used a surface lock, which doesn't need a mortise (catalog number 32H88 from Constantine's, 800-223-8087). The keyhole was formed by drilling several ¼-inch-diameter holes in the proper location, then blending them together with a thin flat file.

6. Assemble the drawer. The drawer parts are nailed together, using the same 2d cut brads—big as they are—used in the box. It works. Just be sure to drill adequate pilot holes. Nail the sides to the front,

and to the back and divider as well. Then lay the bottom (or bottom pieces) overlapping the frame and nail it in place.

7. Install the box top. Before attaching the top, cut a mortise for the lock bolt (and attach the strike, if one was supplied with the lock). This is a simple matter of locating the spot and paring a shallow slot. A strike should be mortised into the top so it won't interfere with the drawer's movement.

If you have had a handle made, install it before attaching the top. Lay the handle on the top, and press the staples into the top to mark where to drill pilot holes. Drill the holes. Insert the staples over the handle and through the pilots; then carefully

DRAWER CONSTRUCTION

TOP VIEW

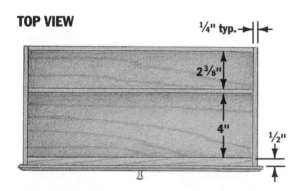

¼" typ.

2⅜"

4"

½"

FRONT VIEW

Form ¼"-wide bevel with block plane.

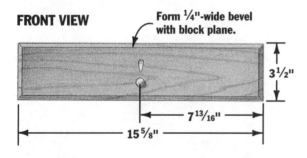

3½"

7¹³⁄₁₆"

15⅝"

SIDE VIEW

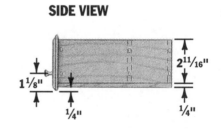

2¹¹⁄₁₆"

1⅛"

¼"

¼"

BOTTOM VIEW

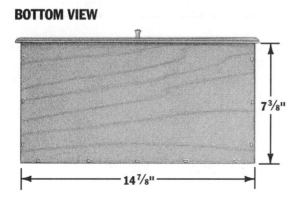

7⅜"

14⅞"

BACK VIEW

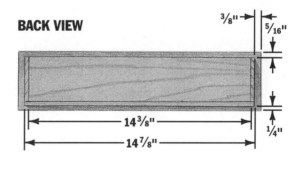

⅜"

5⁄₁₆"

14⅜"

14⅞"

¼"

Making the Handle

Here's how to make a suitable handle and staples for your stage box reproduction. You need a propane torch, a couple pairs of pliers, a ball-peen hammer, and a metal vise (your woodworking bench vise will suffice so long as any nonmetal cauls are removed from the jaws).

The handle is formed from a 36-inch-long piece of $^3/_8$-inch steel rod. To get the bow, make a wooden form. Scribe a $5^1/_8$-inch-radius arc on a scrap of 2 × 12 so the arc cuts across the end grain rather than the long grain. Cut the arc. Clamp the form in your vise, and cold-bend the rod over the form.

You can enhance your leverage if you insert the rod between the vise and the form. Stand to the opposite side of the form. Drop one end of the rod into the loop, and use both hands to pull the rod toward you (left photo below).

After you've bent the rod, cut off the excess at either end.

To form the sharp bends at the ends of the handle, you'll have to heat the metal. An ordinary propane torch will do the job. Concentrate the blue tip of the flame on the spot where you want to make the bend. Hold the rod with a pair of Vise-Grips to avoid burning your hand (right photo below). To position the bend, mark the vise, not the metal—any mark you make on the metal will burn off. The tabs

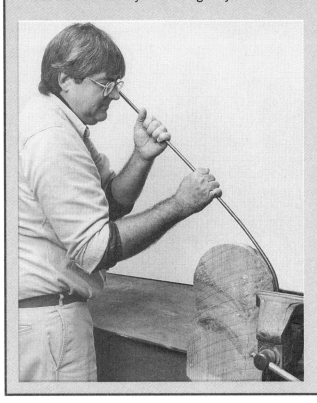
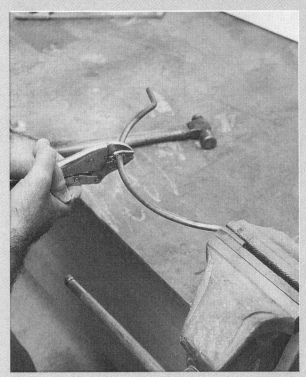

bend the shanks, clinching them across the grain. Be careful not to break the top as you do this.

With this work done, nail the top to the box with the 2d cut brads.

8. Apply the finish. It's fitting, perhaps, given the utility of the stage box, that the original is painted gray. To punch up the color, we used a blue milk paint to finish our reproduction. A step-by-step sequence for applying milk paint can be found in the *ShopSmarts* feature "Country Finishes" on page 305.

After the finish is dry, turn the pull into the drawer front, and install the lock.

on the handle are $1\frac{1}{4}$ to $1\frac{1}{2}$ inches long. Measure from the edge of the jaw, and mark. When the handle rod is red-hot where you want to bend, slide the tip between the jaws, right up to the mark, then tighten the vise. Quickly bend the handle. Do both ends of the handle in this manner.

You can make the necessary staples in a similar fashion, using common fence staples. Straighten out a couple of the staples.

Holding a staple with pliers, heat it with the propane torch. When it's red-hot, hold it against the vise, and strike it with the hammer, drawing it to more of a point. When you have achieved a suitable point on one end, reheat the staple and draw out the other end. When you are done, quench the still-hot metal in water.

Heating the staple anneals it, so that, even when cold, it can easily be bent around the handle to form it back into a staple (left photo below). Drill pilot holes, and drive the staples through the box's top, capturing the handle. With the pliers, carefully bend the very tips of the staple so the tips will dig into the wood when you clinch the staple shanks.

Because the pine is so soft, it will break if you try to hammer the staple to clinch it across the wood. Instead, use your pliers to get the bend started, then tighten the top in your vise, forcing the staple shank against the wood (right photo below).

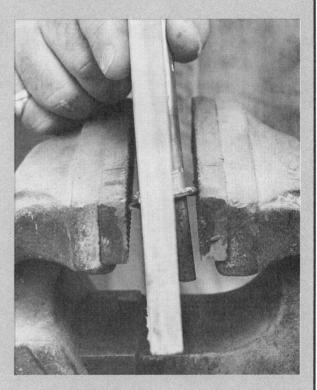

SPLAY-LEG TABLE

More simple to build than it looks, this table is a great weekend project. It's versatile: It could be a bedside table, a chair-side table, even a plant stand. The original's owner uses it as a lamp table next to a wooden settee.

I've seen pieces similar to this one referred to as "country Hepplewhite." The rationale is that George Hepplewhite used the plain tapered leg on many pieces in his furniture design sketchbook, published in London in 1788. In many minds, then, the tapered leg is associated with Hepplewhite. Those same minds recognize Hepplewhite as one of the famous furniture names, right there on the list with Chippendale, Queen Anne, Sheraton, and William and Mary. And so the "country Hepplewhite" label is intended to make the prospective customer think an old table with tapered legs is somehow more special than it is.

This form of marketing hype flows, of course, from the idea that country furniture designs were bastardized forms of sophisticated city furniture designs. Granting truth to that idea—and I'm not inclined to do that—denigrates the design skills of the country woodworker. In this case, then, the country Hepplewhite label suggests that the table so-labeled is the result when a second-rate woodworker tries to copy a sophisticated design. Given that Hepplewhite's stated design objective was "to unite ele-

gance and utility," and having seen samples of his designs, I'd say the country woodworker did a better job of achieving the objective.

You and I don't need a label to recognize the merits of this little table. It is frankly quite plain, with only a bead along the bottom edge of the aprons as a decoration. It uses a minimum of materials and has simple, strong joinery but in its proportions is elegant. To me, it's a positive example of the workman's aesthetic.

The country woodworker, we all know, wasn't necessarily a full-time furniture maker. Making furniture was something he did to supplement income from farming or some other work. Because he didn't work wood every day—or even every month—he never really developed finesse as a woodworker (just like a lot of us hobby woodworkers). So he didn't use complex joinery, and even the simple joints he crafted weren't seamlessly tight. He didn't have the specialized tools, so his creations tended to be plain and unembellished.

But his creations didn't lack an aesthetic. It simply was one shaped by the tools at his disposal and the skills he had mastered. It was shaped, too, by the intended use of the finished piece. This is the so-called workman's aesthetic.

So in the case of this splay-leg table, the design may have grown out of convention

Used in a tavern, the original table (*above*) provided dining accommodation for one. In a contemporary home, the reproduction (*opposite*) serves at the bedside.

EXPLODED VIEW

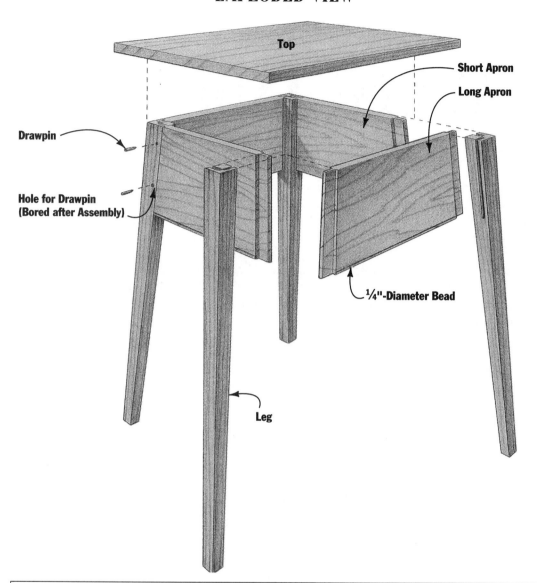

Top

Short Apron

Long Apron

Drawpin

Hole for Drawpin
(Bored after Assembly)

¼"-Diameter Bead

Leg

CUTTING LIST

Piece	Number	Thickness	Width	Length	Material
Legs	4	$1^5/_8$"	$1^5/_8$"	29"	pine
Long aprons	2	$^3/_4$"	$5^7/_8$"	$17^3/_4$"	1-by pine
Short aprons	2	$^3/_4$"	$5^7/_8$"	$15^1/_2$"	1-by pine
Top	1	$^5/_8$"	20"	$23^1/_4$"	1-by pine
Drawpins	16	$^5/_{16}$"	$^5/_{16}$"	$^3/_4$"	hardwood

HARDWARE
6d cut nails

(affecting the table's height, for example), out of the nature of the materials on hand (affecting the kind of wood used, for example, as well as the dimensions of the tabletop, which would dictate the dimensions of the leg-and-apron assembly)), and out of mastered skills (affecting the joinery used). The woodworker used tapered legs because they looked better than straight, square legs and because he could hand plane the leg billets to an attractive taper. No special tools or skills needed.

One thing the woodworker knew was that a small table can be tippy if the legs are too close together. The splay of the legs provides a broader base without making the table larger than the top. It makes the table more stable.

Although the splayed-leg configuration could result in compound angles between legs and aprons, that isn't the case here, because the aprons are angled, too. From a construction standpoint, you work strictly with simple angles. But when you assemble the parts, the result is a complex appearance.

As I said earlier, the table is an excellent weekend project. You can get the table built in a long shop session on Saturday, followed by a relatively short session on Sunday. Working after supper on successive days during the week, you can apply the finish. Within seven days, the table's really all done.

It may take longer to settle on the one place in your house where you want to keep it—bedroom, living room, family room, den. Try it here, try it there. This table looks good no matter where you put it.

---

1. Glue up the tabletop. The dimensions are specified by the Cutting List. Since the part is 20 inches wide, you'll have to edge-glue several narrow boards to form it. A step-by-step sequence for doing this is presented in the *ShopSmarts* feature "Gluing Up Panels" on page 49. Once this part is clamped, it can be set aside to cure, and you can move on to the other parts.

2. Taper the legs. The dimensions of the leg blanks are specified by the Cutting List. These will have to be glued up from 1-by or 5/4 stock or else resawed or planed down from 8/4 stock.

The legs can be tapered most expeditiously on the table saw. The operation is explained fully in the *ShopSmarts* feature "Tapering Legs on the Table Saw" on page 189. Lay out the taper on one of the leg blanks. Note that the legs are tapered from end to end on all four sides. Use the leg to set up the tapering jig, as explained in the *ShopSmarts* feature. Taper the legs.

Sand away any saw marks.

3. Cut the joinery in the legs. Ordinarily, mortises in legs are excavated before the leg is shaped in any way. But in this case, the mortises must be parallel to the tapered surfaces, so it is sensible to cut them *after* the tapers are cut.

Routing mortises is another common woodworking task that's explained fully in a *ShopSmarts* feature. Following the general plan in "Cutting Mortise-and-Tenon Joints" on page 83,

LEG LAYOUTS

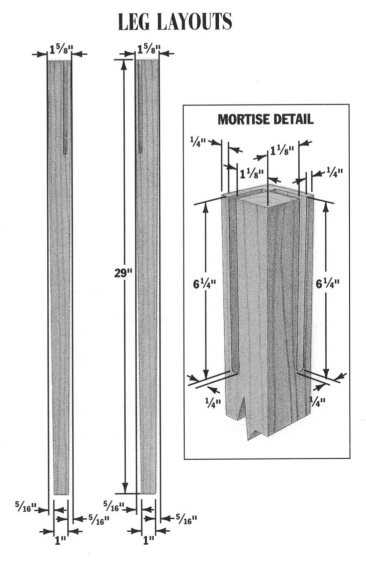

MORTISE DETAIL

PLAN VIEWS

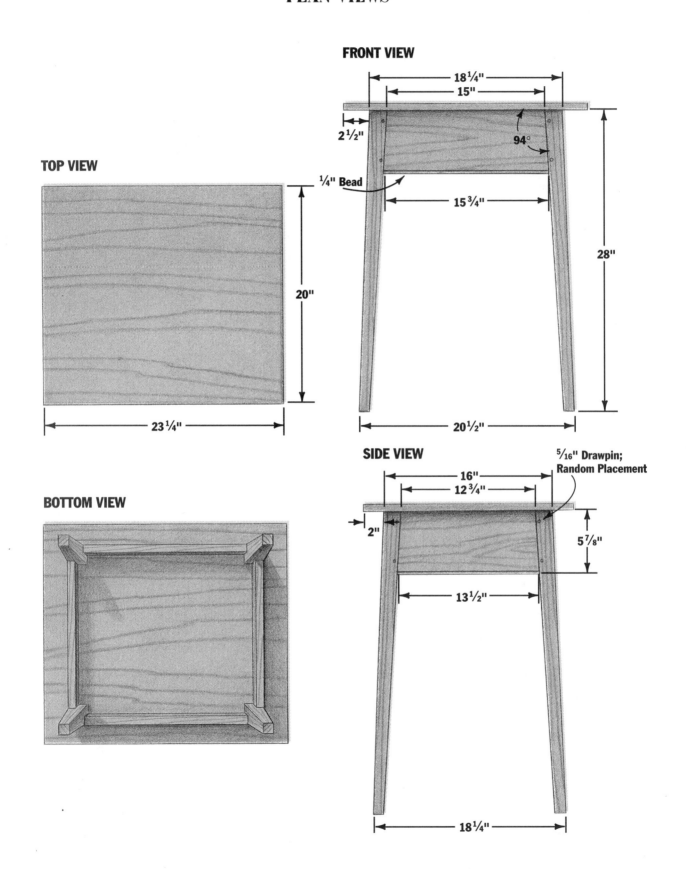

FRONT VIEW

18¼"

15"

2½"

94°

¼" Bead

15¾"

28"

20½"

TOP VIEW

20"

23¼"

BOTTOM VIEW

SIDE VIEW

⁵⁄₁₆" Drawpin;
Random Placement

16"

12¾"

2"

5⅞"

13½"

18¼"

make a mortising fixture to accommodate the legs. Use a plunge router fitted with an edge guide and a ¼-inch straight bit to rout the mortises.

4. Make the aprons. Cut the aprons to the dimensions specified by the Cutting List. Miter the ends of the aprons as shown in *Apron Layouts*.

(Don't reset the gauge after mitering the aprons. Whatever setting you use to miter the aprons can also be used to cut part of each tenon. To complete the tenons, you *will* have to reset the gauge, but don't do that until you've cut one cheek on each of the project's eight tenons.)

To cut the tenons, use a dado cutter. Stack (or adjust) the cutter to produce a cut about ⅝ to ¾ inch wide. Adjust the depth of cut to no more than ¼ inch. Set the table saw's rip fence 1 inch from the outside of the cutter. To guide the workpiece, use the miter gauge, of course. Butt the end of the first apron against the fence, and make the shoulder cut. Back the piece away from the fence and make a second pass, completing the cheek. Repeat the process to cut one cheek on each tenon.

To cut the second cheek, reset the miter gauge. Loosen the locking knob. Butt an apron against the

fence at the new angle, then slide the miter gauge into position, letting the head pivot into the correct new angle. Tighten the knob to lock the head. Now cut the second cheek of each tenon.

Test Cuts Prove the Setup

To get satisfactory tenons, with both shoulders having the same depth, you need to set the height of the dado cutter carefully. Make test cuts on scraps of the apron stock to prove the setup. The length and angle of the cuts are immaterial. Simply nick one face of the scrap, then turn it over, and nick the same area of the second face, forming a projection the same thickness as the tenon will be.

Insert the projection into one of the mortises to check the fit. If it is too loose, lower the cutter a skosh. If it is too tight, raise the cutter. But just remember: The amount of every change will be doubled, since you are cutting twice on each tenon.

APRON LAYOUTS

LONG APRONS

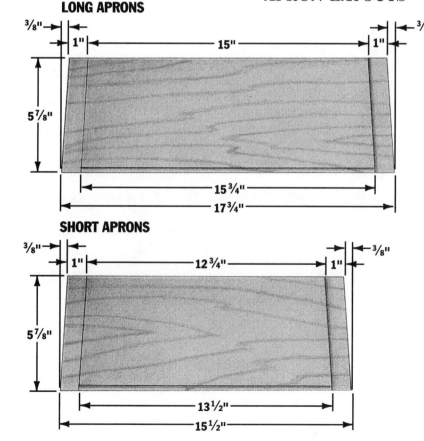

SHORT APRONS

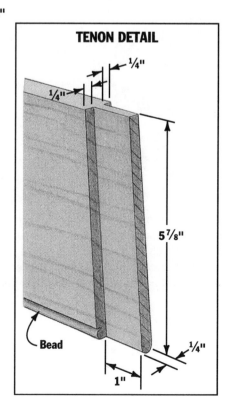

TENON DETAIL

Complete the tenons by rounding-over the bottom edges to conform to the routed mortises. Use a file to do this.

Finally, rout a ¼-inch-diameter bead along the bottom edge of each apron, as shown in the *Tenon Detail* of the *Apron Layouts*.

5. Assemble the legs and aprons. The table now begins to take form. Assemble the legs and aprons without glue to check how the joints fit. Do any necessary trimming.

Cut four pairs of clamping wedges next. Because the legs splay, there are no square surfaces for the clamps. But by making wedge-shaped cauls, you can both protect the legs from clamp damage and give the clamps something to address squarely.

Spread glue on the tenons and in the mortises, and assemble the legs and aprons. Apply pipe or bar

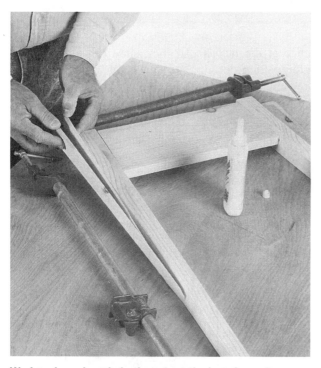

Wedge-shaped cauls both protect the legs from clamp damage and provide the clamps with something to address squarely. In assembling the table, I used the scraps left when the legs were tapered. Double up the scraps, as shown, putting two of the wedges under each jaw.

clamps. Although the shoulders of the tenons are angled while the mortises are square, pine is soft enough to be crushed into a proper fit.

After the glue has cured and you've removed the clamps, pin the joints. Cut 16 drawpins from ⁵⁄₁₆-inch dowel, and whittle a bit of taper on one end of each. Drill two ¹¹⁄₁₆-inch-deep holes into each joint, boring through the leg about ³⁄₈ inch from the seam between leg and apron. Apply glue to the pins, and drive one into each hole. Trim them flush with a chisel.

6. Square the leg ends. This needs to be done for several reasons. First of all, the legs are a little too long, because they were cut a bit long. Then, because of the compound angle between leg and aprons, the leg tops aren't flush with the top edges of the aprons. And finally, because of the leg splay, the legs don't rest flat on the floor.

Trim the leg tops first. Rest a handsaw across the aprons, and thus guided, saw through the leg. When all the legs are trimmed, you can sand them smooth and flat with a belt sander.

Do the bottoms of the legs next. It is likely the table will stand square and even as it is. Set it on the workbench and, if necessary, shim the legs to eliminate wobble or to level the assembly. With a compass set to the fraction that must be trimmed, scribe along the bench top around each leg. Trim the legs with a handsaw or a belt sander.

7. Attach the tabletop. As was the case with many old tables, the original's top was simply nailed in place. Though the nails hold the top securely, there's enough give to allow the top to expand and contract. Use 6d cut nails. You can drive them flush with the surface, or countersink them and cover the heads with wood putty.

8. Apply a finish. Although the original's builder undoubtedly painted it, the original now has a varnish over honey-colored stain finish. We did our best to duplicate that appearance.

A couple of approaches to staining pine that you can try are outlined in the *ShopSmarts* feature "Country Finishes" on page 305.

Tapering Legs on the Table Saw

Tapered legs support a half-dozen of the projects in this book. And there may be at least that many ways to do the job. I've tapered legs on a jointer, on the router table, and on the table saw.

A good—and safe—way to do it is on the table saw with the shop-made tapering jig shown here. As I'm sure you know, there's no one best way to do anything, and tapering legs is no different. But let me outline the genesis of my jig, then you give it a try and make your own judgment. It's an approach *I* like.

Plans for a number of different tapering jigs, including adjustable ones, have been published. All have two drawbacks, as far as I'm concerned.

Calculating the setting is one. The published explanations always involve math equations and terms like "taper per foot" and "rise" and "run." All I have to do is *think* about it, and my wife will nudge me in the ribs and say, "You're grinding your teeth."

Safety is the other concern. To taper a leg, you have to set two pieces together—one the leg billet, the other the jig—and push them by the saw blade. Instinctively, you want to put at least a finger on the leg billet to keep it tightly in the jig. And that puts your finger just a fraction of an inch from the blade. I've tried using a push stick or two for this operation; it brings to mind stilt-walking, and I'm no good at *that* either.

The jig I came up with solves both problems. It's easy to set up, because you use a leg billet with the taper marked on it to set up the jig. And it is safe to use, because two big toggle clamps hold the leg billet in the jig, and at the same time serve as handles for you to use to feed the jig across the saw table.

The jig is made of a good-sized piece of plywood, two toggle clamps, some pickings from the scrap bin, and a handful of drywall screws. The toggle clamps I selected are De-Sta-Co's 207-UL model, and I outfitted them with 3-inch spindles with two check nuts. (The clamps, of course, can be used on other jigs when this one's not in use.)

The step-by-step of tapering a leg begins with the jig setup.

TAPERING JIG

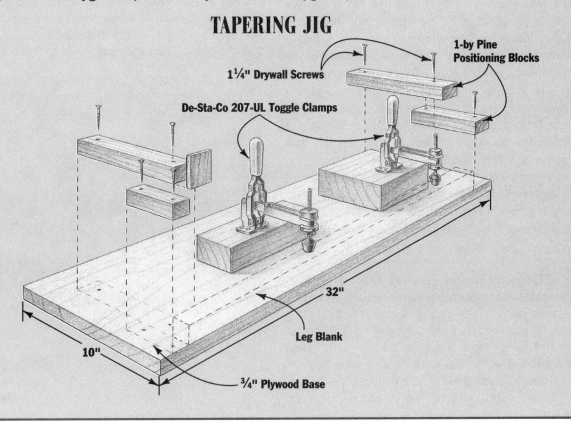

1¼" Drywall Screws

1-by Pine Positioning Blocks

De-Sta-Co 207-UL Toggle Clamps

32"

Leg Blank

10"

¾" Plywood Base

(continued)

Step 1

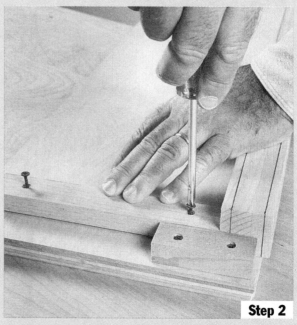

Step 2

1. Set a laid-out leg on the base. To set up the jig, you first must lay out the taper on one face of a leg billet.

Locate and mark the spot at which the taper will begin. If the leg is tapered from end to end, the taper begins at the top. If the leg is square just to the bottom of the apron, then begins to taper, that's the spot you mark. If there's a drop—that is, if the taper begins some distance *below* the apron's bottom edge—then mark that spot.

Lay out the dimensions of the foot at the bottom. With a straightedge and pencil, draw a line from one spot to the other. If the leg is tapered on all four sides, you need to draw two lines on the leg's face, as shown in the Step 1 photo.

Set the leg billet on the 10 × 32-inch piece of ¾-inch plywood that will be the jig's base. Position the leg as shown in the Step 1 photo, with the marked cut line directly over the edge of the base, and with about equal space at each end.

2. Place four blocks of scrap against the leg. As shown in the Step 2 photo, one scrap is butted against each end of the leg to keep it from shifting fore or aft. The other two scraps are positioned to keep the leg from sliding in on the base, away from the edge. Drill pilot holes and drive two drywall screws through each scrap into the base.

Now, when you slide the jig between the rip fence and the blade, the blade will cut off anything extending beyond the edge of the base, to wit, that little wedge of wood that needs to be removed to taper the leg.

3. Add the toggle clamps. Since the leg billet can still jump around a little, we aren't done yet. It can pop up out of place, or slip to the left before you get it to the blade. The toggle clamps keep it in place.

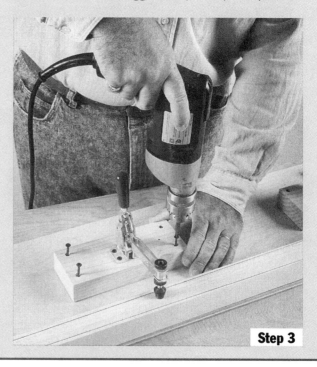

Step 3

I mounted the clamps up on 2 × 4 blocks. One is positioned near the leg's top, the other roughly midway along the taper. I screwed the clamps to the blocks, then screwed the blocks to the base.

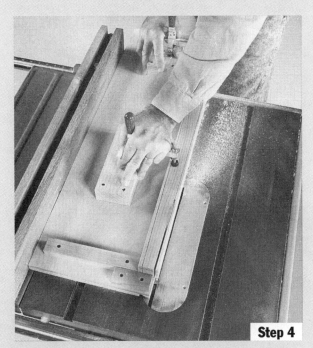

Step 4

Step 5

4. Cut the taper. Set up the table saw for the cut. Use the jig to set the rip fence. Crank the blade high enough to cut through the blank, mounted where it is, up on the jig's base.

Set a leg billet in the jig, and lock the clamps. Switch on the saw and make the cut. The upright handles of the clamps make good handles for feeding the jig across the saw table (and if you angle them slightly, you will be pushing the clamps closed at the same time you are advancing the jig). My usual routine is to make two cuts on one leg before moving to the next.

If your project is, say, the Drop-Leaf Kitchen Table (page 19), the legs are now properly tapered. They're ready to be sanded. If you are tapering legs for the Side Table (page 143), which requires all four sides to be tapered, you still have cuts to make.

5. Adjust the jig for the third and fourth cuts. For the third and fourth cuts, the leg position has to be shifted. Set the laid-out—and partially tapered—leg in the jig, and line up the layout line over the edge of the base. Measure the distance between the cut face and the positioning block. You can cut a little spacer to that thickness, or you can simply back out the two screws holding that positioning block, move it, and redrive the screws. I usually do the latter; it only takes a second.

6. Complete the tapers. With the jig adjusted, you can now make the third and fourth taper cuts quickly *and safely*.

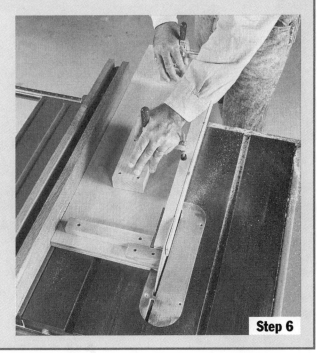

Step 6

BLANKET CHEST

Deciding what to call this project was quite a challenge. Not the "chest" part, of course. That came naturally. But the "blanket" part was hard.

Why? Because chests like this have been called dower chests, blanket chests, storage chests, feed chests. At one time or another in its past, this chest could have been any or all of those. In the time I've owned it, it's been used as a storage chest and a blanket chest. An avid antiquer once swore to me that it was originally a feed chest. Now it holds the television up off the floor.

What this all points up is the versatility and utility of this type of construction. It's a bin with a hinged lid. You put *stuff* in it, and though the *stuff* won't necessarily be organized and easily accessible, it will be collected, protected, and out of sight. If the chest had a lock built into it, as did this one, the *stuff* could be secured as well.

The basic style is known as the six-board chest, a name I like because it doesn't burden the piece with a "usage" connotation. "Use it for whatever purpose that suits," the name says. "All it takes is six boards." (Need I point out that the six boards are the two ends, the two sides, the bottom, and the

lid?) So I was all set to call this example a six-board chest, until I counted the boards. Seven, by strict count. Shoot!

The seventh board, the one that scotched the name, hardly qualifies as a *board* by the standards of the days in which the chest was built. It's a 3-inch-wide ledger, to which the lid is hinged. Held to a strict accounting, any six-board chest built today would be pretty small. To build this one, we had to glue up about five contemporary boards to make a panel as wide as a single board used to be. Even at the turn of the century (the one that switched us from the nineteenth to the twentieth, not the one that's coming up), boards that were 2 feet and more wide were commonplace. A woodworker could literally take six boards and build a chest like this. In fact, that darn ledger just might have been ripped from the lid board.

But the name was still in play. I thought through what I knew of this chest's history.

I bought it a good 30 years ago. I was working for a moving company for the summer, and one of the company's salesmen had opened a second-hand store. He'd give people a cost estimate for moving, then buy up what they didn't want to pay to move. On the

Brass lifts give the reproduction blanket chest (*opposite*) an elegance lacking in the original, with its iron lifts (*above*).

CUTTING LIST

Piece	Number	Thickness	Width	Length	Material
Sides	2	$7/8$"	$23\frac{1}{8}$"	$43\frac{3}{4}$"	5/4 pine
Ends	2	$7/8$"	$23\frac{1}{8}$"	$20\frac{1}{2}$"	5/4 pine
Bottom	1	$7/8$"	$21\frac{3}{4}$"	$43\frac{3}{4}$"	5/4 pine
Ledger	1	$7/8$"	3"	$44\frac{1}{16}$"	5/4 pine
Lid	1	$7/8$"	$18\frac{3}{4}$"	$44\frac{1}{16}$"	5/4 pine
Base molding	1	$3/8$"	$1\frac{3}{4}$"	$44\frac{1}{2}$"	pine
Base molding	2	$3/8$"	$1\frac{3}{4}$"	$22\frac{1}{8}$"	pine
Lid molding	1	$1\frac{1}{16}$"	$1\frac{3}{8}$"	$45\frac{9}{16}$"	5/4 pine
Lid molding	2	$1\frac{1}{16}$"	$1\frac{3}{8}$"	$18\frac{3}{4}$"	5/4 pine
Lid molding	2	$1\frac{1}{16}$"	$1\frac{3}{8}$"	3"	5/4 pine

HARDWARE

2 pr. hinges, $2\frac{1}{2}$" × $1\frac{1}{2}$"

1 chest lock, $5/8$" × $3\frac{15}{16}$" selvedge, $1\frac{3}{16}$" backset, $3\frac{15}{16}$" × $2\frac{1}{8}$" overall. Catalog number 4462 from Paxton Hardware (410-592-8505).

1 escutcheon, $1\frac{1}{8}$" × $1\frac{5}{8}$". Catalog number 248 from Paxton Hardware.

2 brass chest lifts, $4\frac{1}{2}$" boring, $6\frac{1}{2}$" × $2\frac{1}{2}$" overall. Catalog number 5138 from Paxton Hardware.

8d finish nails

6d finish nails

evening I visited his store, the chest was the only piece worth a second look.

Not that I was particularly discriminating. I just saw ten dollars' worth of value in a big chest that would hold a lot of stuff. I regarded the paint as ugly, I know, and stripped it so I could see the wood. I can't really remember what it looked like, but I have a guilty feeling it was grain-painted. The chest was perched on ridiculous little metal casters, which I removed straightaway. The chest had a lock, but it was keyless and disabled.

The chest was and still is a plain, sturdy, utilitarian piece. So much so that the feed chest conceit is believable. A feed chest was a utilitarian form of the classic six-board chest. Stationed in the barn or stable, it was used to store feed grains.

We don't always remember that when the horse was the primary mode of transportation, either under a saddle or hitched to a buggy, lots of nonfarming folks had a horse or two. These would be the folks with feed chests. Farmers needed to store more grain than could be kept in a couple of feed chests.

The old feed chests that have survived usually are classified as primitives. They tend to be rudimentary affairs, just roughly planed boards nailed together. All too often, a feed chest was parked on a dirt floor. Over the years, the wood would just rot away.

But this chest doesn't seem to have come from that past. It's plain, yes, but not primitive. The joinery is simple—rabbets and butt joints, no dovetails—but it's well crafted and strong. The lumber used—it could be southern yellow pine—is still flat and free of defects. The trim—a simple base molding and a larger lid molding that forms a lip to overlap the front side and ends—is low-key but not rudimentary. And the chest shows no evidence of having been anywhere but in warm, dry circumstances.

It all whispers "blanket chest" to me. And so it is.

EXPLODED VIEW

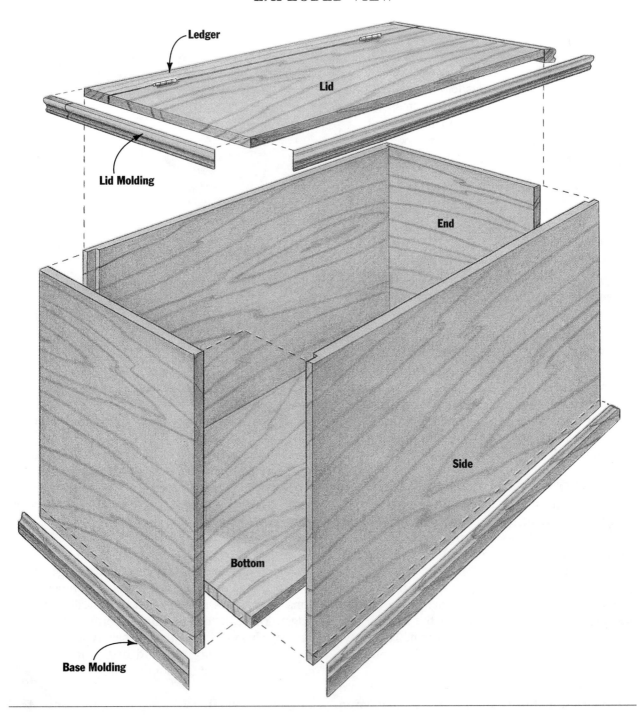

1. **Make the panels.** The original chest was made using ⅞-inch-thick stock, and except for the bottom, all the components were cut from single boards; no gluing up was necessary. You, of course, will need to edge-glue four or more boards to form each of the nearly 2-foot-wide parts for the chest.

Before you do the glue-ups, you must plane down the 5/4 stock. (The boards for the bottom don't necessarily have to be edge-glued.) With the stock properly thicknessed, glue it up. After the glue has cured, scrape off dried squeeze-out, and sand the panels smooth and flat. Rip and crosscut the parts to the dimensions specified by the Cutting List.

Crosscutting with the Plunge Router

You may not think of the plunge router as a crosscutting tool, but it can do an excellent job of trimming the panels for this chest.

Consider what you take on in crosscutting a 2 × 4-foot panel on the typical home-shop table saw. Even with good accessories, such as a big cutoff box and a roller stand, the job can make you feel uncoordinated.

But if a router is your crosscutting tool, the panel can rest on the workbench, and all you have to maneuver is a small, light tool. Clamp a T-square to the workpiece to guide the router. Then run the router back and forth along the T-square, cutting a bit deeper on each pass, until the panel is crosscut clean and square.

2. Rabbet the sides. On this project, the only joint more advanced than the butt joint is the rabbet joint that unites the sides and ends. Because of the size of the side panels, it is easiest to cut the rabbets with a router.

3. Assemble the chest. This is a simple matter of gluing and nailing the sides and ends together, using 8d finish nails, then nailing the bottom to the box. The original has wire nails, so there's no reason for you not to use them. Countersink the nails and putty over them.

Because the butt joints between the bottom and the ends are cross-grain, the builder of the original used individual narrow boards for the bottom, and nailed them, rather than gluing them. That way, the wood's movement wouldn't push or pull the chest apart.

With this in mind, roll the assembled box onto its top edges, and square it up. Nail the bottom in place. You can glue the outermost bottom boards to the sides, since these would be long-grain to long-grain edge joints. But don't apply glue across the ends: Only nail the boards there.

4. Nail the ledger in place. This is the attachment point for the hinges. The lid is fractionally longer than the case so that the lid molding won't bind against the sides. To keep the lines of the lid molding straight, the ledger is the same length as the lid. As you set it in place, keep the overhang on both ends equal.

Like the outermost bottom boards, the ledger can be glued to the top edge of the back side, but it should not be glued to the ends. Drive 8d finish nails through the ledger into the case. Countersink the nails and putty over them.

5. Hinge the lid to the chest. Begin by routing a $^{3}/_{16}$-inch-diameter bead along the lid's hinge edge.

Set the lid in place, and lay out the hinge locations. The hinges are mortised into the lid and the ledger. You can rout the hinge mortises, but it's a job I've always done with a chisel. When the mortises are done, lay out and drill pilots for the mounting screws, and mount the hinges.

6. Make and install the base molding. The base molding is a $1^{3}/_{4}$-inch-high strip applied across the ends and along the front side of the chest, overlapping the seam between the case and the bottom. The molding has a Roman ogee routed along the edge.

Start with strips of $^{3}/_{4}$-inch-thick stock, and rout the profile along the top edge, as shown in *Profiles*. There should not be a fillet at either the top or

PLAN VIEWS

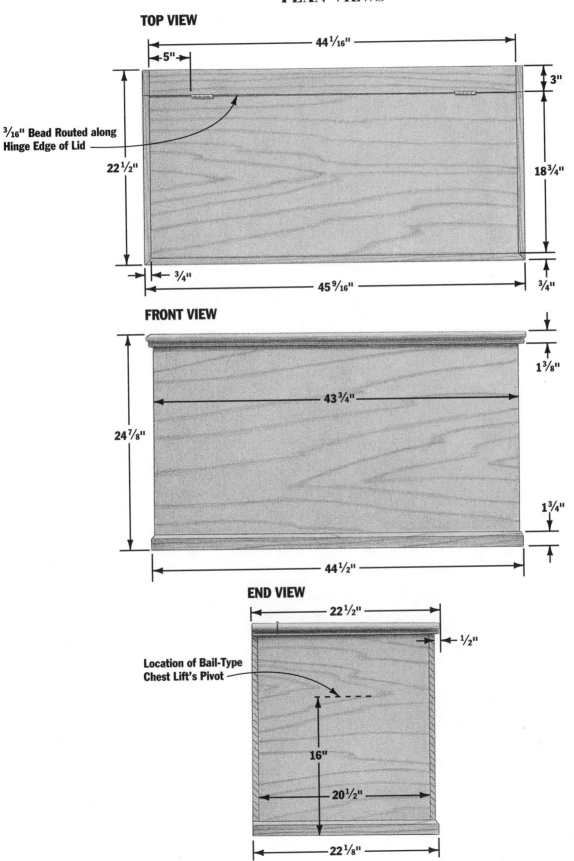

TOP VIEW

44 1/16"

5"

3"

3/16" Bead Routed along
Hinge Edge of Lid

22 1/2"

18 3/4"

3/4"

45 9/16"

3/4"

FRONT VIEW

1 3/8"

43 3/4"

24 7/8"

1 3/4"

44 1/2"

END VIEW

22 1/2"

1/2"

Location of Bail-Type
Chest Lift's Pivot

16"

20 1/2"

22 1/8"

bottom of the profile. Resaw the moldings, reducing them to a thickness of $3/8$ inch.

The molding strips are joined at the corners with miter joints. Miter one end of two strips, and nail them to the ends of the chest. Line up the miters carefully at the front, and allow the square ends to extend beyond the back. Then miter both ends of the front strip, fitting it between the end strips. When you've got the molding trimmed to the perfect fit, nail it to the chest with 6d finish nails. Finally, trim the end moldings flush with the back of the chest.

7. Make and install the lid molding. This molding is applied to the edges of the lid so the seam between the lid and the case is overlapped. Though the profile is quite simple, I couldn't find a single bit that would produce it. Instead, you have to make a series of cuts, alternating between the

---

An Extra Piece May Save Extra Work

When routing moldings, and especially when doing moldings that require a sequence of cuts, always work with strips that are longer than you think you'll need. And always make extras.

The extra length allows you to trim off snipes that often occur at the beginning or end of cuts, especially those on long, thin, narrow, flexible molding strips. The extra pieces offer some forgiveness if you mess up, or if the cutter splinters one of the strips.

---

table saw and the router table, to rough out the molding. Then you have to blend the cuts together with a block plane, file, or sandpaper to finish it.

The sequence of cuts and the setups used are laid out in the *Lid Profile* section of the drawing *Profiles*. Follow those directions to make the necessary molding strips.

When the strips are finished, cut them to fit and apply them to the lid. Cut and apply short pieces to the ends of the ledger.

JOINERY

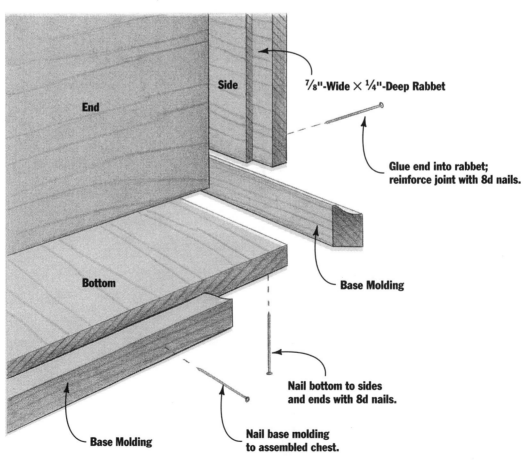

Side

$7/8$"-Wide $\times$ $1/4$"-Deep Rabbet

End

Glue end into rabbet; reinforce joint with 8d nails.

Base Molding

Bottom

Nail bottom to sides and ends with 8d nails.

Base Molding

Nail base molding to assembled chest.

PROFILES

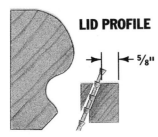

LID PROFILE

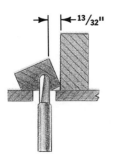

1. Rip the blank to 1¹/₁₆" × 1³/₈", then bevel at 22¹/₂°, as shown, to create a flat for routing.

2. With a ³/₈"-dia. core-box bit in a table-mounted router, plow a groove ⁹/₁₆" deep, positioning it as shown.

3. Rip the blank to a ³/₄" thickness, trimming off portions of the routed face.

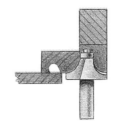

4. With a ¹/₂"-rad. roundover bit in a table-mounted router, form the quarter-round profile on the top edge of the blank.

5. Tilt the saw blade to 45°, and bevel the molding.

6. Sand, plane, or file away waste, fairing the quarter-round into the cove and softening the transition from the cove to the bevel.

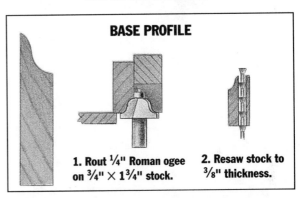

BASE PROFILE

1. Rout ¹/₄" Roman ogee on ³/₄" × 1³/₄" stock.

2. Resaw stock to ³/₈" thickness.

Although all the router and saw cuts are made, the lid molding still isn't completed. There's still too hard an edge between the cove and the bevel and between the nose and the cove. These edges must be softened with sandpaper. Wrap the abrasive around a small block and work the molding by hand, as shown, until all the curves are fair.

8. Apply the finish. The original was painted when I got it, but as I've admitted, I stripped it. What I remember was a golden mustard color, but I selected a green paint for the new chest.

9. Install the hardware. After the finish is dry, install the chest lock and what the hardware maker calls "chest lifts" (I always called them handles). As with many of this book's other projects, it isn't possible to find reproduction hardware to match what's on the original. Catalog numbers and sources for what we did use on our reproduction are in the Cutting List.

NARROW AMISH CABINET

I bought this in a Lancaster County, Pennsylvania, antique store, one of those multidealer emporiums. I never had the opportunity to actually meet the dealer and talk to him about the cabinet. Consequently, I don't know much about the cabinet.

I do take it for a local piece, and the more I study it, the more I'm convinced it's an Amish piece of fairly recent construction. The thing that makes it contemporary, to me, is the use of wire nails with raised cross-hatching of the heads. They're used to fasten the back panel. And there's no evidence that these are a recent addition, or that they're replacements for the original nails.

The Amish, you see, are an odd folk, best known for their continued use of horses and buggies for transportation. They don't have electricity or telephones in their homes. No running water or flush toilets, either. They don't use zippers (or Velcro) in their clothes. Amish woodworkers still adhere to somewhat old-style furniture-making practices. And I think it's pretty easy to mistake a fairly newly made Amish cupboard or cabinet for a well-preserved old piece. They just do some things the old-fashioned way.

The cabinet appealed to me because of its slender conformation, its interesting molding details, some of the joinery details, and the wonderful appearance of the grained paint.

The grain-paint job is so good that at a glance, quite a number of people

have taken it for the wood's natural grain under a clear finish. Gotcha! Then they look closer and are a bit embarrassed to have been fooled.

The engineering of the back is interesting. It's a frame-and-panel affair, wherein the frame has no rails. The stiles are edge-glued to the sides. The beveled back panel is then slipped into the slots in the stiles and nailed to the case's top and bottom. The back thus can expand and contract quite freely.

The door construction is interesting, too. Rather than having the sticking planed directly on the rails and stiles, the sticking is a separate molding strip. The profile stands proud of the door frame's face.

In the original, the sides are joined to the top and bottom with through dovetails. Because the crown and base moldings cover the tails on the sides, you can only see them when you look down on the cabinet top (or upend the piece to look at the bottom). The dovetails used in the case can easily be cut with a router, using the appropriate jig. And they can be fairly easily cut by hand. If the fit isn't perfect, no one will know, because they'll be hidden behind moldings. (And in fact, from what I can see, the ones in the original are pretty rough and gappy.)

If you've got the right kind of dovetail jig, go ahead and dovetail the sides to the top and bottom. Otherwise, follow the step-by-step directions and join the parts in the rabbet joint depicted in the drawings.

The curiously proportioned original (*above*) had no *known* use, yet its reproduction (*opposite*) fits any odd corner, providing useful keeping space.

CUTTING LIST

Piece	Number	Thickness	Width	Length	Material
Sides	2	$3/4$"	$9\,1/8$"	$44\,1/8$"	1-by pine
Top/Bottom	2	$3/4$"	$8\,5/8$"	14"	1-by pine
Back stiles	2	$3/4$"	2"	$44\,1/8$"	1-by pine
Back panel	1	$7/16$"	10"	$44\,1/8$"	1-by pine
Face frame stiles	2	$3/4$"	2"	$44\,1/8$"	1-by pine
Face frame top rail	1	$3/4$"	$2\,7/16$"	$11\,1/2$"	1-by pine
Face frame bottom rail	1	$3/4$"	$1\,7/16$"	$11\,1/2$"	1-by pine
Shelf supports	4	$1/2$"	$1/2$"	$8\,3/8$"	pine
Shelves	2	$3/8$"	$8\,3/8$"	$13\,1/4$"	pine
Crown molding	1	$15/16$"	$1\,7/16$"	$16\,5/8$"	pine
Crown molding	2	$15/16$"	$1\,7/16$"	$10\,13/16$"	pine
Base molding	1	$1/4$"	$7/8$"	$15\,1/4$"	pine
Base molding	2	$1/4$"	$7/8$"	$10\,1/8$"	pine
Feet	4	$2\,1/4$"	$2\,1/4$"	$2\,3/4$"	hardwood
Dowels	8	$1/4$" dia.		$1\,1/4$"	hardwood
Dowels	4	$1/2$" dia.		$1\,3/4$"	hardwood
Door stiles	2	$3/4$"	$1\,7/8$"	$40\,7/8$"	1-by pine
Door rails	2	$3/4$"	$1\,7/8$"	$11\,1/4$"	1-by pine
Door panel	1	$1/4$"	$7\,1/2$"	$37\,1/8$"	pine
Door sticking	2	$7/16$"	$3/4$"	$37\,3/8$"	pine
Door sticking	2	$7/16$"	$3/4$"	$7\,3/4$"	pine
Panel retainers	2	$1/4$"	$3/8$"	$37\,1/8$"	pine
Panel retainers	2	$1/4$"	$3/8$"	$7\,1/2$"	pine

HARDWARE

1 pr. lift-off parliament hinges, $4\,3/4$" high, for doors hinged on right. Catalog number 4048 from Paxton Hardware (410-592-8505).

1 door lock, $7/16$" $\times$ $2\,1/2$" selvedge, $13/16$" backset, $2\,1/2$" $\times$ $1\,5/8$" overall. Catalog number 4440 from Paxton Hardware.

6d cut finish nails

1" $\times$ 18-gauge wire nails

BUILD THE CASE

1. Cut the basic case parts. These include the sides, top, bottom, back stiles, back panel, shelf supports, and shelves. Most of these parts are cut from standard 1-by stock. Cut those parts to the dimensions specified by the Cutting List.

The back panel must be resawed or planed to a thickness of $1/2$ inch or less. The original's is $7/16$ inch. The shelves likewise must be resawed or planed, since they are only $3/8$ inch thick. If you do need to resaw the stock for these parts, you'll need to resaw two narrow boards, then edge-glue them to form the necessary panels. See the *ShopSmarts* features "Resawing on the Table Saw" on page 112 and "Gluing Up Panels" on page 49 for help.

EXPLODED VIEW

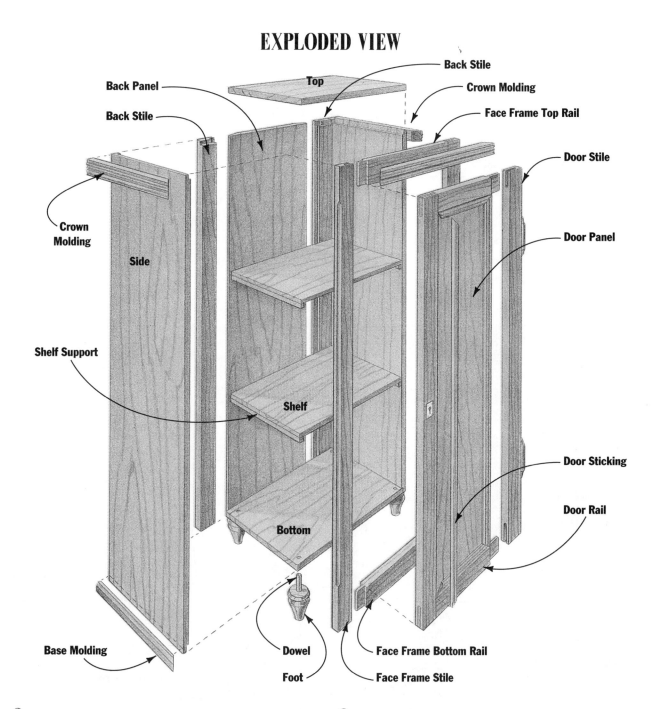

Back Stile

Top

Back Stile

Crown Molding

Back Panel

Face Frame Top Rail

Door Stile

Crown Molding

Side

Door Panel

Shelf Support

Shelf

Door Sticking

Door Rail

Bottom

Base Molding

Dowel

Face Frame Bottom Rail

Foot

Face Frame Stile

2. Rabbet the sides. The rabbet must be wide enough—³/₄ inch—to accommodate the full thickness of the top or bottom. And because the sides are ¹/₂ inch wider that the top and bottom, the rabbets must be stopped ¹/₂ inch shy of the back edges, as shown in the *Joinery Detail* in the *Plan Views*.

Cut these rabbets with a router and straight bit, using either an edge guide or a straightedge clamped to the workpiece to guide the cut. Make the rabbets ³/₈ inch deep. Square the inside corners of the rabbets with a chisel.

3. Make the back stiles. As shown in the *Back Stile Joinery Detail* to the *Back View* drawing, the back stiles are slotted for the back panel and are notched for the top and bottom. Cut the ¹/₄-inch-wide × ³/₈-inch-deep slot on the table saw or with a router.

The notch is a ³/₄-inch-wide × ¹/₄-inch-deep rabbet. Because it is through, it can easily be cut on the table saw. Set the blade height to ¹/₄ inch and cut the shoulder, positioning the cut with the rip fence and guiding the workpiece with the miter gauge. Then reset the fence and the blade height to cut the cheeks.

PLAN VIEWS

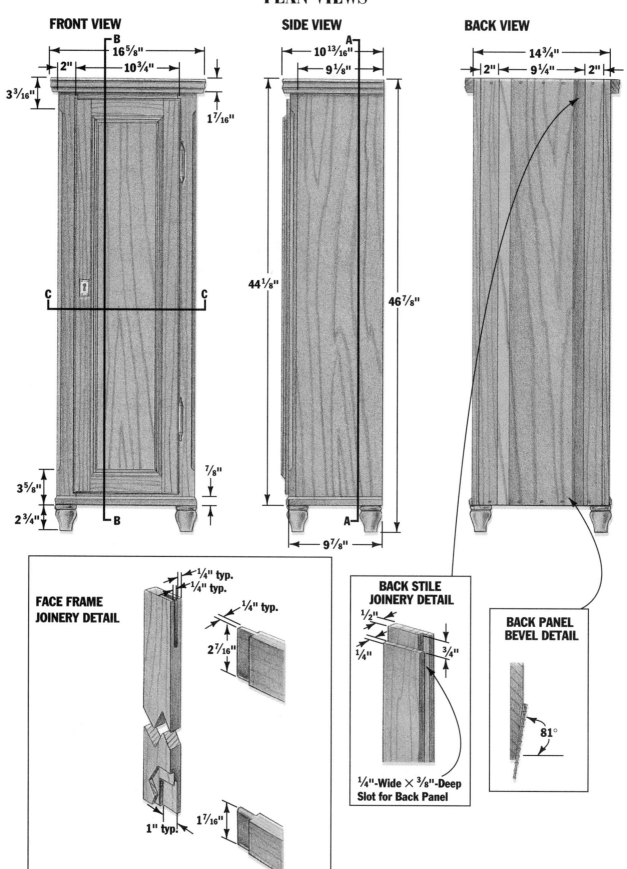

FRONT VIEW

16⁵/₈"
2"
10³/₄"
3³/₁₆"
1⁷/₁₆"
3⁵/₈"
2³/₄"
⁷/₈"
B
C C
B

SIDE VIEW

10¹³/₁₆"
9¹/₈"
44¹/₈"
46⁷/₈"
9⁷/₈"
A
A

BACK VIEW

14³/₄"
2"
9¹/₄"
2"

FACE FRAME JOINERY DETAIL

¹/₄" typ.
¹/₄" typ.
¹/₄" typ.
2⁷/₁₆"
1" typ.
1⁷/₁₆"

BACK STILE JOINERY DETAIL

¹/₂"
¹/₄"
³/₄"
¹/₄"-Wide × ³/₈"-Deep Slot for Back Panel

BACK PANEL BEVEL DETAIL

81°

PLAN VIEWS

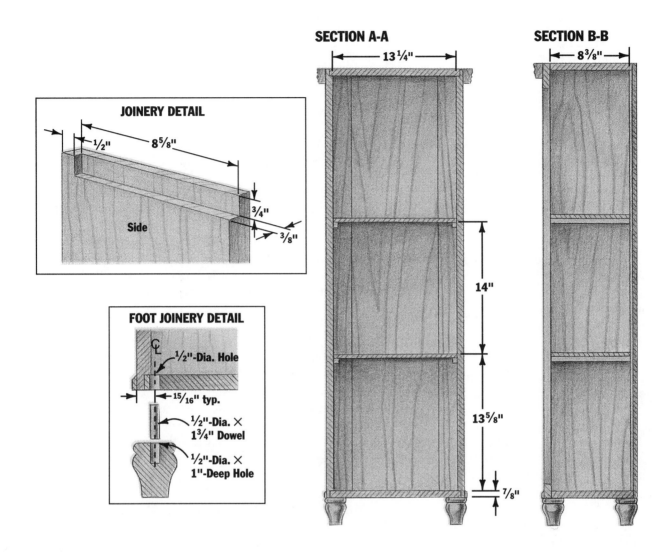

JOINERY DETAIL

1/2" 8⁵/₈"

Side

3/4"

3/8"

SECTION A-A

13¹/₄"

14"

13⁵/₈"

7/8"

SECTION B-B

8³/₈"

FOOT JOINERY DETAIL

C_L

1/2"-Dia. Hole

15/16" typ.

1/2"-Dia. × 1³/₄" Dowel

1/2"-Dia. × 1"-Deep Hole

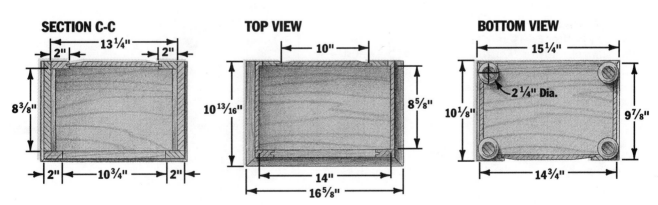

SECTION C-C

2"   13¹/₄"   2"

8³/₈"

2"   10³/₄"   2"

TOP VIEW

10"

10¹³/₁₆"

8⁵/₈"

14"

16⁵/₈"

BOTTOM VIEW

15¹/₄"

2¹/₄" Dia.

10¹/₈"

9⁷/₈"

14³/₄"

4. **Raise the back panel.** As noted, the back panel is $^7/_{16}$ inch to $^1/_2$ inch thick. The long edges are beveled to reduce their thickness so they'll fit into the slots in the back stiles. The quickest way to do this: the table saw.

Position the rip fence where the blade will tilt away from it. Set it $^3/_{16}$ inch from the blade. Tilt the blade 9 degrees, and raise it enough to bevel the stock. Cut the bevels.

5. **Assemble the case.** Use glue to fasten the back stiles to the sides. After the glue has cured, join the sides, top, and bottom, using glue and cut nails. Make sure the case is square. Then slide the back panel into place and secure it with nails driven through it into the top and bottom.

6. **Make the face frame stiles.** Begin by cutting two stiles to the dimensions specified by the Cutting List. The ends of the stiles have open mortises, as shown in *Face Frame Joinery Detail* in the *Plan Views*. These can be routed with a plunge router, as outlined in the *ShopSmarts* feature "Cutting Mortise-and-Tenon Joints" on page 83. If you opt to do them that way, make the fixture shown there to hold the stile while you rout the mortise. Set the stops and adjust the router as detailed in the *ShopSmarts* feature. Then rout the mortises.

Before turning to the rails, rout chamfers on the stiles, as shown in *Front View*. Use a 45-degree chamfer bit. I think it's easiest to do these stopped cuts on the router table.

7. **Make the face frame rails.** Begin by cutting two rails to the dimensions specified by the Cutting List. Cut tenons on the ends, as shown in *Face Frame Joinery Detail* in the *Plan Views*. The tenons can be cut using the tenoning jig shown in the *ShopSmarts* feature "Cutting Mortise-and-Tenon Joints" on page 83. The sequence for cutting tenons with it is presented in the feature.

After the tenons are cut, round one edge with a file to fit it to the routed mortise.

8. **Assemble and install the face frame.** Glue the rails and stiles together. Make sure the assembly is square.

Spread glue on the front edges of the case. Lay the face frame in place on the case. Drill pilot holes and drive nails through the rails into the top and bottom. Then drill $^1/_4$-inch-diameter, $1^1/_4$-inch-deep holes through the stiles and into the case for dowels.

Cut $1^1/_4$-inch pieces of $^1/_4$-inch dowel, one for each hole. One by one, whittle a bit of taper on one end of each dowel, apply a dot of glue, then drive it into a hole. Pare the dowels flush with a chisel.

9. **Nail the shelf supports in place.** Trim the supports to fit inside the cabinet. Nail them in place, as shown in *Section A-A* of the *Plan Views*. Use 1-inch wire nails.

The shelves are not fastened in place. You can set them aside until the cabinet is completed and finished before dropping them in place.

10. **Turn the feet.** Begin by preparing the foot blanks. Use hardwood, such as poplar or maple, for these feet. If you can't find suitable 10/4 hardwood stock, you may have to laminate two or more layers of thinner stock to create the foot blanks. Crosscut the stock into turning blocks, as specified by the Cutting List. Consult *Turned Foot Pattern* for the details of the foot contours. Turn the feet.

11. **Install the feet.** The feet are doweled to the cabinet. Drill a $^1/_2$-inch-diameter, 1-inch-deep hole into the center of each foot. Drill a $^1/_2$-inch-diameter hole into each corner of the cabinet bottom. The centerpoints for these holes are $^{15}/_{16}$ inch from the adjoining edges of the bottom.

Cut four $1^3/_4$-inch lengths of dowel. Glue one into each foot, then glue them to the cabinet bottom.

TURNED FOOT PATTERN

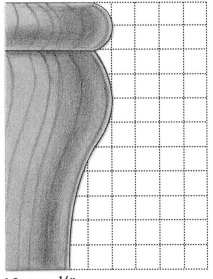

1 Square = $^1/_4$"

MAKE THE MOLDINGS

1. Cut the blanks. The lengths specified by the Cutting List are the lengths for the finished moldings. To create them, you must begin with oversized stock.

2. Make the base molding. The base molding is a saw table exercise. See the sequence in *Base Molding Profile*.

Begin with strips of ¾-inch × 1- to 2-inch stock. Set the blade to a height of only ½ inch, and position the rip fence ¾ inch from the outside of the blade. Now tilt the blade to 39 degrees. Kerf each of the molding blanks.

Reset the blade and the fence to rip each blank to a width of ⅞ inch, as shown in Step 2 of the sequence. Then reset the fence yet again to rip the ¼-inch-thick molding from each blank. Make this cut with the molding to the outside of the blade.

Sand the molding strips to remove any sanding marks.

3. Make the crown molding. The crown molding is made on the router table in three passes.

To make the molding, you need two fences with 45-degree bevels ripped along one edge. You need a ¼-inch straight bit and a ⁵⁄₃₂-inch Roman ogee bit. The *Crown Molding Profile* outlines the routing sequence and details the various setups you need to duplicate.

The process basically is this. On the first pass, you make a small, carefully positioned V-groove in the stock with a ¼-inch straight bit. The reason you get a V-groove with the straight bit is that you use two beveled fences to support the workpiece at a 45-degree angle as you feed it across the bit.

On the next pass, you use a ⁵⁄₃₂-inch Roman ogee bit with the pilot bearing removed. The fences are repositioned and the bit height set so the bit's bearing stem is in the V-groove. You may have to adjust things so that the stem actually scores the workpiece slightly in order to capture the full profile of the bit.

On the third and final pass, the Roman ogee bit is raised considerably and the fences are shifted. The portion of the bit that cuts the fillet is run through that V-groove.

When routing the crown molding, use the most reliable setup approach. Lay out the V-groove on the workpiece. Place the fences on the router table, and clamp one end of each. Set the workpiece in the fences, and swing them as necessary to align the bit with the layout mark, as shown. Clamp the free end of each fence. Adjust the bit height against the layout, too. Then cut the groove.

Setting up for the first cut with the Roman ogee bit follows the same pattern. Remove the bearing from the bit. Lay the workpiece in the fences, and slide it up to the bit. Unclamp one end of each fence, and shift the fences as necessary to align the bearing stem in the V-groove. Adjust the bit height so the bit's entire curve is captured. Reclamp the fences, and rout the profile.

PROFILES

BASE MOLDING PROFILE

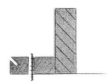

**1. Tilt blade to 39°
and kerf the stock.**

2. Rip stock to ⁷⁄₈" wide.

3. Rip stock to ¹⁄₄" thick.

CROWN MOLDING PROFILE

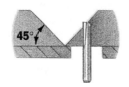

**1. Bevel 2 fences at 45°, and clamp them to the
router table, as shown, to cradle the workpiece.**

**2. With a ¹⁄₄" straight bit, rout
a V-groove in the workpiece.**

**3. Remove the pilot bearing from a ⁵⁄₃₂"
Roman ogee bit. Adjust the bit height
and the fence positions so the bit's
bearing stem aligns with the
V-groove. Rout the workpiece.**

**4. Readjust the bit height and
the fence positions so the bit's
outer edge aligns with the
V-groove. Rout the workpiece.**

**5. Sand the small flat
indicated, blending it
into the profile.**

STICKING PROFILE

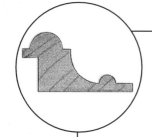

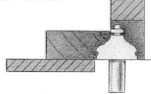

**1. Rout the basic profile using
a French Provincial bit.**

2. Turn over the blank.

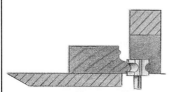

**3. Re-rout the blank
using a bull-nose bit
to form a ¹⁄₄"-dia. bead.**

**4. Rip the profile from the
blank with the profile to the
outside of the blade.**

**5. Cut a ¹⁄₈"-wide ×
¹⁄₄"-deep rabbet.**

4. Make the door sticking. As with the other moldings, you need to begin the task with oversized blanks—both wider and longer than the finished molding. Begin with three blanks—all ¾ inch × 2 inches, two roughly 40 inches long, one about 24 inches long. *Sticking Profile* shows the sequence for creating the molding.

Rout the basic profile using a small French Provincial bit. Although many other manufacturers offer this general profile, only Eagle America (800-872-2511) makes it in the size we used for this door. The bit number is 174-2815.

After routing the basic profile on all the blanks, switch to a ¼-inch-diameter bull-nose bit to amend it. Use this cutter to alter the rounded-over section to a bead. This completes the profile.

Next you must rip the profile from the blank. Be sure the profile is to the outside of the saw blade when you make the cut, so it won't get damaged.

Finally, use the table saw to cut a rabbet in the back. This rabbet will fit over the door's frame members.

5. Apply the crown and base moldings. The crown molding is applied around the very top of the case, and the base molding is applied around the bottom edge, as shown in the *Plan Views*.

In each case, the moldings are simply nailed in place. Fit and miter the strip across the front of the cabinet first. Then miter one end of each side strip and nail it in place.

BUILD THE DOOR

1. Cut the parts. The door is constructed of two rails, two stiles, the sticking, a panel, and four retainers. The frame is joined with bridle joints. The panel "floats" in a groove formed by the sticking and the retainers.

The sticking has already been shaped; set the untrimmed strips aside for now. Cut the other parts to the dimensions specified by the Cutting List. The door panel is only ¼ inch thick. The stock for it will have to be resawed or planed. If you have a planer, you can make the panel from a single board. If you must resaw it, however, you'll have to work with narrower boards and edge-glue them to form the panel. Tips on edge-gluing thin stock can be found in the *ShopSmarts* feature "Gluing Up Panels" on page 49.

2. Cut the bridle joints. The bridle joint is sometimes called the open mortise-and-tenon joint. It uses a standard tenon, but the mortise is simply a slot. You can cut both the tenon and the slot with the tenoning jig shown in the *ShopSmarts* feature "Cutting Mortise-and-Tenon Joints" on page 83.

Cut the tenons first, following the procedure outlined in the *ShopSmarts* feature. Make the shoulder cuts; then, using the jig to carry the workpieces, make the cheek cuts.

Without changing the blade height, use the last tenon cut to adjust the rip fence setting to cut the slot, as shown in the photo on this page. Clamp the first stile in the jig, just as you did the rails, and

Use one of the just-cut tenons in the tenoning jig to reset the jig's position for cutting the open mortise (or slot). Unlock the rip fence and shift it very slightly away from the blade. You want the inside face of the blade to be flush with the tenon's cheek.

make the first cut. Roll the stile, and cut the second cheek of the slot. Cut the cheeks of the other three slots. Now, if there's still a bit of waste in the slots, shift the fence to clean it out with an additional pass.

DOOR CONSTRUCTION

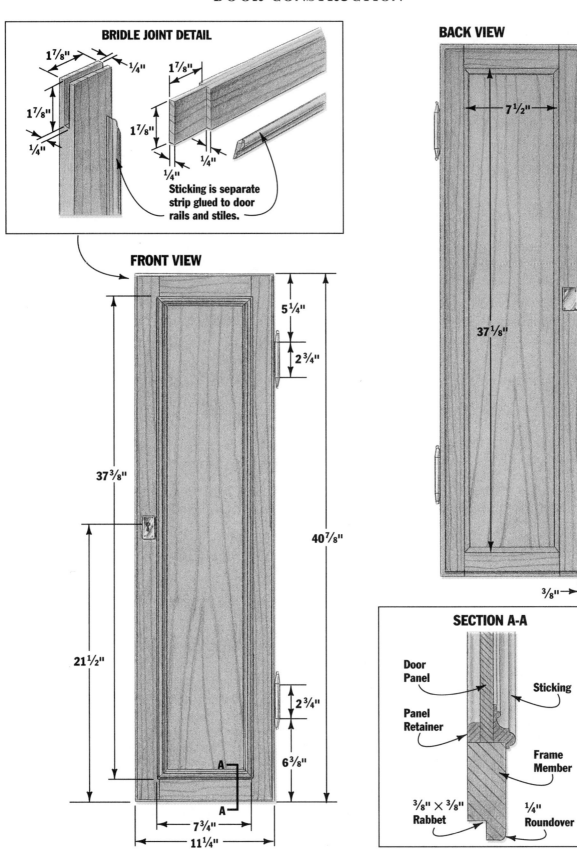

BRIDLE JOINT DETAIL

1⁷⁄₈"   ¼"   1⁷⁄₈"

1⁷⁄₈"   1⁷⁄₈"

¼"   ¼"   ¼"

Sticking is separate strip glued to door rails and stiles.

FRONT VIEW

5¼"

2¾"

37³⁄₈"

40⁷⁄₈"

21½"

2¾"

6³⁄₈"

7¾"

11¼"

BACK VIEW

7½"

37¹⁄₈"

³⁄₈"

³⁄₈"

SECTION A-A

Door Panel

Sticking

Panel Retainer

Frame Member

³⁄₈" × ³⁄₈" Rabbet

¼" Roundover

A

A

After the glue has set, remove the clamps and rabbet the frame. Use a router and a standard $3/8$-inch rabbeting bit.

After the glue has set, remove the clamps and rabbet the frame. Use a router and a standard $3/8$-inch rabbeting bit.

Here's a tip to help you avoid tear-out at the corners. You always want to rout the end grain first, then the long grain. Because of the bridle joints, the end grain at the corners is cut when you rout along the stiles. Do them first, then rout the rails.

Finally, round-over the outer edge of the frame with a $1/4$-inch roundover bit.

4. Apply the door molding. Fit and miter the sticking, and glue it to the door frame. To minimize scraping, especially on the face of the door, use a wet cloth to wipe up any glue squeeze-out immediately.

5. Install the panel. Trim the panel to fit the door frame, and drop it into place. Fit and miter the retainers. Nail them in place, securing the panel. Use the same 1-inch wire nails used for the shelf supports.

6. Install the hardware. With the door lock in hand, cut the necessary mortise and install the lock. Mount the hinges, as shown in the *Front View* of *Door Construction*.

Building a Door That's Flat

There are few more vexing situations than to install your newly made door and discover it is warped.

To avoid this vexation you need to always use the best stock for the door: straight-grained and defect-free. Make sure it is planed *flat* before you cut the joinery.

Sometimes a bit of warp can be introduced during assembly. To make sure the frame is flat, clamp it flat to the workbench until the glue sets. Spread a plastic trash bag on the bench top, and lay the frame on it before clamping it. That way, squeeze-out won't bond the door to the bench.

3. Assemble the frame. Test fit the frame to check your craftsmanship. Assuming it is up to your usual standards, knock it apart and spread glue on the tenon and in the slot. Reassemble the frame and clamp it. Make sure it is square; don't pull it out of square with the clamps.

GRAIN-PAINT THE CABINET

The original cabinet was very skillfully grain-painted. I endeavored to duplicate the style of the original, using a wood-graining tool. Read the *ShopSmarts* feature "Country Finishes" on page 305 for the basics of grain-painting (as well as suggestions for other suitable finishing approaches). I followed the sequence outlined in the feature, starting with sanding and priming, and ending with the top-coat of varnish to protect the finish.

SIDEBOARD

This is an antique that doesn't have the distinctions that museum curators dote on, so you probably won't find one like it in a museum or in arty furniture books. But it is certainly representative of the furnishings that country folk had in their homes from the mid-nineteenth century on.

The dealer who let me measure and photograph this piece, Bob Moyer of Wernersville, Pennsylvania, had acquired it at a farm auction not far from his store—right there in the Berks-Lebanon-Lancaster counties *heart* of Pennsylvania Dutch country. My childhood and years as a newspaper reporter in the region took me into countless small-town homes and farmhouses, and this is unmistakably a piece of the Pennsylvania Dutch country.

The conformation of the main case is very similar to the jelly cupboards built in the region—two drawers over two doors—though it isn't as tall as the typical jelly cupboard. With scrollwork enclosing the middle gallery and topping off the piece, it seems typical of the Pennsylvania Dutch.

The design is functional, and, other than the scrollwork, the ornamentation is pretty restrained. The door frames are chamfered, for example, but the panels are flat, not raised. Small beads turn several seams from structural features into design elements. My hunch is that this sideboard dates from the late 1800s, but hap-

pily, it missed all the design excesses of the Victorian era.

The piece has the utility of a good sideboard, the sort found in every traditional rural home around the region. Behind the left-hand door is a vast area for storing the good dishes. Behind the right-hand door are three drawers, perfect for keeping the good table linens. Silverware, candles, and other table articles are kept in the two drawers above the doors. The main top is a staging and holding area for the big, multicourse family dinners. Up top the cook displays her desserts, and down below, she catches the serving platters bumped off the crowded table.

This vision is from my past, here in the Pennsylvania Dutch country, but I bet there's a similar vision from the past of anyone who favors country furniture.

This is just about the most complicated piece I've included in this country furniture collection. I made the early judgment to include it on emotion. It engendered warm, comfortable, pleasant feelings based on my own past, so I just liked it. And I could argue that it was a practical—and not unattractive—country dining room sideboard.

Being somewhat familiar with case construction, I just assumed from the look that that's how it was constructed. But when I got it

Attractive though the original sideboard (*above*) may be, fancy china and a gorgeous dessert really bring the reproduction (*opposite*) to life.

EXPLODED VIEW

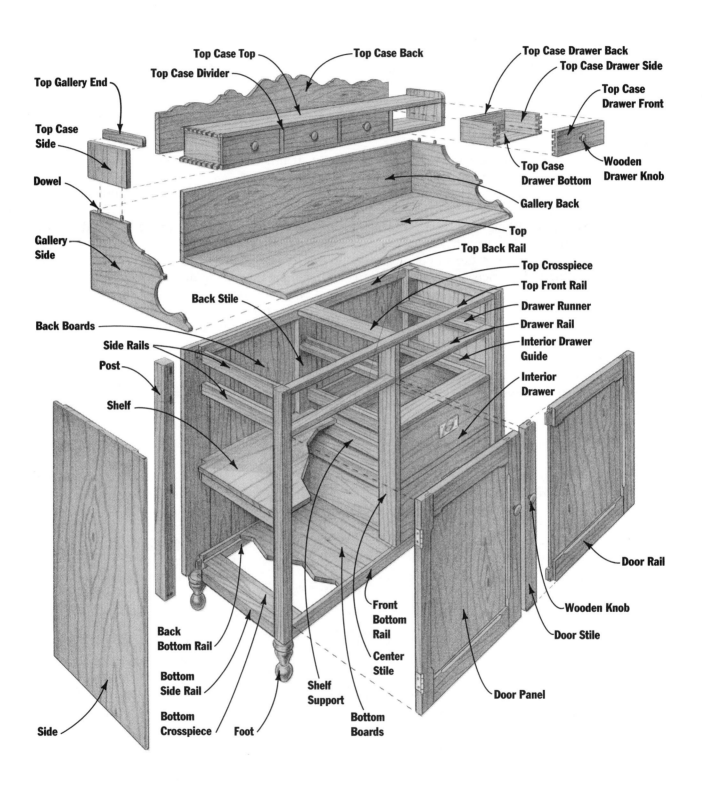

Top Gallery End

Top Case Side

Dowel

Gallery Side

Back Boards

Side Rails

Post

Shelf

Side

Back Bottom Rail

Bottom Side Rail

Bottom Crosspiece

Foot

Shelf Support

Bottom Boards

Front Bottom Rail

Center Stile

Top Case Top

Top Case Divider

Top Case Back

Top Case Drawer Back

Top Case Drawer Side

Top Case Drawer Front

Top Case Drawer Bottom

Wooden Drawer Knob

Gallery Back

Top

Top Back Rail

Top Crosspiece

Top Front Rail

Drawer Runner

Drawer Rail

Interior Drawer Guide

Interior Drawer

Back Stile

Door Rail

Wooden Knob

Door Stile

Door Panel

into the photo studio, pulled out all the drawers, and started to really look at it . . . what a surprise! It's a framework suspended from four posts. Lots of rails that double as drawer guides and supports. Lots of nails securing loose ends. The sides and back are reduced, in the structural scheme, to mere concealment; they're a skin applied to cover the framework.

Another complication is the number of wood thicknesses employed. A nimble craftsman seems to have used up all his odds and ends in this one.

Some of the variations do have design implications. The interplay of thick and thin edges is subtle and may be hard for us to judge. But I think the design would lose something if you simply substituted 3/4-inch stock throughout.

The piece may be somewhat plain, and it may lack special distinction, but it doesn't completely lack sophistication in design or construction. And it is completely representative of country furniture at its best.

BUILD THE CASE

1. Make the posts. There are four posts in the sideboard, but only a single face of the two front posts is visible. Consequently, you can glue-laminate 5/4 stock to make them; the lamination seam won't show. And as long as the knots aren't too hellacious, you can use lower-grade stock.

After scraping off dried glue, joint and rip the post blanks to the final dimensions specified by the Cutting List.

Study the drawing *Post Layouts* carefully. Lay out and rout all the mortises. Use the mortising fixture shown in the *ShopSmarts* feature "Cutting

POST LAYOUTS

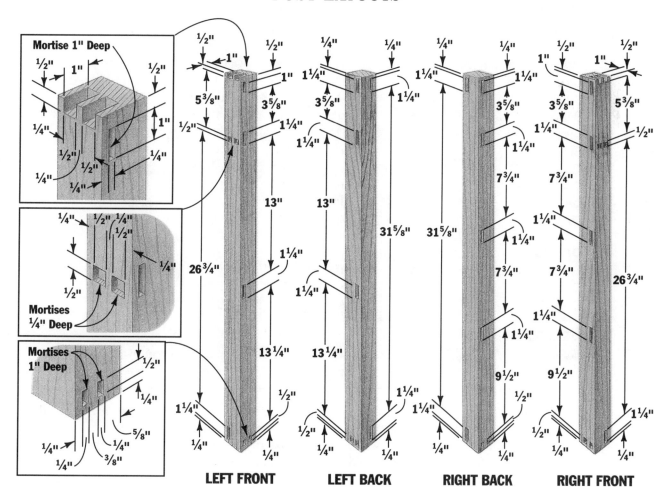

LEFT FRONT   **LEFT BACK**   **RIGHT BACK**   **RIGHT FRONT**

CUTTING LIST

Piece	Number	Thickness	Width	Length	Material
CASE					
Posts	4	1³⁄₄"	1³⁄₄"	34⁵⁄₈"	pine
Top back rail	1	³⁄₄"	1³⁄₄"	45³⁄₈"	1-by pine
Front/back bottom rails	2	1¹⁄₁₆"	1³⁄₄"	45³⁄₈"	5/4 pine
Back stile	1	³⁄₄"	3"	33¹⁄₈"	1-by pine
Bottom side rails	2	1"	1³⁄₈"	16"	5/4 pine
Side rails	7	³⁄₄"	1³⁄₄"	16"	1-by pine
Top front rail	1	³⁄₄"	1³⁄₄"	45³⁄₈"	1-by pine
Drawer rail	1	³⁄₄"	1³⁄₄"	43⁷⁄₈"	1-by pine
Center stile	1	1¹⁄₁₆"	3"	5¹⁄₈"	5/4 pine
Center stile	1	1¹⁄₁₆"	3"	27¹⁄₄"	5/4 pine
Top crosspiece	1	³⁄₄"	1³⁄₄"	15³⁄₈"	1-by pine
Bottom crosspieces	2	1"	3¹⁄₂"	15³⁄₈"	5/4 pine
Drawer runner	1	³⁄₄"	3¹⁄₂"	15³⁄₈"	1-by pine
Drawer runner	2	³⁄₄"	1³⁄₄"	15³⁄₈"	1-by pine
Drawer runner	2	³⁄₄"	1³⁄₄"	14³⁄₈"	1-by pine
Drawer runner	2	³⁄₄"	³⁄₄"	14³⁄₈"	1-by pine
Interior drawer rails	2	³⁄₄"	2³⁄₄"	22³⁄₁₆"	1-by pine
Drawer guide	1	³⁄₄"	1¹⁄₁₆"	13³⁄₄"	1-by pine
Interior drawer guides	2	³⁄₄"	1³⁄₄"	13³⁄₄"	1-by pine
Shelf support	1	³⁄₄"	1³⁄₄"	13³⁄₄"	1-by pine
Shelf	1	³⁄₄"	16³⁄₄"	23¹³⁄₁₆"	1-by pine
Bottom boards	*	³⁄₄"	*	16"	1-by pine
Back boards	†	¹⁄₂"	†	34⁵⁄₈"	1-by pine
Sides	2	³⁄₄"	18"	34⁵⁄₈"	1-by pine
Top	1	³⁄₄"	18¹⁄₂"	46¹⁄₂"	1-by pine
Gallery sides	2	³⁄₄"	10³⁄₄"	19¹⁄₂"	1-by pine
Gallery back	1	¹⁄₂"	10³⁄₄"	47⁵⁄₁₆"	pine
Foot blanks	4	2³⁄₄"	2³⁄₄"	5"	poplar
DOORS					
Stiles	4	³⁄₄"	2³⁄₄"	26¹⁄₈"	1-by pine
Rails	4	³⁄₄"	2³⁄₄"	17⁹⁄₁₆"	1-by pine
Panels	2	³⁄₈"	16⁹⁄₁₆"	21⁵⁄₈"	pine
DRAWERS					
Fronts	2	³⁄₄"	5¹⁄₁₆"	21"	1-by pine
Sides	4	¹⁄₂"	5¹⁄₁₆"	16³⁄₈"	pine

Mortise-and-Tenon Joints" on page 83 to hold the post, and rout the mortises with a plunge router. While the majority of the mortises are ¹⁄₄ inch wide, there are several ¹⁄₂-inch-wide ones, so you'll need both ¹⁄₄-inch and ¹⁄₂-inch straight bits. The setup and sequence for routing a mortise are detailed in the *ShopSmarts* feature.

Most of the mortises are 1 inch deep. The double mortises for the drawer rail, however, are only ¹⁄₄ inch deep, because of the intersecting mor-

Piece	Number	Thickness	Width	Length	Material
DRAWERS—continued					
Backs	2	$1/2$"	$4^9/16$"	20"	pine
Bottoms	2	$3/8$"	$16^1/4$"	$20^1/2$"	pine
INTERIOR DRAWERS					
Fronts	3	$3/4$"	$8^3/16$"	21"	1-by pine
Sides	5	$1/2$"	$8^3/16$"	$15^5/8$"	pine
Backs	3	$1/2$"	$7^{11}/16$"	20"	pine
Bottoms	3	$3/8$"	$15^1/2$"	$20^1/2$"	pine
TOP CASE					
Sides	2	$3/4$"	7"	5"	1-by pine
Dividers	3	$3/4$"	$3^3/4$"	$5^1/4$"	1-by pine
Top/Bottom	2	$5/8$"	$6^1/2$"	$47^1/4$"	pine
Back	1	$1/2$"	$10^1/2$"	$47^1/4$"	pine
Top gallery ends	2	$3/4$"	$1^1/2$"	$6^1/2$"	1-by pine
Drawer fronts	4	$5/8$"	$3^{11}/16$"	11"	pine
Drawer sides	8	$3/8$"	$3^{11}/16$"	$6^1/4$"	pine
Drawer backs	4	$3/8$"	$3^5/16$"	$10^1/4$"	pine
Drawer bottoms	4	$3/8$"	$6^1/8$"	$10^3/4$"	pine
Dowels	4	$5/16$" dia.		1"	hardwood

HARDWARE

2 pr. hinges, $1^1/4$" × $2^1/2$"

3 flush campaign-chest handles, 4" long × $1/2$" deep, brass. Catalog number A19.03 from Garrett Wade, Inc. (800-221-2942). **Note:** These handles are sold in pairs, so you'll need 2 pairs and will have 1 handle left over.

2 wooden knobs, 2" dia. (for drawers)

2 wooden knobs, $1^1/2$" dia. (for doors)

4 wooden knobs, 1" dia. (for top case drawers)

6d cut finish nails

4d cut finish nails

1" headless brads

4 iron dowel screws, $1/4$" × $3^1/2$"

2 bullet catches, $5/16$" dia.

*Glue up several random-width boards to make $46^1/8$"-wide bottom.

†Glue up several random-width boards to make $46^7/8$"-wide back.

tise for one of the side rails. Note that for the same reason, the top side rail mortise in the front post is shorter than the other side rail mortises.

Bore the pilot for the iron dowel screws that fasten the feet to the posts.

2. Cut the frame parts. Refer to the Cutting List, and cut these parts to the dimensions specified: the top back rail, the two front/back bottom rails, the back stile, both bottom side rails, seven side rails, the top front rail, the drawer rail, both center stiles,

(continued on page 221)

PLAN VIEWS

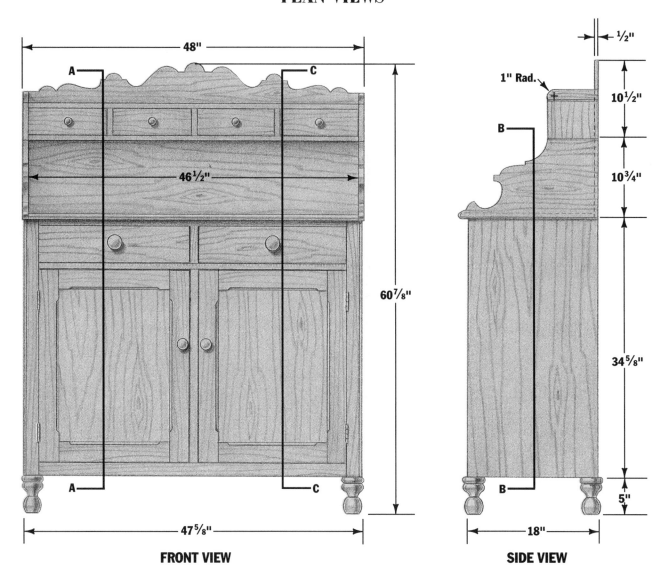

48"

A

C

46½"

60⅞"

A

C

47⅝"

FRONT VIEW

½"

1" Rad.

B

10½"

10¾"

34⅝"

B

5"

18"

SIDE VIEW

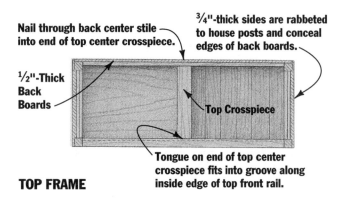

Nail through back center stile into end of top center crosspiece.

¾"-thick sides are rabbeted to house posts and conceal edges of back boards.

½"-Thick Back Boards

Top Crosspiece

Tongue on end of top center crosspiece fits into groove along inside edge of top front rail.

TOP FRAME

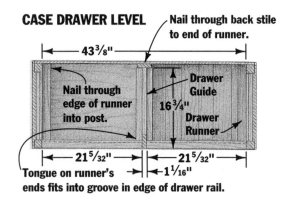

CASE DRAWER LEVEL

Nail through back stile to end of runner.

43⅜"

Nail through edge of runner into post.

Drawer Guide

16¾"

Drawer Runner

21⁵⁄₃₂"

21⁵⁄₃₂"

1¹⁄₁₆"

Tongue on runner's ends fits into groove in edge of drawer rail.

PLAN VIEWS

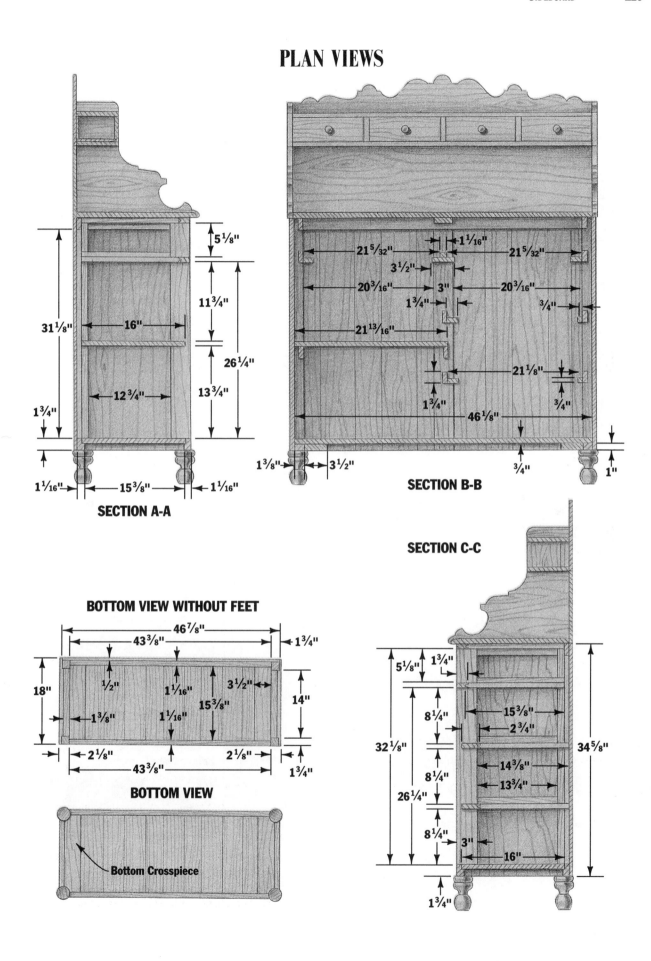

SECTION A-A

$31^1/_8$" $5^1/_8$" $11^3/_4$" 16" $26^1/_4$" $13^3/_4$" $12^3/_4$" $1^3/_4$"

$1^1/_{16}$" $15^3/_8$" $1^1/_{16}$"

SECTION B-B

$21^5/_{32}$" $1^1/_{16}$" $21^5/_{32}$" $3^1/_2$" $20^3/_{16}$" 3" $20^3/_{16}$" $1^3/_4$" $3/_4$" $21^{13}/_{16}$" $21^1/_8$" $3/_4$" $1^3/_4$" $46^1/_8$"

$1^3/_8$" $3^1/_2$" $3/_4$" 1"

BOTTOM VIEW WITHOUT FEET

$46^7/_8$" $43^3/_8$" $1^3/_4$" 18" $1/_2$" $1^1/_{16}$" $3^1/_2$" $15^3/_8$" 14" $1^3/_8$" $1^1/_{16}$" $2^1/_8$" $43^3/_8$" $2^1/_8$" $1^3/_4$"

BOTTOM VIEW

Bottom Crosspiece

SECTION C-C

$5^1/_8$" $1^3/_4$" $8^1/_4$" $15^3/_8$" $2^3/_4$" $32^1/_8$" $8^1/_4$" $14^3/_8$" $13^3/_4$" $34^5/_8$" $26^1/_4$" $8^1/_4$" 3" 16" $1^3/_4$"

FRAMEWORK

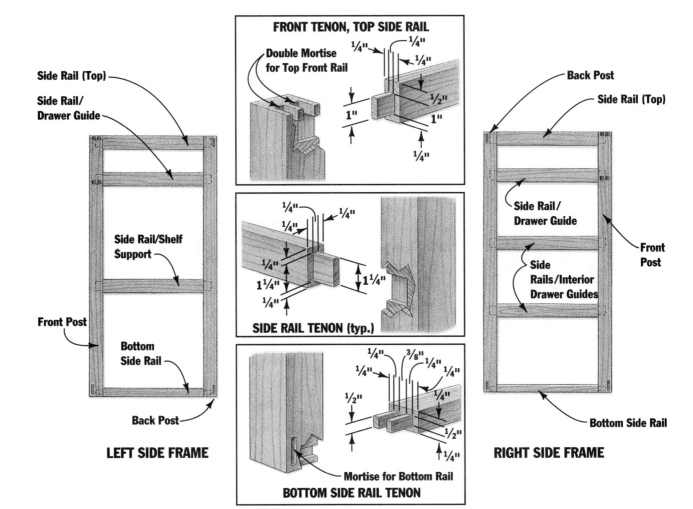

FRONT TENON, TOP SIDE RAIL

Double Mortise for Top Front Rail

1/4" 1/4" 1/4"
1/2"
1"
1"
1/4"

SIDE RAIL TENON (typ.)

1/4" 1/4"
1/4"
1/4"
1 1/4"
1 1/4"
1/4"

BOTTOM SIDE RAIL TENON

1/4" 3/8" 1/4"
1/4" 1/4"
1/2"
1/2"
1/4"

Mortise for Bottom Rail

Side Rail (Top)

Side Rail/Drawer Guide

Side Rail/Shelf Support

Front Post

Bottom Side Rail

Back Post

LEFT SIDE FRAME

Back Post

Side Rail (Top)

Side Rail/Drawer Guide

Side Rails/Interior Drawer Guides

Front Post

Bottom Side Rail

RIGHT SIDE FRAME

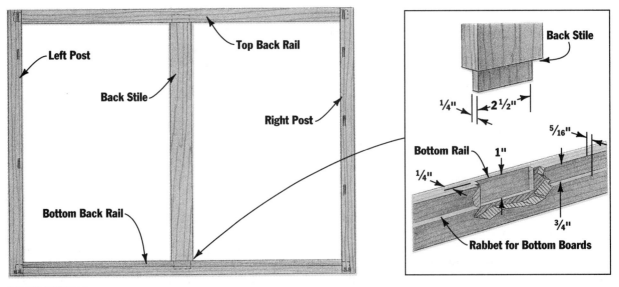

Left Post

Back Stile

Top Back Rail

Right Post

Bottom Back Rail

BACK FRAME

Back Stile

1/4" 2 1/2"

5/16"

Bottom Rail

1"

1/4"

3/4"

Rabbet for Bottom Boards

FRAMEWORK

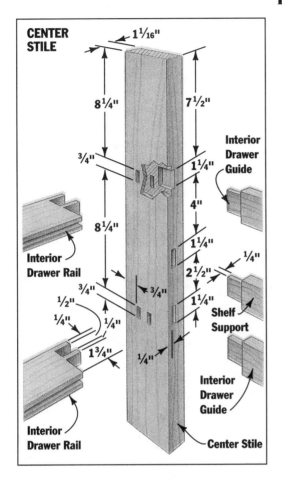

CENTER STILE

1¹/₁₆"

8¹/₄"

7¹/₂"

³/₄"

1¹/₄"

Interior Drawer Guide

4"

8¹/₄"

Interior Drawer Rail

1¹/₄"

³/₄"

³/₄"

2¹/₂"

¹/₄"

¹/₂"

¹/₄"

¹/₄"

1¹/₄"

Shelf Support

1³/₄"

¹/₄"

Interior Drawer Guide

Interior Drawer Rail

Center Stile

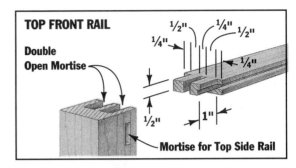

TOP FRONT RAIL

Double Open Mortise

¹/₂" ¹/₄" ¹/₂"

¹/₄" ¹/₄"

¹/₂" 1"

Mortise for Top Side Rail

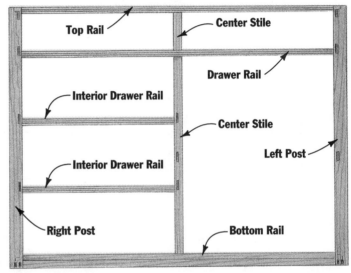

Top Rail

Center Stile

Drawer Rail

Interior Drawer Rail

Center Stile

Interior Drawer Rail

Left Post

Right Post

Bottom Rail

FRONT FRAME

all three crosspieces, both interior drawer rails, both interior drawer guides, the shelf support, and all the drawer runners. While most of these parts are cut from 1-by stock, the front/back bottom rails, the center stiles, and the bottom crosspieces are cut from 5/4 stock. The bottom side rails must be cut from 5/4 stock, then resawed or planed to a 1-inch thickness.

Obviously, there are a lot of parts here, so each should be prominently labeled.

3. Mortise the center stile. Several supports for the sideboard's interior structure are joined to the longer of the two center stile pieces, as shown in the *Center Stile* detail of the drawing *Framework*. Lay out and rout the mortises for these supports in the center stile. Use the same setup used to do the mortises in the posts. Note that the mortises routed into the edge of the stile are offset, not centered.

The short mortises for the interior drawer rails are through. Rather than making a separate fixture for routing these mortises, you can simply clamp the stile atop a scrap and rout the mortises.

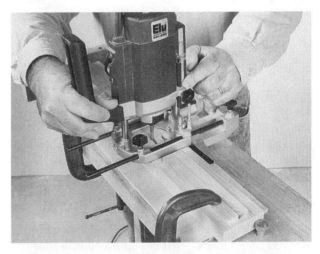

The face of the (long) center stile is wide enough to support the router, so you don't need to use a fixture to hold it while you rout the through mortises for the interior drawer rails. Reference the stile's edge with the router's edge guide to position the mortises, and clamp stops across the workpiece, as shown, to control the length of the mortise. Put a scrap under the workpiece so you won't cut into your bench top.

4. Mortise the back rails for the back stile.
The dimensions and locations of these mortises are
shown in the *Back Frame* detail of the drawing
Framework. Rout the mortises with the same equipment and procedure as used from the other mortises.

5. Cut the tenons. Organization is paramount for
you to get through this step. You must get the correct tenons cut on every part, and there are a
number of variations. All can be cut on the table
saw, using the tenoning jig shown in the *ShopSmarts*
feature "Cutting Mortise-and-Tenon Joints" on page
83. After the tenons are cut, the edges must be
rounded with a file to conform to the shape of the
routed mortises.

Side rails, top back rail, and back stile: Cut
1-inch-long tenons on both ends of all seven side
rails and the top back rail, as well as the back stile.
The tenons should have ¼-inch-wide shoulders all
around. As you round the ends of the tenons with a
file and fit them to their mortises, trim one tenon on
each top side rail to fit the short mortises in the
front posts.

Cutting the double tenons on the bottom side rails is a
relatively simple matter. First cut tenons on both ends of
each rail that are ½ inch thick, ⅞ inch wide, and 1 inch
long. Then, with the rail clamped in the tenoning jig's
front position, set the rip fence so the blade will cut an
inner cheek, forming a tenon ¼ inch wide. After the first
cut, spin the rail around and cut the second inner cheek,
as shown here. After making these cuts on both rails,
reposition the fence so you can clear out that last sliver
of waste from between the two tenons.

Interior drawer guides and shelf support: These
three parts have tenons cut on one end only. The
tenons are the same as those cut on the side rails.

Front/back bottom rails: The tenons on these
parts are the same size as those on the side rails,
but they are offset because of the extra thickness of
these rails. You can thus cut one cheek and both
edges of these tenons with the same setup that you
used for the side rails. But to cut the second
shoulder and cheek, you'll need to adjust the setup.

Bottom side rails: Double tenons are cut on
these parts, as you can see in the *Bottom Side Rail
Tenon* detail of the drawing *Framework*. Though it
may not be immediately obvious, the double tenons
can be cut on the table saw, using the tenoning jig.
First cut the shoulder and cheeks as though you
were forming a tenon ½ inch thick × ⅞ inch wide ×
1 inch long. After forming this tenon on both ends of
the two rails, shift the saw's rip fence position so
you can make additional edge cuts, forming the
inner cheeks.

Top front rail and drawer rail: Both of these have
double tenons that are offset, as shown in the *Top
Front Rail* detail of the drawing *Framework*. As you did
for the bottom side rail tenons, first cut the cheek and
edges of a single tenon, then make additional cuts to
divide the tenon with the workpieces in the edge-
cutting position on the tenoning jig. After the 1-inch-
long double tenons are formed on both rails, trim ¾
inch from the drawer rail tenons so they will properly
fit into the ¼-inch-deep mortises in the front posts.

Interior drawer rails: The last parts to be tenoned
are these. Tenons are cut on one end only. Make the
only shoulder cut with the workpiece on edge. Then
stand the workpiece in the edge-cutting position on
the tenoning jig, and make the three edge cuts. The
gap between the two tenons can be opened by
wasting the wood with repeated saw cuts.

**6. Cut tongue-and-groove joints on the rails
and drawer runners.** The top crosspiece and the
drawer runners are joined to the top rails and
drawer rails with tongue-and-groove joints. The
grooves are ¼ inch wide × ⅜ inch deep. The
tongues should match.

You can cut both the grooves and the tongues
on the table saw. Do the grooves first. Set the blade
height to ⅜ inch, and position the rip fence to
create a ¼-inch-wide shoulder. Test the setup on
scrap. If it's right, cut each groove from end to end
in two passes. Do this on the top front rail, the
drawer rail, and the two interior drawer rails. (This

will nick the tenons on some of the parts; the nick won't show, and it won't weaken the joints.)

Cut the tongues next. Reduce the blade height but keep the fence setting. Cradle the workpiece in the miter gauge, and cut the tongue across the end of it. The fence keeps you from getting the tongue too long. Two or three passes should form each cheek of the tongue. Do one side, then turn the workpiece over to complete the tongue.

Tongues should be cut on one end of each workpiece. Machine the top crosspiece and all seven drawer runners.

7. Rabbet the bottom rails.

The rabbet allows the bottom board to be set into the rails, flush with their top edges. The rabbet is $^5/_{16}$ inch × $^3/_4$ inch, as shown in the detail to the *Back Frame* section of *Framework*.

This task can also be done quickly on the table saw. Set the blade height and fence to make the base cut, and cut both rails. Then reset the blade height and fence position to make the cheek cut.

Safety check! Orient the cut so the waste will come free to the outside of the blade. If it is between the blade and the fence, the blade will surely kick it back, right into your thigh or groin. You'll remember *that!*

8. Assemble the side frames.

With all the joinery cut, it's time to get on with assembly. Do it methodically, working in stages. Do the "side frames" first, gluing together the posts and side rails.

Spread glue in the mortises and on the tenons for one side frame at a time. Insert the rails into one post, then fit the second post in place. Draw the joints closed with bar clamps or pipe clamps. Leave the assembly clamped until the glue sets. Unless your joints are unusually sloppy, the structure should close square and flat.

9. Join the front and back rails to the side frames.

While the glue in the first two subassemblies sets, move on to an element of the back frame. Glue and clamp the back stile between the top and bottom back rails.

After the clamps are off the side frames and the back rail-and-stile assembly, lay one side frame on the floor. Apply glue to its mortises and to the tenons on one end of the top, drawer, and bottom rails. Working quickly, fit these parts in place. Use a mallet, if necessary, to close these joints. Apply glue to the tenons of the back rail-and-stile assembly, and fit it in place, again driving the joints closed.

Apply glue to the remaining tenons and to the mortises in the second side frame. Fit that frame in place. Be sure you get the joints fully closed as expeditiously as possible.

Right the framework, and apply bar clamps or pipe clamps.

10. Make the sides.

The sides are $^3/_4$-inch-thick panels that are rabbeted along both edges for the posts. The front edge of each side is bull-nosed.

Prepare and glue up stock to form the side panels. See the Cutting List for dimensions.

After removing the clamps, scraping off any dried glue squeeze-out, and sanding the panels, rout a $^3/_8$-inch-diameter nose along the front edge. Then cut the rabbets on the table saw. The rabbet along the front edge is $^3/_8$ inch deep × $1^3/_4$ inches wide. The one along the back edge is $^3/_8$ inch deep × $2^1/_4$ inches wide.

11. Nail the bottom in place.

The bottom is composed of 1-by boards of random widths, all measuring 16 inches long. The boards installed at each side must be notched to fit around the posts.

Assembly of the framework can be handled easily by one person. Glue the front rails and the back assembly into one of the side frames, and seat the tenons firmly in their mortises. Apply a bit of glue to each of the remaining tenons, and set the second side frame atop them, as shown. With the second side frame seated firmly, carefully lower the frame onto its back, and apply clamps across the front. Then roll it over and apply clamps across the back.

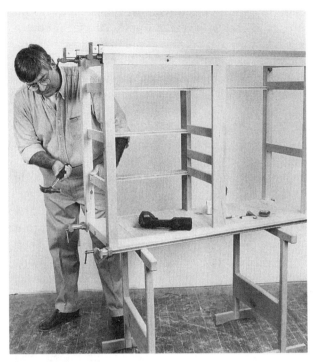

The bottom has been nailed in place. Now the center stile assembly is being installed. The stile has two interior drawer rails jutting from the side, and two drawer guides and a shelf support jutting from the back edge. Line up this assembly as best you can, and drive nails through the side rails and back stile into the ends of the assembly's parts. I found it helps to tack the center itself in position, then to tack one guide to the back stile, and one drawer rail to a side rail. You can spend a little more time getting the parts level and square before drilling pilot holes and nailing the unit solidly together.

Cut the first board to 16 inches, set it into the rabbets in the bottom rails next to the post, and mark it for notching. As you mark the board, bear in mind that the sides are partially recessed between the posts. Because you've already made the sides, you can clamp them temporarily in place to aid you in fitting the first and last bottom boards. (Remove them as soon as you have the notches laid out; it's easier to install the remaining frame parts before installing the sides.) Having cut the notches, nail the first board into place. Cut more boards and nail them in place. Notch the final board, then rip it to fit, and nail it in place.

Finally, cut the bottom crosspieces to fit and install them beneath the bottom, between the front and back rails, tight against the side rails. Toenail through the crosspieces into the front and back rails, and nail through the side rail and the bottom into the crosspieces.

12. Glue up the center stile assembly. Before the center stile can be added to the framework, the interior drawer guides, the shelf support, and the interior drawer rails must be attached to it. Glue and clamp this assembly.

13. Install the center stile assembly. When the glue has set and the clamps are removed from the center stile assembly, fit it into position. To attach it to the framework, drive nails through various frame members into the ends of the assembly parts. For example, drive nails through the bottom into the stile, through the back stile into the guides and shelf support, and through the side rails into the drawer rails.

14. Nail the shelf in place. The shelf is made up of several boards, totaling $16^{3}/_{4}$ inches in width.

The first board to go in must be notched to fit around both the back post and the back stile. As with the bottom, the shelf can't extend out flush with the outer side of the posts. So clamp the side in place to aid you in fitting the shelf boards. The last board to be placed has to be notched to accommodate the post and the center stile. Remember to hold this board $^{3}/_{4}$ inch back from the front edge of the post and stile so it won't interfere with the door.

15. Install the drawer runners. Fit the drawer runners and the top crosspiece in place next. The tongue on the end of the runner is inserted into the groove in the rail. The runner is secured with nails.

Fast-Track Glue-Ups

The usual rule of thumb is that you should leave clamps on an assembly "overnight." But if you are using yellow or white glue, you can safely pop the clamps within an hour of glue-up. These modern glues set quickly—as you may have discovered if you've ever dithered too long with a joint glued but only partly closed. After an hour in the clamps, the set will be secure enough that the joints will withstand considerable stress. When clamps and time are scarce, it's nice to know you don't have to wait until tomorrow to get to the next stage of assembly.

Drive nails through the side rails into the runner adjacent to each. Drive nails through the back stile into the runners abutting it. Drive a couple of nails through the top back rail into the end of the top crosspiece.

Before nailing the 3½-inch-wide drawer runner in place, nail the drawer guide to it.

And after the runners and the top crosspiece are in place, insert the short center stile between the top and drawer rails, and nail it in place.

16. Install the sides. Now that all the internal frame parts are glued and nailed securely in place, you can close in the structure. Start by nailing the

sides to the posts. Use 6d finish nails. Sink the nailheads and putty over them.

17. Nail the back in place. The back is formed of random-width, ½-inch-thick boards, shiplapped edge to edge. Mill stock to the required thickness. Crosscut the boards to length. Then use a dado cutter to cut a ¼-inch-deep × ⅜-inch-wide rabbet along both edges of each board. Cut the rabbet in one face along the first edge, then roll the board over and cut the second rabbet in the other face.

Nail the boards to the top and bottom rails. Because neither the back nor the rails are particularly thick, use 1-inch brads for this purpose.

MAKE AND INSTALL THE FEET

The turned feet on the original are of a general style known as turnip feet. They seem to be poplar, and we used poplar for the reproduction. Making them is a job for an experienced turner. If necessary, glue up poplar stock to make the 2¾-inch-square blocks for turning. Follow the layout

in the drawing *Patterns* to turn the feet.

If you aren't a turner, you can buy turned feet from Osborne Wood Products in Toccoa, Georgia (800-849-8876). The tulip style (catalog number 4100) made by Osborne comes closest to the originals in size, if not exactly in contour.

BUILD THE DOORS

1. Cut the parts. The Cutting List specifies the sizes. The frame parts are ¾ inch thick, so they can be cut from 1-by stock. The door panels must be glued up from ⅜-inch stock resawed (or planed down) from 5/4 stock. (You should be able to resaw two ⅜-inch-thick boards from each piece of 5/4 stock you resaw.) The *ShopSmarts* feature "Gluing Up Panels" on page 49 includes plans for shop-made clamps that are especially well suited to gluing up thin stock.

2. Groove the rails and stiles. The panel "floats" in a ¼-inch-wide × ½-inch-deep groove in the rails and stiles. Cut this groove on the table saw, or on the router table with a straight bit. The groove is offset across the edge of the stock, as shown in a detail to the drawing *Door Construction*.

3. Cut the mortises and tenons. The mortises can be routed using the same fixture used for the framework mortises. You need a ¼-inch straight bit. The mortises, like the panel grooves, are offset.

Cut the tenons on the table saw, using your tenoning jig. Because the mortises are offset, the tenons must be too. This means you must cut one cheek on each workpiece, then reset the table saw

Use One Joinery Cut to Set Up Another

You can make good use of the panel groove in the door frame parts, using it to set the edge guide position and to orient the workpieces in the mortising fixture. With a grooved workpiece clamped in the fixture, you can plunge the bit—with the router switched off, of course—into the groove, trapping the router in the proper position on the fixture for mortising. Slide the edge guide against the side of the fixture, and lock it.

DOOR CONSTRUCTION

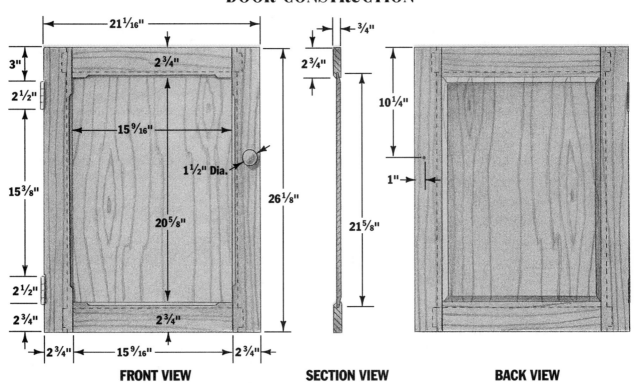

FRONT VIEW

SECTION VIEW

BACK VIEW

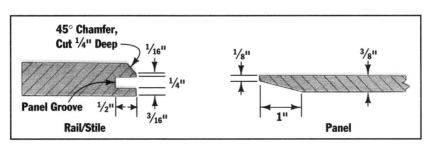

45° Chamfer,
Cut ¼" Deep

1/16"

¼"

Panel Groove   ½"   3/16"

Rail/Stile

1/8"   3/8"

1"

Panel

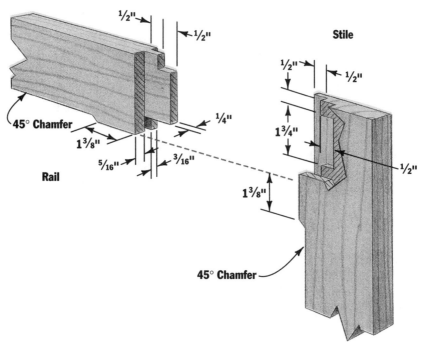

½"   ½"

Stile

45° Chamfer   ¼"

1³/8"

5/16"   3/16"

Rail

½"   ½"

1³/4"   ½"

1³/8"

45° Chamfer

fence before cutting the second. After the tenons are formed, use a backsaw to trim the haunch on each. File the corners of the tenons so they'll fit the mortises.

4. Chamfer the rails and stiles. As shown in *Door Construction*, the rails and stiles have stopped chamfers along their inner edges. With the frames assembled without glue, measure and mark the limits of the chamfers.

Because the chamfer bit's pilot bearing may get lost in the panel groove, you have to rout these chamfers on the router table, guiding the work along the fence. Use a 45-degree chamfer bit.

5. Shape the panels. After the two panels are glued up and trimmed to size, you need only raise them. Since the exposed face of the panel is flat, raising them is done simply to fit them to the panel groove. On the original, the bevels are roughly 1 inch wide. There's no fillet between the bevel and the field. Raise the panels on the table saw.

Position the rip fence where the blade will tilt *away* from it. Raise the blade a little over an inch. Set the fence so that, at the table surface, it is $1/4$

inch from the inside of the blade. Tilt the blade until the top tooth is $3/8$ inch from the fence. This setting should produce the proper bevel. If a test cut proves the setup, cut the panels.

Sand or scrape away all saw marks.

6. Assemble the doors. As a test, assemble the doors without glue. Make any adjustments to the joints that may be necessary. Finish sand all the parts. Then glue up the assembly. Glue the tenons into the mortises, but don't glue the panels in the grooves; they must be free to move a little.

7. Hang the doors. The first step is to ensure that they fit comfortably within the door opening. You need about $1/16$ inch of clearance all around. Plane the door edges as necessary.

The hinges are mortised into the posts and are surface-mounted on the doors. Use a chisel to pare the mortises, then install the hinges.

To keep the doors closed, we used $5/16$-inch-diameter bullet catches. The "bullet" is installed in the edge of the door stile, roughly 1 inch below the knob. The strike is mounted on the center stile.

BUILD THE DRAWERS

1. Cut the parts. There are a lot of drawers in this piece, and of three different sizes. At this stage, make only the five drawers for the case—two exposed drawers and the three concealed behind the right-hand door. Although the dimensions of the two sets of drawers are different, their construction is the same.

Note that the fronts are cut from $3/4$-inch stock; the sides and backs, from $1/2$-inch stock; and the bottoms, from $3/8$-inch stock. Resaw and/or thickness-plane stock for the drawer sides, backs, and bottoms. Edge-glue the stock for the bottoms to form panels of the sizes specified by the Cutting List. Use the same approach used to glue up the door panels.

Crosscut and rip the parts to size. While you don't necessarily need to mark each part, it helps you keep them organized. There are a lot of pieces.

2. Rout the dovetails. The front and sides are joined by half-blind dovetails. In the original, of course, the dovetails were hand cut. For our reproduction, we cut them with a router. Use a $1/2$-inch, 14-degree dovetail bit and a dovetail jig. The

specifics of setting up and using such a jig are laid out in the *ShopSmarts* feature "Routing Dovetails" on page 232.

3. Plow the groove for the bottom. As shown in *Drawer Construction*, the bottoms are housed in a $1/4$-inch-wide × $1/4$-inch-deep groove routed in the sides and front. Cut the groove with a $1/4$-inch straight bit in a table-mounted router.

4. Make the bottom. You've already glued up the bottom panels. After scraping off any dried glue squeeze-out, sand them. The panels are $3/8$ inch thick, while the grooves for them are only $1/4$ inch wide, so the bottoms must be beveled around three sides to reduce the thickness at the edges. You can do this on the table saw, as you did in raising the door panels.

5. Assemble the drawer. With the joinery cut and the parts sanded, proceed with assembly. Glue the sides to the front. Slide the bottom into its groove. Fit the back in place, and drive two or three brads through each side into it. Drive a

DRAWER CONSTRUCTION

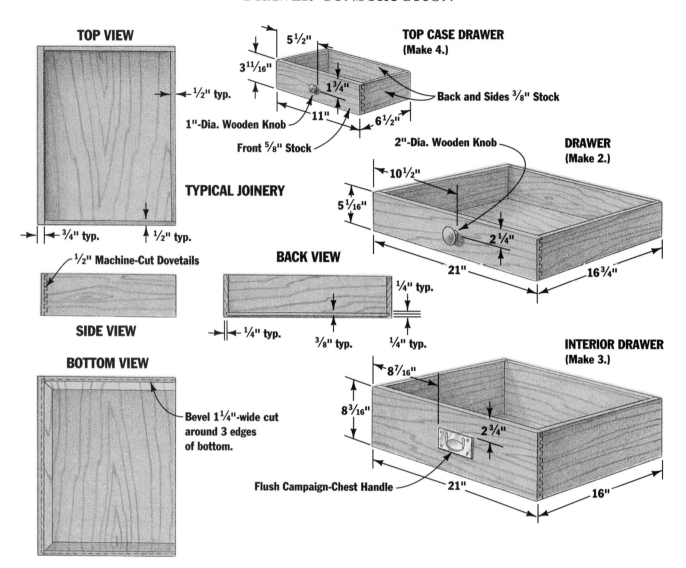

TOP VIEW

½" typ.

¾" typ.   ½" typ.

TYPICAL JOINERY

½" Machine-Cut Dovetails

SIDE VIEW

BOTTOM VIEW

Bevel 1¼"-wide cut around 3 edges of bottom.

5½"

3¹¹⁄₁₆"

1¾"

11"

6½"

TOP CASE DRAWER (Make 4.)

Back and Sides ⅜" Stock

1"-Dia. Wooden Knob

Front ⅝" Stock

BACK VIEW

¼" typ.

¼" typ.   ⅜" typ.   ¼" typ.

2"-Dia. Wooden Knob

DRAWER (Make 2.)

10½"

5¹⁄₁₆"

2¼"

21"

16¾"

INTERIOR DRAWER (Make 3.)

8⁷⁄₁₆"

8³⁄₁₆"

2¾"

Flush Campaign-Chest Handle

21"

16"

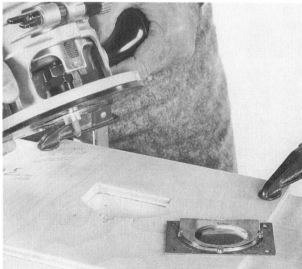

couple of brads through the bottom into the back to keep it in place.

6. Install the knobs. The two drawers for the top of the case have 2-inch-diameter wooden knobs, which can be purchased from any number of retail or mail-order sources. Drill a hole in the center of the drawer front, 2¼ inches from the top edge, and mount these knobs.

The back of the handle used on the interior drawers is shown here. You can see why a recess must be cut in the drawer front. In a piece of plywood, cut an opening to accommodate the handle's "works," and use this template to guide a router equipped with a template guide and a core-box bit. Rout the recess deep enough that the handle's surface plate will sit flat on the drawer front.

The interior drawers have what are called flush campaign-chest handles, which we got from a mail-order supplier. (See the Cutting List.) You need to rout a ½-inch-deep recess for the handle. The easiest way is with a template. Cut the template from a piece of hardboard or plywood. *With the handle in hand*, not simply "on order," cut an opening in the template that's the correct size and in the correct location. Fit a template guide to your router, chuck the appropriate bit in the router, set the depth carefully, then rout the recess.

7. **Fit the drawers to the case.** If necessary, plane the sides or the top edges.

BUILD THE MIDDLE GALLERY

1. **Cut the parts.** The open space between the case and the top case is what I call the middle gallery. It's defined by the case top, the gallery sides, and the gallery back.

All of these parts should be glued up from narrow stock. The top and sides are made from ¾-inch stock, and the back is from ½-inch stock. Resaw and/or plane the stock as necessary, then crosscut, rip, and glue it up, making panels of the sizes specified by the Cutting List.

2. **Shape the top's edge.** The top has what is called a thumbnail formed along its front edge. Use a thumbnail or table-edge bit to rout this shape on the upper surface. Then turn the top over, and complete the edge by routing a ¼-inch roundover along the bottom edge. Use an edge guide to control the cut for this pass, since the surface that the roundover bit's pilot bearing should reference was routed away by the thumbnail bit.

PATTERNS

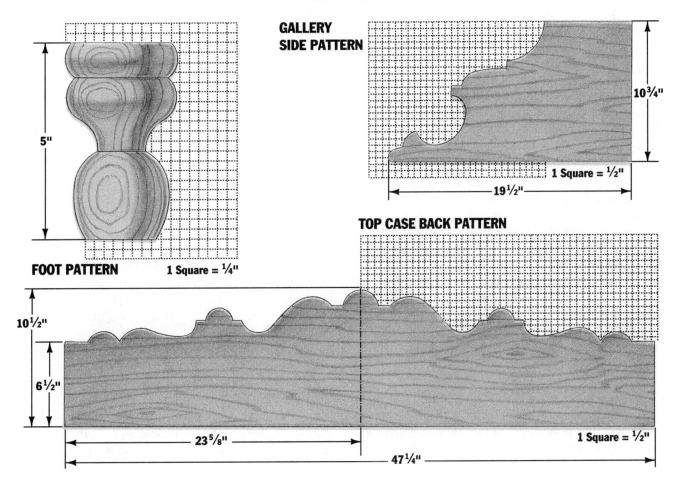

FOOT PATTERN   **1 Square = ¼"**

5"

GALLERY SIDE PATTERN

10¾"

19½"

1 Square = ½"

TOP CASE BACK PATTERN

10½"

6½"

23⅝"

47¼"

1 Square = ½"

3. Shape the sides. The scrolled end is the most obvious shape that each gallery side has, but the sides also have rabbets cut across their back ends for the gallery back and a decorative bead routed along their lower edge.

Rout the beads with a $^3/_{16}$-inch edge-beading bit. Cut the $^3/_8$-inch-deep × $^1/_2$-inch-wide rabbets.

Now enlarge the pattern for the scrollwork, making a full-sized paper or cardboard pattern. Transfer the contour to the workpieces. Cut with a saber saw, and carefully sand the cut edges.

4. Assemble the middle gallery. The parts are simply nailed together with 6d finish nails. Sink the nails and putty over them.

Mount the assembly on the case, again nailing it. Sink the nailheads and putty over them.

Finally, lay out and drill $^5/_{16}$-inch-diameter × $^1/_2$-inch-deep holes for dowels to mount the top case. There are two such holes in each gallery side, one $1^3/_4$ inches from the back, the other $5^5/_8$ inches from the back.

BUILD THE TOP CASE

1. Cut the case parts. The parts include the top and bottom, sides, dividers, back, and top gallery ends. The sides, top gallery ends, and dividers should be cut from $^3/_4$-inch stock to the dimensions specified by the Cutting List.

Stock for the top and bottom must be resawed or replaned to a $^5/_8$-inch thickness. Stock for the back must be resawed or replaned to a $^1/_2$-inch thickness. If necessary—and in the case of the back it probably will be—glue up narrow boards into a panel of the specified width.

2. Rabbet the sides. The sides are $^1/_2$ inch wider than the top and bottom so that the back can overlap the latter parts, while its end grain is concealed by the sides. Cut a $^3/_8$-inch-deep × $^1/_2$-inch-wide rabbet along the back edge of the sides.

3. Rout the dovetails. The top and bottom are joined to the sides by half-blind dovetails. As with the other dovetails in the project, they were hand cut in the original, router cut in our reproduction. Use the same equipment and set as used for the drawer dovetails.

However—and it's a BIG however—the top and bottom are the tail pieces, which means they go in the front of the dovetail jig. And since they are just shy of 4 feet long, you have to really get the jig up off the floor. Standard workbench height won't do.

4. Assemble the case. Glue the sides, top, and bottom together. Slide the dividers into position, flush with the front edges of the case, and drive 4d finish nails through the top and bottom into them. Sink the nails and putty over them.

5. Cut the back. The back is one of the highlights of the sideboard. Enlarge the pattern for the back, making a paper or cardboard template so you can transfer the contour to the back. Cut the contour with a saber saw, and sand the cut edge very carefully.

6. Make the gallery ends. These parts have one corner rounded on a 1-inch radius, and a $^3/_{16}$-inch-diameter bead routed along the bottom edge. The ends have a $^3/_8$-inch-deep × $^1/_2$-inch-wide rabbet cut across them to accommodate the back.

7. Install the back and gallery ends. Set the back in place, and nail it to the case. Nail the ends in place. Toenail through the rounded edge into the top case, and through the side into the back. Sink the nails and putty over them.

8. Mount the top case on the middle gallery. Insert dowel points in the holes bored in the gallery sides. Carefully align the top case on the middle gallery, then press it firmly into the dowel points, transferring the hole locations to the top case.

Upend the top case, and bore a $^5/_{16}$-inch-diameter × $^1/_2$-inch-deep hole at each spot.

Glue a 1-inch-long dowel in each hole in the gallery sides, then set the top case over them.

9. Cut the drawer parts. Although the dimensions are different, these drawers are constructed in the same way as the others in this project.

Note that the fronts are cut from $^5/_8$-inch stock, while the sides, backs, and bottoms are from $^3/_8$-inch stock. Resaw and/or thickness-plane the stock, and crosscut and rip the fronts, sides, backs, and bottoms.

TOP CASE CONSTRUCTION

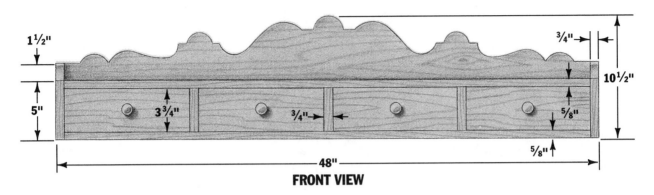

FRONT VIEW

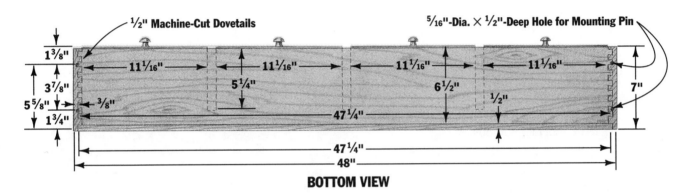

BOTTOM VIEW

10. Rout the drawer dovetails. The front and sides are joined by half-blind dovetails. Rout them in the same way you did those for the other drawers and for the top case.

11. Cut the bottom-panel grooves. As shown in *Drawer Construction*, the bottoms are housed in a 1/4-inch-wide × 1/4-inch-deep groove routed in the sides and front. Cut the groove with a 1/4-inch straight bit in a table-mounted router.

12. Assemble the drawers. With the joinery cut and the parts sanded, proceed with assembly. Glue

the sides to the front. Slide the bottom into its groove. Fit the back in place and drive a couple of nails through each side into it. Drive a couple of nails through the bottom into the back to keep it in place.

13. Install the knobs. The drawers have 1-inch-diameter wooden knobs, which can be purchased from any number of retail or mail-order sources. Drill a hole in the center of the drawer front, 1 3/4 inches from the top edge, and mount these knobs.

14. Fit the drawers to the case. If necessary, plane the sides or the top edges to get a good fit.

APPLY A FINISH

A variety of finishes are appropriate for this piece. Read the options outlined in the *ShopSmarts* feature "Country Finishes" on page 305. It will give you ideas and sketch out the techniques for applying different finishes.

The original was stained and then varnished

long ago. It seems to me that paint was more likely the original finish, so we painted our reproduction a color called pearwood from the Stulb Paint Company's Old Village line.

Whatever finish you use, remove the hinges, catches, and brass handles before applying it.

Routing Dovetails

The dovetail joint is common in country furniture. One hundred to 150 years ago, dovetails were a basic joint. Every woodworker could cut them.

The dovetail joint's strength isn't dependent on glue or mechanical fasteners. At a time when glue wasn't too reliable and when fasteners weren't cheap, that was particularly significant. The dovetail joint allows wood to expand and contract, which is extremely desirable when joining large pieces of wood, such as cabinet cases or chest sides. Bear in mind, too, that back when the country originals shown in this book were built, the woodworkers who made them didn't have power tools. Everything—sawing boards, cutting joints—was done by hand. Even dadoes and rabbets had to be hand cut with a special plane or with a saw and chisel. In that context, cutting dovetails by hand wasn't especially onerous.

In a number of our reproductions, I eliminated casework dovetails because contemporary hobby woodworkers tend to shy away from making the joint. But where they were used in drawers, I kept them in the plans. Half-blind dovetails—the sort used in drawers—are easy to cut with the router. All you need is a dovetail jig and a router.

The typical half-blind dovetail jig, like the Bosch model 92870 shown in the photos, consists of a metal base with two clamping bars to hold the workpieces and a comblike template to guide the router in cutting both pieces at once. (For Bosch distributors, call S-B Power Tool Company at 919-636-4200.) The biggest differences from one brand to another, from one model to another, are the quality of the materials and hardware and the precision with which each is made and assembled. The cheapest ones have stamped parts that tend to flex and buckle, threads that strip quite easily, wing nuts that chew at your fingers. The Bosch model shown has a rigid extruded aluminum base and a durable phenolic template. Its large clamp knobs are easy on the hands during extended dovetailing sessions. Some jigs have extra templates that let you cut $1/4$-inch half-blind dovetails in addition to the standard $1/2$-inch variety, and $1/4$-inch and $1/2$-inch box joints as well.

In addition to the jig, you need a router, a dovetail bit (usually the $1/2$-inch, 14-degree variety), and a guide bushing (usually one with a $7/16$-inch outside diameter, which limits you to a $1/4$-inch-shank bit). Because you have to install the bit after the template guide, there's benefit in using a long-shanked bit, such as Cascade's $2 1/4$-inch-long model (number C1432, available from Cascade Tools, 800-235-0272). The best router to use is a 1- or $1 1/2$-horsepower fixed-base model. The ability to plunge is irrelevant in this operation, and brute power doesn't contribute much, if anything.

Here, step by step, is how to set up the router and jig to cut dovetails.

Step 1

1. Set up the router. Install the $7/16$-inch guide bushing in the baseplate. Then adjust the router so the collet is relatively close to the bushing, and carefully insert the $1/4$-inch-shank bit. Tighten the collet nut. The first thing you'll notice when inserting your $1/2$-inch dovetail bit through a $7/16$-inch guide bushing and into the router collet is that the largest part of the bit doesn't fit through the bushing.

Adjust the depth of cut next. When you do this, turn the bit slowly by hand to absolutely ensure that the bit doesn't contact the bushing. Most guide bushings are steel, which will damage the bit's carbide if the two come into contact. The usual setting is $1/2$ inch, though your jig's instructions may specify some other figure.

TYPICAL DOVETAIL JIG

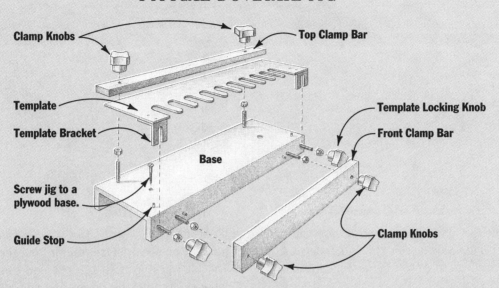

Clamp Knobs

Top Clamp Bar

Template

Template Bracket

Template Locking Knob

Front Clamp Bar

Base

Screw jig to a plywood base.

Guide Stop

Clamp Knobs

2. Set up the jig itself. Most jigs need to be attached to a ³/₄-inch plywood base, which can then be clamped to a workbench. Obviously, the jig has to be positioned at the edge of the bench so that the drawer or box side can be clamped in the jig.

3. Clamp the workpieces in the jig. The workpieces have to be clamped in the jig in a particular way. The socket piece—the drawer front—is clamped to the top of the jig. The tail piece—the

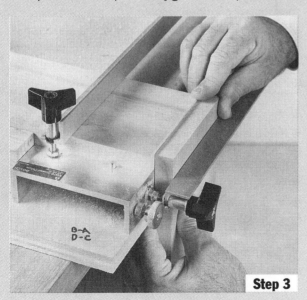

Step 3

drawer side—is clamped to the front of the jig. The socket piece must be butted against the face of the tail piece. The end of the tail piece must be flush with the top surface of the socket piece, as shown in the Step 3 photo.

Here's the easiest way to do it. Roughly position the tail piece in the jig, with its top end well above the jig. Slip the socket piece in the jig, and butt it tightly against the tail piece. Clamp it firmly. Now loosen the clamps holding the tail piece and lower it until its end is flush with the other workpiece. Clamp it firmly.

Both pieces need to be against the alignment pins or stops. These pins align the two workpieces so they are offset exactly ⁷/₁₆ inch. This is the amount they must be offset so that the edges of the assembled joint will be flush. Every jig has these pins—they're adjustable if your jig takes more than one template—and has a pair on the right and on the left. Use the pair on the left for now.

4. Install the template. Fit the template in place next. Typically, the template is screwed to a couple of L-shaped brackets. A slot in each bracket's extension fits over a stud projecting from the jig base. A stop nut serves both to adjust the fore-and-aft position of the template and as a stop against

(continued)

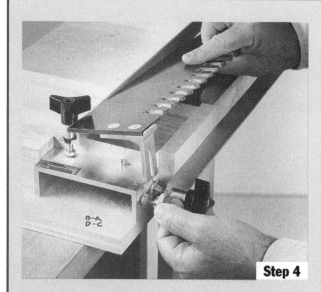

Step 4

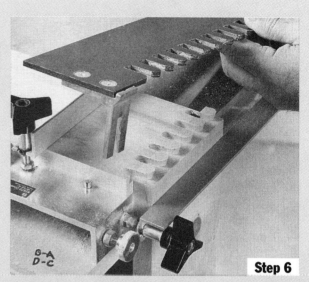

Step 6

which the lock-down nut or knob jams. If you have a choice, adjust it so it will yield a flush dovetail. The template needs to be flat on the workpieces.

5. Rout the dovetails. This will be a test cut. Set the router on the template, its bit free of the work. Switch on the router, and make a quick, shallow scoring cut across the tail piece, feeding from right to left (yes, this is a climb cut). This will help prevent the bit from pulling chips out along the tail piece's shoulder as it exits each cut.

Rout the dovetails, slot by slot, beginning on the left and working to the right. You may want to zip back through them when you are done, just to be sure you didn't pull out of a slot too soon, leaving the work only partially cut.

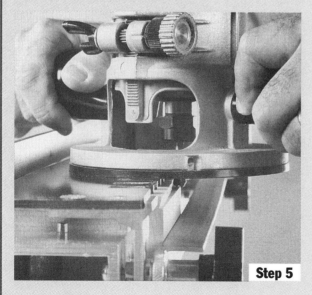

Step 5

6. Check your work before unclamping the parts. Don't just lift the router from the template. The bit will ruin both the cut and the template. Instead, turn off the power and pull the router toward you, getting it well clear of the jig before lifting it. Take a good look at the work and be sure you haven't missed a spot. (If you have, rout it now, before moving anything.) Only then should you remove the template, unclamp the work, and test assemble the joint.

7. Fine-tune the setup. Chances are, your setup needs a little fine-tuning. You slip the two test pieces together, and something's not quite right. Perhaps the fit is too loose. Or too tight. Or the sockets aren't deep enough. Or the parts are a little offset. All of these ills are cured with some fine-tuning.

Fit too tight? The bit's cutting too deep. *Reduce* the depth of cut slightly.

Fit too loose? The bit's not cutting deep enough. *Increase* the depth of cut slightly.

Are the sockets too shallow or too deep? The template is misaligned. To reduce the socket depth, move the template very slightly toward you. To increase the socket depth, move the template away from you. Your jig's instruction sheet should explain exactly how to accomplish these adjustments on your jig. Just remember that as you alter the depth of the sockets, you are also altering the thickness of the tails.

Are the two parts slightly misaligned when

Step 7

assembled? The top and bottom edges should be flush. If they aren't, you may not have had the workpieces snug against the alignment pins. Or the pins may be slightly misadjusted.

Any other problems you have will stem from misalignment of the workpieces in the jig. Make sure the top surface of the socket piece is flush with the top end of the tail piece, that they are at right angles to each other, that the template is square to the workpieces, and so forth.

When you've successfully fine-tuned the setup using the alignment pins on the left, cut a test joint using the right end of the jig. Do any additional tuning needed there.

8. Cut the good wood. Before starting, make sure you're organized for complete success. It doesn't matter whether you are dovetailing one drawer or fifty drawers, it's all too easy to get mixed up and cut the dovetails in the wrong places. After all, you do clamp the work in the jig with the assembly's inside faces exposed, an orientation that seems *calculated* to befuddle.

So do this. Label the parts on what will be their inside faces. If you can read the labels when the parts are in the jig, you've got the orientation correct. If you are doing drawers, the sides *always* go on the front, and the fronts and backs *always* go on the top.

And you need to label more than part names. Consider that each drawer or box has four joints. When you are doing machine-cut dovetails, two of the four joints must be cut on the left side of the jig and two on the right side. You don't want to get them mixed up.

The most simple organizational labeling system I've come across is shown in the drawing. There are few labels, but where you put them is as important as what they are. The labels indicate which is the inner face, and thus which face is up in the jig. The letters are always associated with a particular part. Each letter is placed at the bottom edge of the piece, to indicate which edge goes against the jig's alignment pins. On the jig itself, you mark two two-letter combinations beside each pair of alignment pins, as indicated in the drawing. As you clamp the parts into the jig, orient the letters toward the pins, and check the combination. If it isn't on your list of two, you are at the wrong end of the jig.

ORGANIZING LABELS

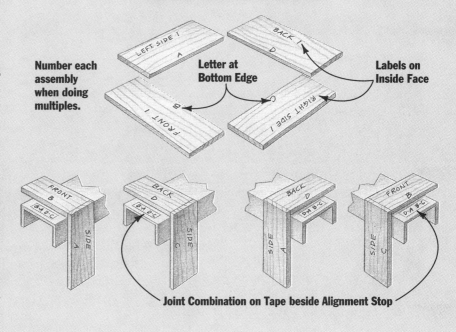

Number each assembly when doing multiples.

Letter at Bottom Edge

Labels on Inside Face

Joint Combination on Tape beside Alignment Stop

BOOKSHELVES

I was drawn to this piece by two things. First, it was a good bookshelf project: easy to make, utilitarian, yet handsome in that country way. Second, I liked the joinery: sliding dovetails. After I was drawn to the piece, I got intrigued by the engineering of it.

Let's look at these attractions.

Shelves. I like books, which shouldn't be a surprise, since I've been writing and editing them for 25 years. I have lots and lots of them, and I can always use more shelf space. This piece responded to a need.

But you can put more than books on these shelves. Whaddaya have? Crocks and baskets? Plants? Everyone's got a few tchotchkes. The project is simple, unassuming, yet attractive. Put it in the family room for videotapes. In the bathroom for linens. Yeah, even in the garage for your motor oil inventory.

It's easy enough to make. This is truly a three-night project: Knock it together the first night, slap on a first coat of paint on the second, and apply the finish coat on the third. With its sliding dovetail joinery, "knocking it together" is meant literally. Make the dovetails just right, and a hint of glue is all you need. A few smacks with a deadblow mallet will drive each shelf into place. Assembly's done.

So the joinery is a draw. I like the sliding dovetail, because it makes assembly a little easier for the Lone Woodworker. The parts won't fall away from one another while you're fumbling with clamps or fasteners. A slightly bowed board can be pulled into line without elaborate clamping configurations. I wanted to include the sliding dovetail in one of the projects in this book, so I was pleased to discover this bookshelf. It proves that the joint was around long before the router made it easy to cut.

Now you're probably wondering, as I did, Is this thing wobbly? There's no triangulation! you're saying. Well, despite that lack, this shelf unit doesn't sway much. Oh, a little. But not what I expected. I think it's that dovetail. It doesn't allow the parts to move the way a plain dado would.

Now if I've sold you on this project, just about all you need is a stack of boards, a saber saw, and a router and dovetail bit. The original is made with full 1-inch boards. We made one in today's 1-by pine (shown in the photo on the opposite page) and one in today's 5/4 pine. Both look good. If you are going to load up the shelves with heavy books, build with 5/4 so the shelves won't sag. For an assortment of books and tchotchkes, 1-by should be satisfactory. And if you have a planer, by all means use 1-inch boards.

Shelves need *stuff* to give them presence. Some books lend weight to the reproduction (*opposite*), but adding collectibles gives resonance.

CUTTING LIST

Piece	Number	Thickness	Width	Length	Material
Sides	2	3/4"	9"	62"	5/4 pine
Shelves	5	3/4"	9"	43½"	5/4 pine

1. Cut the parts. Rip and crosscut the two sides and five shelves to the dimensions specified by the Cutting List.

2. Rout the sliding dovetails. Do the slots first. *Side Layout* shows where to position the slots and how long to make them. The slots are stopped shy of the front edge of the sides. After laying out the slots, rout them. Note especially the width of the groove. The best way to produce a slot of this width

Here's a quick-and-dirty—and savvy—setup for routing tails for sliding dovetails. Its advantage is that you use the same router and bit height setting used for the slots. That's critical to achieving a good fit. Square up a short scrap of 2×4, and rout a recess for the bit at the midpoint. Clamp it to the router base, as shown, with two clamps. Expose just a sliver of the bit, and make test cuts. To deepen the cut, loosen one clamp and tap the block to expose a hair more of the bit.

A good trick for routing the stopped dovetail slots is to use a scrap "starting strip" between two workpieces so that both sides can be routed at the same time, even though both slots are stopped. With the back edge of the baseplate against the fence and the bit poised above the scrap, turn on the machine. Lower the bit into the scrap. Feed the router to the left, cutting to the stop mark. Then feed it back to the right, slotting the second workpiece to the stop mark. Return to the starting position, switch off the router, and tip the bit up out of the cut. Reset the fence to widen the slot.

is to use a ³/₄-inch dovetail bit. With a ¹/₂-inch bit, you have to make two passes to complete each slot.

With the slots done, rout the tails on the ends of the shelves. The bit should just nick the workpiece. You want to form a tail that perfectly fits the slot, and you want to do it with a single pass across each face of the board. Cut tails on the ends of all the shelves.

Pick the front edge of each shelf and mark it. Then trim back the tail ¹/₂ inch.

EXPLODED VIEW

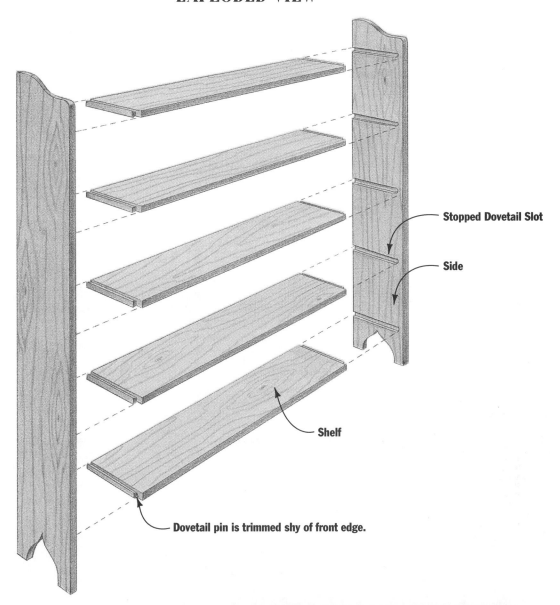

Stopped Dovetail Slot

Side

Shelf

Dovetail pin is trimmed shy of front edge.

3. Cut the tops and feet on the sides. Scale up the *Patterns* and make a template. Trace the top contour on the tops of the sides, and the split-foot contour on the bottom ends. Use a saber saw to cut the contours. Then scrape and sand the cut edges free of all saw marks.

If you like, break the exposed edges of the sides and shelves with a spoke-shave, file, or coarse sandpaper. The idea is to soften the edges and simulate the wear of the ages. You *could* do this

The Dovetail Bit Can Be Fragile

That's because of its pinched waist. Cutting too aggressively in hard wood can snap the bit. Cutting a dovetail slot in incrementally deeper passes isn't possible because of the bit's shape. It's usually a good idea, therefore, to rout a narrow dado with a straight bit, then open it up and reshape it with the dovetail bit.

But white pine is not a particularly hard wood. In most instances, you can save yourself the extra step. Just make a full-depth pass with the dovetail bit.

PLAN VIEWS

FRONT VIEW

SIDE LAYOUT

Cut contour after routing dovetail slots.

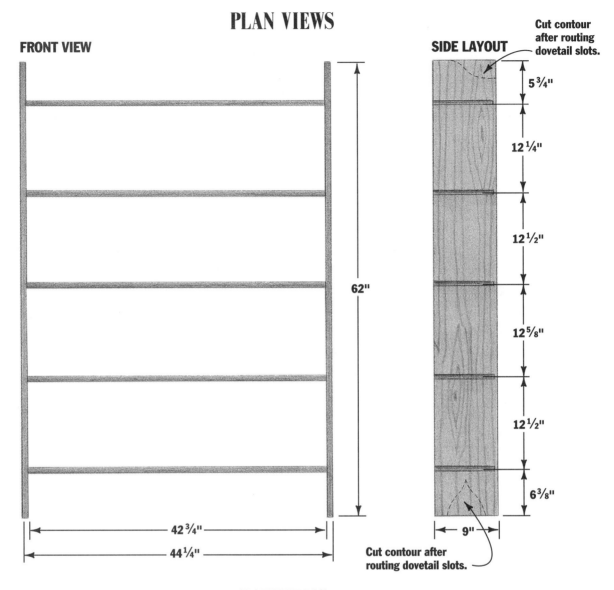

62"

42³⁄₄"

44¹⁄₄"

5³⁄₄"

12¹⁄₄"

12¹⁄₂"

12⁵⁄₈"

12¹⁄₂"

6³⁄₈"

9"

Cut contour after routing dovetail slots.

PATTERNS

TOP

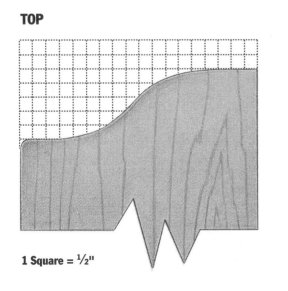

1 Square = ¹⁄₂"

FOOT

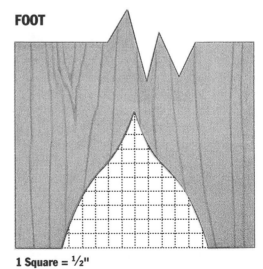

1 Square = ¹⁄₂"

If you can push the shelf into its slots, the fit is too loose. A blow or two with a mallet should be all that's needed to seat the joint. The mechanical lock of the sliding dovetail joint makes it easy to assemble, because the parts won't fall apart while you look for nails or clamps. You only need two hands. *What a concept!*

with a router and roundover bit, but that would produce too consistent an edge, which is what you want to avoid.

Finish sand the parts.

4. **Assemble the shelves.** Apply a dab of glue to the trimmed edge of the tail, start the tail into the slot, and drive it home. You may need a couple of mallet blows to seat the joint. That's not bad.

Get one end of the first shelf joined to the first side. Then insert the other end of that shelf into the second side. The subsequent shelves can be driven into both sides simultaneously. The sides will stay in position, and you won't need to clamp anything or drive in nails or screws. When the last shelf is driven home, you are done but for the painting.

5. **Apply a finish.** You can finish these bookshelves however you like. Our original is stained a dark brown, and we duplicated that with one of our units.

Check out the *ShopSmarts* feature "Country Finishes" on page 305 for information on options for finishes.

JOINERY DETAIL

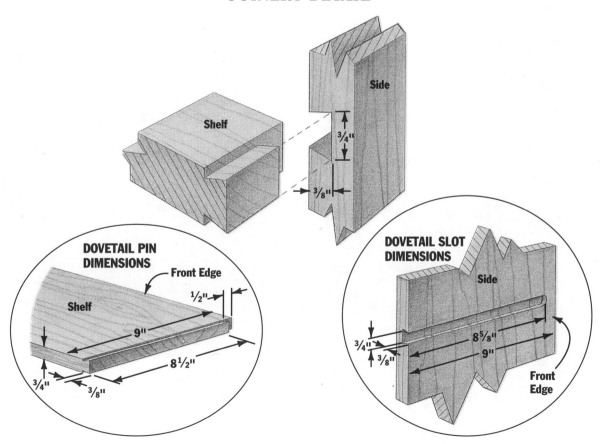

Shelf

Side

3/4"

3/8"

DOVETAIL PIN DIMENSIONS

Front Edge

Shelf

1/2"

9"

8 1/2"

3/4"

3/8"

DOVETAIL SLOT DIMENSIONS

Side

3/4"

3/8"

8 5/8"

9"

Front Edge

FOOTSTOOLS

A footstool is a primitive ottoman. It's not a step stool, which you stand on; it is too small and unstable for that. Rather, it's for propping up your feet.

For today's woodworker, either of these little footstools is a great weekend project. Either is a great gift project. Either is a decent sale-item project. The stools are small, require only a modest amount of stock, are quite easy to make; and yet—when they're all done—they are appealing. The appeal isn't based on practicality. We don't need footstools the way they did two hundred years ago. The appeal must be rooted in the design, maybe nostalgia.

The footstools just look right in a comfortable, country-style home. Not good as a step stool, remember, but great as a plant stand, as an accent to your home's decor.

In the rural home of two hundred years ago, you would prop up your feet for two reasons. One: You'd been on them all day, and you simply wanted to elevate them a bit and let the ache and swelling drain out. Two: You wanted to get them off the cold floor and up out of the draft. The wood fire that ostensibly heated the house usually sent most of the heated air up the chimney. To replace the departing warm air, cold air rushed in through every gap and crack in the house—and there were a lot of those, let me tell you! The footstool, like the wings on the wing chair and the high back on the settle, was calculated to take best advantage of what heat the fireplace generated.

In the country-style home of today, we prop up our feet primarily because we've been on them all day, and we simply want to elevate them a bit. If we don't use footstools for that purpose, it's because the BarcaLounger or the easy chair's upholstered ottoman or even the extra space on the sofa is so much more inviting. With tight construction, good insulation, and central heat, the second reason for the footstool has pretty much gone up the chimney.

So why would you spend a couple of evenings making and finishing such a stool? 'Cause you want one.

My wife remembers using a green footstool as a doll bed. Flip it over, and the legs become headboards and footboards. And I remember a footstool from my

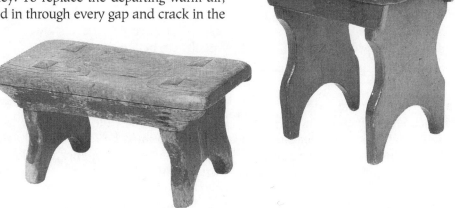

The original footstools (*above*) have been softened and worn by chilled and aching feet, propped before a blazing fire, night after night for a hundred years.

CUTTING LIST

TALL STOOL

Piece	Number	Thickness	Width	Length	Material
Top	1	$3/4$"	$8^3/4$"	12"	1-by pine
Legs	2	$3/4$"	$7^7/8$"	$11^1/2$"	1-by pine
Aprons	2	$1/2$"	$1^3/4$"	$10^7/8$"	pine

HARDWARE
$1^1/2$" headless cut brads

LOW STOOL

Piece	Number	Thickness	Width	Length	Material
Top	1	1"	$7^1/4$"	$15^1/2$"	5/4 pine
Legs	2	$1^1/8$"	$7^1/4$"	$7^3/4$"	5/4 pine
Aprons	2	$1/2$"	$1^3/8$"	$15^1/2$"	pine

HARDWARE
$1^1/2$" headless cut brads

childhood—it was green, too, and it had a penny stuck to the top. It served as the modeling stand in what are known in my family as "The Bubble Gum Pictures," which is a series of color photos my dad took, one night in the late '40s, of my sister, my cousins, and me. Each little kid taking a turn, standing on the footstool wearing my oldest cousin's clodhopper boots, blowing the biggest bubble ever. Now that I think about it, I can still feel the heat from the floodlamps, and hear the teasing and giggling. As I said, nostalgia may be a subtle engine here.

As I traveled from flea market to collector's mall to antique store, scouting out this collection's originals, I saw lots of footstools. More than one dealer had three or four stacked one atop another. The diversity of sizes and designs and finishes was remarkable. When I broke down and bought a couple, I did it because the two, though so different, were remarkably similar. One is low, with a thick top and thick legs. The other is tall and almost square. Yet both are miniature five-board benches, with the legs mortised into the top and secured with aprons. The leg cutouts are virtually the same—a semicircle cut into each edge and into the bottom, forming the two feet.

You may not have a need or desire to prop up your feet, but you do know a lot of people you care about who would love to have one of these footstools. Or, better, the pair.

1. Cut the parts. Although the stools are very similar in appearance and construction, the parts are quite different. The tall stool's top and legs are made of $3/4$-inch stock, while those for the low stool are made of 5/4 stock. The aprons for both are made of $1/2$-inch stock.

It's worth noting that 5/4 stock can range from 1 inch up to $1^3/16$ inches in thickness. Work with what you've got; if it's on the thin side, use it, but remember to reduce the width of the mortises.

Crosscut and rip the parts to the dimensions specified by the Cutting List. The stock for the low stool's top must be resawed and sanded or planed to the required 1-inch thickness. Resaw or plane the stock for the aprons.

2. Make the top template. Study the *Leg Layouts* drawing for the stool you are making. In both cases, the top is shaped and mortised with a router, guided by a $1/2$-inch plywood template. All you do is set it in

EXPLODED VIEW
(LOW FOOTSTOOL)

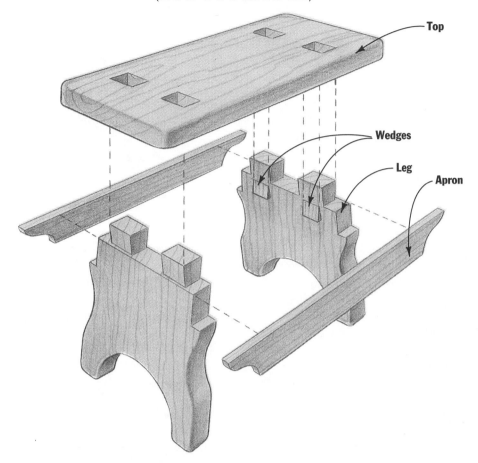

Top

Wedges

Leg

Apron

place, clamp it, and rout. After you rout one end, turn the template 180 degrees to rout the other end.

Note that because of the difference in diameters between the template guide and the bit, the template's guiding edge has to be just slightly different than the workpiece's finished edge. This difference is called the *offset*, and it is equal to half the difference between the diameters of the guide and the bit. Suggested guide/bit combinations that will work with the templates are listed in the *Leg Layouts* drawing.

Lay out the mortising window on the template blank first. You can use a router to rough it out. Pare or file it to the specified dimensions. With the windows cut, saw the template to the specified dimensions.

The corners of the tops are rounded. On the low stool, the curve has a constant radius, but on the tall stool, the curve is a segment of an ellipse, hence the *Pattern* provided for it in the *Plan Views*. Scribe the desired curve on the template, clamp the piece in a vise, and sand to the line. Finally, attach a fence.

3. Rout the mortises in the top. Use a plunge router and the template to cut the mortises and shape the corners. Back up the workpiece (and protect the bench top) by setting it atop a scrap board. Clamp the template to the workpiece. Set up the router with a $^3/_8$-inch (outside diameter) template guide and a $^1/_4$-inch bit—Amana makes a $2^7/_8$-inch-long $^1/_4$-inch straight bit (catalog number 45211) that works well here (available from Amana Tool, 800-445-0077). Set the router on the template, plunge the bit to cut about $^1/_4$ inch deep, and rout. Work the router back and forth, methodically cleaning out the waste. Make several passes to cut completely through the top.

When the mortise has been cut, use the same router to shape each corner. Don't risk damaging the top's edge by hogging straight into the corner. Use discretion. Whittle away at the edge and carefully work it down to the line. When the template guide runs smoothly along the template edge, the top's edge is done.

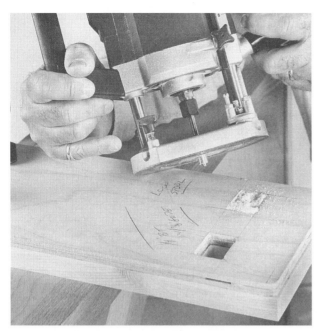

Here's the setup for routing the top. The template is aligned on the top, and the two pieces are clamped at the edge or corner of the workbench, with the area to be routed overhanging the bench top. Note how the mortise cavity fills with chips as you rout. You need to vacuum out the chips, and scrape them out of the corners of the template as well, so the mortise will be accurately sized. Even though it is a through mortise, and most of them will fall through, the chips do get packed in, and it takes some goading to get them all out.

After all the mortises have been routed, use a sharp chisel to square the corners.

4. Make the leg template. The leg templates are made in much the same fashion as the top templates. Follow the specifications shown in the appropriate *Leg Layouts* drawing. The drawing for the low stool shows a sequence for laying out and cutting the template, which may be helpful regardless of which stool you are making.

5. Cut the joinery on the legs. Before you shape the legs using the template and router, cut the tenons and the notches for the aprons. Especially with the low stool, the joinery cuts would be extremely tricky to make after the shaping is done.

Do the work on the table saw. Lay out all the cuts on the legs, and clearly mark the waste. Set the blade height to equal the top's thickness. Attach a tall facing to the miter gauge to help support the workpiece. With the leg standing on end and guided

MORTISING TEMPLATES

TOP VIEW—TALL STOOL

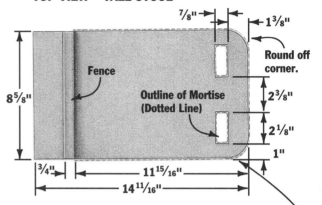

Trimmed workpieces will extend $^1/_{16}$" beyond edge of template because of offset between template guide and bit.

TOP VIEW—LOW STOOL

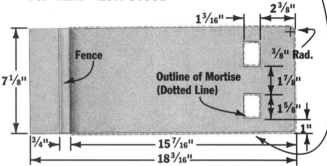

Routing Small Arcs— No Trammel Needed

You can use your router to cut the template's two arcs, even though their radii are probably shorter than that of the router base. Drill a pivot hole in the router's baseplate, as well as the template blank. Fit the pivot pin in the template, then set the router over it.

Remember to measure from the far edge of the bit when locating the pivot hole. (The bit must be to the waste side of the arc.)

To get a fixed-base router started in the cut, scribe the arc with a compass, and drill holes for the bit in the waste area at each end of the arc that the router is to cut.

PLAN VIEWS—TALL STOOL

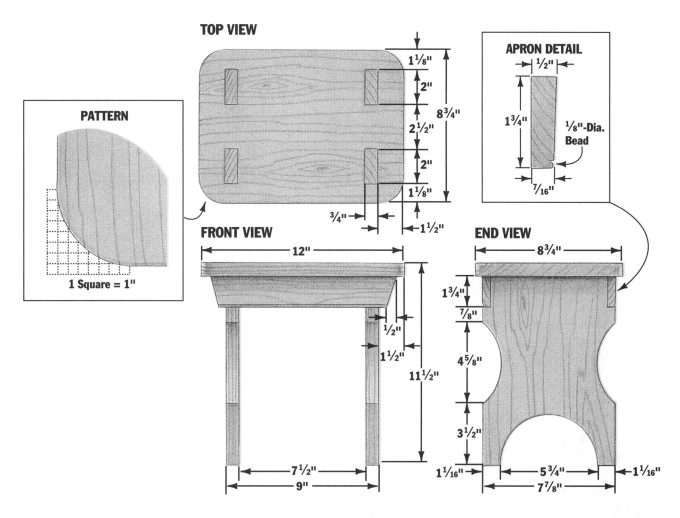

TOP VIEW

$1\frac{1}{8}$"
2"
$8\frac{3}{4}$"
$2\frac{1}{2}$"
2"
$1\frac{1}{8}$"
$\frac{3}{4}$"
$1\frac{1}{2}$"

PATTERN

1 Square = 1"

APRON DETAIL

$\frac{1}{2}$"
$1\frac{3}{4}$"
$\frac{1}{8}$"-Dia. Bead
$\frac{7}{16}$"

FRONT VIEW

12"
$\frac{1}{2}$"
$1\frac{1}{2}$"
$11\frac{1}{2}$"
$7\frac{1}{2}$"
9"

END VIEW

$8\frac{3}{4}$"
$1\frac{3}{4}$"
$\frac{7}{8}$"
$4\frac{5}{8}$"
$3\frac{1}{2}$"
$1\frac{1}{16}$"
$5\frac{3}{4}$"
$1\frac{1}{16}$"
$7\frac{7}{8}$"

by the miter gauge, make the vertical cuts to form the tenons. Make repeated, closely spaced cuts to trim the notch between the tenons.

Adjust the blade height and turn the workpiece onto its edge to cut the tenons' outer shoulders.

In the same manner, cut the notches for the aprons.

6. Kerf the tenons (low stool only). The low stool's legs are angled out 5 degrees. To achieve this angle with square mortises, you merely have to taper the outer face of the tenons, as shown in *Joinery Detail* in the *Plan Views—Low Stool*. A wedge driven into the gap keeps the joint tight.

To taper the tenons, set the table saw blade height equal to the height of the tenons. Adjust the rip fence to the thickness of the leg. Then tilt the blade 5 degrees. Turn on the saw and run the leg, standing on end, along the fence.

When everything is set up correctly, the table saw blade barely creases the tenons. Taper them from full thickness at their tops to just $\frac{3}{32}$ inch less at their shoulders.

PLAN VIEWS—LOW STOOL

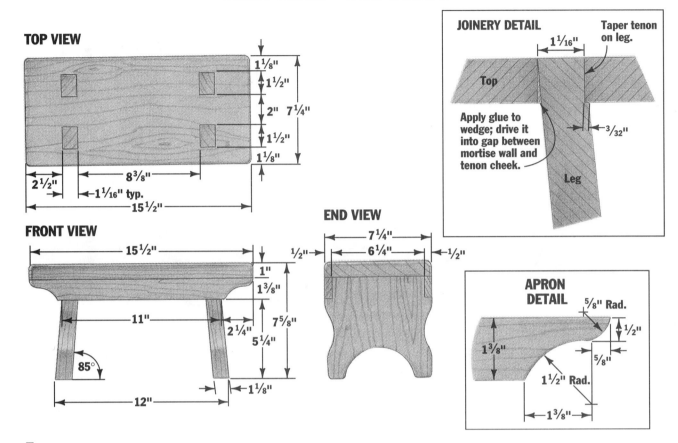

TOP VIEW

FRONT VIEW

END VIEW

JOINERY DETAIL

Taper tenon on leg.

Top

Apply glue to wedge; drive it into gap between mortise wall and tenon cheek.

Leg

APRON DETAIL

---

7. Shape the legs. After all the joinery is cut, you can use the template and router to shape the legs. The routine is like that used to do the top, except that it's advisable to cut the workpiece close to the template with a saber saw before routing. There's quite a bit of waste to be removed, especially in the cutouts. Just don't forget about the offset and cut *too* close to the template.

Lay the leg on a scrap, set the template on top, and clamp them to the bench. Cut with the saber saw, holding the line at least ⅛ inch from the template. With the same guide/bit setup used for the top, rout the leg's edge smooth.

8. Make the aprons. The last step before assembly is to make the aprons. Those for the tall stool are very slightly tapered from top to bottom, as shown in the *Apron Detail* of *Plan Views—Tall Stool.*

Cutting the taper is a resawing operation. Scribe the taper on the end of one apron. Set the table saw blade height and rip fence. Then position the marked workpiece beyond the blade, and tilt the blade until it aligns with the taper marked on the workpiece. Make the cuts.

Rout a ⅛-inch-diameter bead along the edge, as shown in the *Apron Detail* of *Plan Views—Tall Stool.* Cascade sells this small corner beading bit; it's catalog number C1543 (Cascade Tools, 800-235-0272). Then miter the ends, reducing the aprons to their final length.

The low stool's aprons are square, but the ends are cut to an ogee shape. Lay out the line, as shown in the *Apron Detail* of *Plan Views—Low Stool,* and cut it with a saber saw. Sand the cut edges smooth.

9. Assemble the stool. Glue the tenons into the mortises. With the low stool, cut wedges from scrap to fit behind the tenons, and glue them in place. Apply glue to the top edge of each apron and set it in place. If necessary, clamp the apron to the top. Drive cut brads through the aprons into the legs. (Drill pilot holes first if you use headed brads.)

10. Apply a finish. I painted both stools. The originals had been painted, though the finish was completely gone from the top of the low stool. Refer to the *ShopSmarts* feature "Country Finishes" on page 305 for tips on selecting and applying a finish.

LEG LAYOUTS—TALL STOOL

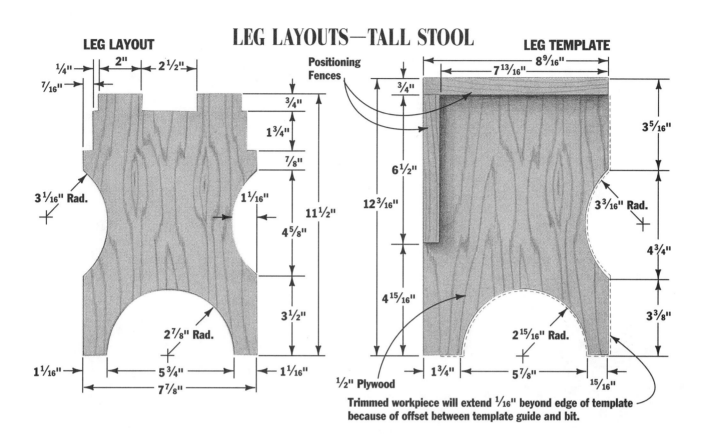

LEG LAYOUT

LEG TEMPLATE

Positioning Fences

¼"   2"   2½"

7/16"

¾"

1¾"

7/8"

3 1/16" Rad.

1 1/16"

11½"

4 5/8"

3½"

2 7/8" Rad.

1 1/16"   5 ¾"   1 1/16"

7 7/8"

8 9/16"

7 13/16"

¾"

6½"

12 3/16"

4 15/16"

½" Plywood

3 5/16"

3 3/16" Rad.

4 ¾"

3 3/8"

2 15/16" Rad.

1 ¾"   5 7/8"   15/16"

Trimmed workpiece will extend ¹⁄₁₆" beyond edge of template because of offset between template guide and bit.

LEG LAYOUTS—LOW STOOL

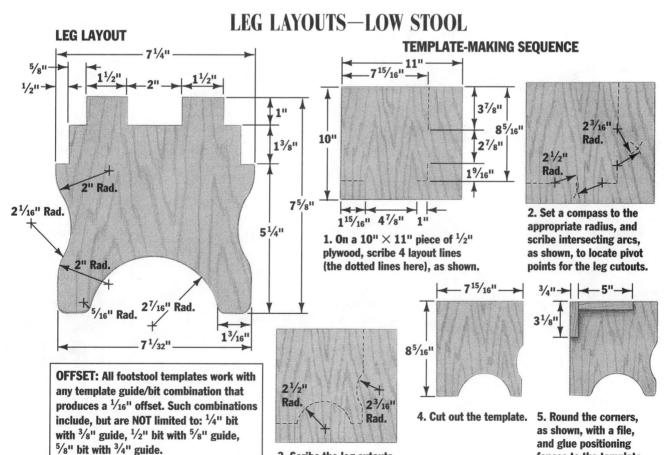

LEG LAYOUT

TEMPLATE-MAKING SEQUENCE

7 ¼"

5/8"

½"

1½"   2"   1½"

1"

1 3/8"

2" Rad.

2 1/16" Rad.

2" Rad.

5/16" Rad.   2 7/16" Rad.

7 5/8"

5 ¼"

1 3/16"

7 1/32"

OFFSET: All footstool templates work with any template guide/bit combination that produces a ¹⁄₁₆" offset. Such combinations include, but are NOT limited to: ¼" bit with ³⁄₈" guide, ½" bit with ⁵⁄₈" guide, ⁵⁄₈" bit with ¾" guide.

11"

7 15/16"

10"

3 7/8"

8 5/16"

2 7/8"

1 9/16"

1 15/16"   4 7/8"   1"

1. On a 10" × 11" piece of ¹⁄₂" plywood, scribe 4 layout lines (the dotted lines here), as shown.

2 3/16" Rad.

2 ½" Rad.

2. Set a compass to the appropriate radius, and scribe intersecting arcs, as shown, to locate pivot points for the leg cutouts.

2½" Rad.

2 3/16" Rad.

3. Scribe the leg cutouts.

7 15/16"

8 5/16"

4. Cut out the template.

¾"   5"

3 1/8"

5. Round the corners, as shown, with a file, and glue positioning fences to the template.

MARITIMES CHEST OF DRAWERS

The order and proportions of the drawers and the form of the pulls attracted me to this old chest of drawers.

The stack of commodious drawers obviously provided lots of compartmented, accessible storage. The top tier of drawers presented an interesting—and unfamiliar—pattern of smaller drawers. While the proportions aren't refined, they are pleasant and they do articulate clearly what this is: a solid, practical, *country* chest of drawers.

And in that light, the meaty pulls are just right.

The chest's provenance is pretty much a mystery. The lack of information about its origins, along with aspects of the chest's current condition, would disappoint the truly serious collector. But it is those very things that, to me, are the essence of country woodworking and its furniture.

Though built in one of Canada's maritime provinces—New Brunswick, Nova Scotia, or Prince Edward Island—this particular chest of drawers was in a back room of an antique store in southern New Hampshire when I measured and photographed it. Clearly, it was not "original."

The base is new, for example. I was told that the "picker" who brought the piece out of Canada made it. Was the old one broken?

Rotted? Don't know. What did it look like? Is the new one a duplicate of the original, or just something easy to make with the materials at hand? Don't know that either, though I suspect the picker didn't try too hard to reproduce the original base.

The finish is new, too. The original was stripped off and replaced with a honey-hued stain and varnish. Who knows what the chest originally looked like? Was it stained and varnished as it is now? Doubtful. Was it used "in the white," which is to say, without a finish? Doubtful. Was it painted? Most likely; pine furniture usually was painted.

One thing I do know is that this chest of drawers saw a *lot* of use. The drawer runners are heavily worn. The picker scabbed new wood over the worst of them. But the level of wear bears testament to how well engineered this chest of drawers is. The drawers, as simply made as they are, are still in good shape. The case is still solid. If the chest hadn't been designed soundly and built properly, it would have come apart as surely as the runners did literally wear away.

And that's the thing about country woodworking as evident in country furniture. The design may be relatively

For the person with lots of clothing, this roomy chest of drawers (*opposite*), a reproduction of a Canadian original (*above*), provides plenty of drawer space.

CUTTING LIST

Piece	Number	Thickness	Width	Length	Material
CASE					
Case sides	2	1"	19$\frac{1}{4}$"	47$\frac{3}{4}$"	5/4 pine
Top	1	$\frac{3}{4}$"	20$\frac{1}{4}$"	42$\frac{1}{4}$"	1-by pine
Top moldings	2	$\frac{3}{4}$"	$\frac{3}{8}$"	20$\frac{1}{4}$"	1-by pine
Bottom	1	$\frac{3}{4}$"	17$\frac{3}{4}$"	41$\frac{1}{2}$"	1-by pine
Battens	5	$\frac{1}{4}$"	2$\frac{3}{8}$"	20$\frac{1}{4}$"	hardwood
Drawer runners	16	1$\frac{1}{8}$"	1$\frac{1}{8}$"	18$\frac{1}{2}$"	1-by pine
Rails	5	$\frac{3}{4}$"	1$\frac{5}{8}$"	41$\frac{1}{4}$"	1-by pine
Top rail	1	$\frac{3}{4}$"	1$\frac{3}{4}$"	41$\frac{1}{4}$"	1-by pine
Bottom rail	1	$\frac{3}{4}$"	2"	41$\frac{1}{4}$"	1-by pine
Drawer stiles	2	$\frac{3}{4}$"	1$\frac{7}{8}$"	6$\frac{1}{2}$"	1-by pine
Top back board	1	$\frac{3}{4}$"	4$\frac{1}{2}$"	41$\frac{1}{2}$"	1-by pine
Bottom back board	1	$\frac{3}{4}$"	6$\frac{5}{8}$"	41$\frac{1}{2}$"	1-by pine
Back boards	5	$\frac{3}{4}$"	7$\frac{5}{8}$"	41$\frac{1}{2}$"	1-by pine
Dowels	18	$\frac{1}{8}$" dia.		$\frac{3}{4}$"	hardwood
BASE					
Base front	1	1"	5"	43$\frac{1}{2}$"	5/4 pine
Base sides	2	1"	5"	19$\frac{7}{8}$"	5/4 pine
Rear feet	2	1"	3$\frac{1}{4}$"	7$\frac{1}{4}$"	5/4 pine
Base cleats	2	$\frac{3}{4}$"	3$\frac{1}{2}$"	42$\frac{1}{4}$"	1-by pine
DRAWERS					
Top center drawer front	1	$\frac{3}{4}$"	6$\frac{3}{8}$"	7"	1-by pine
Top outside drawer fronts	2	$\frac{3}{4}$"	6$\frac{3}{8}$"	15$\frac{1}{2}$"	1-by pine
Top drawer sides	6	$\frac{1}{2}$"	5$\frac{5}{16}$"	18$\frac{7}{16}$"	1-by pine
Top center drawer back	1	$\frac{3}{4}$"	5$\frac{5}{16}$"	5$\frac{1}{2}$"	1-by pine
Top outside drawer backs	2	$\frac{3}{4}$"	5$\frac{5}{16}$"	14"	1-by pine
Top center drawer bottom	1	$\frac{1}{2}$"	18$\frac{7}{16}$"	6$\frac{1}{2}$"	1-by pine
Top outside drawer bottoms	2	$\frac{1}{2}$"	18$\frac{7}{16}$"	15"	1-by pine
Drawer fronts	4	$\frac{3}{4}$"	6$\frac{1}{4}$"	40$\frac{3}{4}$"	1-by pine
Drawer sides	8	$\frac{1}{2}$"	5$\frac{3}{16}$"	18$\frac{7}{16}$"	1-by pine
Drawer backs	4	$\frac{3}{4}$"	5$\frac{3}{16}$"	39$\frac{1}{4}$"	1-by pine
Bottom drawer front	1	$\frac{3}{4}$"	7$\frac{1}{2}$"	40$\frac{3}{4}$"	1-by pine
Bottom drawer sides	2	$\frac{1}{2}$"	6$\frac{7}{16}$"	18$\frac{7}{16}$"	1-by pine
Bottom drawer back	1	$\frac{3}{4}$"	6$\frac{7}{16}$"	39$\frac{1}{4}$"	1-by pine
Drawer bottoms	5	$\frac{1}{2}$"	18$\frac{7}{16}$"	40$\frac{1}{4}$"	1-by pine
Drawer pulls	13	2$\frac{1}{4}$"	2$\frac{1}{4}$"	1$\frac{1}{2}$"	hardwood

HARDWARE

#8 × 1$\frac{1}{4}$" flathead wood screws
6d cut finish nails
3d cut finish nails
3d fine-cut headless brads
Optional: 13 maple pulls, 2" dia., with screw. Catalog number WK-3LB from
    Horton Brasses (203-635-4400).

EXPLODED VIEW

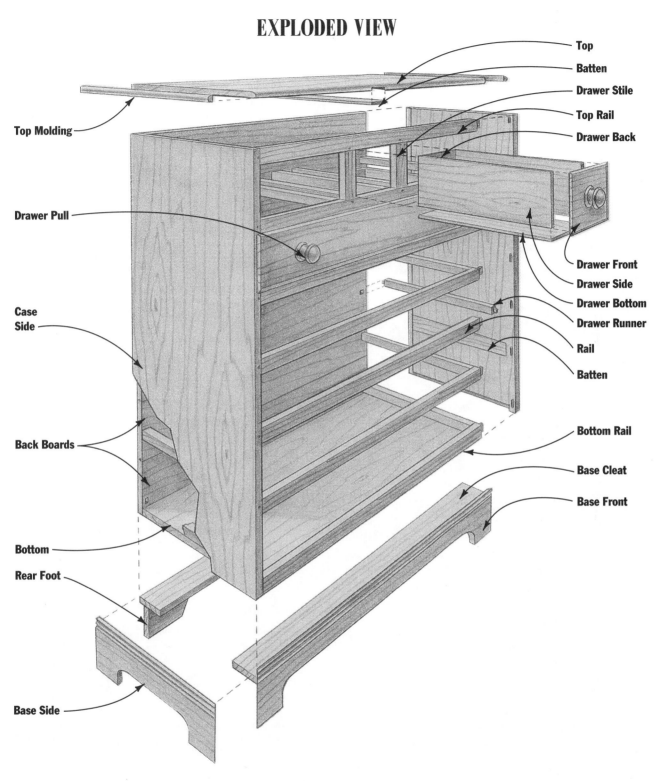

Top

Batten

Drawer Stile

Top Rail

Drawer Back

Top Molding

Drawer Pull

Case
Side

Back Boards

Bottom

Rear Foot

Base Side

Drawer Front

Drawer Side

Drawer Bottom

Drawer Runner

Rail

Batten

Bottom Rail

Base Cleat

Base Front

unsophisticated, but the construction often displays real woodworking savvy. The builder of this chest, for example, dealt well with wood's natural expansion and contraction.

Because the chest of drawers was so well built in the first place, it is still around today despite a century or more of obviously hard use. It got all that hard use because, like most country furniture, it is eminently practical and because, like most country furniture, it is attractive in comfortable, familiar, homey ways. It's practical and attractive still, even by today's standards.

BUILD THE CASE

1. Glue up the sides, top, and bottom. The dimensions for these panels are given in the Cutting List. Tips on gluing up are found in the *ShopSmarts* feature "Gluing Up Panels" on page 49. The sides and top should be free of prominent defects, but because the bottom is unseen, you can use your odds and ends of knotty lumber for that part.

2. Cut the joinery in the sides. The case structure is evident from the drawings. It's somewhat uncommon, yet it's practical and has survived time's tests. The sides and rails are joined by pegged mortise-and-tenon joints; there are no stiles extending from top to bottom as in the typical face frame. The back boards and bottom set into rabbets

Template-Guided Mortising with the Router

Mortise routing can be a template-guided operation. You need a plunge router for this, as you do for other approaches to mortise routing. But you don't need an edge guide or other fences that can be time-consuming to set up. You simply clamp a template to the workpiece, set the router on the template, and rout.

In template-guided work, the bit opening in the router's baseplate is fitted with a guide bushing (sometimes called a template guide). This is a

JOINERY TEMPLATE

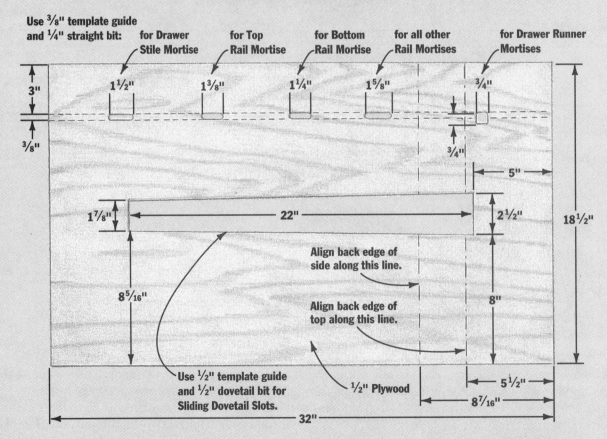

Use ³⁄₈" template guide and ¹⁄₄" straight bit:
for Drawer Stile Mortise — 1½"
for Top Rail Mortise — 1³⁄₈"
for Bottom Rail Mortise — 1¼"
for all other Rail Mortises — 1⁵⁄₈"
for Drawer Runner Mortises — ³⁄₄"

3"   ³⁄₈"   ³⁄₄"   5"   18½"

1⁷⁄₈"   22"   2½"

8⁵⁄₁₆"   8"

Align back edge of side along this line.

Align back edge of top along this line.

Use ½" template guide and ½" dovetail bit for Sliding Dovetail Slots.

½" Plywood

5½"   8⁷⁄₁₆"

32"

cut into the sides. The top overlays the case and is nailed in place.

After the clamps are off the sides, and any glue squeeze-out has been scraped and sanded away, rout the mortises for the rails. These are ½ inch deep and uniformly positioned ¼ inch from the front edges of the side panels. Details of size and location are shown in *Side Layout*. Note that while all are the same width, the top and bottom mortises are different lengths than the other five.

After the mortises are done, cut the rabbets. Be especially careful in cutting the rabbets for the bottom, since they are stopped.

3. Cut the tapered dovetail slots in the sides and top. To keep the sides and top from cupping with changes in temperature and humidity, the original builder drove battens into dovetail slots cut across these wide panels. The slots taper from a width of 2⅜ inches at the back edge to 1¾ inches

(continued on page 258)

Our joinery template is shown here clamped to the side of the chest of drawers. With a cleat clamped to the bottom of the template, it's easy to slide the template along the workpiece from mortise to mortise. The fence ensures all will be the same distance from the workpiece's edge. Lining up the slots for the three different rail mortises makes it easier to rout the slots in the first place, and to rout the mortises.

disk with a precisely sized opening for the bit. The opening has a collar, which catches on the edge of the template, positioning the bit for its cut.

For the typical mortise, the template has a slot routed in it. Because the guide bushing's collar is fractionally larger than the bit, the slot must be slightly wider and longer than the mortise. Position the template on the workpiece so the slot is directly over the spot where the mortise is to be, then clamp it. With the guide bushing's collar caught in the slot, the router can only move where the slot allows.

This approach is especially useful where the workpiece can't easily be clamped in the trough-style fixture shown on page 83 in the *ShopSmarts* feature "Cutting Mortise-and-Tenon Joints." It's useful too where the mortise is wider than the bit's diameter (where it is square, for example). Both of these situations occur in making the Maritimes Chest of Drawers.

For the Maritimes Chest of Drawers, we made one template. See the drawing *Joinery Template*. Made of ½-inch plywood, it has slots for all the mortises, as well as a cutout for the slots for the sliding dovetail battens. For the rail mortises in the sides, rout three slots in the template, each ⅜ inch wide, as shown in the drawing. For the drawer runner mortises in the rails and back boards, the template opening is square, as shown in the drawing. All the mortises are routed with a ⅜-inch-diameter guide bushing and a ¼-inch straight bit.

To use the template, lay out each mortise on the workpiece. Line up the template slot over the layout, centering it by eye. (As an option, you can attach a fence to the template to locate the template in relation to the edge of the workpiece.) Clamp the template securely. Set the router on the template with the guide's collar in the appropriate slot. Turn on the router, plunge the bit, and make the cut.

PLAN VIEWS

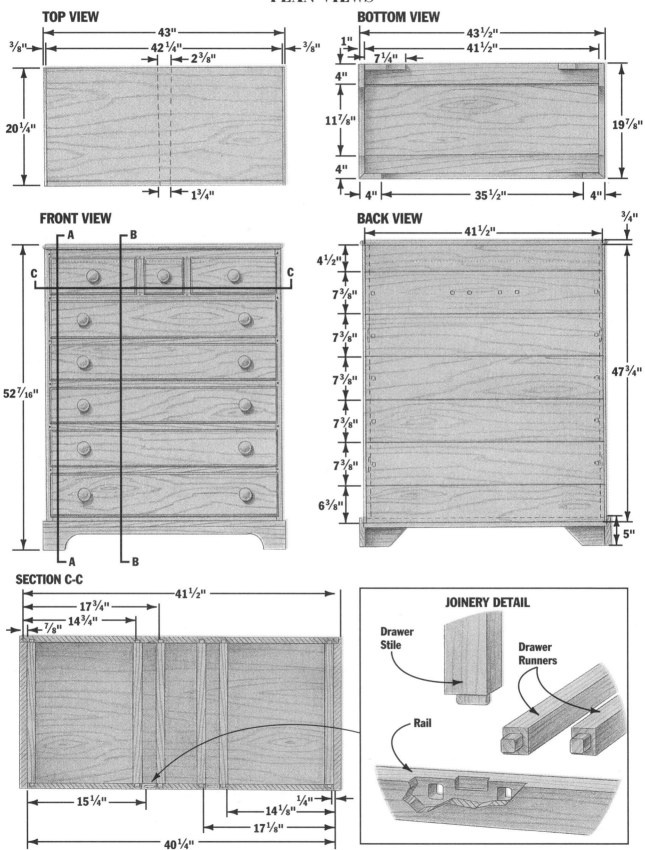

TOP VIEW

3/8" 43" 3/8"
42 1/4"
2 3/8"
20 1/4"
1 3/4"

BOTTOM VIEW

1" 43 1/2"
7 1/4" 41 1/2"
4"
11 7/8" 19 7/8"
4"
4" 35 1/2" 4"

FRONT VIEW

A   B
C   C
52 7/16"
A   B

BACK VIEW

3/4"
41 1/2"
4 1/2"
7 3/8"
7 3/8"
7 3/8" 47 3/4"
7 3/8"
7 3/8"
6 3/8"
5"

SECTION C-C

41 1/2"
17 3/4"
14 3/4"
7/8"
15 1/4"
14 1/8" 1/4"
17 1/8"
40 1/4"

JOINERY DETAIL

Drawer Stile

Drawer Runners

Rail

PLAN VIEWS

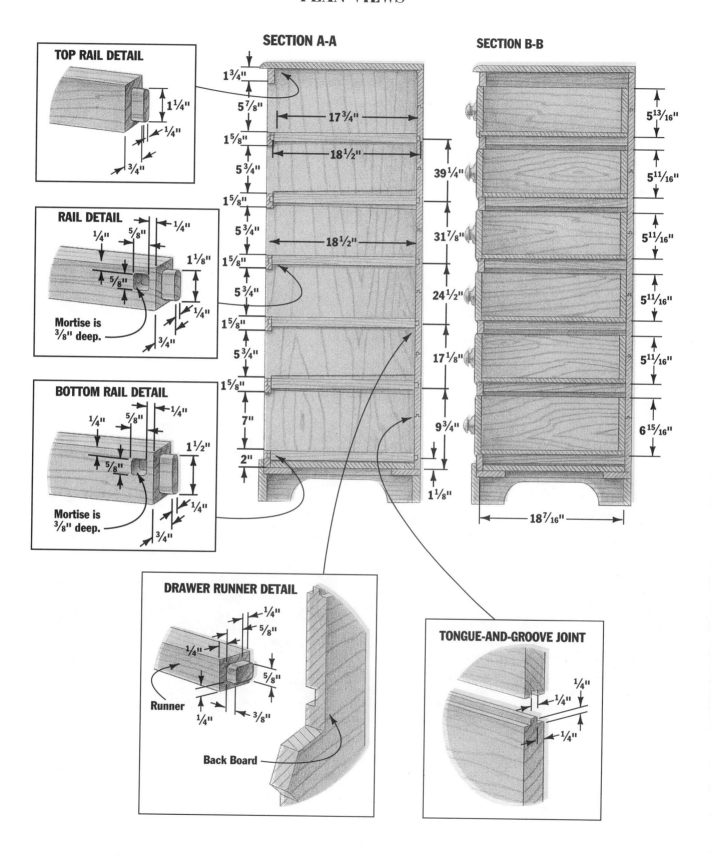

TOP RAIL DETAIL

$1\frac{1}{4}$"
$\frac{1}{4}$"
$\frac{3}{4}$"

RAIL DETAIL

$\frac{1}{4}$"
$\frac{5}{8}$"
$\frac{1}{4}$"
$\frac{5}{8}$"
$1\frac{1}{8}$"
$\frac{1}{4}$"
$\frac{3}{4}$"

Mortise is $\frac{3}{8}$" deep.

BOTTOM RAIL DETAIL

$\frac{1}{4}$"
$\frac{5}{8}$"
$\frac{1}{4}$"
$\frac{5}{8}$"
$1\frac{1}{2}$"
$\frac{1}{4}$"
$\frac{3}{4}$"

Mortise is $\frac{3}{8}$" deep.

SECTION A-A

$1\frac{3}{4}$"
$5\frac{7}{8}$"
$1\frac{5}{8}$"
$5\frac{3}{4}$"
$1\frac{5}{8}$"
$5\frac{3}{4}$"
$1\frac{5}{8}$"
$5\frac{3}{4}$"
$1\frac{5}{8}$"
$5\frac{3}{4}$"
$1\frac{5}{8}$"
7"
2"

$17\frac{3}{4}$"
$18\frac{1}{2}$"
$18\frac{1}{2}$"

$39\frac{1}{4}$"
$31\frac{7}{8}$"
$24\frac{1}{2}$"
$17\frac{1}{8}$"
$9\frac{3}{4}$"
$1\frac{1}{8}$"

SECTION B-B

$5\frac{13}{16}$"
$5\frac{11}{16}$"
$5\frac{11}{16}$"
$5\frac{11}{16}$"
$5\frac{11}{16}$"
$6\frac{15}{16}$"

$18\frac{7}{16}$"

DRAWER RUNNER DETAIL

$\frac{1}{4}$"
$\frac{5}{8}$"
$\frac{1}{4}$"
$\frac{5}{8}$"
$\frac{1}{4}$"
$\frac{3}{8}$"

Runner

Back Board

TONGUE-AND-GROOVE JOINT

$\frac{1}{4}$"
$\frac{1}{4}$"
$\frac{1}{4}$"

SIDE LAYOUT

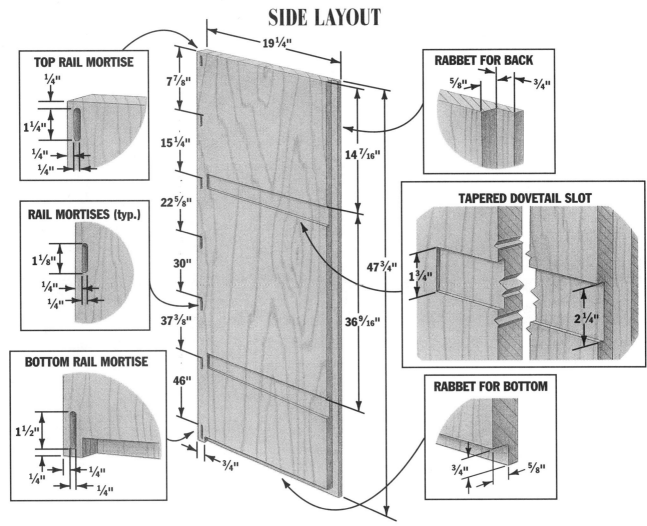

TOP RAIL MORTISE
$\frac{1}{4}$"
$1\frac{1}{4}$"
$\frac{1}{4}$"
$\frac{1}{4}$"

RAIL MORTISES (typ.)
$1\frac{1}{8}$"
$\frac{1}{4}$"
$\frac{1}{4}$"

BOTTOM RAIL MORTISE
$1\frac{1}{2}$"
$\frac{1}{4}$"
$\frac{1}{4}$"

19$\frac{1}{4}$"
7$\frac{7}{8}$"
15$\frac{1}{4}$"
22$\frac{5}{8}$"
30"
37$\frac{3}{8}$"
46"
$\frac{3}{4}$"

RABBET FOR BACK
$\frac{5}{8}$" $\frac{3}{4}$"

14$\frac{7}{16}$"
47$\frac{3}{4}$"
36$\frac{9}{16}$"

TAPERED DOVETAIL SLOT
1$\frac{3}{4}$"
2$\frac{1}{4}$"

RABBET FOR BOTTOM
$\frac{3}{4}$" $\frac{5}{8}$"

near the front edge. Each side has two battens, while the top has one. Refer to *Side Layout* and *Top View* for the specific dimensions and locations of the slots.

The most trouble-free way to cut the slots is with a router, using a template to guide the cuts. The template is shown in "Template-Guided Mortising with the Router" on page 254.

Fit a $\frac{1}{2}$-inch template guide to the router, and install a $\frac{1}{2}$-inch dovetail bit. Carefully set the depth of cut to make the slot $\frac{1}{4}$ inch deep. To rout each slot, clamp the template to the workpiece in the appropriate position. Set the router on the template with the bit clear of the work, switch it on, then

Routing the dovetail slots makes a lot of chips, but there isn't a better way to do it. Clamp the template and the workpiece to the workbench. Feed the router along the perimeter of the template's slot, cutting the slot's outline. Then work methodically back and forth across the slot, clearing the waste from the slot.

move the bit into the work. Rout around the perimeter of the template, then remove the remaining waste to complete the slot.

4. Make and install the tapered dovetail battens. Here's where a strong hardwood might be appropriate, though it isn't absolutely necessary. Whatever species you do use, make it 1/4-inch stock. Cut six or seven blanks to the size specified by the Cutting List (you may need a couple of extras).

Taper each piece on the table saw, just as if it were a table leg. (See the *ShopSmarts* feature "Tapering Legs on the Table Saw" on page 189 for the basics.) After the blanks are tapered, rout the dovetail angle along the edges on the router table. Set the fence so the dovetail bit cuts the angle without reducing the width of the battens.

Fitting the battens into the slots in the sides is a trial-and-error proposition. Ideally, the battens will be just a bit too wide for the slots. Use a block plane to shave the edges until the proper fit is achieved. You want the hand-inserted batten to seize about 3/8 to 1/4 inch short of the slot's end, so it will take a sharp mallet-blow to seat it. When you've got this fit, run the end of the batten across the router table to put the dovetail angle across the end, then round off the corners with a file to match the contour of the slot. Put dots of glue in the two corners of the

slot end, then fit the batten in the slot and drive it home. Trim the batten flush with the shoulder of the rabbet in the back of the side.

Since the slot in the top is through, the batten is a bit easier to fit and install. Apply a little glue to the slot at the front edge of the top panel, and tap the batten firmly into place. Trim the batten flush at both the front and back.

5. Make the face frame. This isn't a separate assembly, but a collection of rails and two short stiles.

In this project, the rails do more than segment the case for the drawers. They also serve as the front supports for the drawer runners. The runners and rails are joined by mortise-and-tenon joints. The mortises for the runners can be routed easily. Use a template to guide the router, as explained in "Template-Guided Mortising with the Router" on page 254. All the rails but the top one have at least two runner mortises. Note that the rail second from the top has four additional runner mortises. See *Sections A-A* and *C-C* with their details in the *Plan Views* drawings.

Rout these mortises.

As previously noted, the rails are joined to the case sides by mortise-and-tenon joints. The two drawer stiles are joined to the top and second rails by mortise-and-tenon joints, too. Lay out and rout

Tenoning with a Dado Cutter

A dado cutter can make quick work of tenoning, especially where the tenon is short—no more than 5/8 inch, say—and where you are removing the same amount of stock from all four surfaces of the workpiece.

The face frame tenons are a very good example. Set up the cutter to make a 3/8-inch-wide cut, and adjust its height to 1/4 inch. Bring the rip fence—with a wooden facing attached to protect the cutter—right up to the cutter.

To form the tenon, guide the workpiece with the miter gauge. Butt the end of the workpiece against the rip fence. One pass cuts the first cheek and shoulder. Roll the workpiece 90 degrees and make another pass. The second cheek and shoulder are now cut. Repeat the roll-and-pass two more times, and the tenon is done.

the mortises for the drawer stiles in the appropriate two rails.

To complete the face frame, cut tenons on the ends of the rails and stiles. All the tenons are $3/8$ inch long with $1/4$-inch shoulders all around. Cut the tenons, then round off their corners with a file (so they'll fit the routed mortises, which don't have square corners).

6. Make the drawer runners.

All the runners are the same. If need be, you can glue strips of standard 1-by stock to produce the thickness needed for the runners. Or you can use 5/4 stock, which is usually somewhere between 1 and $1^{1}/16$ inches thick, and shade the dimensions as necessary to accommodate the thinner stock. Whichever approach you choose, cut the runners to the dimensions specified by the Cutting List.

Set up the table saw with the dado cutter, adjust the depth of cut, and position the rip fence. Guiding the cuts with the miter gauge, tenon the ends of all the runners. See the *Drawer Runner Detail* with *Section A-A* of the *Plan Views* drawings. With a file, round off the corners of the tenons so they'll fit the routed mortises.

7. Complete the top.

Along the front edge, rout a quarter-round profile, cutting deep enough to create a $1/16$-inch step from the top surface. See the *Front* and *Top Views* of the *Plan Views* drawings. To finish off the end grain, nail a strip of bull-nose molding to the ends of the panel. Use a file to shape the end of the molding to blend into the profile along the panel's front edge. (To make the molding, rout a bull-nose profile on the edge of a board, then rip the profile from the board.)

Use Different Woods for Long-Wearing Drawer Runners

According to woodworking lore (or folklore), you should make a drawer runner from a different species of wood than the part that rides on the runner. The parts will wear each other out more quickly if they are made of the same wood species. If you buy this advice, make the chest's many runners from poplar or fir or any wood other than pine.

8. Assemble the case.

The various components are assembled with glue or nails.

Begin by joining the two drawer stiles to the appropriate rails, gluing the tenons in their mortises. Then assemble the rails and sides, again gluing the tenons in their mortises. With bar or pipe clamps securing this assembly, nail the bottom and the top in place.

Pin the rail and stile tenons next. Drill a $1/8$-inch-diameter hole through each mortise-and-tenon joint connecting rail to side and stile to rail. Locate the hole on the midline of the tenon, just $1/4$ inch from the shoulder. (The pins can be seen in the *Front View*.) Drive a dowel pin into each hole, then trim and sand it flush with the face of the chest.

9. Make and install the back boards.

The first step is to rip and crosscut the back boards to the dimensions specified by the Cutting List. (Don't rip the top board just yet; rip it to fit just before nailing it in place.)

Cut tongues and grooves on the boards as indicated in *Tongue-and-Groove Joint* with *Section A-A* of *Plan Views*. Note that the top board is grooved along its bottom edge only, and the bottom board has a tongue formed on its top edge only. All the others have a tongue formed on the top edge and are grooved along the bottom edge.

Lay out and rout the mortises for the drawer runners as you install the back boards. You want the runners to be level. Subtle errors and deviations can easily creep into the construction, so do the mortises board by board as the back is installed. Start at the bottom and work up. Set the first back board in place, and use a level to determine the actual location of the runner on the board. Remove the board from the case, rout the mortises, then fit it—and the runners—to the case and nail it in place. Repeat the process to do the next board. Rip the top board to fit; you will find it easier to install if you bevel the top edge.

To rout the mortises, use the template made for routing the runner mortises in the face frame rails. One back board has six mortises, and the rest have two. The top back board has no mortises.

As you nail the back boards in place, install the drawer runners. Because they are trapped between the rails and the back boards, the runners don't need to be glued, except for the four that overlay the battens. These runners should be glued to the battens to help stiffen them. Just before you set these runners in place, apply a bead of glue to the back.

BUILD THE BASE

1. Cut the parts. The base assembly is a separate unit that is attached to the case with four to six screws. Begin making it by cutting the cleats and rear feet to the dimensions specified by the Cutting List. Trim the rear feet to the shape shown in the *Rear Corner Detail* of *Base Construction*.

Cut the front and sides several inches longer than specified so that you can miter them to their final lengths during assembly.

2. Rout the molded edge on the front and sides. The decorative profile along the top edges of the base front and sides is an integral part of those pieces, rather than being a separate molding. Rout the profile. We used an architectural molding bit from Eagle America (catalog number 175-0302, available from Eagle America, 800-872-2511).

3. Cut the rabbet. Behind the decorative profile is a $3/8$-inch-deep × $1^3/4$-inch-wide rabbet for the cleats and the case. This can be cut easily on the table saw in two passes. Make a shallow cut first to form the bottom of the rabbet; make this cut on all three parts. Reset the blade height and fence position to cut the rabbet's side.

BASE CONSTRUCTION

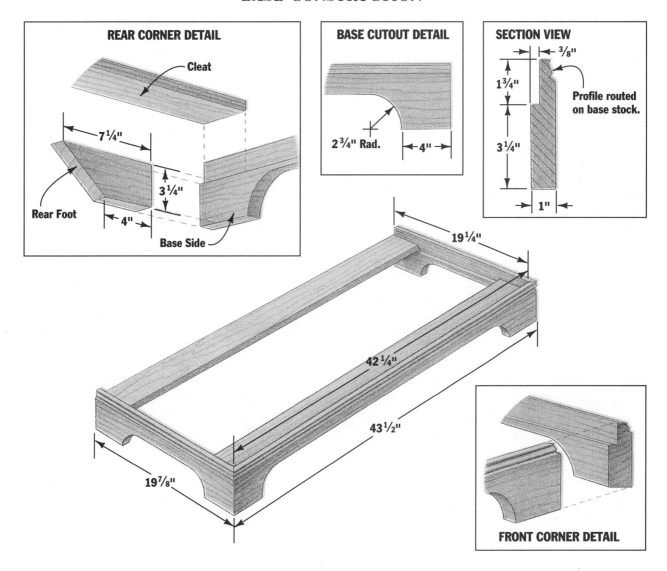

4. Cut the foot profile. Lay out the arcs that form the feet, as shown in *Base Construction*. Cut the contour on the band saw or with a saber saw. Sand the cut edges smooth and straight.

5. Assemble the base and attach it to the case. Miter both ends of the base front, reducing the piece to the length specified by the Cutting List. Miter one end of each side. Then assemble the front, sides, and cleats with glue and cut nails. Attach the rear feet.

With the case resting on its top, set the base in place and drive four to six 1¼-inch screws through the cleats into the case bottom.

BUILD THE DRAWERS

1. Cut the parts. Though there are a lot of drawers in this piece, they are of very simple construction. Moreover, they have enough dimensional similarities to minimize the number of different machine setups. For example, all the drawer sides are the same length, so one stop-block setting will allow you to crosscut *all* the sides.

Note that the fronts and backs are cut from ³/₄-inch stock, and the sides and bottoms from ¹/₂-inch stock.

Crosscut and rip the parts to size. While you don't necessarily need to mark each part, it helps you keep them organized. There are a lot of pieces.

2. Rabbet and shape the fronts. While the order in which you make these cuts isn't important, you should note that you'll need to use a fence—rather than a bit's pilot bearing—to guide whichever cut you do last. The material that the bearing would ride against will have been removed by the first round of cuts.

As shown in the *Drawer Front Detail* of *Drawer Construction*, the dimensions of the rabbets cut into the front are the same on all the drawers.

- Cut a ³/₄-inch-wide × ¹/₂-inch-deep rabbet along the bottom edge of each front for the drawer bottom.
- Cut a ³/₄-inch-wide × ¹/₂-inch-deep rabbet across each end for the drawer sides.
- Cut a ¹/₄-inch-wide × ¹/₂-inch-deep rabbet along the top.

Then rout a ³/₁₆-inch roundover on all four edges of each drawer front, cutting deep enough to create a ¹/₁₆-inch-deep fillet, as indicated in the *Edge Detail* of the *Drawer Construction* drawing.

All of these cuts can be done most efficiently on a router table.

3. Turn the pulls. This is an optional step, since not every woodworker does turning. But you won't find pulls like the ones on the original in stock anywhere. I looked. Either turn them yourself or find someone to do it for you. Follow the *Pull Layout* detail of *Drawer Construction*. Pine doesn't turn well; use poplar or another fairly blond wood.

If you must use stock wooden pulls, I'd suggest looking at the knobs sold by Horton Brasses. (See the Cutting List.)

4. Assemble the drawers. The drawers are simply nailed together. The front and back fit between the sides, and the bottoms overlay the sides, front, and back. No glue is necessary, and in the case of the bottom, it is undesirable.

Lay out and drill holes for the pull-mounting screws. Install the pulls.

5. Fit the drawers to the case. If necessary, plane the sides or the top edges.

FINISH THE CHEST OF DRAWERS

Paint was, most likely, the original finish on this chest of drawers. The finish on the original when I saw it, however, was stain and varnish, and we stuck with that look. We used a gel stain to color the wood, then applied a coat of satin polyurethane varnish.

A detailed step-by-step for applying this finish can be found in the *ShopSmarts* feature "Country Finishes" on page 305.

DRAWER CONSTRUCTION

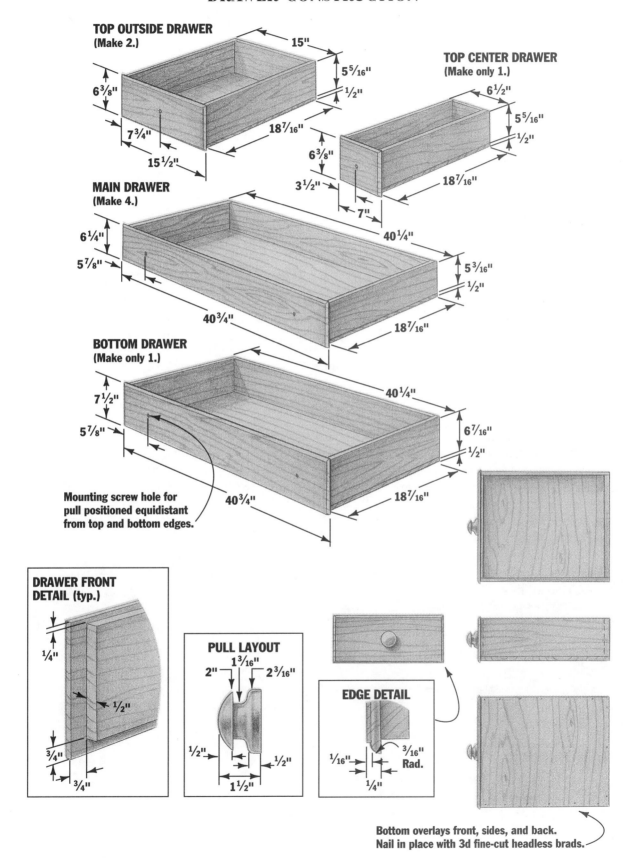

TOP OUTSIDE DRAWER
(Make 2.)

15"
5 5/16"
1/2"
6 3/8"
7 3/4"
18 7/16"
15 1/2"

TOP CENTER DRAWER
(Make only 1.)

6 1/2"
5 5/16"
1/2"
6 3/8"
3 1/2"
7"
18 7/16"

MAIN DRAWER
(Make 4.)

6 1/4"
5 7/8"
40 1/4"
5 3/16"
1/2"
40 3/4"
18 7/16"

BOTTOM DRAWER
(Make only 1.)

7 1/2"
5 7/8"
40 1/4"
6 7/16"
1/2"
40 3/4"
18 7/16"

Mounting screw hole for
pull positioned equidistant
from top and bottom edges.

**DRAWER FRONT
DETAIL (typ.)**

1/4"
1/2"
3/4"
3/4"

PULL LAYOUT

1 3/16"
2"   2 3/16"
1/2"   1/2"
1 1/2"

EDGE DETAIL

1/16"   3/16"
Rad.
1/4"

Bottom overlays front, sides, and back.
Nail in place with 3d fine-cut headless brads.

Routing an Edge Joint

The first step in preparing any edge joint is to joint the edges of the mating boards. You can joint boards quickly and accurately on the jointer; but if you don't have a jointer, the router with a straight bit can help. With the proper jig, it does a special job of preparing two (or more) boards for edge-joining. A well-conceived and well-executed routed edge joint will virtually disappear.

In brief, the technique is this: You clamp a fence atop the first workpiece and, guiding the router base against the fence, trim about $1/16$ inch from the workpiece. Then you secure the second workpiece directly opposite the first. By guiding the router along the same fence—you haven't moved it—you trim the second workpiece and produce an edge on it that's a negative image of the edge milled on the first workpiece. The two boards should fit together perfectly.

To execute the technique, you should have an edge-routing platform and fence. You can make one from a third of a sheet of good-quality $3/4$-inch plywood. I have one that's 4 feet long, sufficient for the work I've done using this technique. But you are limited only by plywood's sheet sizes.

Use whatever router you have, though a $1^1/2$-horsepower fixed-base machine is ideal. If possible, use a large-diameter shear-cut straight bit with a $1/2$-inch shank.

Step 1

1. Router-joint the first board. To router edge-joint two boards, set one on the wider half of the platform. Set the fence on it, and adjust its position on the board so you'll be routing away no more than $1/16$ inch of stock. Clamp the fence and the work to the platform. (If the work is narrow, you may need to shim the fence; just be sure both the work and the fence are clamped so neither will move.)

Stand with the fence in front of you, as shown in the Step 1 photo. Rout from right to left, pulling the router against the fence as you go. Check the edge. If it is less than smooth, square, and clean, shift the fence a tad and make a second pass.

ROUTER EDGE-JOINTING PLATFORM

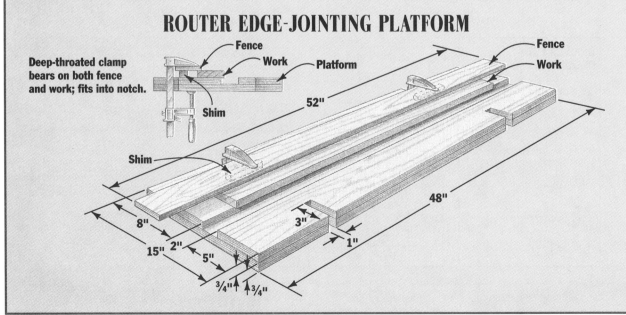

Deep-throated clamp bears on both fence and work; fits into notch.

Fence Work Platform Fence Work

Shim

Shim

52"

48"

8" 3"

15" 2" 1"

5"

$3/4$" $3/4$"

Step 2

Step 3

2. Router-joint the second board. When the first board is done, leave it right where it is. You don't move it or the fence: You simply position the second board along the opposite side of the platform, parallel to the first piece. You need a gap between the two boards that's $1/16$ inch less than the diameter of the bit you are using. Got the gap set? Clamp down the second board.

Now the router will rest on both boards. The bit, however, shouldn't fit between them (if it does, check that gap again!).

To rout the second board, stand in the same place as before. But this time, you have to feed the router left to right. Pull it against the fence as you move it. Make the cut in a single, continuous pass. If you interrupt the cut for any reason, it's likely to be botched. You can rescue the work, of course, simply by finishing the cut, then shifting the board slightly and making another attempt.

3. Join the two boards. When the second board is machined, unclamp it—but NOT the first piece or the fence—and pull it against the first piece. The two should mate perfectly. You may have to juke the second piece back and forth fractionally to get the two in sync, for there's only one correct alignment. A bump on the first piece should fit into a corresponding hollow in the second piece. That's because any imperfections in the fence are telegraphed into the two workpieces differently—in effect, in positive form to one, in negative form to the other. When the two are in sync, they'll virtually merge together.

To help you line them up for gluing, slash a pencil line or two across the seam.

Of course, if the two pieces *don't* mate perfectly, it may be that you've failed to rout deeply enough. I'd try another pass on the second board, and if that didn't cure the mismate, I'd go back to the beginning and repeat the process.

Make the Platform

Cut three 4-foot-long strips of $3/4$-inch plywood. One should be about 15 inches wide, the second about 8 inches wide, and the last about 5 inches wide. Glue the two narrower pieces atop the widest, as shown in the drawing. The 2-inch-wide channel formed allows the bit to cut below the working stock without marring the platform. It also gives all the chips and dust generated by the operation a place to go.

Cut a fence about 6 inches wide and about 4 inches longer than any stock you anticipate router edge-jointing. (Although the platform shown here is only 4 feet long, you can use it to machine boards longer than 4 feet. The essential point is that the fence be longer than the workpieces.)

To use the platform, you have to rest it across sawhorses or some other support(s) that permit you to clamp the work to both sides. A regular workbench will probably be too wide for this.

BENCH TABLE

My wife was the champion of this project. She gets the credit.

With one "opening" left in this book's project lineup, I was looking for something easy. I already had the proverbial 9 pounds 15 ounces of drawings, photos, and sentences for this 5-pound bag. So "real easy" was the pivotal criterion. Too, my deadline was looming. Thus, real easy, to me, translated to a bootjack. You know, nail a couple of small boards together and slap some paint on.

But Judi had seen a bench table with a round top, and she felt it was the ideal candidate. She lobbied. I'd talk about looking for a bootjack, and she'd come back with this bench table idea. And I had to concede that a bench table could be easy to make. Only a few parts, real simple joinery. Start it one weekend, finish it the next. Yeah, easy to make.

Yet it would be useful as well as attractive. The roots of the bench table (or the settle table, as it's sometimes called) are grounded in medieval practicality. Shelters were small and drafty back in the Middle Ages. Every piece of furniture was dear; each was made by hand with man-powered tools. If a piece of furniture could serve more than one purpose, so much the better. So *Hooray!* for the bench table. With the tabletop lowered, it's a table. With the tabletop raised, it's a seat. Placed before the fireplace, the tabletop-back would reflect the fire's heat, creating a warm alcove, while at the same time warding off drafts.

As furniture evolved, the bench table became more sophisticated in appearance and construction. Some versions even added storage to the uses, by incorporating a drawer or a bin under the seat. Many people today associate them with old-time taverns and rooming houses, and their multipurpose nature did distinquish them in such settings.

Life has changed some since the Middle Ages. Today we've got spacious homes with central heat. But a bench table is still practical. It can be a seat. It can be a table.

Bench or table? Well, which do you need? Both reproduction (*opposite*) and original (*above*) are set as benches. But lower their backs, and each becomes a table.

CUTTING LIST

Piece	Number	Thickness	Width	Length	Material
Bench sides	2	$1\frac{1}{2}$"	$13\frac{1}{4}$"	$27\frac{3}{4}$"	1-by pine
Seat	1	1"	$11\frac{3}{4}$"	$36\frac{1}{4}$"	5/4 pine
Aprons	2	$\frac{3}{4}$"	$3\frac{3}{4}$"	$36\frac{1}{4}$"	1-by pine
Tabletop center board	1	$\frac{7}{8}$"	12"	$47\frac{3}{4}$"	5/4 pine
Tabletop boards	2	$\frac{7}{8}$"	11"	$47\frac{3}{4}$"	5/4 pine
Battens	2	$1\frac{3}{4}$"	$2\frac{5}{8}$"	$31\frac{5}{8}$"	pine
Pins	3	$1\frac{1}{4}$"	$1\frac{1}{4}$"	$5\frac{1}{2}$"	pine

HARDWARE

8d cut nails

Optional: 3 wooden knobs, $1\frac{1}{4}$" dia., with three $4\frac{1}{2}$" lengths of $\frac{5}{8}$"-dia. wooden
doweling (for pins)

And what're ya gonna do with a bootjack?

So I went shopping for what I prayed would be that last easy-to-make project. It was a bright Sunday. I drove from cavernous antiques mall to crowded flea market to high-tone antiques shoppe, looking through the morning and into the afternoon. There were a few worthy candidates: a crusty old hardware case, a tabletop desk. I made mental notes.

Then I saw my bootjack. It was in a huge barn that was gussied up as a multidealer antiques market in Mount Joy, Pennsylvania. It really was a bootjack. Pine, too. Worn. Easy to make. Two small boards nailed together.

And looming over it was . . . a bench table.

I studied the price tag. I noted the "20 percent off" signs posted everywhere. I secretively counted the cash in my wallet. I looked at the price tag again. I calculated. When Ed came by, we talked about the piece. It just happened to be his. He'd acquired it near Milton, Pennsylvania. It still had the original red paint, though that was under a couple of more-recent coats, one green, the surface coat an olive-brown. He gave his best price and it *was* better than 20 percent off. I dickered a little. He was eager for the sale. I had my bootjack.

Except it was the bench table.

Bench tables have always been country. I've never seen a high-style one. And this particular version is unabashedly primitive. It has no embellishments, no enhancement like storage capacity, no designer touches like scalloped edges. It's straight practicality—a five-board bench with a tabletop accessory. Yet it doesn't look like a Crate City special. It's got country's charm.

I can attest that it is an easy project to build. The bench sides and tabletop battens need to be glue-laminated, and each of the three tabletop boards must be glued up. With all the clamp time, these gluing processes lend themselves to relatively brief shop sessions spread over a week. I started on the reproduction on a Monday evening, and I spent less than an hour on that and each of the next three evenings gluing up panels and glue-laminating the sides and battens. On Saturday, I assembled and primed the piece. A few days later, with the paint barely dry, it was in the vestibule, festooned with Christmas garlands.

I got my last project. It met the easy-to-make criterion. I met my deadline. Judi loves it. (And consequently me.) So it was a good deal all around.

And what're ya gonna do with a bootjack, anyway?

EXPLODED VIEW

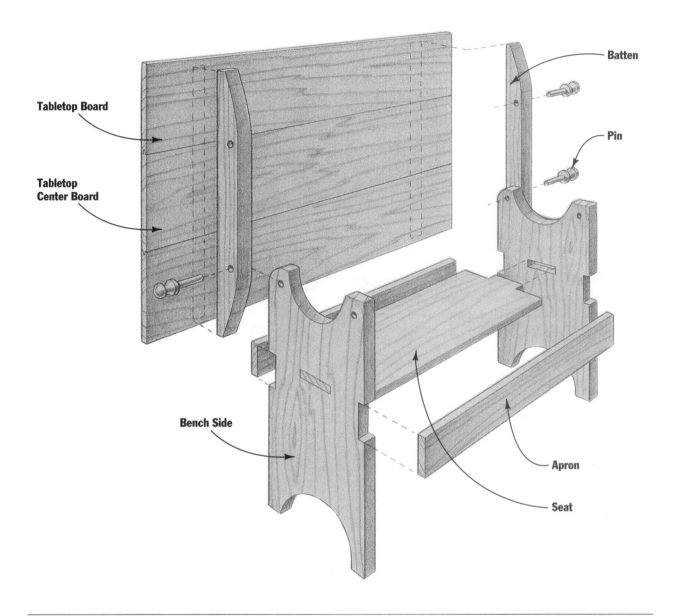

Tabletop Board

Tabletop Center Board

Bench Side

Batten

Pin

Apron

Seat

MAKE THE BENCH

1. Cut the bench parts. As I mentioned, this is essentially a five-board bench, composed of two legs (or sides, as I've labeled them here), a seat, and two aprons.

The aprons are simply ripped and crosscut to the dimensions specified by the Cutting List.

The seat is too wide to be taken from a single board; it has to be glued up. Use 5/4 stock, and don't fret if your 5/4 is thicker than the 1 inch specified by the Cutting List. An extra sixteenth or so of

thickness won't make a difference in this part. Crosscut the stock, and edge-glue the boards to form the seat. (Helpful tips on doing this work can be found in the *ShopSmarts* features "Gluing Up Panels" on page 49 and "Routing an Edge Joint" on page 264.)

The sides are 1½ inches thick. If you can find 8/4 pine that's affordable, you can use that stock. I glue-laminated the sides from 1-by stock. As with the seat, the sides are too wide to be taken from a single board, so you first have to edge-glue panels. Rip and crosscut enough 1-by boards to form four panels approximately 14 × 29 inches.

2. Glue up the sides. Making the sides begins as an edge-gluing enterprise. Glue up the 1-by boards for the sides into the four panels. After the clamps are off the panels, scrape off any dried squeeze-out and sand them smooth and flat. But don't trim them to final dimensions yet.

Glue-laminate the sides next. Apply glue to the face of one panel, making sure to get thorough coverage around the edges. Set a second panel atop it. Orient the two panels so the glue joints in one are

In gluing two ¾-inch-thick panels face-to-face to form a side, take advantage of pine's usually maddening tendency to cup. Orient the crowned surfaces in. As you apply clamps along the edges, the bow in the panels will spread the clamp pressure across the entire surface, giving you a good glue bond. And the bowing of one panel will counteract that of the other, leaving you with a flat side piece.

SIDE LAYOUTS

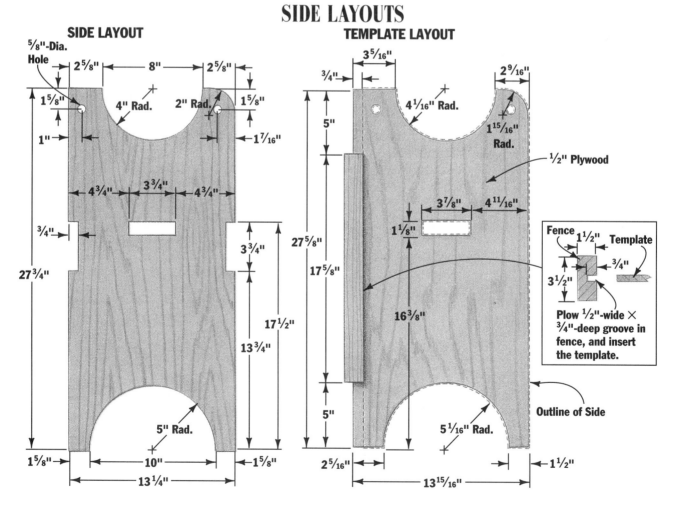

SIDE LAYOUT

⅝"-Dia. Hole

2⅝" — 8" — 2⅝"

1⅝"   4" Rad.   2" Rad.   1⅝"

1"   1⁷⁄₁₆"

4¾"   3¾"   4¾"

¾"   3¾"

27¾"   17½"

13¾"

5" Rad.

1⅝"   10"   1⅝"

13¼"

TEMPLATE LAYOUT

3⁵⁄₁₆"

¾"   2⁹⁄₁₆"

4¹⁄₁₆" Rad.

5"   1¹⁵⁄₁₆" Rad.

½" Plywood

3⅞"   4¹¹⁄₁₆"

1⅛"

27⅝"

17⅝"

16⅜"

5"

5¹⁄₁₆" Rad.

2⁵⁄₁₆"   1½"

13¹⁵⁄₁₆"

Fence   1½"   Template
¾"
3½"
Plow ½"-wide × ¾"-deep groove in fence, and insert the template.

Outline of Side

PLAN VIEWS

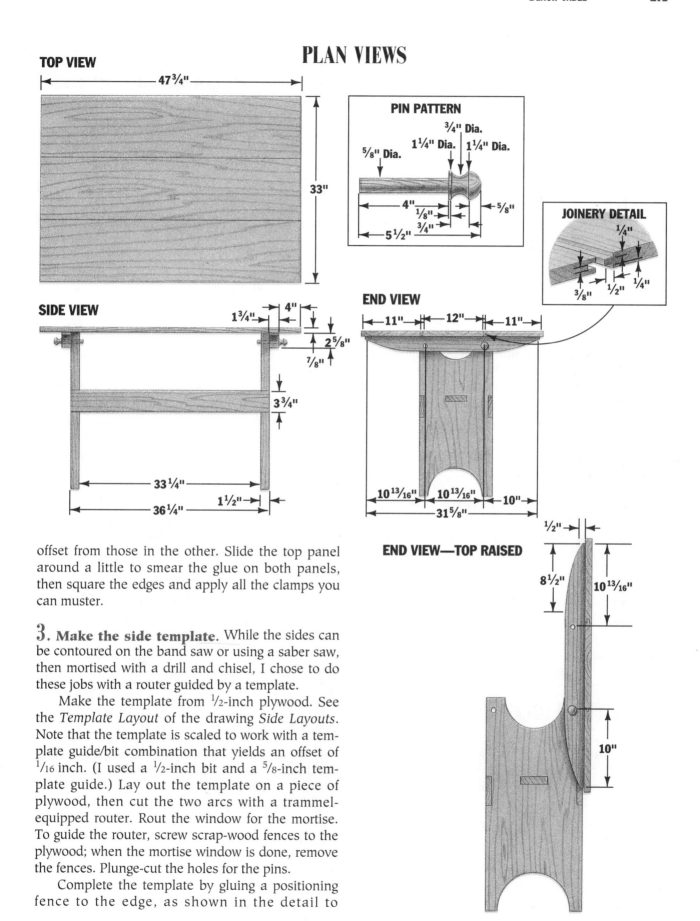

TOP VIEW

47¾"

33"

PIN PATTERN

⅝" Dia.   1¼" Dia.   ¾" Dia.   1¼" Dia.

4"

⅝"

⅛"

5½"   ¾"

JOINERY DETAIL

¼"

⅜"   ½"   ¼"

SIDE VIEW

4"

1¾"

2⅝"

⅞"

3¾"

33¼"

1½"

36¼"

END VIEW

11"   12"   11"

10¹³⁄₁₆"   10¹³⁄₁₆"   10"

31⅝"

END VIEW—TOP RAISED

½"

8½"   10¹³⁄₁₆"

10"

offset from those in the other. Slide the top panel around a little to smear the glue on both panels, then square the edges and apply all the clamps you can muster.

3. **Make the side template.** While the sides can be contoured on the band saw or using a saber saw, then mortised with a drill and chisel, I chose to do these jobs with a router guided by a template.

Make the template from ½-inch plywood. See the *Template Layout* of the drawing *Side Layouts*. Note that the template is scaled to work with a template guide/bit combination that yields an offset of ¹⁄₁₆ inch. (I used a ½-inch bit and a ⅝-inch template guide.) Lay out the template on a piece of plywood, then cut the two arcs with a trammel-equipped router. Rout the window for the mortise. To guide the router, screw scrap-wood fences to the plywood; when the mortise window is done, remove the fences. Plunge-cut the holes for the pins.

Complete the template by gluing a positioning fence to the edge, as shown in the detail to

Template Layout. This fence allows you to clamp the template to one side of the workpiece, rout about halfway through, then switch the template to the workpiece's other face to complete the job. The bench sides are 1½ inches thick, remember. With the thickness of the template added in, you'll need a bit with a 2-inch-long cutting edge to do the work from one side.

4. Make the sides. After removing the clamps from the sides, rip and crosscut each side to square it up and reduce it to its final 13¼ × 27¾-inch dimensions. Sand the faces.

Lay a side on the workbench with scrap under it, so the router bit won't cut the bench top when it breaks through. Set the template on the side, align it carefully, and clamp it. Set up the plunge router with the appropriate bit and template guide, and adjust the plunge depth. Rout around the perimeter of the workpiece in a series of passes, cutting fractionally deeper on each pass. Rout the mortise and pin holes. After every couple of passes on the mortise, stop and vacuum the chips from the cavity.

If you have a long enough bit, you can cut all the way through. Otherwise, cut as deep as you can. Then remove the template, turn the workpiece over, and reposition and reclamp the template. Repeat the routing steps until all the cuts are completed.

Cut the apron notches next. Lay an apron across the side, aligning it with the top edge of the seat mortise. Scribe along its top and bottom edges, thus marking the tops and bottoms of the notches.

Move to the table saw, and use the apron to set the blade height. Cut the notches by standing the side on edge and guiding it into the saw blade with the miter gauge. Cut the notch with repeated passes.

Really Long Router Bits

Half-inch straight bits with more-than-2-inch-long cutting edges are available from both Freud and Amana. Freud's is catalog number 12-130; Amana's is 45427. Both manufacturers sell through dealers; for the name of one near you, call Freud at 800-472-7307 and Amana Tool at 800-445-0077.

5. Lay out and cut the seat tenons. The most accurate way to lay out the tenons on the ends of the seat is from the mortises. Lay the seat atop the side, its end square with the mortise. Mark the left and right mortise edges on the seat. Use a square to extend these marks, laying out the tenon. Repeat the process with the second side to lay out the second seat tenon.

The tenons are cut the same way the apron notches were cut in the sides. Use one of the sides to set the saw blade height. Stand the seat on end and guide it with the miter gauge. Make repeated saw cuts to remove the waste on each side of the tenon.

6. Assemble the bench. The bench is assembled with glue and cut nails. Apply glue to the edge of the seat tenon, and insert it into the appropriate side. Do the same to join the second side to the seat.

With the assembly resting on its edges, square the sides to the seat. Set an apron in place, and nail it to the sides and the seat. Turn the assembly over, and nail the second apron in place. The original had nails driven through the sides into the ends of the seat. With properly fitted mortises and tenons, however, these nails shouldn't be necessary.

MAKE THE TABLETOP

1. Cut and glue up the tabletop parts. The original's tabletop is composed of three wide boards, joined with tongue-and-groove joints and nailed to two battens. Holes drilled through the batten sides align with holes in the bench sides. Turned pins inserted through these holes connect the bench and tabletop.

Begin making the tabletop by cutting and gluing up the battens. Each batten can be formed by glue-laminating a piece of 5/4 and a piece of 1-by. Cut the plies to rough size, and glue them together. After the glue has set, trim the battens to the dimensions specified by the Cutting List.

In cutting the tabletop boards, the choice you face is how to mimic the original. Do you glue up stock to form three wide boards, which you then join with tongue-and-groove joints? Or do you mill tongues and grooves on the boards you have, and use as many as you need to compose the tabletop?

I chose to make three wide boards so I could

reproduce the joinery as it is on the original. The center board has tongues on both edges, while the outer boards are grooved. Before edge-gluing narrow 5/4 boards, resaw or plane them to a ⅞-inch thickness. (See the *ShopSmarts* feature "Resawing on the Table Saw" on page 112.) After the glue has cured, scrape and sand them, then rip and crosscut them to the dimensions specified by the Cutting List.

2. Make the batten template. The lower edges of the battens are curved, as you can see in *End View*. There are a bunch of ways to form the curves, but in keeping with the table saw-and-router conceit of this book, I chose to cut them with a router guided by a template.

Make the template from ½-inch plywood. The template needs only one arc; you can shift it from location to location. Just make it long enough to provide clamping space clear of where the router rides on it. With a layout bow, like the one shown in the photo on page 280, form an arc that will connect the points indicated in *End View–Top Raised*. Trace the arc from the bow to the template material. Cut to the line with a saber saw, then file and sand the edge to eliminate any nicks, dimples, or bumps.

3. Make the battens. The battens are already "made." You merely need to form the curves on the lower edges. Position the template on the batten, and clamp it. Using the plunge router with the same bit-and-template guide combination used in making the bench sides, rout the curves. If bit-length limitations require you to work from both sides of the batten, do so. If misalignment of the template creates a ridge in the routed edge, you can always sand the edge smooth with a belt sander.

4. Drill the pin holes. As previously noted, the tabletop assembly and the bench are connected by pins inserted through matching holes drilled in the battens and the bench sides. The holes were routed in the bench sides. It is easiest to bore the holes in the battens before the tabletop is assembled.

Clamp the battens to the bench, and transfer the hole positions from the bench. I used a brace and auger bit to bore the holes in the battens while they were clamped to the bench, but you may choose to mark the hole locations, unclamp the battens, and drill the holes in the battens.

5. Cut the joinery on the tabletop boards. As indicated in the *Joinery Detail* to the *End View* drawing, the tongue-and-groove joints between the tabletop boards are ⅜ inch wide × ½ inch deep. Note also that the center board has two tongues, no grooves. The outside boards have the grooves.

You can cut the joinery with a router and slot cutter. I did it on the table saw.

6. Assemble the tabletop. Use no glue; just nail the parts together. Reclamp the battens to the bench sides, and put a thin shim between batten and side to provide clearance. Set the center board in place first. Drive cut nails through it into the battens. Add the outer boards and nail them.

7. Turn the pins. The pins that came with the bench table were not the originals. Those were, apparently, lost long ago. The dealer told me the family from whom he had acquired the piece had been using clothespins. He asked a turner to make new ones.

Having no others, I've provided a pattern for the "new" pins. If you are a turner, follow the *Pin Pattern* in the *Plan Views* and make pins for your project.

If you aren't a turner, you can buy wooden knobs and bore holes in them for ⅝-inch-diameter dowels. Glue a 4½-inch length of dowel in each.

APPLY THE FINISH

As I mentioned, the original bench table is painted an olive-brown color and has areas where green and red paint is visible. I *think* the red is the original color, the green a later paint job. The top surface of the tabletop is completely devoid of finish.

I painted the bench, the pins, and the underside of the tabletop brick red, using Old Village paint sold by the Stulb Paint Company. The top surface and the edges of the tabletop I stained Minwax's colonial maple. Read over the *ShopSmarts* feature "Country Finishes" on page 305 for sequences for priming and painting and for "conditioning" and staining pine. I followed those sequences in finishing the reproduction.

DOME-TOP CHESTS

These chests are fraternal triplets. Each is individual, with little features unique to it. Yet all are clearly alike.

Obviously, the biggest differences from one chest to another are the dimensions and the finishes. Look closer, though, and you notice that the largest chest has a base molding that the others lack. The midsized chest has lifts and a matching escutcheon, which the others lack. There are additional differences inside. The largest chest has a double rabbet forming a seal between lid and chest, and it has a till. Each of the two smaller chests has strips nailed around the inside of the chest to form a seal between the lid and chest.

The largest and smallest of the three hail from New Hampshire, while the midsized chest I found in Pennsylvania.

Yet the dominant impression is that this is a matched set of chests. You almost expect each to nest inside the next largest.

What creates this impression are the domed lids. Despite their different sizes and their different origins, all share the same lid design. The thickness of top panel and the degree to which it curves are pretty much the same on all three chests. It seems that you can bend a ⅜-inch-thick pine board just so much, and country woodworkers knew just how much that is.

As woodworking projects, these chests are great. The chest bodies are pretty simple to build. Rabbet joints connect the fronts and backs to the ends. The bottoms either overlay or fit flush. Glue and cut nails secure things. How hard is that?

Then there are the lids. How do you get that panel to bend over the top?

The dome-top chests (*opposite*) are so much alike, it's hard to believe the originals (*above*) were made by craftsmen working in different states.

CUTTING LIST

SMALL CHEST

Piece	Number	Thickness	Width	Length	Material
Front/Back	2	$5/8$"	$7\frac{1}{2}$"	$18\frac{1}{2}$"	1-by pine
Ends	2	$5/8$"	$8\frac{1}{4}$"	$8\frac{3}{4}$"	1-by pine
Bottom	1	$1/2$"	$9\frac{3}{8}$"	$18\frac{1}{2}$"	1-by pine
Top	1	$5/16$"	$9\frac{5}{8}$"	$18\frac{1}{2}$"	1-by pine
Lip	2	$1/4$"	$5/8$"	$17\frac{1}{4}$"	1-by pine
Lip	2	$1/4$"	$5/8$"	$8\frac{1}{8}$"	1-by pine

HARDWARE

1 pr. wrought brass butt hinges, 1" × 1". Catalog number 4080 from Paxton Hardware (410-592-8505).

8 brass flathead wood screws, #3 × $3/8$"

1 brass half-mortise lock, $1/4$" × $1\frac{7}{16}$" selvedge, $5/8$" backset, $1\frac{7}{16}$" × $7/8$" overall. Catalog number 4446 from Paxton Hardware.

4d cut finish nails

$3/4$" × 18-gauge wire brads

MEDIUM CHEST

Piece	Number	Thickness	Width	Length	Material
Front/Back	2	$5/8$"	$10\frac{7}{8}$"	$23\frac{1}{4}$"	1-by pine
Ends	2	$5/8$"	$11\frac{3}{4}$"	$11\frac{7}{8}$"	1-by pine
Bottom	1	$5/8$"	$11\frac{1}{4}$"	22"	1-by pine
Top	1	$3/8$"	12"	$23\frac{1}{4}$"	1-by pine
Lip	2	$3/8$"	$1\frac{1}{4}$"	$11\frac{1}{4}$"	1-by pine
Lip	2	$3/8$"	$1\frac{1}{4}$"	22"	1-by pine

HARDWARE

1 pr. brass butt hinges, $1\frac{1}{2}$" × 1"

1 steel half-mortise lock, $1/2$" × $2\frac{9}{16}$" selvedge, 1" backset, $2\frac{9}{16}$" × $1\frac{9}{16}$" overall. Catalog number 4445 from Paxton Hardware.

2 chest lifts, $2\frac{1}{4}$" × $3\frac{1}{2}$", flat black iron. Catalog number CL-5S from Horton Brasses (203-635-4400).

It turns out that those country woodworkers knew you could harness pine's natural tendency to cup. You don't need steam to bend the top panel. You just let dampness cup the top. Once it starts cupping, you set it on the chest, use a couple of band clamps to coax it down into place, and nail it. How hard is that?

Well, the answer is that none of it is hard. But it is different, and a little dicey, 'cause after all, you could coax a little too aggressively and crack the

MEDIUM CHEST HARDWARE—*continued*

1 iron escutcheon, 3½" × 2¼". Catalog number CL-5SE from Horton Brasses.

4d cut finish nails

¾" × 18-gauge wire brads

LARGE CHEST

Piece	Number	Thickness	Width	Length	Material
Front/Back	2	¾"	15⅛"*	29"	1-by pine
Ends	2	¾"	16¼"*	15"	1-by pine
Bottom	1	¾"	14¼"	27½"	1-by pine
Top	1	⅜"	16"	29"	1-by pine
Base foot	2	¾"	½"	17¼"	1-by pine†
Base fingernail	2	¾"	1¼"	17¼"	1-by pine†
Base cap	2	¾"	1"	17¼"	1-by pine†
Base foot	2	¾"	½"	30½"	1-by pine‡
Base fingernail	2	¾"	1¼"	30½"	1-by pine‡
Base cap	2	¾"	1"	30½"	1-by pine‡
Till bottom	1	5/16"	3¹³/₁₆"	15"	pine
Till front	1	5/16"	2⅜"	15"	pine
Drawer shelf	1	5/16"	3¹³/₁₆"	15"	pine
Drawer front	1	¾"	1½"	13⅜"	1-by pine
Drawer bottom	1	5/16"	3"	13⅜"	pine
Drawer back	1	5/16"	1³/₁₆"	13⅜"	pine
Drawer sides	2	5/16"	1½"	3¾"	pine
Till false front	1	¾"	5⅛"	15"	1-by pine

HARDWARE

1 pr. brass butt hinges, 1½" × ⅞", with screws. Catalog number 4201 from Paxton Hardware.

1 steel half-mortise lock, ½" × 2⁹/₁₆" selvedge, 1" backset, 2⁹/₁₆" × 1⁹/₁₆" overall. Catalog number 4445 from Paxton Hardware.

6d cut finish nails

¾" × 18-gauge wire brads

*This allows ⅜" extra width for routing chest top from chest bottom, leaving the interlocking lips.

† After routing appropriate profile, edge-glue 3 pieces to form base molding (¾" × 2¾" × 17¼").

‡ After routing appropriate profile, edge-glue 3 pieces to form base molding (¾" × 2¾" × 30½").

board. It isn't a given that the board will just go limp and drape itself over the chest. But, see, that's the fun. Without spending too much time and risking too much expensive wood, you get to expand your woodworking universe.

When you are done, you have a nifty chest to show off to relatives, friends, and neighbors. You've got a wonderful canvas for displaying your grain-painting skills. And you've got a handsome storage container.

EXPLODED VIEW
(MEDIUM CHEST)

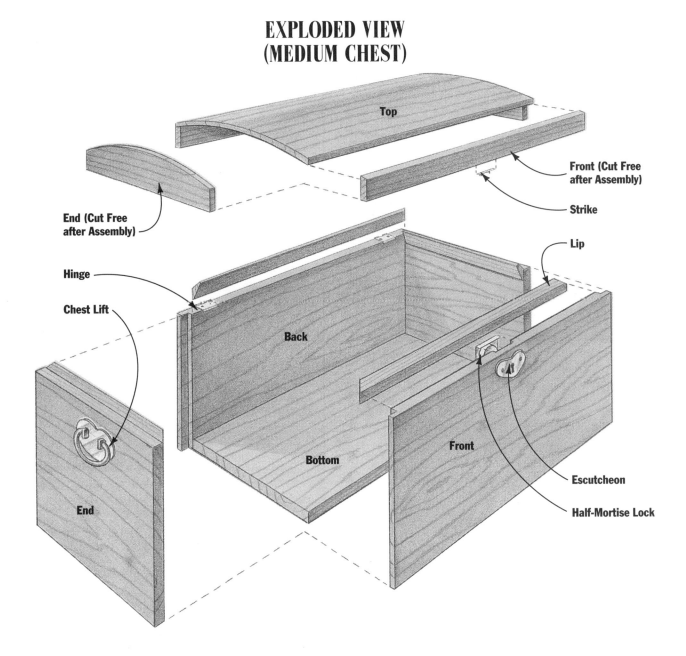

Top

Front (Cut Free after Assembly)

Strike

Lip

End (Cut Free after Assembly)

Hinge

Chest Lift

Back

Escutcheon

Half-Mortise Lock

Front

Bottom

End

The dome-lid design of the chests relates them to sea chests, though none is as burly as I picture a real sea chest being. But the domed lid of a sea chest would shed water, helping to keep its contents dry. The two smaller chests were originally a form of luggage, I'm sure, and their domed lids were designed for practicality, offering some weather resistance. The smaller chest could be carried under an arm, but the midsized chest has those lifts. It was intended to be moved.

The largest chest, with its base molding, seems more fixed, more a piece of furniture that was put in a spot, say in a bedroom, and left there. It could be

moved, but I don't see it as luggage. No lifts. Contributing to this perception is that this chest has a till, a common feature of blanket and dower chests. Typically, a till is a narrow, shallow trough extending from front to back along one end of the chest. Even in a full-sized blanket chest, the till is only 5 to 6 inches wide and deep. Usually the till has a lid that doubles as a prop to hold the chest lid open.

In the case of this large domed chest, the till lacks a lid, but it does have another special feature: a hidden drawer.

As you can see, these chests are individuals. But you won't be able to build just one.

CHEST CONSTRUCTION

1. Cut the parts. Regardless of the chest you build, you must resaw or plane at least some stock. None of the tops is thicker than 3/8 inch, and in the small and medium chests, the stock for the rest of the project is under the standard 3/4-inch thickness. You may also have to edge-glue stock to make broad panels, particularly for the large chest. Resaw, plane, and joint the stock as necessary.

Now rip and crosscut the parts to the dimensions specified by the Cutting List. If necessary, glue up narrow stock to make boards of sufficient width for the project.

2. Cut the joinery. In all three chests, the front and back are joined to the ends with rabbet joints. In all cases, the front and back are the parts rabbeted. Get the dimensions of the rabbet from the appropriate *Plan Views* drawing, then cut the rabbet.

If you are building the large chest, cut the first of the so-called lid separation dadoes. As shown in a detail of *Plan Views—Large Chest*, the lid of this chest is rabbeted, as is the top edge of the case. You cut the dado into the inner faces of the front, back, and ends. After the chest is assembled, you cut the second dado, this one around the outside. It has to be placed with care, because it simultaneously separates the lid from the chest and completes the rabbets. The dimensions given by the Cutting List for the chest front, back, and ends include an allowance for these dadoes. The *Layout Detail* of *Till Construction* shows the location of this first dado. (Mark the location of this dado on the outside faces of the workpieces so that you can easily position the second dado after the chest is assembled.)

Note: If you are building the large chest, now's the time to rout the joinery for the till. Refer to "Till with a Hidden Drawer" on page 284 for specifics.

PLAN VIEWS—SMALL CHEST

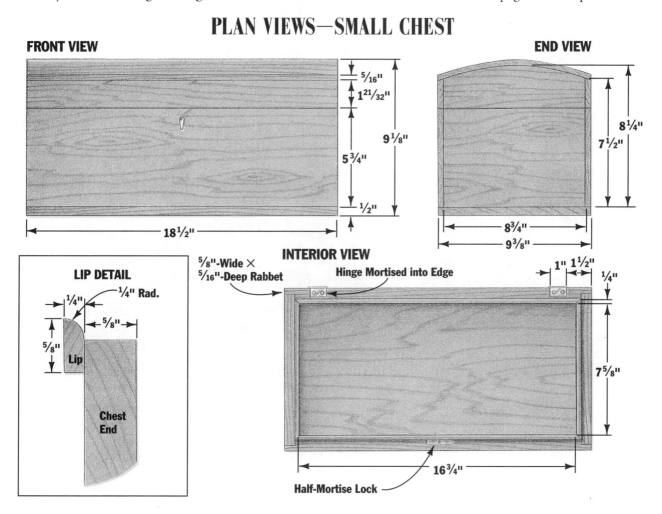

FRONT VIEW

5/16"
1²¹/₃₂"
9¹/₈"
5³/₄"
¹/₂"
18¹/₂"

END VIEW

8¹/₄"
7¹/₂"
8³/₄"
9³/₈"

LIP DETAIL

¹/₄" Rad.
¹/₄"
⁵/₈"
⁵/₈"
Lip
Chest End

INTERIOR VIEW

⁵/₈"-Wide × ⁵/₁₆"-Deep Rabbet
Hinge Mortised into Edge
1" 1¹/₂"
¹/₄"
7⁵/₈"
16³/₄"
Half-Mortise Lock

PLAN VIEWS—MEDIUM CHEST

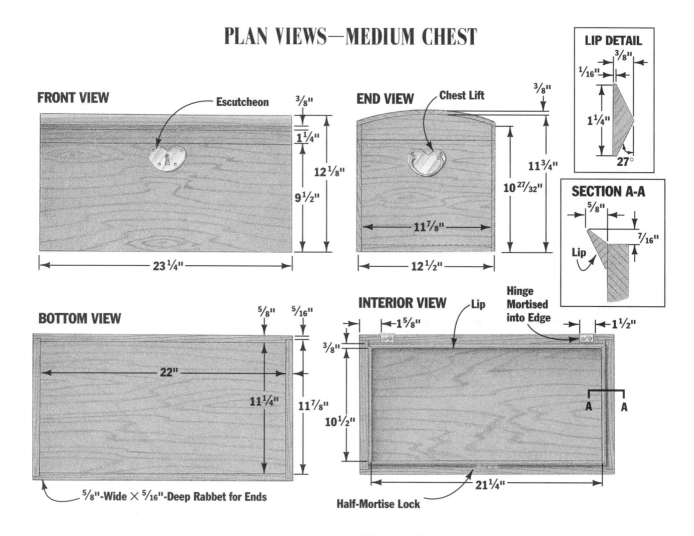

FRONT VIEW — Escutcheon

$3/8"$
$1 1/4"$
$12 1/8"$
$9 1/2"$
$23 1/4"$

END VIEW — Chest Lift

$3/8"$
$11 3/4"$
$10 27/32"$
$11 7/8"$
$12 1/2"$

LIP DETAIL

$3/8"$
$1/16"$
$1 1/4"$
$27°$

SECTION A-A

$5/8"$
$7/16"$
Lip

BOTTOM VIEW

$5/8"$ $5/16"$
$22"$
$11 1/4"$ $11 7/8"$
$5/8"$-Wide × $5/16"$-Deep Rabbet for Ends

INTERIOR VIEW — Lip — Hinge Mortised into Edge

$1 5/8"$
$3/8"$
$1 1/2"$
$10 1/2"$
$21 1/4"$
A   A
Half-Mortise Lock

3. Cut the arch on the ends. Lay out the arch by lining up a flexible straightedge with the end points, then bowing it until it aligns with the high point of the arch. An assistant can then scribe along the straightedge and capture the arch on the workpiece.

Cut the arch with a scroll saw.

After laying out and cutting the first end, use it to lay out the second. Cut it too.

4. Assemble the chest. Join the ends to the front with glue and cut finish nails. Set the nails flush. Add the back. Finally, glue and nail the bottom in place.

Note: To make the chest with the till, you have to install the till parts during this assembly process. Refer to "Till with a Hidden Drawer" on page 284 for specifics.

5. Apply the top. This is a lot easier than you might think. Take a down-to-earth

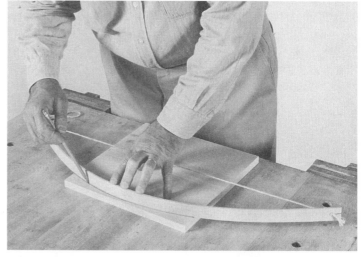

The arches are easy to lay out with a shop-made bow. Kerf the ends of a strip of thin stock. Catch a knotted string in one kerf. Bow the strip as desired, then capture the arc by pulling the string through the other kerf, looping it around the strip and through the kerf a second time. Then you can position the bow on the workpiece and trace the arc.

PLAN VIEWS—LARGE CHEST

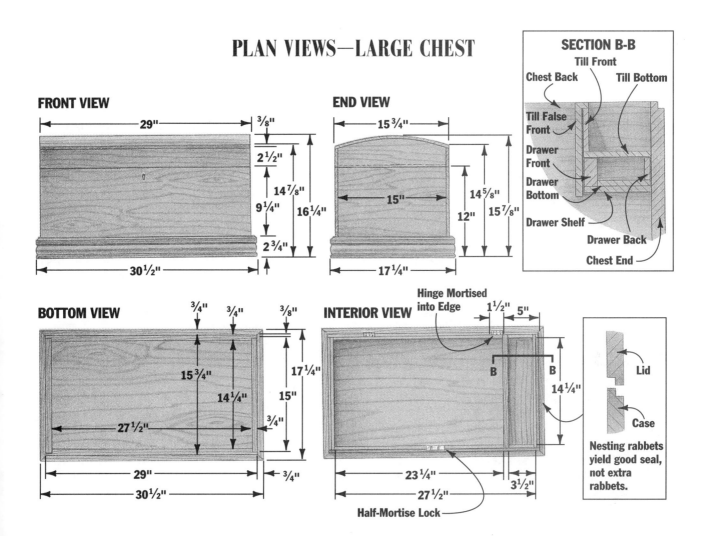

FRONT VIEW

29"   3/8"   2 1/2"   14 7/8"   9 1/4"   16 1/4"   2 3/4"   30 1/2"

END VIEW

15 3/4"   15"   14 5/8"   12"   15 7/8"   17 1/4"

SECTION B-B

Till Front
Chest Back   Till Bottom
Till False Front
Drawer Front
Drawer Bottom
Drawer Shelf
Drawer Back
Chest End

BOTTOM VIEW

3/4"   3/4"   3/8"
15 3/4"   17 1/4"
14 1/4"   15"
27 1/2"   3/4"
29"   3/4"
30 1/2"

INTERIOR VIEW

Hinge Mortised into Edge   1 1/2"   5"
B   B
14 1/4"
23 1/4"   3 1/2"
27 1/2"
Half-Mortise Lock

Lid
Case
Nesting rabbets yield good seal, not extra rabbets.

country tack: Lay the top panel on a wet cloth for an hour or so, and carefully bend it while it's thoroughly damp on one side. (See the photos on page 282.) Each chest has a top made of stock no more than 3/8 inch thick, so this simple approach really works.

Start the process by resawing and/or planing stock for the top to the required thickness. Select the wood for the top very carefully. Not only do you need to avoid defects, you need to select stock with straight grain. Rift-sawn or quarter-sawn stock is best, but we did work successfully with flat-sawn stock. If necessary—and it doubtless will be—glue up narrow boards to form the top panel. If you follow the dimensions specified by the Cutting List, the panel will be long enough and wide enough to overhang the chest about 1 inch all around, which is what you want.

About an hour before you're going to apply the top, wet a towel and lay the panel on it. Within a few minutes, the board will probably start to cup. Work with it!

Apply a bead of glue along the top edges of the chest case. Center the panel over the case. Obviously, you'll orient the cupped face down. A couple of band clamps can be tightened alternately to work the panel down onto the chest. Being too abrupt may crack or break the board, even if it is wet and somewhat pliable, so work cautiously. Drill a pilot hole for each nail. Orient cut nails so the wide section is parallel to the grain, so it won't split the wood.

And if you should break the panel, start the whole process over, making a new panel. (Ultimately, the top panel may well crack. Two of our three old chests *are* broken. But with neither of them is your eye seized by the crack. You see that crack, yet it doesn't bother you.)

6. Cut the top from the chest. Give the top panel a few hours to dry out before trimming the edges flush with the case sides. Use a saber saw to remove the bulk of the waste, then use a block plane or belt sander to finish the job.

Here's our panel-cupping setup, with the panel just about ready for bending. The panel rests on a wet towel. (A plastic trash bag keeps the bench top dry.) Scrap strips under the towel along the panel's edges keep it up against the panel as it cups. And a little heat from an ordinary lightbulb helps force the issue by driving some moisture out of the panel's top surface. The cupping may not appear severe, but even this degree of cupping helps a *lot* in bending the panel onto the chest without breaking it.

Pull the top panel tightly against the chest case with band clamps before nailing it. (Notice the overhang all around.) Nail the ends first.

To separate the lid from the chest on the small and medium chests, you saw it on the table saw. Cut the short ends first, then cut one of the long sides. To keep the lid square to the chest (so it doesn't pinch the blade and damage the edges), pause to insert shims in the kerfs, securing them with masking tape, before making the final cut.

With the large chest, you have to use a router or a dado cutter to cut the lid free of the chest. Position this cut just below the dado that's inside the chest, so they just intersect. (See the photos on the opposite page.)

7. Install the hinges and the lock. All three chests have simple brass butt hinges, with the leaves mortised into the case and lid. Lay out the hinge locations, pare the hinge mortises with a chisel, and install the hinges.

Two of the original chests—the small and medium—have what I'd call hasp locks. They are a lot like suitcase latches, only bigger. Nice, but I simply wasn't able to find reproductions of these *anywhere*.

So on all three reproduction chests we used what locks we could find. All thus have locks like that found on the original of the large chest. With the lock *in hand* (not just on order), cut a mortise to accommodate it. A half-mortise is easily chopped out with a chisel and mallet. Drill the keyhole, then install the lock.

8. Cut and install the lips. The large chest has a seal between the lid and the case formed by the rabbet joint, but on the two smaller chests you need to make and install strips around the inside of the case.

To make the strips for the small chest, plane a 2- to 3-inch-wide × 18-inch-long clear board to a thickness of 5/8 inch. Rout a 1/4-inch roundover along one edge, then rip a 1/4-inch strip (with the rounded edge, of course) from the workpiece. That's your first "lip." Repeat the steps until you have as many strips as you need. Cut the strips to fit the chest, mitering the ends. Glue and nail (with brads) the strips to the inner edge of the case, as shown in *Plan Views—Small Chest.*

The lips for the medium chest are beveled on the table saw. Rip a batch of 3/8-inch × 1 1/4-inch strips, enough for all the lips. Tilt the table saw blade to 27 degrees and rip bevels on the strips, as shown in *Plan Views—Medium Chest.* Cut the strips to fit the chest, mitering the ends. Then glue and nail (with brads) the strips to the inner edge of the chest.

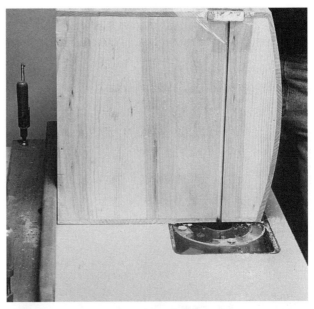

Successfully routing the lid from the large chest depends most upon how accurately you mapped the dado around the inside of the chest. Line up the bit by the marks you made on the chest's outer surface, then set the fence against the chest bottom and clamp it. Set the bit height (*left*) against the seam between the front and the end, so the depth of cut equals half the stock thickness. With the bit height and fence position set, rout the dado

around the chest (*right*). As you did in sawing the lid from the other chests, rout across the ends first, then along the front and back. On the final cut, you want to prevent the lid from shifting as it is freed from the chest. To fix the lid at the top corners, I attached cardboard shims with packing tape. And I made the cut with dispatch. As you get to the last 5 or 6 inches of the cut, don't hesitate. Push the chest through the cut!

9. Apply a finish. All three chests have basically the same finish: paint. Blue milk paint was used on the small chest. The medium chest was subtly grain-painted in a brown over a yellow base color. The large chest had several different paint jobs in its time, most recently a coat of dark green.

We followed these precedents.

Step-by-step sequences for applying milk paint and for grain-painting can be found in the *ShopSmarts* feature "Country Finishes" on page 305.

Note: The base molding should be attached to the large chest before a finish is applied.

BASE MOLDING (LARGE CHEST ONLY)

The large chest has a base molding. The complete profile is not complicated, but it does have to be created from three separate strips, referred to here as the foot, fingernail, and cap.

1. Rout the profiles. For best results, the stock for the molding should be clear. The beginning dimensions are such that you should be able to glean satisfactory strips from #2 or #3 stock. Mill and rip the strips to the dimensions specified by the Cutting List, but crosscut them longer than specified—give yourself room for error.

Do the routing on the router table. Refer to the drawing *Base Molding Detail*. The foot and cap

pieces both have $1/8$-inch beads, so do these cuts first. Switch to a $1/4$-inch beading bit, and rout this profile on the cap piece next. Finally, switch to a fingernail bit (sometimes called a half-radius bullnose bit) and rout the fingernail profile.

2. Glue up the molding. This is a simple edge-gluing procedure. Keep the backs of the three elements flush.

3. Install the molding around the chest. The molding should be cut to fit, with the ends of each piece mitered.

BASE MOLDING DETAIL

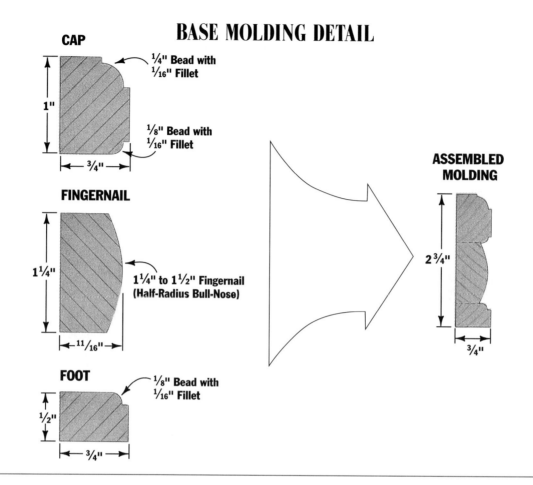

CAP

¼" Bead with
¹⁄₁₆" Fillet

1"

⅛" Bead with
¹⁄₁₆" Fillet

¾"

FINGERNAIL

1¼"

1¼" to 1½" Fingernail
(Half-Radius Bull-Nose)

¹¹⁄₁₆"

FOOT

⅛" Bead with
¹⁄₁₆" Fillet

½"

¾"

**ASSEMBLED
MOLDING**

2¾"

¾"

TILL WITH A HIDDEN DRAWER (LARGE CHEST ONLY)

1. **Cut the parts.** With the exceptions of the false front and the drawer front, the till parts are all taken from ⁵⁄₁₆-inch-thick stock. To economize on lumber, you can resaw 1-by stock on the table saw, producing two usable pieces from each board. (See the *ShopSmarts* feature "Resawing on the Table Saw" on page 112.) Ideally, the resawed stock should be run through a planer to flatten it and to plane it parallel to the opposite face. But in this application, you can sand away saw marks and, so long as the faces aren't dramatically out of parallel, you'll be okay.

Rip and crosscut the stock to the dimensions specified by the Cutting List.

2. **Rout the joinery in the chest front and back.** The till front and bottom and the drawer shelf fit into dadoes routed into the front and back of the chest. The dadoes must be cut before assembly, of course. The dimensions and positions are shown in the *Layout Detail* of *Till Construction*.

To cut the till joinery, clamp a fence to the work to guide the router. Rout the dadoes for the till front first, then do the cuts for the bottom and drawer shelf.

3. Install the till bottom and drawer shelf. These two parts must be installed when the chest is assembled. The front can be glued into place after the lid is cut free of the chest; but because the bottom and drawer shelf are trapped between the front and the back, they must be placed during assembly. Spread a bit of glue along the edge of each piece that contacts the chest end.

4. Install the front. After the lid is cut from the chest, spread a little glue along one edge of the front, drop it into its dadoes, and bond it to the till bottom. Push a couple of brads through the front into the chest front and back.

5. Build the drawer. Drill two ³⁄₄-inch-diameter stopped holes into the drawer front for finger holes. You can improve the gripability of these finger holes by angling them toward each other. If you have one, use a Forstner bit.

The drawer joinery is almost primitive. Edge-glue the back to the bottom, and the bottom to the front, as indicated in *Till Construction*. After the glue has cured, attach the sides with brads.

Check the drawer's fit in the till. Plane the assembly as necessary for a good fit.

6. Make and install the false front. The principal task here is to cut the rabbet that conceals the till front and the drawer. A good way to do this is to begin with a board that's about an inch wider than specified. On the router table or with a dado cutter, excavate a 4³⁄₄-inch-wide × ³⁄₈-inch-deep recess from one end of the board to the other. Leave a ³⁄₈-inch-wide shoulder along what will be the top of the false front. After the recess is cut, rip the false front to its final width, trimming away the shoulder along the bottom of the piece.

Fit the false front to the till. Plane or sand the part as necessary to achieve a good fit.

TILL CONSTRUCTION

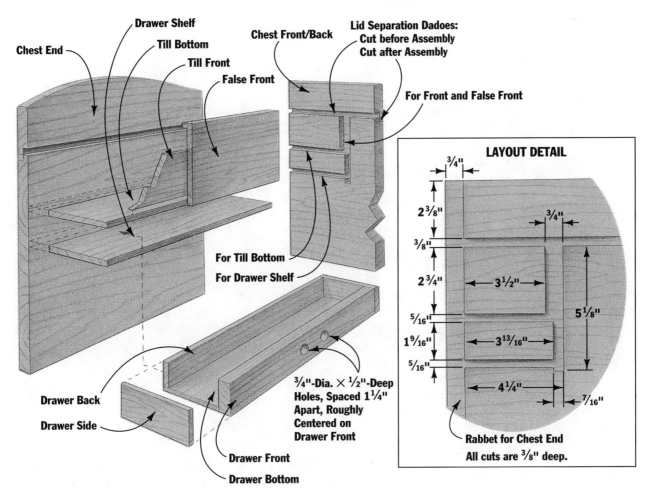

Chest End
Drawer Shelf
Till Bottom
Till Front
False Front
Chest Front/Back
Lid Separation Dadoes:
Cut before Assembly
Cut after Assembly
For Front and False Front
For Till Bottom
For Drawer Shelf
Drawer Back
Drawer Side
³⁄₄"-Dia. × ¹⁄₂"-Deep Holes, Spaced 1¹⁄₄" Apart, Roughly Centered on Drawer Front
Drawer Front
Drawer Bottom

LAYOUT DETAIL

³⁄₄"
2³⁄₈"
³⁄₈"
2³⁄₄"
5⁄₁₆"
1⁹⁄₁₆"
5⁄₁₆"
³⁄₄"
3¹⁄₂"
3¹³⁄₁₆"
4¹⁄₄"
5¹⁄₈"
⁷⁄₁₆"

Rabbet for Chest End
All cuts are ³⁄₈" deep.

AMISH WARDROBE

When Jeff Day and I carried the old wardrobe (upon which this project is based) into the office shortly after I started work on this book, it immediately attracted a gathering of woodworking writers and editors.

The paint had been stripped off, and in none too delicate a fashion. So it doesn't have an eye-catching finish. Isn't in pristine shape either—nicks and dents and gouges, some splitting of the stiles, and lots of wear about the feet. But it *is* big, and it attracts attention.

The basic features were quickly assessed, then the skepticism surfaced.

Jeff, an old colleague of mine, had found the piece in what was more a used furniture store than an antiques store. Only interesting piece there. All the dealer knew about the piece—that he'd share—was that it came out of Pennsylvania's Lancaster County. Sooo . . . The piece is roomy (and Jeff's house has no real closets). It has a few nice moldings, nothing really ornate or heavy. A good, relatively primitive, country piece. In pine. And the price wasn't bad. So he had bought it.

As we looked it over, Jeff pointed out the hand-carved hooks inside and the novel drawer locks that he especially liked. And we, too, were taken with them.

The wardrobe doesn't have a rod inside for hangers. Rather, it has a batten across the back with 8 wooden hooks mortised into it. Where the hanger rod would be is a 1 × 3 with another 15 hooks: 8 jutting toward the front, 7 toward the back. From all indications, the hooks were sawed to a basic, fairly uniform shape, then whittled by hand to soften and smooth the edges, and probably to form a round tenon.

The drawers are kind of wacky; the locking system is stone simple and works like a charm. The drawer fronts are asymmetrical, in that each front is flush with the side on its outer side but partly overlaps a compartment divider in the center. So the outer side is joined to the front with half-blind dovetails, and the inner side is joined to it with a sliding dovetail. I do call that wacky. So practical and well engineered that it's wacky.

Each drawer's lock is a turned pin that's inserted in a hole in the floor of the wardrobe. It extends into a hole in the drawer front. Can't open the drawer unless you withdraw the pin. And when the wardrobe's door is closed and locked, you can't get to the pin. Ta da!

The large cove molding forming the cornice is not attached to the case. It's part of a separate assembly that just drops over the top of the case.

The original wardrobe (*above*) had been stripped, but we grain-painted the door and drawers of the reproduction (*opposite*) to give it some snap.

The piece has almost no metal fasteners. I counted a dozen nails in the drawers, fastening sides to backs. The door hinges are fastened in place with eight more nails. And the door lock has a couple of untapered screws mounting it to the door. The bead moldings around the top are secured with wire brads, but the sill and base moldings are attached with wooden pegs. The same kind of wooden pegs secure the face frame to the case, the sides to the top, bottom, and shelf, and even hold the back in place.

So it seemed to be a pretty old piece to our eyes.

Then someone pointed out the planer marks on the sides. Not plane marks, *planer* marks. And then we realized that the sides were formed by gluing up relatively narrow boards. If the piece were really old, it would have been made of single wide boards.

What *did* we have here? A fake? Someone's high school shop project?

A fake it isn't. If you are going to counterfeit an antique, you produce a copy of a $10,000 piece or a $100,000 piece. To be in that marketplace, it's got to have the original finish. The wardrobe, nice as it is, is not in the $100,000 marketplace, even if it were to still have its original finish.

Yes, antiquity is suggested by all the handwork details: the whittled hooks, the pegged construction, the hand-cut dovetails, and hand-cut mortise-and-tenon joints. But it's unlikely that someone building a utilitarian piece like this would lavish all this handwork on it. For the price Jeff paid, a woodworker couldn't have made a cent if counterfeiting were his motivation. He had to have another motivation. And that's what made us accept this as an Amish creation.

It's hard to explain the Amish in a sentence or two. Members of a religious sect that came to the United States to escape persecution in Germany in the 1700s, the Amish are known for their plain clothing (and their gloriously colorful quilts), their horses and buggies, their rejection of much of modern culture and technology. They live apart from the public school systems, hold government at arm's length, and refuse Social Security (and any other part of the welfare state). Amongst themselves, they still speak Pennsylvania Dutch. Everything they are and do emanates from their interpretation of the Bible.

And they are Lancaster County, Pennsylvania's main tourist attraction.

Many, many things the Amish do the old-fashioned way. Even more things they do in quirky new-old ways. Woodworking is in the quirky realm, and I think this wardrobe is one of its products. While by no means new, the wardrobe is newer than we editors wanted to believe at first look.

MAKE THE CASE

1. Glue up the case panels. The case incorporates seven panels that have to be created by gluing up narrow boards. These are the top, the bottom, the shelf, the two sides, and the two back panels. Their finished dimensions are given in the Cutting List.

Make these panels first. An edge-gluing sequence is given in the *ShopSmarts* feature "Gluing Up Panels" on page 49.

2. Cut the remaining case parts. The back stile is cut from 5/4 stock, the face frame rails and stiles from 1-by stock. Though you may not intuitively think of drawer guides and runners and the base divider as case parts, now's the time to cut them. The dimensions of all these parts are given in the Cutting List.

3. Cut the case joinery in the sides. In the original, the top, sides, and bottom are dovetailed together. The shelf seems to have been dropped into place and secured with more wooden pegs.

I opted to use rabbet joints instead of the dovetails, as shown in *Section B-B* of the *Plan Views*. The rabbets can be cut on the table saw using a dado cutter, but I think it's easier, given the size of the side panels, to cut the rabbets with a router. Guide the router with a T-square or an edge guide, and make the cut with a 3/4-inch straight bit.

4. Cut the back joinery. The back is composed of the two back panels and a back stile. The panels are joined to the stile with dado-and-rabbet joints, and this assembly overlays the case formed by the top, bottom, and sides. Because the stile is thicker than the panels, the top, bottom, and shelf must be notched to accommodate it.

Begin by plowing a 3/8-inch-wide × 3/8-inch-deep groove in each edge of the stile. The grooves should be centered on the edges. This operation

EXPLODED VIEW

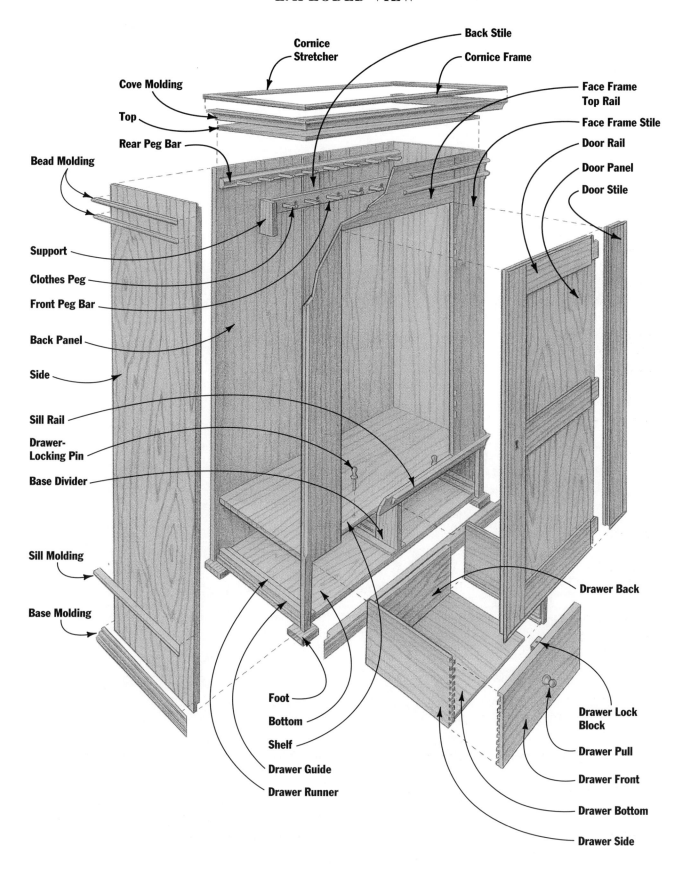

Cornice
Stretcher

Cove Molding

Top

Rear Peg Bar

Bead Molding

Support

Clothes Peg

Front Peg Bar

Back Panel

Side

Sill Rail

Drawer-
Locking Pin

Base Divider

Sill Molding

Base Molding

Back Stile

Cornice Frame

Face Frame
Top Rail

Face Frame Stile

Door Rail

Door Panel

Door Stile

Drawer Back

Drawer Lock
Block

Drawer Pull

Drawer Front

Drawer Bottom

Drawer Side

Foot

Bottom

Shelf

Drawer Guide

Drawer Runner

CUTTING LIST

Piece	Number	Thickness	Width	Length	Material
CASE					
Sides	2	3/4"	19 1/2"	72"	1-by pine
Top/Bottom	2	3/4"	19 1/2"	42 1/8"	1-by pine
Shelf	1	3/4"	19 1/2"	41 3/8"	1-by pine
Back panels	2	3/4"	19 5/8"	72"	1-by pine
Back stile	1	1 1/16"	4 3/8"	72"	5/4 pine
Face frame stiles	2	3/4"	7 3/8"	72"	1-by pine
Face frame top rail	1	3/4"	8 3/4"	30 1/8"	1-by pine
Sill rail	1	3/4"	1 7/8"	30 1/8"	1-by pine
Pegs	30	3/16"	3/16"	1 1/4"	hardwood
Feet	4	1"	3 3/4"	3 3/4"	5/4 pine
Rear peg bar	1	1 1/4"	1 3/4"	41 3/8"	1-by pine
Front peg bar	1	3/4"	2 1/2"	41 3/8"	1-by pine
Supports	2	3/4"	2 1/4"	6"	1-by pine
Clothes pegs	23	5/8"	3/4"	2 5/8"	poplar
MOLDINGS					
Base molding	1	1 1/8"	1 5/8"	44 5/8"*	5/4 pine
Base molding	2	7/8"	1 1/8"	21 7/8"*	5/4 pine
Sill molding	1	7/8"	1 1/8"	44 5/8"*	5/4 pine
Sill molding	2	7/8"	1 1/8"	21 7/8"*	5/4 pine
Bead molding	2	3/8"	7/16"	43 5/8"*	1-by pine
Bead molding	4	3/8"	7/16"	21 3/8"*	1-by pine
Cove molding	1	1 3/4"	1 3/4"	46 3/4"*	5/4 pine
Cove molding	2	1 3/4"	1 3/4"	23"*	5/4 pine
Cornice frame	1	1/2"	2 3/4"	47"	1-by pine
Cornice frame	2	1/2"	2 3/4"	23 1/16"	1-by pine
Cornice stretcher	1	1/2"	1 1/4"	43 1/2"	1-by pine
DOOR					
Door stiles	2	3/4"	4 1/2"	51 3/4"	1-by pine
Door rails	3	3/4"	4 1/2"	22 7/8"	1-by pine
Door panels	2	1/2"	20 7/8"	20 1/8"	1-by pine

can be done on the router table with a straight bit or a slot cutter, or on the table saw with a dado cutter.

Rabbet the panels next, doing just one edge of each panel. Cut the rabbet 3/8 × 3/8 inch. If it is necessary to fit the tongue into the groove in the stile, make the rabbet a little deeper.

The final bit of back joinery is to cut the notches for the stile in the top, bottom, and shelf. Lay out and cut them with a saber saw.

5. Assemble the case and back. Join the top, bottom and sides with glue and 6d nails. (Although the original seems to have been assembled with

Piece	Number	Thickness	Width	Length	Material
DRAWERS					
Base divider	1	$3/4$"	5"	$9^1/4$"	1-by pine
Drawer guides	2	$3/4$"	1"	$19^1/2$"	1-by pine
Center drawer guide	1	$3/4$"	1"	$14^3/16$"	1-by pine
Drawer runners	4	$3/8$"	1"	$19^1/2$"	1-by pine
Drawer fronts	2	$1^1/16$"	$9^3/16$"	$19^{13}/16$"	5/4 pine
Drawer sides	4	$3/4$"	$9^3/16$"	$19^9/16$"	1-by pine
Drawer backs	2	$3/4$"	$8^1/4$"	$18^3/16$"	1-by pine
Drawer bottoms	2	$3/8$"	$19^7/16$"	$18^{11}/16$"	1-by pine
Drawer pulls	2	$1^3/8$"	$1^3/8$"	$2^3/8$"	poplar
Drawer lock blocks	2	1"	$1^1/2$"	$2^1/2$"	5/4 pine
Drawer-locking pins	2	$7/8$"	$7/8$"	$3^3/16$"	poplar

HARDWARE

1 pr. lift-off parliament hinges, $4^3/4$" high. Catalog number 4048 for doors hinged on the right, number 4049 for doors hinged on the left, from Paxton Hardware (410-592-8505).†

1 surface-mounted door lock, $2^1/8$" × $3^1/2$" overall, $1^1/8$" backset. Catalog number 4496 from Paxton Hardware.

8d cut finish nails

6d cut finish nails

4d cut finish nails

8d finish nails

$7/8$" headless cut brads

4 wood screws, #10 × $1^1/2$-inch (for peg bars)

Optional: 2 drawer pulls, $1^1/4$"-dia. knob, $3/8$"-dia. shank, maple. Catalog number WK-6LS from Horton Brasses (203-635-4400).

Optional: 2 drawer-locking pins, $7/8$" dia. × $1^5/8$" knob height, $3/8$"-dia. shank, maple. Catalog number WK-1 from Horton Brasses.

*These are finished lengths. It's smart to crosscut the stock several inches longer than specified, then trim it to fit the case as it is being applied. It's also smart to make an extra stick or two of the molding, to cover yourself in case of a mismeasurement or miscut while you are trimming out the case.

†The original wardrobe has the door hinged on the right, and the drawings reflect this. I hinged the reproduction's door on the left.

wooden pegs, the nails are a lot easier to use, and they won't show in the finished piece.) You can use corner clamps to hold the components in position while you drive the nails.

Glue the back stile in the notches cut for it in the top and bottom. Then drive a couple of 8d cut finish nails through each end into the case. Fit the panels in place next, and fasten them to the case with 6d cut finish nails.

6. **Install the drawer runners and the shelf.** Use 4d cut finish nails to attach the runners and guides. Position them as shown in *Sections B-B* and *C-C* of the *Plan Views*.

(continued on page 294)

PLAN VIEWS

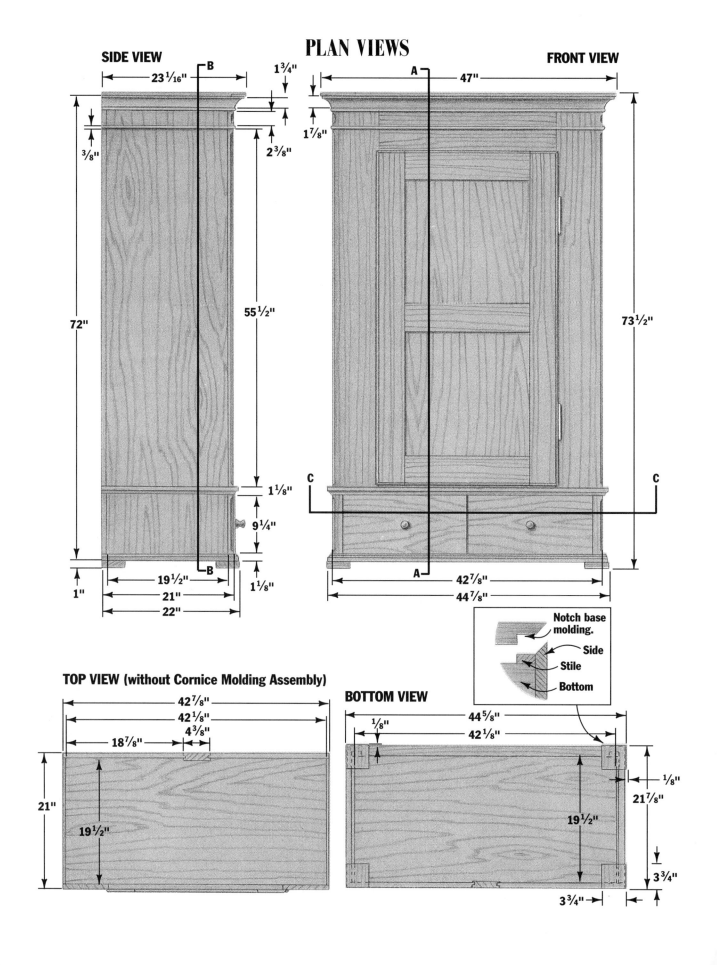

SIDE VIEW

B

23 1/16"

1 3/4"

3/8"

2 3/8"

72"

55 1/2"

1 1/8"

9 1/4"

B

19 1/2"

21"

22"

1 1/8"

1"

FRONT VIEW

A

47"

1 7/8"

73 1/2"

C

C

A

42 7/8"

44 7/8"

Notch base molding.

Side

Stile

Bottom

TOP VIEW (without Cornice Molding Assembly)

42 7/8"

42 1/8"

4 3/8"

18 7/8"

21"

19 1/2"

BOTTOM VIEW

44 5/8"

1/8"

42 1/8"

1/8"

21 7/8"

19 1/2"

3 3/4"

3 3/4"

PLAN VIEWS

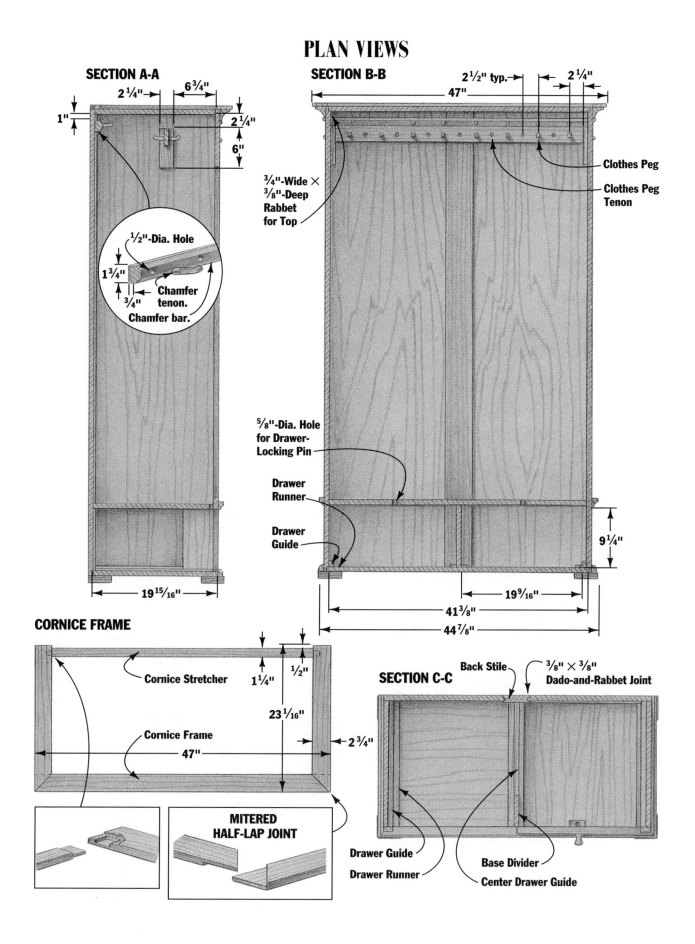

SECTION A-A

2 1/4"

6 3/4"

1"

2 1/4"

6"

1/2"-Dia. Hole

1 3/4"

Chamfer tenon.

3/4"

Chamfer bar.

19 15/16"

SECTION B-B

2 1/2" typ.

47"

2 1/4"

Clothes Peg

Clothes Peg Tenon

3/4"-Wide × 3/8"-Deep Rabbet for Top

5/8"-Dia. Hole for Drawer-Locking Pin

Drawer Runner

Drawer Guide

9 1/4"

19 9/16"

41 3/8"

44 7/8"

CORNICE FRAME

Cornice Stretcher

1 1/4"

1/2"

23 1/16"

Cornice Frame

2 3/4"

47"

MITERED HALF-LAP JOINT

SECTION C-C

Back Stile

3/8" × 3/8" Dado-and-Rabbet Joint

Drawer Guide

Drawer Runner

Base Divider

Center Drawer Guide

With the case resting on its back, position and install the shelf. Use a couple of corner clamps to hold the shelf while you drive 6d cut finish nails through the sides into it. Fit the base divider into place, and secure it with nails driven through the shelf and the bottom. Move the case off its back, and drive three to five nails through the back assembly into the shelf.

7. **Cut the face frame joinery.** The face frame parts are joined by mortise-and-tenon joints. Refer to the *ShopSmarts* feature "Cutting Mortise-and-Tenon Joints" on page 83 for general directions on making these joints. The dimensions of the different joints are shown in the drawing *Face Frame Construction*.

Rout the mortises using a ¼-inch straight bit and a plunge router. Secure the workpiece in the type of fixture shown in the *ShopSmarts* feature to rout the mortises.

Cut the tenons on the table saw using the tenoning jig shown in the *ShopSmarts* feature. Cut the tenons to size, then round the corners with a file so the tenons will fit the routed mortises.

8. **Chamfer and notch the face frame stiles.** The stiles of the face frame are embellished with three stopped chamfers. These can be routed with a standard 45-degree chamfer bit. Set the depth of cut so the chamfer is about ⅜ inch wide. Refer to *Face Frame Construction* for the locations of the starting points and for the lengths of these chamfers. Lay out the chamfers, then rout them.

The stiles are also notched to accommodate the drawers. Lay out the notches and cut them with a saber saw.

FACE FRAME CONSTRUCTION

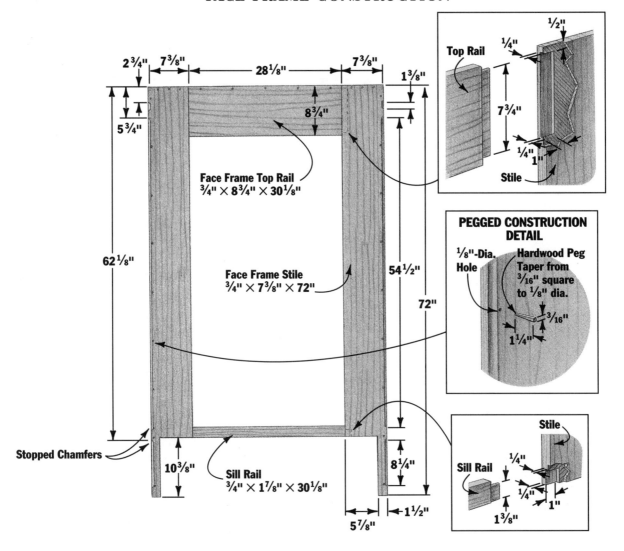

Face Frame Top Rail
¾" × 8¾" × 30⅛"

Face Frame Stile
¾" × 7⅜" × 72"

Stopped Chamfers

Sill Rail
¾" × 1⅛" × 30⅛"

Top Rail

Stile

PEGGED CONSTRUCTION DETAIL

⅛"-Dia. Hole

Hardwood Peg Taper from ³⁄₁₆" square to ⅛" dia.

Sill Rail

Stile

9. Assemble and install the face frame. Apply glue to the mortise-and-tenon joints, assemble the rails and stiles, and clamp the face frame assembly until the glue sets.

Lay the case on its back. After the clamps are off the face frame, spread glue along the case edges and position the face frame on the case. Secure it with bar or pipe clamps. Lay out the locations of the peg holes. Spot them about ³/₈ inch from the edge. Those in the stiles are roughly 2 inches from the top and bottom and 8¹/₂ inches apart; exact placement isn't critical, and neither is the exact number you use. Since the cornice's cove molding will conceal the top edge of the face frame, I used 6d nails here. Drill ¹/₈-inch-diameter holes for the pegs, making them about 1³/₈ inches deep.

Next, whittle some pegs. Prepare strips of ³/₁₆-inch-square hardwood and cut a batch of 1¹/₄-inch pieces. Whittle each peg, as indicated in the *Pegged Construction Detail* of *Face Frame Construction*, tapering it from its full, square girth at one end to a diameter of ¹/₈ inch or less at the other.

When the pegs are ready (or as each one becomes ready), drive each one into its hole. Apply a bit of glue to the round end, insert it in a hole, then tap it home. Trim each peg flush (or nearly flush) with a chisel.

Here's what a face frame peg should look like. Saw the square stock into pieces, then whittle the taper on one end with a utility knife. Put just a spot of glue on the tapered section, and insert it in the pilot hole. A few hammer blows will drive the whole thing into the hole.

Cutting out the clothes pegs with a hand-held saber saw is not nearly as easy as cutting them out with a table-mounted saber saw. Just screw a router-table mounting plate to the shoe of the saber saw, and hang the saw in your router table. Use a template to lay out the pegs, tenon to tenon, as shown, and cut them out.

10. Make the clothes pegs. Make the pegs from poplar rather than pine. Pine's pretty brittle; I think giving a peg-hung garment too boisterous a yank would easily snap the peg.

The pattern for the clothes pegs is shown in *Patterns and Profiles*. Convert it into a template, but make the template durable, since you have to trace it onto 23 blanks.

Trace the pattern onto the pieces and cut them out. This can be a challenge if you don't have a scroll saw or band saw. Try hanging your saber saw in your router table. (See the photo above.)

After the pegs are roughed out, refine the shape and soften the edges with a carving knife, a file, or just sandpaper. Use a file or chisel to round off the corners of the tenons, shaping them into approximate rounds.

11. Make the peg bars. There are two peg bars inside the case. One is attached to the back, about 1 inch below the top. The other is suspended between the sides, roughly midway between the front and back and about 2¹/₄ inches below the top. Cut the bars to the dimensions specified by the Cutting List.

Fit the rear bar into the case and transfer the

location of the back stile to the bar, so you can notch the bar to accommodate the stile. Chamfer the edges of this bar, as shown in the detail accompanying *Section A-A* of the *Plan Views*.

Lay out the locations of the holes (technically, they're round mortises) for the clothes pegs. See *Section B-B* for the layout. Drill the holes with a ½-inch-diameter bit.

One by one, apply glue to the tenons of the clothes pegs and force them into the holes in the bars. Bear in mind that the pegs alternate on the front peg bag. That is, you install eight pegs in one side of the bar—the two outside holes and every other hole in between. Then you turn the bar over and install the remaining seven pegs in the other side.

12. Install the peg bars. The rear bar should go in first. It is simply screwed to the back (yes, there are screws used in the original). Four #10 × 1½-inch wood screws should do it. Drill and countersink pilot holes, then drive the screws. Locate one screw near each end of the bar, and the other two evenly spaced in between.

The front bar is suspended in notches in the two supports, which are nailed to the sides. Cut the supports to the dimensions specified by the Cutting List, then notch each to accommodate the peg bar. The supports are positioned as indicated in *Section A-A*. Bear in mind that you can't nail the supports in place and then drop the bar into the notches, since the supports are too close to the top.

APPLY THE MOLDINGS

The wardrobe has four different moldings. Around the very bottom of the case is a base molding. The sill molding is aligned with the bottom edge of the door sill. At the top are two fine bead moldings. And crowning the case is a cornice molding (which is actually a separate, removable assembly).

Profile sections of all these moldings are shown in *Patterns and Profiles*.

1. Rout the base molding. Prepare the stock first. The molding strips on the sides are ⅞ × 1⅛-inch stock, which is easy enough to plane or resaw from 5/4 stock (which usually is 1 1/16 inches thick). But the strip for the front must be 1⅛ × 1⅝ inches, so it must either be planed down from 6/4 or 8/4 stock or be glued up from 1-by or 5/4 material. In any case, prepare the stock to the required sizes, and crosscut the strips a couple of inches longer than what's specified by the Cutting List.

Rout the bead on the stock on the router table. Use a 5/16-inch beading bit.

2. Apply the base molding. The front section of the base molding must be notched near the ends to accommodate the face frame stiles, then mitered at the very ends. See the detail to the *Bottom View* drawing.

Lay out the notches by holding the molding against the case and marking it at the inner edges of the stiles. Make sure you have the piece centered so you have plenty of overhang on either side of the

case. (And be sure you have it bead-side up.) Mark the depth of the notch, as shown in the *Bottom View* of the *Plan Views*. Use a square to complete the layouts from these marks. Cut the notches with a saber saw.

Miter the front piece next. Fit it in place, then mark it at the outer surfaces of the sides. Miter the ends. Tack the molding in place.

Miter one end of each side piece. Fit each piece to the case, and check the tightness of the miter joint between it and the front piece. (The strip should be long enough that the square-cut end extends beyond the case back at this point.) Recut one or both pieces as necessary to achieve the tightness you want. Then mark and crosscut the side piece to length. Nail it to the case with 6d cut finish nails. Finally, nail the front piece to the case.

3. Attach the feet. With the case still on its back across sawhorses, nail the feet to the case using 6d cut finish nails.

4. Rout the sill molding. As you can see from the profile section, the sill molding is simply a ⅞ × 1⅛-inch strip with a ½-inch-radius cove along one edge. Cut the stock to the girth specified, and cut overlong pieces for the front and sides. Rout the cove on the router table, using either a ½-inch cove molding bit or a 1-inch core-box bit.

5. Apply the sill molding. As previously noted, the molding is aligned with the bottom edge of the

PATTERNS AND PROFILES

COVE MOLDING

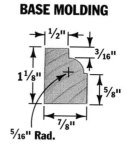

BEAD MOLDING

SILL MOLDING

BASE MOLDING

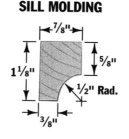

DRAWER-LOCKING PIN PROFILE

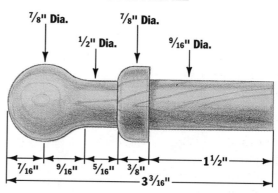

CLOTHES PEG PATTERN

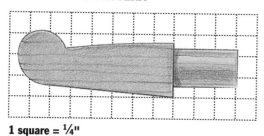

1 square = $\frac{1}{4}$"

face frame's sill stile. Hold the front piece against the case, cove down, and mark it for mitering. Miter it (both ends) and the side strips (one end each).

Tack the front molding in place, and hold the side strips in place to check the tightness of the miter joints. Trim them as necessary, then nail the molding to the case with 6d cut finish nails.

6. Rout the bead molding. The finished bead moldings are very thin and flexible, and altogether frail. You won't have much success trying to nose narrow strips of $\frac{3}{8}$-inch stock. There are a lot of alternatives, but here's an approach that's worked for me: Rout a $\frac{3}{8}$-inch nose on both edges of a 2-inch-wide strip of 1-by stock, then resaw it.

To rout the nose on this stock, work at the router table and use a $\frac{3}{16}$-inch roundover bit. Round-over both edges on one side of the stock, then turn it over and work the edges of the second side. On this side, however, make successive

passes, cutting the profile deeper and deeper into the material, until you have a perfect bull-nose with a $\frac{3}{8}$-inch flat beside it.

Then resaw the stock on the table saw, preserving the $\frac{3}{8}$-inch-thick portion with the nosed edges. Rip this into the $\frac{7}{16}$-inch-wide bead molding strips.

7. Apply the bead molding. Work as you did in applying the sill molding. Fit the strips to the case and mark them for mitering. Then nail them in place; use cut brads for these strips. See *Front View* and *Side View* for the specific positions of the bead moldings.

8. Cut the cove molding. This is a table saw project. Turn to the *ShopSmarts* feature "Coving on the Table Saw" on page 170 for the particulars of setting up the table saw and cutting the cove. On this particular molding, the cove is 2 inches wide.

Before actually cutting the cove, you need to make up blanks for the molding. Glue-laminate a couple of pieces of 5/4 stock to form each blank. After the clamps are off and any dried squeeze-out scraped off, rip each blank to 1³/₄ inches square, then rip a 2-inch-wide chamfer on it.

Here's how to cut the chamfer: Crank the blade to a height of about 2¹/₂ inches. Position the rip fence 2 inches away from the blade. Then tilt the blade to 45 degrees (it should be tilting toward the fence). Adjust the blade height if necessary to prevent it from contacting the fence. Make the cut.

Now cut the cove, positioning it on the 2-inch-wide chamfer.

9. Cut the cornice frame joinery. Cut the three cornice frame pieces and the cornice stretcher to the dimensions specified by the Cutting List. Then check the *Cornice Frame* drawing in the *Plan Views*. Note that the front and sides of the frame are joined by mitered half-laps, while the stretcher is joined to the sides by mortise-and-tenons.

When cutting the mitered half-lap on the long cornice frame piece, the miter gauge should be set at 45 degrees. Line up the very corner of the workpiece with the cutter, and form the shoulder of the lap with the first pass. Then back the workpiece away from the cutter, and make a second pass, clearing more waste from the lap. A third pass should finish the lap. The depth of cut, of course, should equal half the thickness of the workpiece.

Cut the laps on the table saw, using a dado cutter. Set up the cutter to clear a swath about ⁵/₈ to ³/₄ inch wide. Set the depth of cut to ¹/₄ inch (or half the thickness of the working stock). Make test cuts on two scraps and check the fit.

To avoid confusion, mark the shoulders of the laps on the three workpieces. On the long cornice frame piece, the shoulders must be angled at 45 degrees. On the shorter two pieces, the shoulders are square. Make the cuts, guiding the workpiece with the miter gauge. Several passes will be required to clear all the waste from each lap.

When the laps are cut, switch the saw to the regular blade. Miter the ends of the short workpieces.

Rout the mortises, using the trough-style fixture to hold the frame member for the operation. Use a ¹/₄-inch bit in a plunge router to make the cuts.

Cut the tenons on the table saw, using the tenoning jig described in the *ShopSmarts* feature "Cutting Mortise-and-Tenon Joints" on page 83.

10. Assemble and install the cornice frame. Begin with the cornice frame. Glue the mortise-and-tenon joints, joining the frame sides and the stretcher. Then glue the frame front in place. Pulling mitered half-laps tight can be a bit vexing; try bringing the parts together with corner clamps, then applying a hand screw to the joint to seat the parts.

The assembled cornice should simply rest atop the case. It can be pulled to the front, and it can be lifted off the case. But as a practical matter, it will stay where you put it.

To achieve this fit, you should fit the cove molding to the front of the case, and mark where the miters would be if you were attaching the molding tightly to the case. Cut one miter, then shift the second miter about ¹/₁₆ inch farther away from it *so the molding is slightly long*. Now miter one end of the two short cove moldings. Don't cut them to finished length; leave them long, but miter one end.

Glue the moldings to the cornice frame. Attach the long molding first, aligning it parallel to the frame's front edge, and insetting it about ⁵/₁₆ inch. After the glue has set, add the two short moldings. Apply glue to the mitered surfaces. (You can glue the moldings to the frame because the joints are long grain to long grain.)

After the glue sets, fit the assembly to the case. Mark and trim both the cove molding and the cornice frame so both are flush with the back of the case.

MAKE THE DOOR

1. Cut the door parts. The door is a frame-and-panel composition, made up of three rails, two stiles, and two panels. The rails and stiles are ³/₄-inch stock, the panels ¹/₂-inch. Since the rails and stiles can be made from single boards, cut stock to the dimensions specified for them by the Cutting List.

The panels will have to be glued up. Resaw or plane enough ¹/₂-inch stock to form the panels. In crosscutting the individual boards, be sure to make them 2 or 3 inches overlong so you'll have some margin for trimming and squaring the panels. After the stock is ready, glue up the panels; an edge-gluing sequence is presented in the *ShopSmarts* feature "Gluing Up Panels" on page 49.

2. Plow the panel grooves in the rails and stiles. This can be done a variety of ways: on the router table using a ¹/₄-inch straight bit or a slot cutter, with a hand-held router and a slot cutter, on the table saw with a dado cutter. Whichever method you use, try to center the groove on the edges of the stock. The stiles and top and bottom rails are grooved on one edge only; the middle rail, on both edges.

3. Rout the mortises. The sizes and locations of the mortises are shown in *Door Construction*. All of the mortises are 1¹/₂ inches deep and are squarely in the groove.

Use the mortising fixture shown in the *ShopSmarts* feature "Cutting Mortise-and-Tenon Joints" on page 83 to hold the stile, and rout the mortises with a plunge router and a ¹/₄-inch straight bit. The setup and routing sequence is detailed in the *ShopSmarts* feature.

4. Cut the tenons. Because the stiles are grooved from end to end, the tenons on the top and bottom rails must be haunched. The cheeks are cut on the table saw, using the tenoning jig shown in the *ShopSmarts* feature on the mortise-and-tenon. Set up the saw and jig, and make the cuts outlined there.

Cut the haunches with a backsaw. Two cuts on each tenon is all it takes.

Finally, to fit the tenons to the routed mortises, round their edges with a file.

5. Raise the panels. When the glue has set, pull the clamps from the door panels and carefully scrape off any dried glue. Sand the panels flat and smooth, then trim the panels to square them and reduce them to their final size.

The backs of the panels are raised to reduce the edge thickness to ¹/₄ inch so that the panels will fit the grooves in the door frame. The width of the bevel created when the panels are raised isn't all that important, but the depth of the grooves is pivotal here. Ordinarily, you could do this job on the router table as well (or better) than on the table saw. But panel-raising bits form a lip on the edge of the panel that's too short for this door's panel groove. (See the *ShopSmarts* feature "Raising Panels" on page 140.) So you almost have to do the job on the table saw.

The *ShopSmarts* feature goes into more detail, but in brief, the panel-raising routine is this: Set the fence where the blade will tilt *away* from it. Position it ³/₁₆ inch from the blade. Set the blade height at about 2 inches. Tilt the blade until the highest tooth is just over ¹/₂ inch from the fence. (Hold the workpiece beyond the blade, and sight across the blade to set the degree of tilt.) Make the four cuts required to raise each panel.

Sand away any saw marks, and test the fit of the panels in the grooves of the door frame parts.

6. Assemble the door. As a test, assemble the door without glue. Make any adjustments to the joints that may be necessary. Finish sand all the parts. Then glue up the assembly. Glue the tenons into the mortises, but don't glue the panels in the grooves; they must be free to move a little.

7. Shape the door edge. After the clamps are off the door and any dried glue has been scraped off, trim the assembly to reduce it to its final dimensions as well as to make it square.

Worried about crosscutting something as big as the door on your table saw? Square the door with the router instead. Select the cleanest long edge as the baseline. To guide the router, set a fence at right angles to that edge. Use the largest-diameter straight bit you have to make the cut, and remove the bare minimum of material necessary to achieve your goal—a smooth, straight edge. Working off the

DOOR CONSTRUCTION

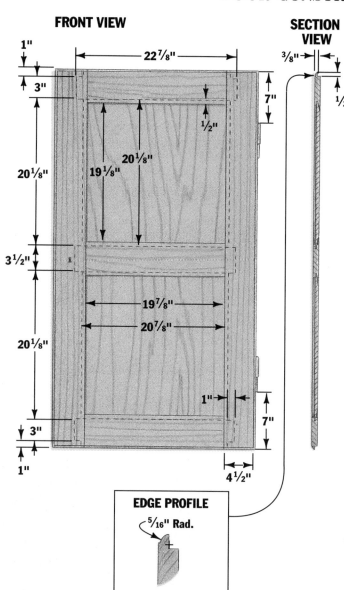

FRONT VIEW

1"

22⁷⁄₈"

3"

¹⁄₂"

7"

20¹⁄₈"

20¹⁄₈"

19¹⁄₈"

3¹⁄₂"

19⁷⁄₈"

20⁷⁄₈"

20¹⁄₈"

1"

7"

3"

1"

4¹⁄₂"

SECTION VIEW

³⁄₈"

¹⁄₂"

EDGE PROFILE

⁵⁄₁₆" Rad.

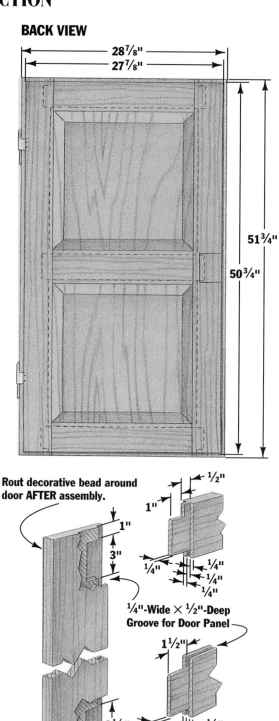

BACK VIEW

28⁷⁄₈"

27⁷⁄₈"

51³⁄₄"

50³⁄₄"

Rout decorative bead around door AFTER assembly.

¹⁄₂"

1"

1"

3"

¹⁄₄" ¹⁄₄" ¹⁄₄" ¹⁄₄"

¹⁄₄"-Wide × ¹⁄₂"-Deep Groove for Door Panel

1¹⁄₂"

3¹⁄₂"

¹⁄₄" ¹⁄₄" ¹⁄₄" ¹⁄₄"

Cut rabbet around back of door AFTER assembly.

baseline edge, trim the top and bottom edges of the door. Then if necessary, work off those edges to trim the remaining long edge.

After the door is square, use the router and a rabbeting bit to cut the rabbet around the door's edge, as indicated in the *Section View* of *Door Construction*. Then check how the door fits the case. If necessary, widen the rabbet to achieve the right fit.

Finally, chuck a ⁵⁄₁₆-inch roundover bit in a table-mounted router, and rout the edge profile around the door. Because of the rabbet, the bit's pilot bearing has no stock to contact, so you have to use the router-table fence to guide the cut.

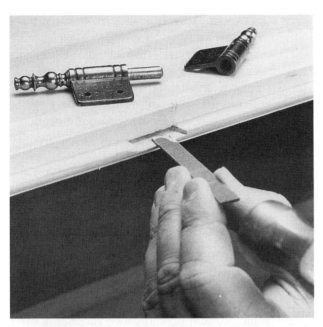

Mounting the hinges on the wardrobe door is pretty crude woodworking. Here the leaf mortise has been pared in the door-edge rabbet, and the slot has been started. The scrap-metal punch has no tapered cutting edge; the tip has been ground square and blunt. You'll probably extract some wood fibers from the slot, but mostly you'll be crushing the wood, forcing that slot into it. (The hinges' two parts can be seen on the door. The part with the pin is mounted on the case; the other part, on the door.)

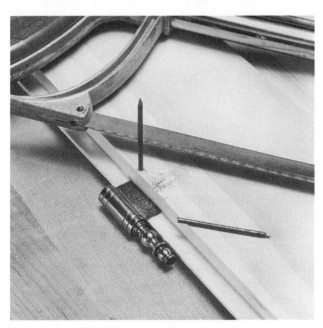

Here's a good look at the almost-completed installation. The hinge is in place, and the mounting nails have been driven through the door stile from the front side. One has been cut flush. If you don't get the nails cut quite flush, file them down.

8. Hang the door. The door of the original features a very unusual hinge that is installed in a very unusual fashion. (Interestingly, both pieces in this collection that I attribute to the Amish have the same hinges installed in the same way.) The only place I know of that sells these hinges is Paxton Hardware (see the Cutting List), and Paxton labels them parliament hinges. Their advantage is that you can easily remove the door, simply by lifting it off the pins. Half the hinge (the part with the pin) is mounted on the case; the other half, on the door.

In this project, the hinges are mounted in a way that Paxton never envisioned, I'm sure.

Mount the hinges on the door first. Take the hinge locations from the drawings, and lay them out on the door. With a chisel, pare a leaf mortise into the base of the rabbet around the inner face of the door. The depth of the mortise should match the thickness of the hinge leaf. Obviously, the leaf is wider than the rabbet, so you next must pound a slot into the edge of the door, as shown in the photo. To make the slot, use a 2- to 3-inch piece of $1/8 \times 3/8$-inch steel. Grind the working end square and blunt. Hammer this "punch" into the door's edge, crushing the pine and creating a slot. This is crude, but it works. When the slot is done, you'll set the leaf in the mortise, then force it into the slot,

Punching the hinge slot in the case is done with the same "tools" and techniques. The clamps secure a scrap to the inside of the case, backing up the area being punched, minimizing tear-out (you'll still have some). Keep punching and probing until the slot is just wide enough for the hinge leaf.

> ## *Deliberate Misalignment Makes Assembly Easier*
>
> Install parliament hinges in perfect alignment, and you probably won't be able to install the door. Hard to believe?
>
> Bear in mind that to install the door, you have to align the door's two hinge barrels directly over the case's two hinge pins. The hinge pairs are about $2^{1}/_2$ feet apart. The chances that you'll be able to align both barrels directly above both pins and keep them aligned as you lower the door are slim to none.
>
> Make your life easier. Deliberately mount the two hinge pins about $^{1}/_{16}$ inch farther apart than are their mates on the door. This will allow you to get one hinge started, then shift your focus to the other.

until the barrel is tight against the edge of the door's roundover.

Transfer the hinge locations to the case next. You don't want the door to bind, so you need to shim it up from the sill and then shift it away from the hinge-side stile $^{1}/_{16}$ to $^{1}/_8$ inch. Hold the door in the opening and see how much play you have, then tape shims of the appropriate thickness to the sill and the hinge-side stile. Set the door in

place, tight to the shims, and mark the locations of the hinges.

Transform these marks into full layouts for slots to be made for the hinges. Clamp a scrap behind the stile to minimize tear-out when you pound the slots through, using the same crude technique used to slot the door. Two tips are worth mentioning here.

One, drill a string of holes the length of the slot to ease the blunt-end chiseling necessary. Just remember that the slot isn't supposed to be wider than the thickness of the hinge leaf.

Two, if the slot does get punched a little wide, push a shim into the slot with the hinge. This allows you to adjust the hinge position very slightly.

With the hinges fitted, secure them with 8d finish nails (wire nails, not cut nails). Hold the hinge against the wood surface and mark where to drill pilot holes. I slipped the hinges into place before drilling so that I could gauge whether or not I had the pilot aligned as I drilled. You can feel the bit contact the hinge and get channeled through the screw hole. Drive the nails. The nails can be driven completely into the edge of the stile. Those driven into the door will stick out, of course. Use a hacksaw to cut them flush.

9. Install the lock. With the lock in hand, lay out and cut the required open mortise for it. Drill the keyhole. Install the lock. Lay out and chisel the necessary mortise for the bolt in the face frame stile. If your lock has a strike—not all do—install it.

MAKE THE DRAWERS

1. Cut the drawer parts. The wardrobe's two drawers have some unusual features. Most obvious is the joinery: One side is dovetailed to the front, while the other is joined to the front by a sliding dovetail. But the drawers also have a bead profile cut along the top edges of the sides, and the fronts are equipped with lock blocks.

Begin constructing the drawers as you do most projects, by cutting the parts to the sizes specified by the Cutting List. The drawer fronts are cut from 5/4 stock, the sides and backs are from $^{3}/_4$-inch stock, and the bottoms are glued up from stock that's been resawed or planed down to $^{3}/_8$ inch.

2. Rout the sliding dovetail joint. This joint is relatively easy to cut with a table-mounted router,

but it can be used only where the front overhangs the side. (The side of the dovetail slot will break out if the slot is too close to the end of the board.) The side of the drawer that's adjacent to the base divider meets this requirement. The fronts overhang the sides just enough to conceal the divider.

As you can see in the drawing *Drawer Construction*, the slot in the drawer front is stopped. The slot should end about $^{5}/_8$ inch shy of the front's top edge. The centerline of the slot is $^{3}/_4$ inch from the end of the front, and the slot is $^{3}/_8$ inch deep. Chuck a $^{1}/_2$-inch dovetail bit in the table-mounted router, set the bit height to $^{3}/_8$ inch, and set the fence $^{3}/_4$ inch from the center of the bit. To make the cut in one front, you feed the workpiece from right to left. To cut the second, you feed the workpiece

DRAWER CONSTRUCTION

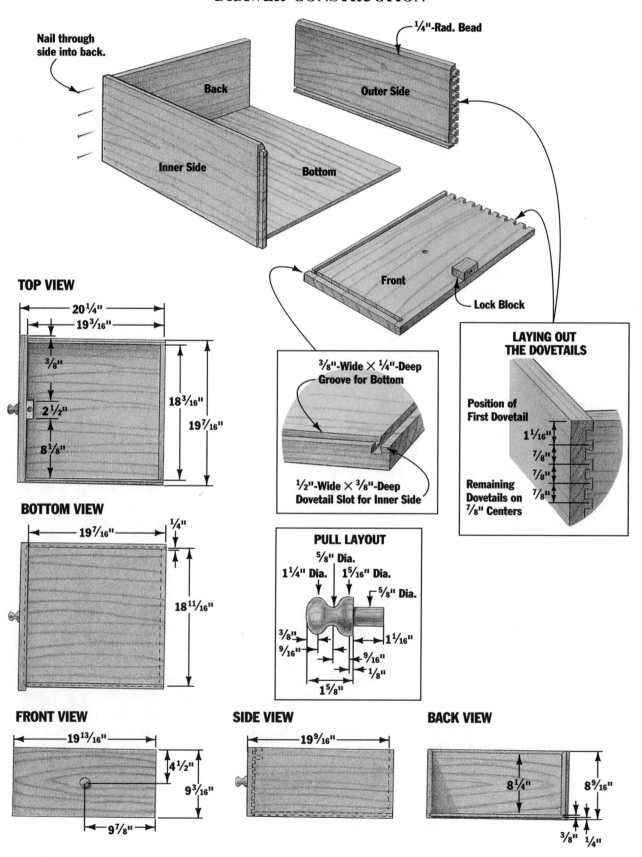

Nail through side into back.

¼"-Rad. Bead

Back

Outer Side

Inner Side

Bottom

Front

Lock Block

TOP VIEW

20¼"
19³/₁₆"
³/₈"
2½"
8⅛"
18³/₁₆"
19⁷/₁₆"

BOTTOM VIEW

19⁷/₁₆"
¼"
18¹¹/₁₆"

FRONT VIEW

19¹³/₁₆"
4½"
9³/₁₆"
9⁷/₈"

³/₈"-Wide × ¼"-Deep Groove for Bottom

½"-Wide × ³/₈"-Deep Dovetail Slot for Inner Side

PULL LAYOUT

⅝" Dia.
1¼" Dia.   1⁵/₁₆" Dia.
⅝" Dia.
³/₈"
9/₁₆"
1¹/₁₆"
9/₁₆"
⅛"
1⅝"

SIDE VIEW

19⁹/₁₆"

LAYING OUT THE DOVETAILS

Position of First Dovetail
1¹/₁₆"
⅞"
⅞"
⅞"
Remaining Dovetails on ⅞" Centers

BACK VIEW

8¼"
8⁹/₁₆"
³/₈"   ¼"

from left to right. You need to be particularly careful when moving the work from right to left, since the bit will tend to grab the work.

With the slots routed, cut the tails. Use the same bit and bit height setting, but reset the fence so just the very edge of the bit projects beyond it. Stand the appropriate drawer side on end, and slide it along the fence. Turn the side around and cut the second face, forming the dovetail pin. Check the tail's fit in the slot, and if necessary, reset the fence and make additional passes to get the tail to fit. When that's done, trim the top edge of the tail to conform to the stopped slot.

3. Rout the dovetails. A full explanation of the procedure is given in the *ShopSmarts* feature "Routing Dovetails" on page 232. In this instance, you cut $1/2$-inch half-blind dovetails on the outer side of each drawer (*not* the side that will be adjacent to the base divider). You'll clamp one drawer in the left side of the jig to dovetail, while the other drawer will be clamped in the right side of the jig for dovetailing. Set up your router with the appropriate template guide, chuck the bit, and make all the fine-tuning adjustments outlined in the *ShopSmarts* feature. When the setup is right, rout the dovetails for the two drawers.

4. Rout the grooves for the bottom. The size and location of the grooves is shown in *Drawer Construction*. While you can cut these grooves in the table saw, you can easily stop the groove in the drawer front—so it won't show in the assembled drawer—if you do it with a table-mounted router.

5. Assemble the drawers. Before you glue the drawer parts together, rout a $1/4$-inch bead along the inner top edge of all the sides. Assemble each drawer without glue to check how everything fits, then glue the sides and fronts together, insert the bottom in its groove—don't glue it—and nail the back in place. A nail through the bottom into the back will secure the bottom.

6. Turn the pulls and locking pins. This really is an optional step. A lot of woodworkers have turning equipment and skills, and they enjoy producing all the wooden parts for a project. If this describes you, check the *Pull Layout* of the *Drawer Construction* drawing and the *Drawer-Locking Pin Profile* of the *Patterns and Profiles* drawing, then turn your own. If you are not a turner, you can use purchased wooden pulls (described in the Cutting List).

7. Fit the drawers and install the pulls. Fitting the drawers should involve little more than sanding or lightly planing the edges so each drawer slides smoothly and easily in and out of the case.

To install the pulls, drill a hole for the shank of each pull and glue the pull in place.

8. Install the lock blocks and drill the locking-pin holes. Glue a lock block to the top inside face of each drawer, as shown in *Drawer Construction*. After the glue has set, fit the drawers in place, then drill a hole through the shelf of the case into the lock block. Make the hole deep enough that the locking pin drops into it up to its hilt.

APPLY A FINISH

All traces of finish had been stripped from the original wardrobe before Jeff Day got it. After months of hemming and hawing (something I'm good at), I settled on a two-tone red paint job. Paint clearly was the original finish material, and it's not unlikely the paint would have been brown or maroon. However, the Amish don't avoid bright colors, and they do grain some furniture. So a two-tone paint job with some graining seemed reasonable.

After priming the wardrobe and sealing the knots, I applied two coats of Old Village's New England red to the case. I painted the cornice assembly, the drawer fronts, and the door with Old Village's Rittenhouse red paint. This is the equiva-

lent of fire-engine red. The New England red is a more maroon red.

After the paint had dried, I brushed a coat of the New England red over the door frame, drawer fronts, and cornice assembly. This was the glazing. I used a graining comb to rake the rails and stiles of the door, the drawer fronts, and the cornice assembly, uncovering streaks of the brighter red. I then used a sponge to apply New England red to the door panels, patting it on so that a mottled texture resulted, with the brighter red showing through.

Read the *ShopSmarts* feature "Country Finishes" on page 305 for a little more information on graining and on other finishing options.

Country Finishes

Paint was the finish of choice for pine when the originals upon which this collection is based were built. But it was the choice from an underwhelming array of available finishing materials.

Consider: The country woodworker could use milk paint or oil paint, either of which he'd mix up himself. Or he could use varnish or shellac, either of which would have to be purchased for a lot of money. The paints would add some color to an otherwise dark, drab decor. The clear finishes would add more of the same to that decor. The paint would be a durable, washable finish. Both shellac and the varnishes of the day were delicate.

Consider too: Pine was not a wood valued for its color and figure. It was utilitarian lumber. So covering pine wasn't a scurrilous act.

It's easy to lose sight of this when you look at old originals in flea markets and antique stores. Much of the old pine furniture that still exists has been refinished. The original paints were stripped off and replaced with sprayed-on stains and varnishes. In some cases, the refinishing was done so long ago that, since then, the wood's taken on an aged glow.

Trying to stain pine to reproduce that natural patina can be enormously frustrating and unrewarding. Pine is just not a wood that takes stain predictably.

The focus here is on three main country finishes: milk paint, paint, and stains. A subset of painting that I'll cover briefly is graining.

Milk Paint

Milk paint really uses milk. The original country woodworker would mix milk, lime, and earth pigments to make it. Today's country woodworker can buy it in powdered form. Like powdered milk, you add it to water and mix it, let it stand a short time, and voila! you've got a milk product. It's nontoxic. But store it too long after it's mixed, and you've got a *sour* milk product.

In finishing a number of the projects in this book—the Drop-Leaf Kitchen Table (page 19), the Candle Shelf (page 89), and the Post-and-Panel Chest (page 131), among others—I used the milk paint made and sold by The Old Fashioned Milk Paint Company (508-448-6336). The paint is available in 16 colors, and supplemental materials, such as a crackle finish product, are also sold. The directions supplied are first-rate. If you're accustomed to buying paint at the local K-Wal, it may strike you as pricey, but you don't need much for any of these projects. In powdered form, the paint can be stored indefinitely. Mix a small quantity for the job at hand, and store the rest of the powder for the next project.

Before using milk paint for the first time, I was prepared, based on something I'd read, to find it somewhat vexing to apply. It's going to be like painting a sponge, I thought. It will soak into the wood so quickly I won't be able to draw it out, the way you can with other paints. It'll be real thin and blotchy. I'll have to apply three or four coats to get good coverage.

Then I tried it.

I was misinformed. It's great stuff.

The paint goes on easily, and it does dry *fast*. It does dry *flat*. The color is uneven, but not dramatically so. After the first coat, the project has color, but the wood's figure and texture is still evident. To the Post-and-Panel Chest, we applied only one coat; that was just enough. Other projects got two coats, but none of them needed more than two coats. And because of the speed of drying, we were able to apply both coats the same day.

Milk paint is susceptible to watermarking, so even the manufacturer recommends using a protective, clear topcoat. Anything you use will slightly alter the color of the milk paint, and of course it will alter the surface quality of it. On the Post-and-Panel Chest, the topcoat we used was a polyurethane wiping varnish. I used commonplace polyurethane varnish on the Drop-Leaf Kitchen Table.

(continued)

Step 2

Here, step by step, is how to finish one of your projects with milk paint.

1. Prepare the wood's surface. Since milk paint binds best to fresh, raw wood, begin by sanding the portions of the project that are to be painted. Make sure you remove all traces of glue squeeze-out. Use 220-grit sandpaper, and wipe the surfaces clean with a tack rag.

2. Mix the milk paint. The manufacturer recommends mixing equal parts water and powder. I fished a couple of jars out of the recycling bins in the garage. Put warm water in one, an equal quantity of powder in the other. Add the powder to the water and stir for a couple of minutes. The paint tends to be lumpy, but in my experience, the little flecks have never been a problem. If they bother you, strain the paint through cheesecloth. Let the mixture stand for about 10 to 15 minutes before applying it; this allows it to thicken.

3. Wet down the wood. Just before brushing on the paint, wipe the entire project with a clean, wet cloth. The paint flows over a damp wood surface better than over a dry one.

Step 3

If you want to seal the knots, so they won't show through the paint, now is the time to do it. Use shellac.

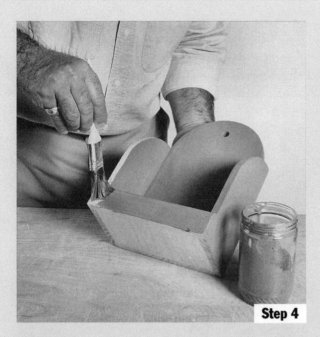

Step 4

4. Apply the first coat of paint. Use a natural-bristle brush to apply the paint. It won't flow like an oil or latex paint, but you shouldn't have trouble drawing it out. Because the moisture in the milk paint will be absorbed by the wood, the paint will dry quickly. The first coat usually dries down thin, streaky, and blotchy, so don't be put off by its appearance.

Step 5

5. Prepare the painted surface for the second coat. This can be done as soon as the first coat is dry, which is usually within a half-hour in a warm shop. To smooth the painted surfaces, buff them lightly with #000 or finer steel wool. Remove the bulk of the dust with a shop vac, then wipe the project with a tack cloth to clean up every last mote.

6. Apply the second coat. Because the first coat seals the wood, this coat can be drawn out with the brush more easily. Upon drying, the appearance of the second coat is much more uniform than the first.

Milk paint dries quite flat. To give it a sheen, brush on a coat of something—boiled linseed oil, wiping varnish, or polyurethane. If the project is something that will get day-to-day handling—a project like a table, for example—use a topcoat that will protect the milk paint. Polyurethane takes a lot of verbal abuse from "fine woodworkers," but it sheds that abuse as well as it does the abuses of everyday use.

Paint

Everyone, surely, has done painting. You've painted a room, or the house trim. You've painted an old piece of furniture. So you know how to do it, right?

Well, you probably do. But familiarity breeds laxity. Sure, you're just joking when you say you're going to "slap some paint on it." But say it enough times, and that's just what you end up doing. The resulting slappy paint job doesn't match the effort you invested in constructing the piece.

A good paint job involves good surface preparation, priming the wood, sealing any knots, and carefully applying a couple of finish coats. It requires the same attention and care from you that cutting the parts and routing the joinery does.

In painting the reproductions, I tended to choose standard colors from the Old Village line by the Stulb Paint Company (215-654-1770), simply because the convenient local paint store maintains a good inventory of it. I could look at a color chart and make a pick appropriate to the project's era and style. Even though all the colors reproduce in this book as shades of gray, you may have noticed that I did suggest specific colors for individual painted pieces. Can't find Old Village paint? Look for any "reproduction" paints. Failing that, just find a chart

(continued)

of colonial-era colors. Have the paint technician mix you a quart of the color you want, in the paint you want—oil-based or water-based.

While you are at the paint store, get primer (and have it tinted), stain sealer of some sort, and a decent brush. If you are using oil-based paints, get mineral spirits for cleanup.

Here, step by step, is how to finish one of your projects with paint.

1. Prepare the wood's surface. Sand the piece of furniture until all machine and tool marks are completely eliminated, finishing up with 220-grit paper. Brush and vacuum away the major part of the dust, then wipe the surface with a tack rag to get the last few motes.

Step 2

2. Apply the primer. Before the piece is painted, its surface should be primed. Primer is formulated specifically to bond to raw wood, providing good adhesion for the paint layers that follow. (Because the primer sticks well to wood, but not necessarily to other surface coatings, I apply the knot sealer onto it, rather than it onto the knot sealer.) Primer can be water-based or oil-based; I usually use latex, because it dries more quickly than oil-based.

Ideally, you should have the primer tinted the same color as the paint. Not only does this give

the best coverage, it prevents a nick or scratch from exposing white primer. As a practical matter, I don't like to have nearly full cans of custom-tinted primer aging on the shelf. Instead, I buy latex primer by the gallon and have it tinted gray, which covers more easily than white.

Apply your primer with a good natural-bristle brush, always working in the direction of the grain.

Step 3

3. Seal the knots. It is almost inevitable that a project built of pine will have a few exposed knots. If you just paint over a knot, its yellow-brown color will eventually bleed through the paint, announcing the knot's presence. You have to seal the knot with shellac, pigmented shellac, or some other stain sealer.

When the prime coat is completely dry, sand lightly with 220-grit paper, and remove all sanding dust by brushing and vacuuming. Look over the piece; you'll be able to pick out the knots. Brush the sealer over any and all knots. In the Step 3 photo I'm using Kilz, which is a brand of pigmented shellac. Though I didn't do it, you can have the sealer tinted to match the primer. The shellac-based sealers dry quickly, so you can apply a couple of coats of sealer in a short time.

After the sealer has dried and you are ready to paint, sand the sealed areas lightly and remove the dust with a tack rag.

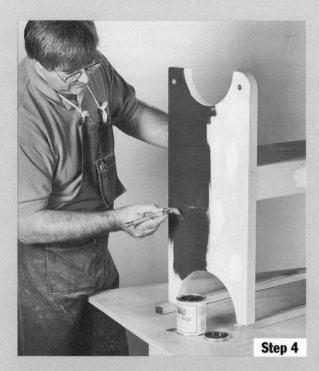

Step 4

4. Apply the paint. Don't try to complete the job with a single heavy coat. Instead, figure that you'll need to apply two coats to get complete coverage, and brush on the paint accordingly.

Use a high-quality brush. Begin in the middle of a surface, drawing the paint in both directions along the wood's grain. Level out the paint with long strokes of the brush tip.

Allow the first coat to dry completely. Run your hand over it; if, while drying, it collected dust, rub it down with #000 steel wool or 400-grit sandpaper. Wipe it down with a tack rag, then apply the second coat.

Grain-Painting

As often as not, a piece of country furniture would have something beyond a solid-color painted finish. Decorative moldings or other embellishments would be painted in a contrasting color. Decorative motifs—flowers, birds, or simple geometric designs—would be painted on panels or drawer fronts. Elaborate scenes might be painted on otherwise blank panels. It was a form of folk art that carried well beyond "finishing" as a woodworking procedure.

Grain-painting is a subset of such folk finishes. It's a way of colorfully decorating a piece of furni-ture. Strictly speaking, grain-painting is the technique of using paint to reproduce the figure of wood. Particularly in the 19th century, skilled artisans known as grainers produced all sorts of false finishes. Not only would furniture made of pine or poplar be painted to look like walnut or mahogany, but plaster walls would be painted to look like marble. The skilled practitioners of the art were artists and could deceive with their work.

But a lot of the unique "grain-painted" pieces preserved in museums and private collections are far more impressionistic than realistic. Some surviving examples look downright bizarre.

Several of the reproductions we built display variations of grain-painting that most any woodworker can master. The Narrow Amish Cabinet (page 201) is really grained; that is, the intent was to mimic wood grain. The large Candle Box (page 55) has a combed finish. The Amish Wardrobe (page 287) combines solid-color areas with combed and sponged embellishments. The sides and ends of the large Tool Tray (page 115) have a fanciful finish created with kitchen plastic wrap. And the medium Dome-Top Chest (page 275) has a swirling finish created with a wadded sheet of newspaper.

To duplicate each finish, the process is the same. The project is painted a base color, often called the ground color. After the ground is dry, a glaze is brushed on. While wet, the glaze is manipulated with a graining tool to expose some of the ground.

You can use paint or gel stain for the glaze, but you'll probably get better results if you use real glazing. Here's why: Paints want to level, by which I mean, paints are formulated to even out, to make those brush strokes disappear. But when you are graining, you want the strokes to stay, you want the distinct ridges and the texture.

Where do you get glaze? You pretty much have to mix it yourself. A limited variety of glazes may be found at a good paint store. For example, we used Zar Antiquing to grain the Narrow Amish Cabinet. The limitation is in color choice—only dark shades like walnut are available. It is for "antiquing," after all, which means making things look old and dirty. For colorful glazes, buy a quart of clear glazing liquid and some tubes of artist's oil

(continued)

paints. Pratt & Lambert calls its glazing liquid Lyt-All; McCloskey's is called Glaze Coat. There are undoubtedly other brands available. Add the artist's oil paint to the glazing liquid, mix thoroughly, and you're ready to grain.

Here, step-by-step, is how to grain-paint a project.

1. Apply the ground. In other words, turn back to the section "Paint" on page 307. Follow the step-by-step presented there: Sand, then clean the wood surface; prime the wood; seal the knots; apply one or two coats of paint.

Step 2

2. Choose a glaze and a graining tool. Rather than tint an entire quart of liquid glaze, spoon a modest amount into a small container. Add a small amount of the artist's color, and mix it thoroughly into the glaze. Evaluate the hue. If necessary, add more of the artist's color and mix. Evaluate again. Just keep tinting and mixing until you have the color of glaze you want. And if you inadvertently add too much color, you can lighten the shade of the glaze by adding white.

With the glaze mixed, choose your graining tool. In the Step 2 photo, you see a selection of commercial tools—metal graining combs (three textures in each of four widths), a triangular rubber-edged comb, and an arched grainer, along with a bristle brush and a couple of sponge brushes. The

latter can produce some interesting effects. Remember that you can also use a feather, a wad of paper, a ball of putty, a strip of plastic wrap, a sponge, and all sorts of other contrived "tools" to manipulate the glaze after it's applied.

3. Apply the glaze and "grain." Use a brush to apply the glaze, coating a defined area, such as the end of the large Tool Tray (page 115) shown in the following photos. Immediately start to work the glaze with the graining tool you've selected. If you don't like what you create, brush out the glaze and start over.

Step 3

A mock wood grain effect is produced with a tool that has concentric half-circle ridges on an arched surface. You slide the tool's working surface across the glazed wood, and as you do, you rock the tool. It may take two or three passes to get the hang of it. And beyond that, it may take five or six passes to get a crisp, clean, attractive wood-figure appearance. But if a strong wood grain effect is what you are after, this tool can produce it. We used this tool on the Narrow Amish Cabinet (page 201), but with a very light touch to subdue the strength of the figure.

Combs scratch away the glaze in parallel lines. This can be pretty boring, but an infinite variety of effects can be achieved with a little creative comb choreography. Moving the comb from side to side

Step 3

as you drag it across the glaze produces waves, as shown in the second Step 3 photo. Try different cycles of movements to see what different waves you can create. Comb geometric patterns into the glaze. Experiment. Remember, you just have to re-brush the glaze to start over.

Try other tools, especially the homemade kind. Daub at the glaze with a wad of paper or a sponge to get a mottled appearance. Daub the glaze with a ball of putty, or draw the putty into a strand and

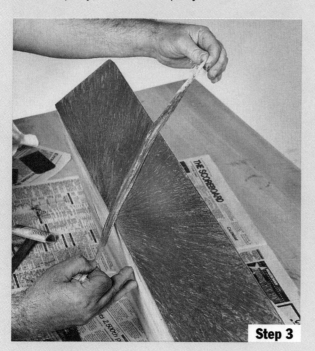

Step 3

roll it across the glazed surface. Twist a piece of plastic wrap into a strand and stroke across the surface, as shown in the third Step 3 photo, to create a burst effect. Caress the glaze with a feather to get random sweeps and swirls of color. Stab it with a pencil eraser to punctuate. And by all means, leave your fingerprints on your work.

4. Apply a protective clear topcoat. After the glaze has dried, you should apply a coat or two of varnish to protect it.

The graining process can be random and free-wheeling, or it can be precise, repetitive, methodical, and ultimately tedious. The colors you choose, the tool you use, and especially the way you use it produce the finish. My advice is to start with a small canvas, rather than a large one. Choose a project like one of the Candle Boxes (page 55) or the small Dome-Top Chest (page 275). Or select particular features of a larger piece to decorate. Move on to the larger canvas only after you've got some experience.

Stain

Pine can be enormously frustrating to stain. In addition to the problems that attend any staining venture, there are problems special to pine. At its very worst, stain turns a substantial piece, one you spent a month or two of Saturdays and Sundays building, into an eyesore. And you can experience this disaster even after you've diligently applied the stain to test boards before tackling the project itself.

The root problem is that pine's density varies dramatically. Clearly, it can change from board to board, but it varies too across a single board. Most obviously, the density of the (soft) early-wood differs from that of the (hard) latewood. But it also varies randomly from one area to another. The porous areas soak up stain readily, becoming dark, while the more dense areas don't. The result is a pronounced color reversal in the pine's grain pattern, which has the effect of emphasizing the grain. The dark blotches produced by random density variations exacerbate the dreadful appearance.

What to do?

(continued)

Avoidance is good. Paint that cupboard. Remember that the fellows who built the country originals undoubtedly used paint as the final finish, not stain.

Patience is good, too. As it ages, pine develops a beautiful orange-brown patina. Give your reproduction a decade or so to mellow, and that patina will ripen to the color you see (and probably admire) on many pine antiques. Unfortunately, leaving the wood unfinished entirely will allow it to accumulate fingerprints and smudges and dirt. You can varnish the piece. As long as it isn't water-based, a varnish will warm the wood's natural coloring, and though it will retard the growth of a natural patina, it won't arrest it completely. Thus, as the pine ages, its color will grow darker and richer.

Impatient and confrontational, are you? Here are two approaches to try. They are not foolproof.

1. Apply a wood conditioner—a process called washcoating—then, while the conditioner is still wet, the stain.

2. Use the thickest gel stain you can find.

Before you try using either of these approaches, be very sure you've sanded or scraped the wood flawlessly. It is all too easy to overlook a patch of cross-grain sanding marks or to completely miss sanding an edge. Paint may conceal such shortcomings, but stain will accentuate them. So if you plan to stain your project, be especially attentive to these details.

As you start to apply stain, divide the project into discrete areas, and work one area at a time. This will help you get a more consistent appearance. You won't get hung up at one corner of the piece and inadvertently allow the stain to sit too long on another surface, thus getting it too dark. Separate the areas at seams or edges. In staining the Schoolmaster's Desk (page 123), I did two legs, a side, and the front, then the other legs, the other side, and the back. Then I did the top surfaces.

Washcoating is, after preparing the wood's surface carefully, a simple two-step process.

1. Apply the wood conditioner. According to the label on McCloskey's Stain Controller, which I used on the Schoolmaster's Desk, the product has a tung-oil base. It isn't surprising, then, that you apply it as you would an oil finish. That is, you

Step 1

flood the surface with the conditioner and let it soak in. I use a bristle brush to apply the conditioner, as you can see in the Step 1 photo. Monitor the area you've treated, and reapply conditioner wherever it soaks in completely. You want to keep the surface wet, just as you would in applying an oil finish.

Step 2

2. Apply the stain before the conditioner dries. After about 10 or 15 minutes, wipe the excess conditioner from the wood, and apply the stain. The kind of stain you use isn't important. On the Schoolmaster's Desk, I used an oil-based pigmented stain, largely because it gave me the tone